Cyber Crime and Cyber Terrorism Investigator's Handbook

Cyber Crime and Cyber Terrorism Investigator's Handbook

Edited by

Babak Akhgar

Andrew Staniforth

Francesca Bosco

ELSEVIER

AMSTERDAM • BOSTON • HEIDELBERG • LONDON
NEW YORK • OXFORD • PARIS • SAN DIEGO
SAN FRANCISCO • SINGAPORE • SYDNEY • TOKYO

Syngress is an Imprint of Elsevier

SYNGRESS.

Acquiring Editor: Steve Elliot
Editorial Project Manager: Benjamin Rearick
Project Manager: Priya Kumaraguruparan
Designer: Mark Rogers

Syngress is an imprint of Elsevier
225 Wyman Street, Waltham, MA 02451, USA

Library of Congress Cataloging-in-Publication Data
Akhgar, Babak.
   Cyber crime and cyber terrorism investigator's handbook / Babak Akhgar, Francesca Bosco,
Andrew Staniforth.
      pages cm
   Includes bibliographical references and index.
   1. Computer crimes–Investigation. 2. Cyberterrorism–Investigation. 3. Computer crimes–
Investigation–Case studies. 4 Cyberterrorism–Investigation–Case studies. I. Bosco, Francesca
II. Staniforth, Andrew. III. Title.
   HV8079.C65A37 2014
   363.25'968–dc23

                                                                                        2014017880

British Library Cataloguing-in-Publication Data
A catalogue record for this book is available from the British Library

ISBN: 978-0-12-800743-3

For information on all Syngress publications,
visit our website at http://store.elsevier.com/syngress

This book has been manufactured using Print On Demand technology. Each copy is produced to order
and is limited to black ink. The online version of this book will show color figures where appropriate

Acknowledgments

The editors wish to thank the multidisciplinary team of experts who have contributed to this book, sharing their knowledge and experience. Thanks are also extended to Lord Carlile of Berriew CBE QC for supporting this work. We would also like to take this opportunity to acknowledge the contribution of the team at CENTRIC (Centre of excellence in terrorism, resilience, intelligence, and organized crime research, at Sheffield Hallam University) and for the support provided by West Yorkshire Police, the Office of the Police and Crime Commissioner for West Yorkshire, and the United Nations Interregional Crime and Justice Research Institute (UNICRI).

And finally, we express our gratitude and appreciation to Dr. Eleanor Lockley. Her contribution and dedication has made this edited volume possible.

We would particularly like to acknowledge the following organizations and individuals for their support:

Sheffield Hallam University
West Yorkshire Police
Office of the Police and Crime Commissioner for West Yorkshire
United Nations Interregional Crime and Justice Research Institute

Endorsements

"This authoritative volume provides all security practitioners with a trusted reference and resource to guide them through the complexities of investigating cyber crime and cyber terrorism."

Lord Carlile of Berriew CBE QC

"The global multi-disciplinary team of expert contributors have compiled an excellent operational reference and resource to support the new generation of cyber investigators."

John D Parkinson OBE

Chair of Centre of Excellence in Terrorism, Resilience, Intelligence & Organised Crime Research (CENTRIC)

Contents

Contributors

Babak Akhgar
Director of CENTRIC, Sheffield Hallam University, UK

Ameer Al-Nemrat
University of East London, UK

P. Saskia Bayerl
Rotterdam School of Management, Erasmus University,
The Netherlands

Francesca Bosco
University of Milan, Italy

Giovanni Bottazzi
Dipartimento di Ingegneria Civile e Ingegneria Informatica,
Unversita di Roma 'Tor Vergata', Roma

Ben Brewster
CENTRIC, Sheffield Hallam University, UK

Emelyn Butterfield
Lecturer, Leeds Metropolitan University, UK

Daniel Cohen
Research Fellow, The Institute of National Security Studies,
Tel Aviv University, Israel

Alan Cook
Agenci Information Security (AIS) Consultancy, UK

Mohammed Dastbaz
Dean of the Faculty of the Arts, Environment and
Technology, Leeds Metropolitan University, UK

Ruairidh Davison
Human Systems Integration Group, Coventry University, UK

David Day
Senior Lecturer, Sheffield Hallam University, UK

Konstantinos Domdouzis
CENTRIC, Sheffield Hallam University, UK

Helen Gibson
CENTRIC, Sheffield Hallam University, UK

Edward Halpin
Leeds Metropolitan University, UK

Bruno Halupeau
European Crime Centre EC3, Eurpol

Gary Hibberd
Agenci Information Security (AIS) Consultancy, UK

Amin Hosseinian-Far
Williams College, UK

John Huddlestone
Coventry University, UK

Hamid Jahankhani
Director of Research and Consultancy Development,
Williams College, UK

Eleanor Lockley
Researcher, CENTRIC, Sheffield Hallam University, UK

Eric Luiijf
TNO Networked Organisations Principal Consultant C(I)IP&
Cyber Ops Networked Organisations, The Hague,
The Netherlands

Alessandro Mantelero
Polytechnic University of Turin, Italy

Gianluigi Me
CeRSI, Research Center in Information Systems,
LUISS Guido Carli University, Roma

Dale Richards
Senior Lecturer, Human Technology Centre, Coventry
University, UK

Fraser Sampson
Chief Executive and Solicitor of the Office of Police and
Crime Commissioner, West Yorkshire Police, UK

Siraj A. Shaikh
Digital Security and Forensics (SaFe) Research Group,
Coventry University, UK

Andrew Staniforth
West Yorkshire Police, UK

Alex W. Stedmon
Reader in Human Factors, Human Systems Integration
Group, Coventry University, UK

Giuseppe Vaciago
Polytechnic University of Turin, Italy

Sufian Yousef
Anglia Ruskin University, UK

Author Biography

BABAK AKHGAR

Babak Akhgar is Professor of Informatics and Director of CENTRIC (Center of excellence in terrorism, resilience, intelligence and organized crime research) at Sheffield Hallam University and Fellow of the British Computer Society. Akhgar graduated from Sheffield Hallam University in Software Engineering. He gained considerable commercial experience as a Strategy Analyst and Methodology Director for several international companies. Prof. Babak Akhgar obtained a Master degree (with distinction) in Information Systems in Management and a PhD in Information Systems. He has more than 100 referred publications in international journals and conferences on information systems with specific focus on knowledge management (KM). He is member of editorial boards of a number of international Journals, Chair and programme committee member of several international conferences. Akhgar has extensive and hands on experience in development, management and execution of KM projects and large international security initiatives (e.g., Application of social media in crisis management, intelligence-based combating of terrorism and organised crime, Gun crime, cyber security, Public Order and cross cultural ideology polarization) with multimillion Euros budgets.

In addition to this he is the technical lead of two EU Security projects; "Courage" which focuses on Cyber Crime and Cyber Terrorism and "Athena project" which focuses on the application of social media and mobile devices in crisis management. He has co-edited a book on Intelligence management (Knowledge Driven frameworks for combating Terrorism and Organised crime). His recent books are titled Strategic Intelligence Management (National Security Imperatives and Information and Communications Technologies) 2013 and Emerging Trends in ICT Security 2014. Prof. Akhgar is also a member of academic advisory board of SAS UK.

ANDREW STANIFORTH

Detective Inspector Andrew Staniforth has extensive operational counter-terrorism experience in the UK. As a qualified teacher he has designed national counter-terrorism exercise programmes and delivers training to police commanders from across the world at the UK College of Policing. He is the author of the *Blackstone's Counter-Terrorism Handbook* (Oxford University Press, 2013), the *Blackstone's Handbook of Ports and Borders Security* (Oxford University Press, 2013), the *Routledge Companion to UK Counter-Terrorism* (Routledge, 2012) and *Preventing Terrorism and Violent Extremism* (Oxford University Press, 2014). Andrew is a Senior Research Fellow at the Centre of Excellence for Terrorism, Resilience, Intelligence and Organised Crime Research (CENTRIC), and a Visiting Fellow at the School of Law, University of Leeds. He currently leads a research team at West Yorkshire Police progressing multi-disciplinary international security projects.

FRANCESCA BOSCO

Francesca Bosco earned a degree in International Law and joined UNICRI in 2006 as a member of the Emerging Crimes Unit. In her role in this organization, Bosco is responsible for cybercrime prevention projects, and in conjunction with key strategic partners, has developed new methodologies and strategies for researching and countering computer-related crimes.

She has collaborated on different cybercrime-related projects such as the Hackers Profiling Project (HPP), SCADA (Supervisory Control and Data Acquisition) Security, a multi-level training program for ICT and security professionals, lawyers, and law enforcement agencies. Bosco has also participated as a speaker in various conferences and training seminars on the topic of child online pornography and has contributed to the development ITU Child Online Protection (COP) guidelines.

More recently, Bosco has been researching and developing technical assistance and capacity building programs to counter the involvement of organized crime in cybercrime, as well as on the legal implications and future scenarios of cyber terrorism and cyber war. She is also researching and managing projects on hate speech online and on data protection issues related to automated profiling. Bosco is one of the founders of the Tech and Law Center and she is currently a PhD candidate at the University of Milan.

Foreword

It is a real privilege to be invited to write the Foreword for the *Cyber Crime and Cyber Terrorism Investigators' Handbook.* This new volume provides an authoritative and accessible guide of substantial practical and operational value which, for the very first time, ensures all security practitioners have a trusted reference and resource to navigate them through the challenges and complexities of investigating cyber crime and cyber terrorism.

The growing role of cyberspace in society has opened up new threats as well as new opportunities. A growing number of individuals and groups are looking to use cyberspace to steal, compromise or destroy critical data, and the national security machinery of governments have no choice but to find ways to confront and overcome these threats if they are to flourish in an increasingly competitive and globalized world.

As citizens put more of their lives online, the safety of cyber space matters more and more. People want to be confident that the networks which support their nation's security, their prosperity, and their own private lives as individuals, are both safe and resilient. The scale of citizen and state dependence on cyber space now means that our economic well-being, our key infrastructure, our places of work and our homes can all be directly affected.

There are, of course, crimes that only exist in the digital world, in particular those that target the integrity of computer networks and online services. But cyberspace is also being used as a platform for committing crimes such as fraud, and on an industrial scale. Identity theft and fraud online now dwarf their offline equivalents. The internet has also provided new opportunities for those who seek the sexual exploitation of children and the vulnerable.

Cyberspace allows criminals to target countries from other jurisdictions across the world, making it harder to enforce the law. Cyber criminals can operate from anywhere in the world, targeting large numbers of people or businesses across international boundaries, and there are challenges posed by the scale and volume of their crimes, the technical complexity of identifying the perpetrators as well as the need to work internationally to bring them to justice. The internet has unfortunately enabled aspiring criminals to commit offences, based on a belief that law enforcement struggles to operate in the online world.

The internet has also changed—and continues to change—the very nature of terrorism. The internet is well suited to the nature of terrorism and the psyche of the terrorist. In particular, the ability to remain anonymous makes the internet attractive to the terrorist plotter. Terrorists use the internet to propagate their ideologies, motives and grievances as well as mounting cyber attacks on critical infrastructures. Modern terrorism has rapidly evolved, becoming increasingly nonphysical, with vulnerable "home grown" citizens being recruited, radicalized, trained and tasked online in the virtual and ungoverned domain of cyber space.

To support the emergence of cyber-based investigations, the *Cyber Crime and Cyber Terrorism Investigators' Handbook* is enriched with case studies, explanations of strategic responses and contextual information providing the theoretical underpinning required to effectively tackle cyber crimes. This unique volume serves to explore and explain the responsibilities of law enforcement agencies to address online criminal and terrorist activity. Authored and edited by a multi-disciplinary team of experts from academia, law enforcement and private industry, this new volume shall be a welcome introduction to the resource library of cyber investigators.

Lord Carlile of Berriew CBE QC

Preface

The *Cyber Crime and Cyber Terrorism Investigators' Handbook* is an authoritative and accessible collection of chapters which provides security practitioners with a trusted reference and resource to guide them through the complexities and operational challenges of effectively investigating cyber crime and cyber terrorism (CC/CT). Enriched with case studies, explanations of key challenges and strategic responses, this unique volume shall support the increasing role and responsibility of all Law Enforcement Agencies (LEAs) to tackle online criminal activity and prepare for cyber-based attacks.

This book is divided into three interrelated parts:

Part one consists of eight chapters. They address the fundamental aspects of cyber crime and cyber terrorism (CC/CT) from a practitioner's perspective. This section also addresses the notion of cyberspace for LEAs and considers the definition of CC and CT from multi-jurisdictional representation. It also provides an overview of the investigative considerations for tackling CC and CT, addressing the key investigation processes, principals and workflows needed for understanding of CC/CT.

Part two consists of five chapters and explores some of the key case studies related to CC/CT. The case studies help to provide the reader with a broad knowledge of the previous instances of CC/CT and cyber attacks. Lessons learnt from existing cases provide practitioners and LEAs with the knowledge and understanding of the diversity across the subject area. The chapters focus on how the internet is being used for cyber crime and terrorist activity and is essential reading for all cyber investigators. Two chapters provide classification tools focusing upon human centric taxonomy for cyber crime motives and the classification system from a technological perspective.

Part three consists of five chapters and addresses some of the contemporary topics in the context of CC/CT such as Big Data and social media, considering these in the framework of LEAs environment. It explores and informs the reader on the wider facets of CC/CT which remain important contextual elements for all cyber investigators' understanding of their operating environment.

The three parts of the volume can be considered independently, and each chapter can also be considered and used independently but collectively, they provide the practitioners with a holistic view of the operational challenges of contemporary CC/CT. This new volume shall be accompanied by additional online learning support materials which will provide the reader with up-to-date resources, so they can stay informed on issues related to CC/CT.

This new contribution to CC/CT knowledge shall be a welcome introduction to the resource library of LEAs and security professionals, following a multi-disciplinary philosophy, being supported by leading experts across academia, private industry, and government agencies. The *Cyber Crime and Cyber Terrorism Investigators' Handbook* juxtaposes practical experience and, where appropriate, policy guidance, with academic commentaries and technical advice to illustrate the complexity of cyber investigations. The reading of this volume shall ensure all security practitioners are better informed to carry out their CC/CT investigative responsibilities to protect the citizens they serve.

Cyberspace: The new frontier for policing?

Fraser Sampson

Published in 2011, the UK Cyber Security Strategy states that:

> Our vision is for the UK in 2015 to derive huge economic and social value from a vibrant, resilient and secure cyberspace, where our actions, guided by our core values of liberty, fairness, transparency and the rule of law, enhance prosperity, national security and a strong society.

That the United Kingdom even has a cyber security strategy is telling. Governments and their agencies—not only in the United Kingdom but worldwide—have struggled to distinguish criminality that specifically relies on the use of the hyper-connectivity of global information technology from "ordinary" crime that is simply enabled by using information and communication technology. Despite legislative interventions such as the Council of Europe Convention on Cybercrime (for an analysis of which see Vatis, 2010, p. 207) in 2001, cyberspace remains a largely unregulated jurisdictional outpost.

The first piece of criminal legislation to address the use—or rather the misuse—of computers in the United Kingdom was enacted in 1990. The recital to the Computer Misuse Act 1990 states that it was an act "to make provision for securing computer material against unauthorized access or modification; and for connected purposes." This narrow, pre-Internet focus was very much predicated on the concept of a computer as a functional box (or network of boxes) containing "material" that required protection (Sampson 1991a, p. 211). Although the Act addressed unauthorized access, the concept of causing a computer to perform a function in furtherance of other crimes was also a central part of the new legislation (Sampson, 1991b, p. 58) which, for the first time in the United Kingdom, sought to catch up with computer technology that was becoming part of people's everyday lives—a race in which the legislative process did not stand a chance.

While the legislation was amended in 2006 with the introduction of a new criminal offence of unauthorized acts to impair the operation of a computer or program, etc., looking back through today's digital prism, the legislation has a decidedly analog look to it. When the legislation came into force we had little idea of the impact the "information super-highway" would have on our everyday lives, still less the engrenage effect of social media.

According to the UK's 2011 Cyber Security Strategy, at the time of its publication 2 billion people were online and there were over 5 billion Internet-connected devices in existence. During that same year, the number of people being proceeded against for offences under the Computer Misuse Act 1991 in England and Wales, according to a document from the Ministry of Justice, was nine (Canham, 2012) with no people being proceeded against for the two offences under s.1(1) and s.1(3). Perhaps as surprisingly, the records from the Police National Legal Database (PNLD) used by all police forces in England and Wales for offence wordings, charging codes, and legal research show that during two weeks (chosen at random) in 2013 the Computer Misuse Act 1990 and its constituent parts were accessed as follows:

Between 4th and 10th March—907 times
Between 10th and 16th November—750 times

Reconciling these two data sets is difficult. While it is clear from the PNLD access data that law enforcement officials in England and Wales are still interrogating the 1990 legislation frequently (on average, around 825 times per week or 118 times per day or annually 42,900 times), the number of prosecutions for the correlative offences is vanishingly small. One of the many challenges with cybercrime and cyber-enabled criminality is establishing its size and shape.

THE SHAPE OF THE CHALLENGE

Just as the shape of our technology has changed beyond all recognition since 1990, so too has the shape of the challenge. The almost unconstrained development of Internet-based connectivity can be seen, on one hand, as a phenomenological emancipation of the masses, an extension of the Civil Data Movement and the citizens' entitlement to publicly held data (see (Sampson and Kinnear, 2010). On the other hand, the empowerment it has given others (particularly sovereign states) to abuse cyberspace has been cast as representing the "end of privacy" prompting a petition to the United Nations for a "bill of digital rights."

Steering a predictably middle course, the UK strategy sets out the key—and, it is submitted, most elusive—concept within the document: that of a "vibrant, resilient, and secure cyberspace." The aspiration must surely be right but how can resilience and security be achieved within a vibrant space run by computers? In terms of both computers and our reliance upon them, we have moved so far from the original notion of boxes, functions, commands and programs, along with the consequences that can be brought about by their use, that a fundamental re-think is needed.

So what—and where—is cyberspace? Much has been written recently on the threat, risk and harm posed by "cybercrime," "e-crime," "cyber-enabled" criminality but the legislation has been left a long way behind. The EU has a substantial number of workstreams around its "Cybersecurity Strategy" and its own working definition of "cyberspace" though its own proposed Directive has no legal definition but rather one for Network and Information Security to match the agency established in

2004 with the same name. In the United Kingdom, a parliamentary question in 2012 asked the Secretary of State for Justice how many prosecutions there had been for "e-crime" in the past 5 years. In response, the Parliamentary Under Secretary of State gave statistics for ss 1(4), 2 and 3(5) of the Computer Misuse Act while the correlative Hansard entry uses the expression "cybercrime" in its heading.

Wherever it is, constitutional lawyers around the world have wrestled with the applicability of their countries' legislation with the borderlessness of the virtual word of the Internet; the application of "analog" territorial laws to the indeterminable digital boundaries of the infinite global communications network is, it seems, proving to be too much for our conventional legal systems. Here is why.

When it comes to interpreting and applying law across our own administrative jurisdictional boundaries, an established body of internationally agreed principles, behavior, and jurisprudence has developed over time. Some attempts have been made to apply these legal norms to cyberspace. For example, the International Covenant on Civil and Political Rights sets out some key obligations of signatory states. In addition, activities executed within or via cyberspace should not be beyond the reach of other community protections such as those enshrined in the European Convention of Human Rights or the EU Charter of Fundamental Rights, particularly where issues such as online child sexual exploitation are involved. The first basic challenge that this brings however, is that of jurisdiction.

Cottim has identified five jurisdictional theories and approaches in this context, namely (Cottim A. 2010):

1. *Territoriality theory*: The theory that jurisdiction is determined by the place where the offence is committed, in whole or in part. This "territoriality theory" has its roots in the Westphalian Peace model of state sovereignty that has been in place since 1684 (see Beaulac, 2004, p. 181). This approach has at its heart the presumption that the State has sovereignty over the territory under discussion, a presumption that is manifestly and easily rebuttable in most "cyberspace" cases.
2. *Nationality (or active personality) theory*: Based primarily on the nationality of the person who committed the offence (see United States of America v. Jay Cohen; Docket No. 00-1574, 260 F.3d 68 (2d Cir., July 31, 2001) where World Sports Exchange, together with its President, were defendants in an FBI prosecution for conspiracy to use communications facilities to transmit wagers in interstate or foreign commerce. The defendants were charged with targeting customers in the United States inviting them to place bets with the company by toll-free telephone call or over the Internet). While the Antiguan Company was beyond the jurisdiction of the court, the President was a US citizen and could, therefore, be arraigned before an American criminal court.
3. *Passive personality theory*: While the "nationality theory" deals with the nationality of the offender, the "passive personality theory" is concerned with the nationality of the victim.

In what Cottim calls "the field of cybercriminology," a good example of this jurisdiction assumption can be seen in a case where a Russian citizen who lived in

Chelyabinsk, Russia was sentenced by a court in Hartford Connecticut for hacking into computers in the United States.

4. *Protective theory*: Cottim's "protective theory" (also called "security principle" and "injured forum theory") deals with the national or international interest injured, assigning jurisdiction to the State that sees its interest—whether national or international—in jeopardy because of an offensive action. Cottim sees this rarely used theory as applying principally to crimes like counterfeiting of money and securities.

5. *Universality theory*: In his final theory, Cottim identifies the approach of universality based on the international character of the offence allowing (unlike the others) every State to claim of jurisdiction over offences, even if those offences have no direct effect on the asserting State. While this theory seems to have the most potential for applicability to cyberspace, there are two key constraints in the way it has been developed thus far. The first constraint is that the State assuming jurisdiction must have the defendant in custody; the second is that the crime is "particularly offensive to the international community." While this approach has, Cottim advises, been used for piracy and slave trafficking there is considerable practical difficulty in defining the parameters of the universality approach even in a conventional context and the possibility of extending it to cover cyberspace offending and activity is as yet unexplored.

When it comes to conventional extra-territorial challenges, the device of focusing on key elements such as the nationality of the offender and the geographical location of the causal conduct or consequent harm has produced some successful prosecutions for (and perhaps thereby deterred) some conventional cyber-enabled offending. For example, Cottim cites a case where the Managing Director of CompuServe Information Services GmbH, a Swiss national, was charged in Germany with being responsible for the access—in Germany—to violent, child, and animal pornographic representations stored on the CompuServe's server in the United States. The German court considered it had jurisdiction over the defendant, although he was Swiss, he lived in Germany at the time. The Amtsgericht court's approach has been criticized as not only unduly harsh but as unsustainable and it is difficult to argue with Bender who says "it must be noted that the 'law-free zones' on the Internet cannot be filled by a ruling like this, but need a new self-regulatory approach" (Bender, 1998).

In some cases litigants also use the jurisdictional differences to argue down the gravity of the sanction or the extent of their liability, particularly where the perpetrator from one jurisdiction brings about consequence in another. A good recent example is Klemis v Government of the United States of America [2013] All ER (D) 287 where the UK defendant allegedly sold heroin to two men in Illinois, USA. One of the men subsequently died and raised questions at the point of sentencing as to how the different legislatures in the two jurisdictions had set the requirements for the relevant actus reus (criminal act) and the mens rea (culpable state of mind) differently. Another recent example of trans-jurisdictional friction is Bloy and Another v Motor Insurers' Bureau [2013] EWCA Civ 1543. In that case a road traffic collision in the

United Kingdom had been caused by a Lithuanian national who had been uninsured at the time. The Motor Insurers' Bureau is the UK compensation body for the purposes of the relevant EU Directive and was obliged to pay compensation where a UK resident had been injured in a collision in another Member State caused by an uninsured driver. In such cases, the Directive enabled the Bureau to claim reimbursement from the respective compensatory body in the other Member State. However, under the domestic law of Lithuania the liability of the compensatory body was capped at €500k. The Bureau argued that its liability to pay the victim should be capped by Lithuanian domestic law even though the collision happened on an English road.

Clearly the challenges of unauthorized access and use of data obtain; so too do the jurisdictional challenges of locus of initiators and consequences. However, these have to be understood in the context of the much more pernicious and truly viral threats such as denial of service attacks, malware, data espionage and what Cottim calls the scareword of "cyber-terrorism" which has now become formally adopted by many law enforcement agencies, politicians and commentators. The reality is that, with the requisite knowledge and motivation, a teen with a laptop can alter the "use by" dates on food products in a packing plant on the other side of the world, or command the central heating system of a neighbor's Internet-connected home to overheat, or send the traffic lights in a far away city into a frenzy. The further reality is that the wattle-and-daub constructs of conventional law making in common law countries, along with their correlative law enforcement practices, will not provide the answer to these threats and risks and even staples such as "crime scenes" and "perpetrators" are no longer adequate within the new frontier of cyberspace.

However, it is not just the domination and manipulation of cyberspace by criminals that has caused public concern. The aftermath of the Edward Snowden revelations about intrusive governmental espionage demonstrated that cyberspace is regarded as a potentially perilous place by private users not just in fear of becoming victims of remote criminality. There is also a real fear that the technological environment allows state agencies to operate in highly intrusive yet anonymous and unaccountable ways, prompting the CEOs of some of the world's leading IT companies to write an open letter to the President of the United States demanding reform of cyberspace surveillance based on a series of overarching principles that guarantee the free flow of information yet limit governmental authority and impose a substantial degree of oversight (Armstrong et al., 2013).

What then is the size of the challenge presented by this amorphous construct of cyberspace?

THE SIZE OF THE CHALLENGE

The population of cyberspace is estimated by the UK government to be >2 billion. While we do not accurately know the frequency or longevity, this means that one-third of Earth's population visit cyberspace and billions more are anticipated to join them over the next decade, exchanging over $8 trillion in online commerce.

According to the Commissioner of the City of London Police, "cyber" fraud (broadly offences of dishonesty committed by use of computer networks) costs the UK £27 billion per year while "cyber breaches" (presumably involving the unauthorized infiltration of a private or public computer network) have been recorded by 93% of small and medium businesses in the United Kingdom in 2013, an increase of 87% on the previous year.

Aside from some of the peculiar criminological features unique to crime committed in cyberspace (such as the absence of any real motive for anyone—individual or corporate victims or their Internet Service Providers—to report crimes involving fraud) the basic challenge facing us now seems to be how to get to grips with the concept of cyberspace—vibrant, resilient, secure or otherwise. Having separated cybercrime from cyber-enabled crime in the same way we might separate crime within a transport network from crime where the transport network is merely an enabler, surely we need to begin to treat cyberspace for what it is: a separate socio-spatial dimension in which people choose not only to communicate, but also to dwell, trade, socialize and cultivate; to create intellectual property, generate economic wealth, to begin and end relationships; to forage, feud and thrive; to heal and harm. Viewed in this way cyberspace is another continent, vast, viable and virtual, a distinct jurisdiction requiring its own constitution and legal system, its own law enforcement agents and practices. The Director of Operational Policing Support for Interpol's General Secretariat, Michael O'Connell, has compared the movement across cyberspace with "the 2 billion passenger movements across the world." The reality is that cyber travelers move around the borderless virtual globe with almost immeasurable speed, almost zero cost and almost total anonymity.

The challenge of tackling cyber security stretches way beyond simply standardizing our legal frameworks. The UK Government has also recognized that "Without effective cyber security, we place our ability to do business and to protect valuable assets such as our intellectual property at unacceptable risk." In the report commissioned by the UK Government, Price Waterhouse Coopers estimate that there are over 1000 different global publications setting out cyber standards. Moreover, their assessment of the standards situation across organizations looked patchy and incomplete.

While the awareness of cyber security threats and the importance placed on them was generally found to be high, the efforts to mitigate cyber security risk differ significantly with the size of the organization and its sector. The report found that only 48% of organizations implemented new policies to mitigate cyber security risks and only 43% conducted cyber security risk assessments and impact analysis to quantify these risks. The report also found that 34% of organizations who purchased certified products or services did so purely to achieve compliance as an outcome.

Although the authors are clear in pointing out that the online survey reached an audience of ~30,000 organizations, it produced around 500 responses, not all of them complete. Nevertheless, the picture that emerges from the report is one of a fragmented and nonstandardized response to a global threat.

THE RESPONSE

Aside from stretching and reworking legal principles such as jurisdiction and issuing strategies, there have been several key responses to the challenges of cybercrime and cyber-enabled criminality. For example, the Metropolitan Police Service was recently reported as having substantially expanded its E-crime unit to a reported 500 officers in response to the threat of "cybercrime" having become a Tier One National Security threat. This is consistent with the responses having effect across the UK law enforcement community. The Police Reform and Social Responsibility Act 2011—the legislation that created elected police and crime commissioners—also introduced the concept of the Strategic Policing Requirement (SPR). The SPR is published by the Home Secretary and sets out those national threats that require a coordinated or aggregated response in which resources are brought together from a number of police forces; it applies to all police forces in England and Wales and is referred to by other law enforcement agencies throughout the United Kingdom.

The SPR identifies how police forces and their governance bodies often need to work collaboratively inter se, and with other partners, national agencies or national arrangements, to ensure such threats are tackled efficiently and effectively.

The SPR contains five areas of activity and threat that are, if at a Tier One or Tier Two risk level in the National Security Risk Assessment, covered. These are:

- Terrorism (Tier One)
- Other civil emergencies requiring an aggregated response across police force boundaries
- Organized crime (Tier Two)
- Threats to public order or public safety that cannot be managed by a single police force acting alone
- A large-scale cyber incident (Tier One) including the risk of a hostile attack upon cyberspace by other states

The SPR recognizes that there may be considerable overlap between these areas. For example, there may be a substantial organized crime element involved in a cyber incident and vice versa. All elected police and crime commissioners and their respective chief police officers must have regard to the SPR in their planning and operational arrangements. This is an important legal obligation for reasons that are discussed below.

Having set out these key risks to national security, the SPR requires policing bodies to have adequate arrangements in place to ensure that their local resources can deliver the requisite:

Capacity
Capability
Consistency
Connectivity and
Contribution

to the national effort (the five "'Cs").

Given the legal and practical difficulties that are explored infra, the extent to which local policing bodies are in a position to meet these criteria in a meaningful way in relation to "cyber incidents"—whether "upon" or within cyberspace is questionable. For example, while it is a relatively simple task to assess the capacity and capability of a group of local police force (even a large one such as the Metropolitan Police) to tackle large-scale public disorder, and to measure the connectivity of their resources in preparing for such an event, it is far harder to demonstrate that the same forces meet the five C requirements (capability, connectivity, and so on) required to understand and respond to even a highly localized cyber incident, still less a cyber attack sponsored by another state. This too is important because the courts in the United Kingdom have interpreted the expression "have regard to" a government policy as meaning that public bodies fixed with such a duty must above all properly understand that policy. If a government policy to which a public body must have regard is not properly understood by that body this has the same legal effect as if that body had paid no regard to it at all. Further, if a public body is going to depart from a government policy to which it must "have regard," that body has to give clear reasons for doing so, such that people know why and on what grounds it is being departed from. While the EU might have a series of arrangements in place which require Member States to notify them of "incidents" that "seem to relate to cyber espionage or a state-sponsored attack" and invoke the relevant parts of the EU Solidarity Clause, there is little evidence that most police areas would be in a position confidently to make that assertion, promptly or at all.

Quaere: how well are all affected police agencies in England and Wales able to demonstrate that they have properly understood the threat of a cyber attack in the context of the SPR? If the answer to this is anything other than an unqualified "yes," then they might do well to issue a notification to that effect to their respective communities and stakeholders.

CONCLUSION

Tackling computer-enabled criminality has generally focused on the physical presence of those controlling, benefiting, or suffering from the remote activity—it has been concerned with input and output. The European Union has a proposed Directive to require Member States to ensure they have minimum levels of capability in place, along with Computer Emergency Response Teams (CERTs) and arrangements for effective coordination of "network and information systems." At the same time the Budapest Convention has been in force for almost a decade to provide a model for the many signatory nations (including the United States) to draft their domestic "cybercrime" legislation and the correlative cyber security industry is vast and burgeoning. But is there not a pressing need to tackle what is taking place in cyberspace itself? Using existing jurisdictional theories is arguably not enough; what is needed is not a partial application of some extra-cyberspace laws adapted to suit some extra-cyberspace consequences. Continuing to apply the traditional criminological approaches to technological innovation in the context of cyberspace is, it is submitted, rather like separating criminality that takes place within an underground transport network from that where the offender uses the London Underground to facilitate their offending. In the first situation the setting is a key component of the offending while, in the second, it is a chosen part of the wider modus operandi and the offender might just as easily have chosen to take the bus, a taxi or to walk to and from the locus of their crime. This is the fundamental difference between cyber-enabled offending and offending within cyberspace. Policing the exits and entrances is never going to be a complete or even satisfactory answer to the latter. Aside from the practical and jurisprudential reasons, there are also important political imperatives beginning to emerge. For example India's Telecom and IT Minister Kapil Sibal asserted recently that there should be "accountability and responsibility" in the cyberspace in the same way as in diplomatic relations:

> *If there is a cyberspace violation and the subject matter is India because it impacts India, then India should have jurisdiction. For example, if I have an embassy in New York, then anything that happens in that embassy is Indian territory and there applies Indian Law.*

For this approach to go beyond the conventional jurisdictional approaches considered supra would require a whole new set of processes, procedures and skills; it would take more than the publication of a set of agreed standards or an agreed recipe for domestic legislation. There needs, it is submitted, to be a new presence in cyberspace, a dedicated cyber force to tackle what the Director-General of the National Crime Agency, Keith Bristow, calls "digital criminality." Perhaps what is needed is not a new way of overlaying our conventional law enforcement assets and techniques on cyberspace or a new way of extending our two-dimensional constructs of jurisdiction to fit a multi-dimensional world, but a new wave of cyber assets—"cyber constables" as it were—to patrol and police the cyber communities of the future. However, given our global experience of the ways in which some state agencies have operated within cyberspace, in the post-Snowden era that perennial question of democratic law enforcement "quis cusodiet" sits just as fixedly above cyber policing as it has in every analog setting to date.

REFERENCES

Armstrong, T., Zuckerberg, M., Page, L., Rottenberg, E., Smith, B., Costelo, D., 2013. An Open Letter to Washington. 9 (December 2013).

Beaulac, S., 2004. The Westphalian model in defining international law: challenging the myth. Austral. J. Legal History 7, 181–213.

Bender, G., 1998. Bavaria v. Felix Somm: the pornography conviction of the former CompuServe manager. Int. J. Commun, Law Policy Web-Doc 14-1-1998.

Canham, D., 2012. Freedom of Information Request to Secretary of State for Justice. (accessed 24.10.2012). https://www.whatdotheyknow.com/request/computer_misuse_act_2.

Cottim, A., 2010. Cybercrime, cyberterrorism and jurisdiction: an analysis of article 22 of the COE convention on cybercrime. Eur. J. Leg. Stud. 2 (3), European University Institute, San Dominico de Fiesole, Italy.

Sampson, F., 1991a. Criminal Acts and Computer Users Justice of the Peace. Chichester 155 (14), 211.

Sampson, F., 1991b. Criminal Acts and Computers. March 1991, Police Requirements Support Unit Bulletin 39, 58, Home Office Science & Technology Group, London.

Sampson, F., Kinnear, F., 2010. Plotting criminal activity: too true to be good crime mapping in the UK. Oxford J. Policing 4 (1), 2–3.

Vatis, M.A., 2010. Proceedings of a Workshop on Deterring Cyberattacks: Informing Strategies and Developing Options for U.S. Policy. National Research Council, The National Academies Press, Washington, DC, pp. 207–223.

Definitions of Cyber Terrorism

2

Eric Luiijf

INTRODUCTION

The phrase cyber terror appeared for the first time in the mid-eighties. According to several sources, Barry C. Collin, a senior person research fellow of the Institute for Security and Intelligence in California, defined cyber terror at that time as "the convergence of cybernetics and terrorism"—an elegant and simple definition. That definition, however, was not specific enough to make a clear distinction with terms like cybercrime, cyber activism (hacktivism), and cyber extremism.

The first glimpses of the cyber revolution, the next wave after the industrial revolution, were much debated in the eighties (e.g., Toffler, 1980). It was therefore no surprise that the first discussions were raised in that decade about cyber terror and terrorism in the envisioned new world. In the nineties, the debate about the cyber revolution widened to phenomenon such as information warfare and information superiority. That reinforced the idea again that terrorists could enter cyberspace and use that as a domain for terroristic actions. This idea was reflected by the National Research Council (1991): "Tomorrow's terrorist may be able to do more damage with a keyboard than with a bomb." As a result, cyber terrorism was added to the list of serious national threats to the United States.

The unexpected outcome of the 1993 battle of Mogadishu (Bowden, 1999) showed the potential of an asymmetric threat with a major political impact, and with the millennium uncertainties, further widened the societal uncertainty about a possible terrorist initiated risk from cyberspace for the public. Since then, the term cyber terror has helped to create dramatic and attention grabbing newspaper headlines. This chapter subsequently asserts that, based on a definition developed from previous definitions, the world has not yet experienced a real cyber terror impacting event.

THE CONFUSION ABOUT CYBER TERRORISM

Around the millennium, many experts from different disciplines showed interest in the potential of cyber terrorism. For that reason, a wide range of moderate definitions for cyber terrorism were proposed, especially in the period between 1997 and 2001. The reason for the incoherence of the definitions stems from the fact that their origin lay in quite different expert fields such as law enforcement, international studies, anti-terror, information security, and information operations. The popular press even creates more confusion. Below several of these definitions will be discussed to show examples of the confusion. From these definitions we can derive elements for an encompassing definition of cyber terror as stated in the following sections. The definitions also demonstrate that no act of cyber terror has occurred yet.

In 1997, Mark Pollitt of the FBI defined cyber terrorism as:

> *The premeditated, politically motivated attack against information, computer systems, computer programs, and data which result in violence against non-combatant targets by sub-national groups or clandestine agents (FBI, 1997).*

The emphasis in this definition lies on the what, and whom. The terror-related aspect of fear is lacking as well as the use of threatening with an attack. Combatants are excluded, which reflected FBI's mandate but did not help to derive the comprehensive definition. In 2004, the FBI (Lourdeau, 2004) redefined cyber terrorism as:

> *A criminal act perpetrated by the use of computers and telecommunications capabilities, resulting in violence, destruction and/or disruption of services, where the intended purpose is to create fear by causing confusion and uncertainty within a given population, with the goal of influencing a government or population to conform to a particular political, social or ideological agenda (FBI, 2004).*

This definition focuses on the criminality of the act, the traditional information and communication technology (ICT) means, the intended impact, and motivation. The definition lacks a wider view on newer ICT, such as those embedded in for instance critical infrastructures, cars, and medical equipment. The impact in the definition is limited only to raising fear and uncertainty whereas terrorism may aim at disrupting the economy, the environment, international relationships, and governmental governance processes as well.

In 2000, the information security expert Professor Dorothy E. Denning defined cyber terrorism as:

> *an attack that results in violence against persons or property, or at least causes enough harm to generate fear (Denning, 2000).*

This definition has its focus on the possible impact of cyber terrorism. Why terrorists would perform an act of cyber terrorism and the how are not discussed. After 09/11, she redefined cyber terrorism in (Denning, 2001) as:

> *unlawful attacks and threats of attack against computers, networks, and the information stored therein when done to intimidate or coerce a government or its people in furtherance of political or social objectives (Denning, 2001).*

This definition stems clearly from an information security point of view. Its focus is on the integrity and availability of information. This definition does not cover physical effects as a result of an affected cyber layer. The definition also fails to make a clear distinction with cyber activism (hacktivism).

In 2002, the US Center for Strategic and International Studies defined cyber terrorism as:

The use of computer network tools to shut down critical national infrastructure (such as energy, transportation, government operations) or to coerce or intimidate a government or civilian population (Lewis, 2002).

This definition is imprecise. For instance, this definition suggests that a critical infrastructure operator who shuts down a (part of) critical infrastructure for technical or safety reasons from his/her operating station could be a cyber terrorist. At the same time, hacktivists trying to impress governmental decision-makers are cyber terrorists as well—and are not included.

When reflecting on press headlines from the last 25 years, it immediately becomes apparent that each new disruption related to our cyber world is labeled by popular press as "cyber terror." Then with hindsight, the "cyber terror" event is hardly remembered a couple of years later. At most it is regarded as a simple act of cybercrime or activism. In instances where it was a denial-of-service attack, the sustained bandwidth of daily annoying attacks to organizations is often factored higher than the simple cyber surface scratching event which was labeled as a cyber-terror event in the press.

Another source of confusion stems from the use of the term "cyber terror" for all use of cyberspace activities by terrorists and terrorist groups. It is the combination of cyberspace as a possible target and a weapon used by terrorists and terrorist groups of the communication commodity services we all use. Terrorists use cyberspace for their command and control, global information exchange and planning, fundraising and attempts to increase their support, community, propaganda, recruitment, and information operations (Bosch et al., 1999) to influence the public opinion (NCTb, 2009). Some of this use may be considered crime or even cybercrime by national governments, but it will not be considered "terrorism" according to the various national legal systems.

CYBER TERRORISM DEFINITION

As discussed in the previous section, large differences are visible between the previous and many more definitions of cyber terrorism. Some of the proposed definitions are restricted by the mandate and thus the confined view of an organization; others concentrate on specific ICT technologies, targets, or motivations of the actors.

What is needed is a definition which clearly defines cyber terrorism from ordinary cybercrime, hacktivism, and even cyber extremism. From the above, it will be clear that elements which need to be part of the definition are:

- The legal context (intent, conspiracy, just the threat or act?)
- Cyberspace being used as a weapon or being a target
- The objective(s) of the malicious act which include a kind of violence with far-reaching psychological effects to the targeted audience
- The intent combined with the long-term goal (e.g., societal or political change; influencing political decision-making) which drives the terrorist or terrorist group.

With respect to cyberspace—systems, networks and information—as a weapon or a target, we can distinguish cyber attacks by cyber terrorists on (or a combination of):

- The integrity of information (e.g., unauthorized deletion, unauthorized changes) causing the loss of trust in ICT and society. Targets could be databases that are critical to society: person records, vehicle registration, property ownerships, and financial records and accounts.
- The confidentiality of information. Large-scale breaches of personal privacy and organizations' confidential information could create societal disorder, e.g. the publication of the complete health records of HIV-infected persons in a nation could initiate a sequence of harassments and suicides. The response by a government may breach the privacy of citizens and result in the amplification of the intended terrorist objectives.
- The availability of ICT-based services through ICT-means, for example by a long duration denial-of-service attack, an unauthorized disruption of systems and networks, or physical or electromagnetic attack on data centers and critical ICT-system components.
- ICT-based processes which control real-world physical processes, e.g. a nuclear power plant, refinery, vehicles and other forms of transport, health monitoring and control, smart grids and smart cities (see Chapter 3 on New and Emerging Threats).

In order to provide a more precise definition of cyber terrorism based on all elements identified before, we first need to look at the definition of terrorism which shall encompass the cyber terrorism definition. Unfortunately there is no generally agreed international definition of terrorism, see for instance Saul (2005).

UK's Terrorism Act (UK, 2000) defines terrorism as:

The use or threat of action designed to influence the government or an international governmental organisation or to intimidate the public, or a section of the public; made for the purposes of advancing a political, religious, racial or ideological cause.

It involves or causes:

- *serious violence against a person;*
- *serious damage to a property;*
- *a threat to a person's life;*
- *a serious risk to the health and safety of the public; or*
- *serious interference with or disruption to an electronic system (UK Terrorism Act 2000).*

Interestingly this definition includes a cyber aspect as well. The definition contains some weak points, for instance a political party trying to influence the government to reintroduce smoking at offices by cancelling the anti-smoking laws is involved with a serious risk to the health and safety of the public. This definition states that such a party is a terror organization.

In 2010, the Netherlands government changed its terrorism definition to align the definition used by its justice system with the operational definition of its intelligence services. At the same time the Dutch government tried to align with the terrorism definition provided by European Council (2002) and the United Nations. The Dutch working definition of terrorism (NCTb, 2014) is:

threatening, making preparations for or perpetrating, for ideological reasons, acts of serious violence directed at people or other acts intended to cause property damage that could spark social disruption, for the purpose of bringing about social change, creating a climate of fear among the general public, or influencing political decision-making.

However, when comparing the UK's considered terroristic impact part with elsewhere defined national interests, the UK's "damage to a property" sounds weak. The Dutch, for example, consider "disruptive economic damage," "serious negative impacts to the ecological security," and "a serious change of social and political stability" as elements to be mitigated national risk.

On the basis of preceding considerations, terrorism probably can be better defined as:

The use, making preparations for, or threat of action designed to cause a social order change, to create a climate of fear or intimidation amongst (part of) the general public, or to influence political decision-making by the government or an international governmental organisation; made for the purposes of advancing a political, religious, racial or ideological cause; and it involves or causes:

- *violence to, suffering of, serious injuries to, or the death of (a) persons(s),*
- *serious damage to a property,*
- *a serious risk to the health and safety of the public,*
- *a serious economic loss,*
- *a serious breach of ecological safety,*
- *a serious breach of the social and political stability and cohesion of a nation.*

From that, we can derive a definition of cyber terrorism as:

The use, making preparations for, or threat of action designed to cause a social order change, to create a climate of fear or intimidation amongst (part of) the general public, or to influence political decision-making by the government or an international governmental organisation; made for the purposes of advancing a political, religious, racial or ideological cause; by affecting the integrity, confidentiality, and/or availability of information, information systems and networks, or by unauthorised actions affecting information and communication technology-based control of real-world physical processes; and it involves or causes:

- *violence to, suffering of, serious injuries to, or the death of (a) persons(s),*
- *serious damage to a property,*
- *a serious risk to the health and safety of the public,*

- *a serious economic loss,*
- *a serious breach of ecological safety,*
- *a serious breach of the social and political stability and cohesion of a nation.*

HAS CYBER TERRORISM EVER OCCURRED?

Using the final definition above, there is only a limited set of actions after the mid-eighties which may have neared a real cyber terror act. A first one was during the Nagorno-Karabakh conflict around 1999. Following unconfirmed reports, hackers modified blood types in patient records in a hospital database causing the risk of people dying through receiving the wrong blood transfusion. A second one may be the 2006–2007 preparations by an Al Qa'ida-related terrorist group which planned to physically target the Telehouse telecommunications centre and internet exchange in the London Docklands area. In August 2006, the potential societal effect of such an attack was demonstrated by a small power disruption at Telehouse. This technical disruption took down tens of thousands websites and hundred thousand customers of Plusnet internet services for a number of hours (Wearden, 2006). The societal effects of a possible long-duration disruption which could have been the result of a successful physical attack can only be guessed but probably would have been minor given the redundancy of systems, networks, backed up information, and services.

All other cyber disruptions that took place were labeled as cyber-terror acts by the news media, were (although for the public and organizations sometimes disturbing and annoying) ICT-disruptions caused by acts of cybercrime or hacktivism, or turned out to be technical in nature.

CONCLUSIONS

This chapter discussed the elements which are required to classify an event as a cyber-terroristic act and derives a definition of cyber terror.

Despite the many media headlines, it is asserted that based on the definition shaped above, that no clear act of cyber terrorism has occurred yet. We need to be prepared, however, for acts of cyber terror as the increasing societal critical reliance on ICT will make ICT systems and services as well as embedded ICT an interesting target for future terrorists.

REFERENCES

Bosch, J.M.J., Luiijf, H.A.M., Mollema, A.R., 1999. Information Operations. Netherlands Annual Review of Military Studies (NL ARMS). Tilburg University Press, Tilburg, The Netherlands.

Bowden, M., 1999. Black Hawk Down: A Story of Modern War. Atlantic Monthly Press, Berkeley, CA, USA.

Denning, D.E., 2000. Cyberterrorism—Testimony before the Special Oversight Panel on Terrorism Committee on Armed Services U.S. House of Representatives. House of Representatives, Washington, DC, USA. http://www.fas.org/irp/congress/2000_hr/00-05-23denning.htm (accessed 23.02.14).

Denning, D.E., 2001. Is Cyber Terror Next? Social Science Research Council, Washington, DC, USA. http://www.fas.org/irp/congress/2000_hr/00-05-23denning.htm (accessed 23.02.14).

European Council, 2002. Council Framework Decision 2002/475/JHA of 13 June 2002 on combating terrorism. Council of the European Union, Brussels (Belgium). http://eur-lex.europa.eu/LexUriServ/LexUriServ.do?uri=CELEX:32002F0475:EN:NOT (accessed 23.02.14).

Lewis, J.A., 2002. Assessing the Risk of Cyber Terrorism, Cyber War and Other Cyber Threats. Center for Strategic and International Studies, Washington, DC, USA. http://csis.org/files/media/csis/pubs/021101_risks_of_cyberterror.pdf (23.02.14).

Lourdeau, K., 2004. Testimony of Keith Lourdeau, Deputy Assistant Director, Cyber Division, FBI before the Senate Judiciary Subcommittee on Terrorism, Technology, and Homeland Security, February 24, 2004, Senate, Washington, DC, USA. http://www.fbi.gov/news/testimony/hearing-on-cyber-terrorism (accessed 23.02.14).

National Research Council, 1991. Computers at Risk: Safe Computing in the Information Age. National Academy Press, Washington, DC, USA.

NCTb, 2009. Jihadists and the Internet (2009 update). National Coordinator for Counterterrorism, Den Haag, The Netherlands. http://www.fas.org/irp/world/netherlands/jihadists.pdf, (accessed 23.02.14).

NCTb, 2014. What is Terrorism? National Coordinator for Counterterrorism, Den Haag, the Netherlands. http://english.nctb.nl/themes_en/Counterterrorism/what_is_terrorism, (23.02.14).

Pollitt, M.M., 1997. Cyberterrorism—Fact or Fancy? In: Proceedings of the 20th National Information Systems Security Conference, Baltimore, USA. http://www.cs.georgetown.edu/~denning/infosec/pollitt.html, (accessed 23.02.14).

Saul, B., 2005. Attempts to define 'terrorism' in international law. T.M.C. Asser Press, the Netherlands. Netherlands Intern. Law Rev 52 (1), 57–83.

Toffler, A., 1980. The Third Wave. Bantam Books, Morrow, USA.

UK, 2000. Terrorism Act 2000. UK Legislation, London, UK. http://www.legislation.gov.uk/ukpga/2000/11/contents (accessed 23.02.14).

Wearden, G., 2006. Power outage knocks ISPs offline. Zdnet, United Kingdom. http://www.zdnet.com/power-outage-knocks-isps-offline-3039281211/, (accessed 23.02.14).

New and emerging threats of cyber crime and terrorism

3

Eric Luiijf

INTRODUCTION

Advancements in information and communication technologies (ICT) inextricably bring new threats to the end-users and society. However, the last 40 years have shown that many of the same cyber security design and programming failures occur over and over again when a new ICT innovation and development cycle takes place. Unfortunately, this allows us to predict new cyber security failures in the next innovation cycle. The reason is that with each new ICT advancement developers and programmers fail to take previously identified cyber security lessons into account. They grow up in the totally new ICT-development cycles and environments. They are even motivated and encouraged to disregard "old school" ICT.

Firstly, a short historic overview about some of the developments in cyber threats and related cybercrime is provided. This serves as a basis for the next section which discusses previous ICT innovation cycles show the recurrence of cyber security failures with patching and fixing afterwards, and the lack of learning the previously identified cyber security lessons. A section about organizational issues is presented, and based on the lessons identified in the past, a final section discusses new ICT innovations and predicts new and emerging threats as well as disguised old threats in a new fabric which may be exploited by cyber criminals, hacktivists, industrial spies, and states.

SOME HISTORIC MILESTONES

When discussing cyber-related crime EC (2007) recognized three different types of cybercrime, overlooking the fourth one added below:

1. traditional forms of crime using cyber relates to, e.g., forgery and web shop and e-market types of fraud,
2. illegal content, e.g., pirated music and child pornography,
3. crimes unique to electronic networks such as hacking and denial-of-service attacks,
4. crimes unique to cyberspace which intent to have effects to physical systems and or in the physical world, e.g., the cyber manipulation of process control systems in the gas transport grid causing a pipeline rupture and subsequent explosions.

Many people today think that cybercrime is recent problem. The contrary is true as the following examples show:

- According to DHS (2014), "Beginning in 1970, and over the course of three years, the chief teller at the Park Avenue branch of New York's Union Dime Savings Bank manipulated the account information on the bank's computer system to embezzle over $1.5 million from hundreds of customer accounts." Many more types of cybercrimes (e.g., forgery and fraud) have followed since then.
- Although the first replicating computer codes were developed in the 1960s, it took until 1971 before Bob Thomas developed the Creeper virus which infected other systems in the Arpanet. Although unwillingly running computer code at systems owned by another organization, his "experiment" was not yet considered a crime at that time.
- In early 1977, an insider over a weekend stole hundreds of original computer tapes and their back-ups from the computer center and back-up storage of a chemical industry company called ICI. He tried to extort ICI and requested 275.000 pound sterling (Geelof, 2007). After the perpetrator was apprehended, the newspaper headline stated "The theft of computer data of ICI marks a new era of criminality" (Korver, 2007).
- On November 2, 1988, Robert T. Morris released the first computer worm on the Internet which infected thousands of systems. In 1990, Morris was convicted under the 1986 Computer Fraud and Abuse Act. He was sentenced to three years of probation, 400 h of community service, and a fine of 10,000 USD (Markoff, 1990).
- In 1994, Russian hackers made 40 transfers which totaled over 10 million USD from Citybank to bank accounts in Finland, Russia, Germany, the Netherlands, the United States, Israel and Switzerland. All but $400K of the money was recovered (Harmon, 1995). This case showed that cybercrime could result in unauthorized transfers of high amounts of money.
- In 1995, the first phishing attempts took place.
- In 1997, the Electronic Disturbance Theater (EDT) was formed. EDT created tools to establish an electronic version of sit-ins on the internet. On April 10, 1998, their Floodnet tool was used by protesters from many nations to perform denial-of-service attacks on the website of the President of Mexico and later on the White House (Wray, 1998).
- In January 1998, a disgruntled system operator remotely manipulated the SCADA system of a coal-fired power plant putting it in emergency mode and removed the SCADA system software.
- In 2005, the air conditioning system of a European bank's computer center was deliberately hacked. The computer room temperature slowly increased and caused a shutdown of all computer system services.
- In 2006, the Russian Business Network (RBN) started. Soon after its inception, RBN was a central point for offering cybercrime tools and services for spam, phishing, Trojans and more.
- In July 2010, the existence of the one month earlier detected Stuxnet process control system worm became widely known. Stuxnet specifically targeted

the Siemens process control systems of the uranium enrichment plant in Natanz, Iran. Its effect was that it covertly cybotaged the speed control of the ultracentrifuges resulting in extreme wear and tear (Falliere et al., 2010) (for further reference to this case please see Chapters 9 and 13).

- In 2011, British intelligence agencies replaced a webpage with a recipe for making bombs by a recipe for making cup cakes (Huff Post Food, 2011).

If we neglect the traditional forms of crime and the illegal content type of cyber-crime, the examples above show cybercrime, hacktivism, and (state) cyber operations which exploited the ICT-vulnerabilities of technology, of organizations, and of human behavior.

CYBER SECURITY LESSONS NOT LEARNED FROM PREVIOUS ICT INNOVATION CYCLES

ICT has gone through a number of innovation cycles since its start in World War II. New ICT developments are adopted by industry and society in a way which reflects the technology adaption lifecycle model coined by Bohlen and Beal (1957). Early adopters take up the innovations. After the breakthrough of an ICT innovation, a fast uptake by users and organizations can be recognized. Later on, a mainstream phase occurs in which the negative drawbacks of the new innovations have been overcome.

It was shown by Venkatesh et al. (2003) and Venkatesh and Bala (2008) that adopting ICT innovations largely relates to the ease of use and its usefulness to the end-users and their organizations; in short, user-friendly functionality. The cyber security aspects of ICT innovations do not play a role according to their findings. After the many ICT innovation cycles we have gone through, one could expect that cyber security requirements would have come more to the forefront, but that is obviously not the case. The main reason is that no cyber security lessons are learned from earlier ICT innovation cycles and that the same mistakes are repeated over and over again as the driving forces for ICT innovation come from outside security-aware communities.

In the 1960s, one could walk to a terminal and start typing a username and password to log-in. If the username was entered wrongly, a new user environment was created. The usernames and passwords were stored clearly on the system and the password file often was accessible to all users and system programs. Over time, the security of computer access was improved and the number of times one could try passwords for a certain username became limited. The manifold of security problems posed by buffer overflows and lack of input validation allowing hackers to elevate their access level to system resources were fixed in the operating systems of mainframes in the mid-seventies. However, each new operating system version contained the same type of design and coding errors in newly developed functionality and patching of those holes was required.

In the seventies, existing and new computer companies caused an ICT revolution by bringing mini computers and midi computers to department levels of organizations. As these systems were intended to be used in small cooperative environments, ease of use was their advantage point. One could walk up to the system, reboot the system and run ones' programs without any computer security measure other than the physical access to the room. Multi-user use was added in a simplistic way as seen from a computer security aspect. For example, the original UNIX/etc/passwd file was world-readable. It showed the usernames, and their related one-way encrypted passwords and the random salt value. The one-way encryption process was supposed to provide strong system access security as the process was irreversible. The claim was right; however as the encryption process was public, hackers simply used brute force processing of all character permutations through the fast password algorithm and compared the outcome with the encrypted passwords in the password file. Out of the box thinking resulted in a simple way to reveal usernames and passwords. Moreover, Moore's law caused an increase in processing speed each year and thus decreased the password strength and time needed to break username-password combinations.

Other operating systems at that time allowed the user to interrupt a program which had access to the password file and created a memory dump containing all passwords in plain text.

Moreover, similar to earlier mainframes, the operating systems in minis and midis were not secured against hackers as bad coding practices were used, e.g., buffer overflows and lack of input validation. Providing new functionality in the operating system had priority over security.

Apple launched its Apple II in 1977. IBM followed with the Personal Computer (PC) in 1981. The initial disk operating systems did not provide any security other than a read-only bit to protect against the accidental overwriting of a file. It was personal computers after all.

Networking of PCs onwards from 1983, e.g., with Novell and LAN Manager, required more security to be added in hindsight to the PC. The increase in malware such as viruses and worms required additional security measures to be added to the PC platform—which was not intended to be secure at all—and its subsequent Windows operating systems. Major failures in computer security were found in simple access to the memory of system and other applications, disk scavenging, clear text passwords on the network, and too simple implementations of security measures that dealt with legacy protocols. An example was the legacy support for LAN Manager in Windows/NT where one easily could determine the length of a users' password. In a similar manner, the protection of the Windows/NT password file and file system was based on internal system protection, it failed when hackers out of the box used of a Unix-based bootable floppy disk and application to access the system device.

It took until after the millennium before manufacturers like Microsoft started to take the security of their server operating systems serious. At the same time, design failures occurred in the encryption processes of wireless networking technology. The push to the world-wide market and of the new functionality was more important than proper cyber security. In a fast sequence, the wireless encryption protocol WEP was shown to be insecure causing the need for their replacement which was broken soon thereafter. Why did the system designers and programmers not learn from the lessons identified with earlier security failures? Why did they only look for functionality?

In parallel, ICT found its way in the automation of physical and real-world processes such as in the chemical industry, switching of rail points, and the control of the power, gas and water grids. The Supervisory Control And Data Acquisition (SCADA) and similar process control protocols were designed without many security considerations. The software was proprietary and no one else was interested in its detailed working. The process control networks were closed, therefore no hackers would have access. The same manufacturer root password which one could not change was embedded in thousands of units all over the world. The Stuxnet case was a case in making use of such a design and deployment error (Falliere et al., 2010).

The design, implementations of SCADA protocols and the protection of systems in the field did not keep pace with the security considerations ahead of their field. Connectivity with public networks, ease of teleworking, and tools like Shodan which identify vulnerable process control systems connected to the internet create the access paths for cyber criminals to critical infrastructures such as our energy grids (Averill and Luiijf, 2010).

Only some years ago, testing a SCADA network with the ICT-network tool Nmap at a large inhomogeneous SCADA installation caused one-third of the SCADA implementation to crash and another one-third to stop communication. The SCADA protocol implementations could not deal with an unexpected byte more or less in a received packet. It failed to validate the received protocol packets as the implementation expected a benign operating environment.

These are just some examples of ICT innovations and adaptation cycles where the system designers did not properly take security considerations into account and the programmers failed to learn from cyber security lessons identified in earlier ICT adaptation cycles. Failing to protect against buffer overflows, no input validation, not cleaning of sensitive information from re-usable memory buffers, and embedding system passwords are just some examples of errors—and thus disguised old threats—that occur over and over again with each ICT innovation cycle.

Moreover, new ICT-functionality itself provides unknown backdoors. For example, new versions of Programmable Logic Controller (PLC) boards nowadays may contain an embedded web engines. Often such new PLC boards replace old defective PLC boards. The new functionality, however, allows access to all PLC functions unless someone takes the time to lock the web interface entry.

More examples of these and other threats to process control systems can be found in Luiijf (2010).

ORGANIZATIONAL ASPECTS NOT LEARNED FROM PREVIOUS ICT INNOVATION CYCLES

When we take a look at the end-user side, early adopters of ICT innovations mainly focus on effectiveness increases, "cool" applications, and ease of use. Therefore, manufacturers are rewarded by early adopters for being first on the market with their cool new functionality, for not bringing months later a secured, well tested, and less easy to use innovation empowered by the use of ICT.

During the mainstream phase of an ICT innovation cycle, the whole chain (from manufacturer, sales force, and acquisition process at the end-user, system integrator, installer, third-party maintenance organization, and the daily operations by the end-user) largely fails to take cyber security into account. The whole process is focused on providing functionality, not on a secure operational environment. It starts with the manufacturer's installation guide which discusses electromagnetic compatibility on the first pages, then where to connect the power cord and network plug. Security, if at all, is loosely documented after page 60. It even may be surprising that standard manufacturer passwords sometimes have been modified. Where ICT is almost hidden as part of easier to functionality, people are "unconsciously insecure." An extensive discussion on this phenomenon and some detailed examples of avoidable cyber security failures can be found in Luiijf (2013).

EMERGING THREATS

From the above, it will be clear that any next ICT innovation cycle will result in new threats to end-users and our society. The bright new ICT inventors focus on the new functionality, increased efficiency and effectiveness of people and organizations, and ease of use. They lack any historic understanding of previous secure design failures and of earlier lessons identified in good coding practices.

This means that emerging threats can be predicted in new fields of ICT, especially where ICT is deeply embedded in functional systems. Often the threats are old threats disguised in a new look. These will allow cybercriminals, hacktivists, cyber spies, and states to enter ICT-based systems in an unauthorized way by making use of:

- Weaknesses in the validation of input values and protocol elements causing unexpected inputs to be used as a can opener.
- Buffer overflows allowing elevation of access rights to system manager (root) level.
- Man in the middle attacks to near field and wireless communication channels.
- The addition of self-configuring hardware modules to an existing system or network providing a backdoor.
- Publically known manufacturer and other default passwords.
- Unconfigured functionality which provides a backdoor.
- Unconsciously insecure managed ICT, often embedded in functions where people do not understand that it contains ICT under the "hood."

The above forms a basis to understand the large number of next innovation areas where ICT is embedded and which may provide or already provides such security threats and new attack routes. We can distinguish mass products and essential parts of critical sectors:

1. Modern living: Increasingly, digital TVs are connected to public networks and the internet. The many millions of digital TVs with sets of fast video processing engines are an attractive source of processing power for cyber criminals, e.g., to make them part of botnets. The digital TV soon will become

an open platform; see for instance the Wyplay developments, making the TV the heart of multi-media, gaming and other new digital services. Obviously, there is not yet a clear concern about the cyber security threats of the digital TV until it will be too late.

2. Modern living: Domotics (domestic robots) will take off soon. An increasing number of early adopters currently monitor and change temperature settings in their home or office remotely from their smart phone. This is just a first step in the remote management of the home. No one discusses the cyber security threats related to these functions.

3. Health sector: An increasing number of ICT-based systems are used to monitor the health of persons. Pacemakers and insulin pumps already have been hacked through their wireless interface. The designers did not take into account that hackers might be interested in manipulating such small systems. The wrong settings, however, may have a life-threatening effect (Stigherrian, 2011).

4. Soon, devices which monitor persons with a health problem on a 24/7 basis will be connected to the global grid with mobile and wireless technologies. If functionality goes first, manipulated data may cause all such patients automatically be phoned to report immediately at the hospital, or may cause wrong levels of medicines to be prescribed to patients.

5. Health monitoring and other medical equipment in hospitals is increasingly connected to the hospitals' core network. As the protection of such networks may be weak for reasons discussed above, patients may be at risk. Impossible? In the Netherlands, a health monitoring system in a hospital emergency room was found to be a member of the Kazaa music sharing network. Thinking about cyber security seems to be discouraged near medical equipment. Is that because the cyber threat raises one's pulse rate beyond healthy limits? Actually it is the unconsciously insecure phenomenon again.

6. Financial sector: Near Field Communication (NFC) chips provide a new form of identification and authentication for the holder of a smart phone. This forms the basis for contactless micro payments. It can be expected that cybercrime will take advance of the payment function by remote manipulation of the smart phone.

7. Transport sector: Modern cars and trucks contain an enormous amount of lines of code in its increasing number of electronic control units (ECU). According to TRB (2012), they are literally "computers on wheels." The code modules monitor an increasing number of sensors and control and activate many actuators from brakes to windscreen wipers, from lights to collision avoidance systems. As many manufacturers develop modules, the interfaces between them need to be open. They presume a benign closed environment without hackers. However, if not already in your current car, network interfaces with public networks soon will provide automatic emergency call services such as Assist™ and eCall. Other services will follow which means that mobile data and mobile internet interfaces will open the car platform for two-way communication. Cybercrime will follow in due time.

Note that cars may not only be used for their mobility function. The battery may be used as temporary storage for locally produced power which can be used later to sell it at a much higher price to the power grid. Cyber criminals may try to disrupt such mechanisms in order to affect the cyber-physical grid behavior and energy market prices.

Another expected innovation stimulated by the authorities may be the activation of all car horns in a selected area. They may be an alternate to the hard to maintain, costly and in rural areas ineffective emergency siren system. Such functionality may be of interest to hackers to show their abilities (probably in the mid of the night).

Experiments with collaborative and fully automatic driving of cars and trucks take place in the USA and EU. Safety is an issue, but ICT security aspects seem to be of less concern despite many successful hacking attacks on cars in laboratory settings (Rouf et al., 2010). Moreover, the threat to the security of the transport system, e.g., due to malware affecting a specific car type or specific type of ECU, has not been addressed upfront. Once again, earlier identified lessons are not taken into account. Moreover, mechanics that perform the software upgrades to your car during maintenance have not been trained in cyber securing the laptop they hook up to cars, another unconsciously insecure risk. A more detailed analysis of threats to ICT systems in and around cars can be found in Bijlsma et al. (2013).

Another innovation is that of the next generation digital red light/speed trap camera. It will require only a power source. A wide range of wired and wireless connectivity means it provides for remote access. As the camera can be programmed remotely to read number plates and decide upon the information that is stored and transmitted for a picture for issuing a fine, it will be an attractive functional box for hackers to create havoc, e.g., take a photo of each taxi independent of its speed during the green phase.

8. Energy and drinking water sectors: Smart meters are rolled out now in a number of nations. They will form the first smart interface between the utility grids (such as power, gas, drinking water) and the local utility system within properties. Smart meters make it feasible for utility customers to have very flexible contracts based on greenness, time of day and day of the week. As prosumers they may sell locally generated power to the grid at the best time. Manipulation of smart meters, however, provides a business model to (cyber) criminals, as has already been shown in the USA by KrebsOnSecurity (2012). As smart meters often use mobile telecommunication technologies to communicate with neighboring concentration points and there will be many of those concentration points per local area, the investment in technology and therefore in cyber security needs to be cheap. On the other hand, equipment needs to function for years while one is not prepared for massive security upgrades in case of malware or other cyber security failures affect the smart meter function.

Some smart meters allow for a remote turn-off of the customer services. Cyber criminals or hacktivists may find a way to turn-off utility services at a large scale, for instance to extort a utility company. Note that in many nations, it is legally not allowed to remotely activate utility services to a property as that may endanger the safety of persons. A large-scale event therefore may take up to days to recover from.

9. Smart living: Smart appliances will be part of our homes soon. The smart fridge, dish washer, washing machine, and so on will start communicating with the smart grid and find the greenest or the cheapest time to use power and water. The even smart fridges will keep track of consumables and order supplies at the local super market. The design of such appliances, which have an expected lifetime of at least 15 years, do not take cyber security updates into account. Moore's law, however, will cause an invalidation of any cryptographic protection mechanism in probably half of such a lifetime. With weak security, smart appliances may become a new distributed denial of service platform attacking either via ICT systems connected to the ICT layer, or the smart (power) grid. For example in the latter case an attack could provide false information to the grid on a massive scale about when how much power is required in a certain area. The question then remains how can we manage the security posture of millions of fridges, dish washers, and washing machines, including their update status, and their license to operate in the smart grid system? This becomes a cyber-security challenge equivalent to what Bijlsma et al. (2013) stated for the automotive sector.

10. All sectors: Smart (energy) Grids and Smart Cities require the cooperation of a large number of stakeholders who connect their mostly physical services though a management layer with its large ICT base. Risk management across a chain of organizations is a problem, especially because it is often vague who is responsible for them. Making the chain (cyber) resilient is an even larger challenge. But, at the higher level on information exchanges between organizations, the earlier identified cyber security lessons are not applied. Lacking validation of information acquired from another organization and verifying it was allowed and expected values may cause decisions to be taken with major consequences. Criminals may take advantage of such weak interfaces, e.g., by careful crafting of service price jumps.

11. Health and care sector: After a slow start, fixed position robots are applied in flexible industries such as the automotive sector. Currently, a first-generation mobile robot is on the market. A fast innovation cycle is expected as these robots are expected to become part of the workforce in hospitals and homes for elderly people. They will provide flexible services at lower costs and fill the current gaps in the availability of nurses and people providing personal care. The pressure to provide robots to the market may cause a main focus to be on safety aspects while cyber security aspects are overlooked. It can be predicted from the earlier identified cyber security lessons that cyber security failures will occur in the protection of communication channels between the robot and the main controlling station in validating commands to the robot. Who is liable when due to a cyber-attack a robot provides the wrong medicine or shakes up a bed with person enwrapped in plaster? Moreover, robots will be managed by a department which is likely to be unconsciously insecure.

It will activate the robots without a properly secured configuration as the configuration handbook will only discuss robot safety issues and will not discuss cyber security issues at length.

12. All sectors: The next ICT innovation cycle is the Internet of Things (IOT). Almost any device will have an internet address, communicate what it senses, and may activate its actuators. Futurists dream about amazing new ICT functions and bright technical people implement them. In some cases they even inject an RFID chip under their skin to identify themselves as authorized users of innovative ICT-based services. Once again, more elaborate thoughts about cyber security are not in the designers' mind set.

CONCLUSIONS

This chapter showed that earlier cyber security lessons identified about threats and risk to current and previous ICT innovation cycles do not make their way into the next ICT innovation cycle. The old cyber security lessons will be identified again. Patches will be used to plug the holes in the "Swiss cheese" design.

People with the bright innovative ideas are not educated in cyber security, neither are many of the programmers who implement their ideas. They neglect the old threats which provide attack paths to cyber criminals.

New and emerging threats can therefore be predicted as long as this innovation cycle without proper cyber security is not broken. The only advantage is that cyber-crime investigators can prepare themselves for the next innovation cycle by becoming an early adopter and preparing the right set of forensic tools.

REFERENCES

Averill, B., Luiijf, E.A.M., 2010. Canvassing the cyber security landscape: why energy companies need to pay attention. J. Energy Security, May.

Bohlen, J., Beal, G.M., 1957. The Diffusion Process. Agriculture Extension Service. Iowa State College, Ames.

Bijlsma, T., de Kievit, S., van de Sluis, J., van Nunen, E., Passchier, I., Luiijf, E., 2013. Security challenges for cooperative and interconnected mobility systems. In: Luiijf, E., Hartel, P. (Eds.), Critical Information Infrastructures Security, 8th International Workshop, CRITIS 2013, Amsterdam, Lecture Notes in Computer Science, vol. 8328. Springer, Heidelberg, pp. 1–15.

DHS, 2014. US Secret Service Written testimony of U.S. Secret Service for a Senate Banking, Housing and Urban Affairs Subcommittee on National Security and International Trade and Finance hearing titled "Safeguarding Consumers' Financial Data". DHS, Washington, DC. http://www.nationaljournal.com/library/110188 (accessed 15.02.14).

EC, 2007. Towards a general policy on the fight against cyber crime. COM(2007) 267 final, Commission of the European Communities, Brussels, Belgium. http://eur-lex.europa.eu/LexUriServ/LexUriServ.do?uri=COM:2007:0267:FIN:EN:PDF (accessed 15.02.14).

Falliere, N., O Murchu, L., Chien, E., 2010. W32.Stuxnet Dossier. Symantec, Cupertino, USA. http://www.symantec.com/content/en/us/enterprise/media/security_response/whitepapers/w32_stuxnet_dossier.pdf (accessed 15.02.14).

Geelof, A., 2007. Chantage om gegevens uit computer. The Netherlands, Telegraaf 12-01-1977, pp. 1 and 9.

Harmon, A., 1995. Hacking Theft of $10 Million From Citibank Revealed. August 19, 1995, Los Angeles Times, Los Angeles. http://articles.latimes.com/1995-08-19/business/fi-36656_1_citibank-system (accessed 15.02.14).

Huff Post Food, 2011. British Spies Replace Terrorists' Online Bomb Instructions With Cupcake Recipe. June 2011. http://www.huffingtonpost.com/2011/06/03/british-spies-terrorist-bomb-cupcake-recipe_n_870882.html (accessed 15.02.14).

Korver, H., 2007. Met diefstal computer gegevens ICI trad tijdperk in van nieuw soort criminaliteit. Telegraaf 22-01-1977, pp. 17, The Netherlands.

KrebsOnSecurity, 2012. FBI: Smart Meter Hacks Likely to Spread. http://krebsonsecurity.com/2012/04/fbi-smart-meter-hacks-likely-to-spread (accessed 15.02.14).

Luiijf, H.A.M., 2010. Process Control Security in the Cybercrime Information Exchange. NICC, The Hague, The Netherlands. http://www.cpni.nl/publications/PCS_brochure-UK.pdf (accessed 15.02.14).

Luiijf, E., 2013. Why are we so unconsciously insecure? Int. J. Crit. Infrastruct. Protect. 6, 179–181.

Markoff, J., 1990. Computer Intruder is Put on Probation and Fined $10,000. New York Times. May 5, 1990, http://www.nytimes.com/1990/05/05/us/computer-intruder-is-put-on-probation-and-fined-10000.html (accessed 15.02.14).

Rouf, I., Miller, R., Mustafa, H., Taylor, T., Oh, S., Xu, W., et al., 2010. Security and Privacy Vulnerabilities of In-CarWireless Networks: A Tire Pressure Monitoring System Case Study. USENIX'10, p. 16, https://www.usenix.org/conference/usenix-security10/security-and-privacy-vulnerabilities-car-wireless-networks-tire-pressure (accessed 15.02.14).

Stigherrian, 2011. Lethal medical device hack taken to the next level. CSO Online, Australia. http://www.cso.com.au/article/404909/lethal_medical_device_hack_taken_next_level/ (accessed 15.02.14).

TRB, 2012. TRB Special report 308: The Safety Challenge and Promise of Automotive Electronics: Insights from Unintended Acceleration. Transportation Research Board, National Academies Press, Washington DC. http://www.nap.edu/catalog.php?record_id=13342 (accessed 15.02.14).

Venkatesh, V., Morris, M., Davis, G., Davis, F., 2003. User acceptance of information technology: toward a unified view. MIS Q 27 (3), 425–478.

Venkatesh, V., Bala, H., 2008. Technology acceptance model 3 and a research agenda on interventions. Decision Sci 39 (2), 273–315.

Wray, S., 1998. The Electronic Disturbance Theater and Electronic Civil Disobedience. June 17, 1998, http://www.thing.net/~rdom/ecd/EDTECD.html (accessed 15.02.14).

Police investigation processes: practical tools and techniques for tackling cyber crimes

4

Andrew Staniforth

INTRODUCTION

The Internet has brought, and will continue to bring, huge benefits to industry, individual citizens and their communities around the world. Unfortunately, there are a small but increasing minority of people who seek to exploit new opportunities for their chosen criminal purpose. Cyber criminals are quick to spot the potential vulnerabilities of new technologies and use them to commit offences, or try to frustrate detection of their activities (HM Government, 2011). Cyber crime and cyber terrorism is no longer about those who simply seek to access computer systems to prove it can be done. Cyber threats are real and damaging. The criminals and terrorists behind contemporary cyber threats to society are well organized, and seek to take advantage of those using Internet services. Whether this is for financial gain, in pursuance of extremist ideologies or as threats to children, the impact on the victims can be devastating. The most vulnerable members of our society are all too often the victims of cyber crimes—from young people threatened by bullying or sexual predators, to the elderly who provide easy prey for organized fraudsters (HM Government, 2010).

To tackle the phenomenon of cyber crime and cyber terrorism, governments across the world have invested substantial resources in homeland security, resulting in significant law enforcement and intelligence agency responses to online threats. Designed to detect, deter and disrupt all manner of cyber-related hazards, new cyber policing units have been rapidly established to investigate cyber crimes (Awan and Blakemore, 2012). Such investment fulfils the first duty of governments to protect the security and safety of their country, citizens and their wider interests. The focus and investments made to tackle cyber crime and cyber terrorism are welcomed but no one in authority can afford to be complacent. The threat from cyber crime and cyber terrorism is constantly evolving—with new opportunities to commit "old" crimes in new ways as well as high-tech crimes which did not exist several years ago (HM Government, 2011). Cyber criminals are becoming more sophisticated, and they continue to develop malicious software and devise improved methods for infecting computers and networks (HM Government, 2011). Cyber criminals are also continually adapting their tactics as new defenses are implemented. To counter new cyber criminal activities, law enforcement agencies must continue their efforts to ensure cyber space is a hostile environment for them to operate.

The complex nature and sophistication of cyber crime and cyber terrorism demands a dedicated response, especially from investigators who are critical to the success of tracking cyber criminals and bringing them to justice. Therefore, this chapter shall focus upon the role of the cyber investigator, addressing the challenges they encounter and the methods, models and investigative doctrine they should use to become an effective cyber detective. Although this chapter does not focus on the technical role and responsibility of those specialist hi-tech investigators, it will provide them with the tools and techniques to develop their core investigative skills. This chapter shall also serve as a timely reminder for the police officer and traditional criminal detective investigator, many of whom now find themselves thrust into investigating online crimes with little or no training and experience in this domain.

This chapter consequently considers five pertinent areas of core investigative competencies which provide the foundations upon which professional cyber investigations, indeed all criminal investigations, should be conducted. The key investigative skills of decisions making, problem solving, developing hypothesis, embracing innovation, and the importance of contact management are all explored in the context of contemporary cyber investigations.

INVESTIGATIVE DECISION MAKING

Making sound judgments is a core role and important attribute of any successful cyber investigator, particularly those Senior Investigating Officers (SIO) charged with the responsibility of managing and directing large-scale investigations. Effective decision making, particularly at the very outset of cyber investigations, will ensure opportunities are not missed and potential lines of enquiry are identified and rigorously pursued. In reality, law enforcement officers who are engaged in the early developments of an investigation do have to cope with a lack of sufficient information to begin with, and some important decisions may need to be made quickly and intuitively. According to Cook and Tattersall (2010)

> *A key skill involves the tenacity of the investigator being able to recognise when there is insufficient time to gather further information. Intuition however, derives from knowledge and experience and can be prone to bias, therefore investigative decisions must always be based on reasoning and analysis to avoid subjectivity (p. 33).*

The commencement of a cyber-based investigation, especially any complex investigation which may be high profile and is being conducted under the glare of the media will be frenetic. Nothing should prevent the professional cyber investigator from being able to progress their tasks at a pace which ensures they can perform their roles to the highest professional standards. Investigators must be afforded the time to complete their investigations and this requires them to not get caught up in the pace of the wider investigation but to slow things down where necessary. This approach will assist key decision making processes which is vital to the success of any investigation. According to Cook and Tattersall (2010):

> *Investigative decision making must always be directed at reaching goals or objectives. In order to ensure that good decisions are made towards achieving particular aims, it should at the earliest point in the investigation be determined what the primary investigative objectives are. A generic example of how such objectives may look are as follows:*

- *Establish that an offence has been committed or has not been committed.*
- *Gather all available information, material, intelligence and evidence.*
- *Act in the interests of justice.*
- *Rigorously pursue all reasonable lines of enquiry.*
- *Conduct a thorough investigation.*
- *Identify, arrest and charge offenders.*
- *Present all evidence to prosecuting authorities (p. 34).*

It is effective practice to record the primary investigative objectives of a cyber investigation into an investigative policy decision making log at the early stages of the investigation. This ensures that rationale for key investigative decisions are captured at the time they were made in light of all information that was readily available. The primary investigative objectives must be disseminated to all other officers and investigators who have an operational requirement to know the strategic direction of the cyber investigation. During the process of investigations, investigators and senior officers will be using their skills to analyze, review and assess all the information and material that is available. This is an extremely important process as the accuracy, reliability, and relevance of material being obtained will influence decision making. Any changes to the primary investigative objectives should be recorded and again disseminated to all officers progressing the investigation. According to Caless et al. (2012):

> *The golden rule is for investigators to apply what is known as the 'ABC' principle throughout the life of an investigation as follows:*

A. Assume nothing
B. Believe nothing
C. Challenge and check everything (p. 271).

All investigators, especially those progressing complex cyber investigations, must ensure that nothing is taken for granted and it cannot be assumed that things are what they seem or that processes have been performed correctly (Caless et al., 2012). Looking for corroboration, rechecking, reviewing, and confirming all aspects of the investigation are hallmarks of an effective cyber detective, and shall ensure that no potential line of enquiry is overlooked during a dynamic and fast-moving cyber investigation.

INVESTIGATIVE PROBLEM SOLVING

Essential to the core investigative skills of decision making are elements of problem solving. A logical approach to making decisions to effectively resolve problems within cyber investigations is demonstrated by the Cyber Investigators Staircase Model (CISM). Adapted for law enforcement from leadership and management models, the CISM contains important and sequential elements to ensure effective problem solving shown in Figure 4.1.

The model works on the basis that it is preferable to choose a particular course of action out of a range of possible "options" (Staniforth, 2014). The basic point here is that a cyber investigator should not assume there is only one option available, there are always alternatives, especially in cyber investigations which have a tendency to quickly gather large volumes of data. Information lies at the heart of an investigation and gathering sufficient information helps to populate the number of options which can then be worked through a decision making processes as to which option is the most compelling.

In order to gather and collect information to satisfy the requirements of Step 2 on the CISM, a set of interrogative pronouns, commonly known in the law enforcement field as the "5× WH+H" method—Who, What, When, Where, Why+How can be put to good use (Cook and Tattersall, 2010). This formula helps to organize

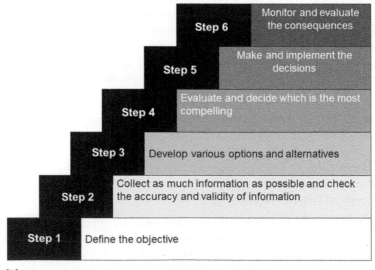

FIGURE 4.1

Cyber Investigators Staircase Model.

the investigative information and to identify where there are knowledge gaps. For a cyber crime investigation this may look as follows:

- Who is the victim?   – Victim details and why this victim?
- What happened?   – Precise details on incident/occurrence
- When did it happen?   – Temporal issues such as relevant times
- Where did it happen?   – Geographic locations, national/international?
- Why did it happen?   – Motivation for crime or terrorism
- How did it happen?   – Precise modus operandi details

This information can then be developed into a useful investigative matrix which will help identify the gaps in information by setting out all the relevant details in a logical sequence which is easily understood. The matrix can then be populated as the cyber investigation develops and used as a source of reference for the basis of applying the CISM and any associated decision making that is required. The matrix must be a living document, being regularly updated as the investigation progresses. The matrix can then be cross-referenced to decisions as and when they are made and will serve to illustrate just what was known or not known at the time any particular decision was made. This is a very important point for justifying why a particular course of action was, or was not, taken by the investigator.

The $5 \times WH + H$ structure can also be useful when being briefed or updated about an incident or set of circumstances. Investigators can pose questions using the $5 \times WH + H$ headings in order to establish sufficient detail about what may already be known. The method can be used to ensure clear and concise information is supplied in a systematic rather than a random approach. To support investigators engaged in progressing complex cyber cases, the Scanning, Analysis, Response and Assessment (SARA) model for problem solving, shown in Figure 4.2, provides an effective process for police officers (Caless et al., 2012).

The SARA analytical methodology offers a staged process for identification, understanding and resolution of specific problems through scanning, analysis, response, and assessment. The four-staged process is used by a number of law enforcement agency practitioners to provide a framework to guide them through the challenges of finding solutions to complex problems. It is an approach that works well for problems and challenges arising during cyber crime and cyber terrorism investigations. Of course, in reality, no theoretical model can cover all potential issues when attempting to dynamically solve problems during complex cyber investigations with international dimensions, but the model provides a methodical approach that shall support and inform key investigative decisions (Staniforth, 2014). It must also be recognized that stages of the SARA cycle may overlap, repeat themselves and some can remain undeveloped while others move to completion. This mirrors the pace of cyber investigations as some strands of a complex investigation can develop rapidly, while others require more time to progress. It is also acknowledged that when addressing problems police officers do not go steadily round the four stages of the SARA cycle, but instead cut across some stages when experience informs them it is expedient and in the interests of the wider investigation to do so. That being said, the

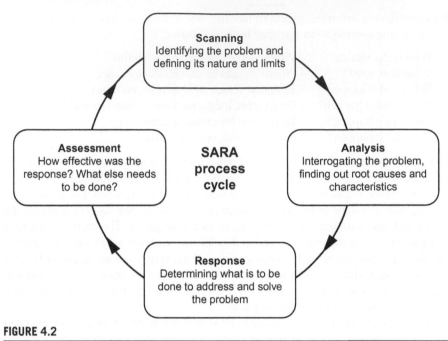

FIGURE 4.2

The SARA process cycle.

SARA cycle provides a methodical approach upon which to frame problem solving activity. Those officers charged with the responsibility of investigating cyber-related crimes would be well advised to adopt such a model which provides confidence and clarity to their problem solving decision making processes.

DEVELOPING INVESTIGATIVE HYPOTHESIS

Decisions to effectively progress cyber investigations may have to be based on or guided by a hypothesis. For cyber investigations, Cook and Tattersall (2010) recommend that:

> *a hypothesis is a proposition made as a basis for reasoning without the assumption of its truth and supposition made as a starting point for further investigation of known facts. Developing and using hypothesis is a widely recognised technique amongst criminal investigators which can be used to try to establish the most logical or likely explanation, theory, or inference for why and how a cyber crime has been committed. Ideally, before cyber investigators develop hypothesis there should be sufficient reliable material available on which to base the hypothesis such as details of the victim, precise details of the incident or occurrence, national or international dimensions of the offence, motives of the crime and the precise modus operandi (p. 43).*

Of course, knowledge and experience of previous cases will also greatly assist in constructing relevant hypothesis. Generating and building hypotheses is an obvious and natural activity for cyber investigators, particular during the early stages of an investigation. Clearly, if there is sufficient information or evidence already available then there will be no need to use the hypothesis method. However, cyber investigators are being increasingly called to establish the most basic of facts at the commencement of investigations, such as whether a crime has been committed or not. Hypotheses are important to provide initial investigative direction where there is little information to work with. All cyber investigators must "keep an open mind" and remember that it is better to gather as much information as possible before placing too much reliance on any speculative theory (Cook and Tattersall, 2010). It is a mistake for cyber investigators to theorize before sufficient data is collected as it is easy to fall into the trap of manipulating and massaging facts to suit theories, instead of ensuring that theories suit the facts.

Cook and Tattersall (2010) provide professional police investigative practice guidance which is commonly used by law enforcement officers across the world. Their advice, based on extensive investigative experience in the UK, includes checklists for consideration when building hypothesis. Cook and Tattersall (2010) recommend that when developing theoretical assumptions, cyber investigators would be well advised to give due consideration to the following:

- Beware of placing too much reliance on one or a limited number of hypotheses when there is insufficient information available.
- Remember the maxim 'keeping an open mind'.
- Ensure a thorough understanding of the relevance and reliability of any material relied upon.
- Ensure that hypotheses are kept under constant review and remain dynamic, remembering that any hypothesis is only provisional at best.
- Define a clear objective for the hypothesis.
- Only develop hypothesis that 'best fit' with the known information and material.
- Consult with colleagues and experts to discuss and formulate hypothesis.
- Ensure sufficient resources are available to develop or test the hypothesis (Cook and Tattersall, 2010, p. 45).

Progressing cyber investigations is a collaborative effort and police officers must consult, listen and consider the advice and guidance provided by specialist hi-tech investigators. Any cyber investigator who ignores specialist advice does so at their peril.

INVESTIGATIVE INNOVATION

Cyber crime and cyber terrorism investigators, especially those officers leading and managing investigative teams, must be capable of having or recognizing good ideas and using them to make things happen. This is an extremely useful skill for any police investigator progressing traditional criminal enquiries but is essential for cyber investigators given the sheer size, scale, scope and sophistication of online criminality. To detect, deter and disrupt cyber criminal activity all cyber investigators need to draw upon their experience, skill and ingenuity. Innovative approaches to tackling cyber crime and cyber terrorism are essential, and investigators should bring or introduce new methods and ideas for implementation as part of the investigative process.

It is imperative that cyber investigators and senior leaders create an effective team working environment. Every lesson of every cyber investigation has revealed that no one single investigator can effectively progress cyber investigations on their own. Only by working together and bringing individual skills and expertise to bear in concert with one other, will a team of cyber investigators be able to tackle cyber crime and cyber terrorism effectively. Therefore, officers engaged in investing cyber crimes must create a consistent culture of positively finding solutions and new ideas to problems and challenges. The need to share and support new ideas is a necessary component of any cyber investigative team and innovative ideas that enliven and arouse the spirit of investigators is essential. Assumptions based on traditional beliefs and prehistoric knowledge should be challenged in favor of finding new ways of doing things, with new tactics, techniques and technology. This is not to say that traditional methods do not work when they are clearly tried and tested, but adopting a more radical, less risk averse approach and embracing innovative ideas to bring cyber criminals to justice is absolutely necessary for the continued professional development of cyber crime policing policy, practice and procedure.

INVESTIGATORS CONTACT MANAGEMENT

Within policing, and especially in cases of issues related to the investigation of cyber crime, one of the key points from which all perceptions of the police derives is that of the contact between the public and the police (Caless et al., 2012). This first contact with the public, whether victims or witnesses of cyber crimes, is critical for the effective delivery of cyber policing at every level. Whether this contact is by calling the police via telephone or meeting a police officer in person, for the member of the public initiating the interaction and coming forward, it is a time of crucial importance. The member of the public contacting the police, implicitly or explicitly to report cyber crime, asks themselves three questions as follows:

- Will my concern be taken seriously?
- Will I receive the service I expect?
- Will I get satisfaction from what has occurred?

If this initial contact is well handled, then the subsequent actions are based on an established foundation. To tackle all manner of cyber criminality, law enforcement agencies require the full support of the public, so when members of the public have the courage and conviction to come forward to report and discuss cyber crime issues, police officers must have due regard to positive contact management. Cyber crime contact management must be a priority not just for those law enforcement officers who are public-facing, but for all of police officers, including cyber crime investigators. By simply ensuring that reports from the public are appropriately prioritized, taken seriously, and the member of the public is kept informed and is satisfied with the police response, will best serve the efficiency of the initial investigation.

All police officers must understand that first impressions really do count. The courteous, professional and positive contact with members of the public is important for all policing activities, including the investigation of cyber crime. Above all else, matters reported to the police regarding cyber crime must be taken seriously. There is no room for complacency in tackling cyber crime. When dealing with reports concerning cyber crime, all officers must:

> **LISTEN** (Staniforth, 2014) to members of the public:
> **L**isten to citizens and take their concerns seriously
> **I**nspire confidence and provide reassurance
> **S**upport with information, advice and guidance
> **T**ake ownership and record citizen concerns
> **E**xplain what you shall do and why
> **N**otify supervision and report concerns

During all cyber investigations, the public must be put first. The victims of cyber crimes must be managed professionally and specialist care and support provided as required. Complainants of cyber crimes must be regularly updated as to the progress of the investigation. By listening to members of the public and providing a police service of the highest professional standards will increase confidence of the public in the law enforcements commitment and determination to tackle cyber crimes.

INVESTIGATING CRIME AND TERROR

When Metropolitan Police officers raided a flat in West London during October 2005, they arrested a young man, Younes Tsouli. The significance of this arrest was not immediately clear but investigations soon revealed that the Moroccan born Tsouli was the world's most wanted "cyber-terrorist" (Staniforth and PNLD, 2009). In his activities Tsouli adopted the user name "Irhabi 007" (Irhabi meaning "terrorist" in Arabic), and his activities grew from posting advice on the internet on how to hack into mainframe computer systems to assisting those in planning terrorist attacks (Staniforth, 2012). Tsouli trawled the internet searching for home movies made by US soldiers in the theatres of conflict in Iraq and Afghanistan that would reveal the inside layout of US military bases. Over time these small pieces of information were collated and passed to those planning attacks against armed forces bases. This virtual hostile reconnaissance provided insider data illustrating how it was no longer necessary for terrorists to conduct physical reconnaissance if relevant information could be captured and meticulously pieced together from the internet.

Police investigations subsequently revealed that Tsouli had €2.5million worth of fraudulent transactions passing through his accounts which he used to support and finance terrorist activity. Pleading guilty to charges of incitement to commit acts of terrorism Tsouli received a 16-year custodial sentence to be served at Belmarsh High Security Prison in London where, perhaps unsurprisingly, he has been denied access to the Internet. The then National Coordinator of Terrorist Investigations, Deputy Assistant Commissioner Peter Clarke, said that Tsouli:

> *provided a link to core al Qa'ida, to the heart of al Qa'ida and the wider network that he was linking into through the internet", going on to say: "what it did show us was the extent to which they could conduct operational planning on the internet. It was the first virtual conspiracy to murder that we had seen (Staniforth and PNLD, 2013).*

The case against Tsoouli was the first in the UK which quickly brought about the realization that cyber-terrorism presented a real and present danger to the national security of the UK. A decade has now passed since the arrest of Tsouli, and law enforcement practitioners have come to understand that the internet clearly provides positive opportunities for global information exchange, communication, networking, education, and is a major tool in the fight against crime, but a new and emerging contemporary threat continues to impact upon the safety and security of the communities they seek to protect. The Internet has been hijacked and exploited by terrorists not only to progress attack planning but to radicalize and recruit new operatives to their cause (Awan and Blackmore, 2013).

The case against Tsouli served to raise concerns amongst security professionals that there was a distant lack of understanding by police investigators between the disciplines of crime and terrorism, at both a strategic and tactical level. To provide clarity, investigators must understand that first and foremost terrorism is a crime, a crime which has serious consequences and one which requires to be distinguished from other types of crime, but a crime nonetheless. Individuals who commit terrorist-related offences contrary to domestic and international law are subject to the processes of a criminal justice system and those who are otherwise believed to be involved in terrorism are subject to restrictive executive actions. However, the key features of terrorism that distinguish it from other forms of criminality are its core motivations. Terrorism may be driven politics, religion, or a violent and extremist ideology (Staniforth, 2012). These core objectives are unlike other criminal motivations such as for personal gain or in the pursuit of revenge. Terrorists may be driven by anyone or any combination of the core motivations but the primary motivator is political. Terrorism is a very powerful way in which to promote beliefs and has potentially serious consequences for society. If allowed to grow and flourish, terrorism can undermine national security, it can cause instability to a country, and in the most extreme of circumstances can lead to war. Terrorism seeks to undermine state legitimacy, freedom, and democracy. These are a very different set of motivations and outcomes when compared against other types of crime. This is the very reason why tackling terrorism nationally and internationally is an endeavor led by intelligence agencies of government, regarded as "higher policing" activity within the secret and sensitive domain of nation security. The primacy afforded to the intelligence apparatus of governments to tackle terrorism therefore means that countering terrorism is different to investigating other types of criminality. The potential impact on a nation's security is why terrorism, in all of its forms, requires a covert, pre-emptive and intelligence-led approach to prevent it.

While it is important for the cyber investigator to distinguish between crime and terrorism, it must also be recognized that both cyber crime and cyber terrorism investigations are very different to other types of traditional criminal investigations. There are three key differences to consider, first of all, cyber investigations have a global reach. Every major cyber crime or cyber terrorism investigation has the potential for enquiries to be conducted in multiple locations. One enquiry for one single cyber terrorist for example, may lead investigators to several police jurisdictions in separate regions of the same country and then to numerous countries in Europe, the Middle East, Africa and around the world as investigators pursue lines of enquiry. Secondly, the scale of an investigation can rapidly grow as multiple victims and suspects are identified residing anywhere in the world. To resource this level of investigation where there is a critical requirement for intelligence and evidence capture can quickly go beyond the capacity of traditional investigative teams established for the most serious of criminal offences. Thirdly, the complexity of such an investigation is not only evident in the cross-border of trans-national protocols but that intelligence and evidence is being collected simultaneously. Evidence is required to support successful prosecutions and intelligence may be required urgently to support ongoing covert operations for intelligence agencies around the world (Staniforth and PNLD, 2009).

CONCLUSION

The impact of cyber crime and cyber terrorism has forced intelligence and law enforcement agencies across the world to enter into a new era of collaboration to effectively tackle cyber threats together. Despite cyber investigations having reach, scale and complexity beyond that experienced in other large-scale enquiries, their effectiveness relies upon thorough investigative police work. This chapter serves to illustrate that although investigators in specialist cyber crime and counter-terrorism units do have unique skills and abilities to perform their roles, it is their attention to detail combined with a professional and practical application to their role as an investigator which is critical to their success. Focusing upon the core investigative tools and techniques described in this chapter is essential for the effective investigation of cyber crime and cyber terrorism.

Cyber crime shall continue to evolve at a rapid pace and all security practitioners must recognize that they are now operating in a world of low impact, multiple victim crimes where bank robbers no longer have to plan meticulously the one theft of a million dollars; new technological capabilities mean that one person can now commit millions of robberies of one dollar each (Wall, 2007). Paradoxically, effective contemporary cyber investigations rely upon a collaborative, multi-disciplinary and multi-agency approach where police detectives, hi-tech investigators, forensic analysts and experts from academia and the private sector work together to tackle cyber threats. The complex nature and sophistication of cyber crime and cyber terrorism continues to demand a dedicated and determined response, especially from investigators who are critical to the success of tracking cyber criminals and bringing them to justice. A professionally trained, highly skilled cyber investigative workforce is now required. This workforce must prepare and equip itself for the cyber challenges that lie ahead and the reading of the chapters which follow provide an excellent starting point. Most importantly however, cyber crime and cyber terrorism investigators—no matter how complex and technical cyber investigations become in the future—must develop their expertise founded upon the core investigative competencies outlined in this chapter.

REFERENCES

Awan, I., Blakemore, B., 2013. Policing Cyber Hate, Cyber Threats and Cyber Terrorism. Ashgate Publishing Ltd, Surrey.

Caless, B., Harfield, C., Spruce, B., 2012. Blackstone's Police Operational Handbook: Practice and Procedure, second ed. Oxford University Press, Oxford.

Cook, T., Tattersall, A., 2010. Blackstone's Senior Investigating Officers' Handbook, second ed. Oxford University Press, Oxford.

Government, H.M., 2010. A Strong Britain in an Age of Uncertainty: The National Security Strategy, London Stationary Office, London.

Government, H.M., 2011. The UK Cyber Security Strategy—Protecting and Promoting the UK in a Digital Age, London Stationary Office, London.

Staniforth, A., 2014. Preventing Terrorism and Violent Extremism. Oxford University Press, Oxford.

Staniforth, A., PNLD, 2013. Blackstone's Counter-Terrorism Handbook, third ed. Oxford University Press, Oxford.

Staniforth, A., PNLD, 2009. Blackstone's Counter-Terrorism Handbook. Oxford University Press, Oxford.

Staniforth, A., 2012. The Routledge Companion to UK Counter-Terrorism. Routledge, Oxford.

Wall, D., 2007. Cybercrime—The Transformation of Crime in the Information Age. Polity Press, Cambridge.

Cyber-specifications: capturing user requirements for cyber-security investigations

5

Alex W. Stedmon, Dale Richards, Siraj A. Shaikh, John Huddlestone, Ruairidh Davison

INTRODUCTION

In many security domains, the "human in the system" is often a critical line of defense in identifying, preventing, and responding to any threats (Saikayasit et al., in print). Traditionally, these domains have been focused in the real world, ranging from mainstream public safety within crowded spaces and border controls, through to identifying suspicious behaviors, hostile reconnaissance and implementing counter-terrorism initiatives. In these instances, security is usually the specific responsibility of front-line personnel with defined roles and responsibilities operating to organizational protocols (Saikayasit et al., 2012; Stedmon et al., 2013).

From a systems perspective, the process of security depends upon the performance of those humans (e.g., users and stakeholders) in the wider security system. Personnel are often working in complex and challenging work environments where the nature of their job is that specific security breaches may be very rare and so they are tasked with recognizing small state changes within a massive workflow, but where security incidents could have rapid and catastrophic consequences (e.g., airline baggage handlers not identifying an improvised explosive device in a passengers luggage).

Furthermore, with the increasing presence of technology in security provision there is a reliance on utilizing complex distributed systems that assist the user, and in some instances are instrumental in facilitating decisions that are made by the user. However, one of the significant benefits of deploying dedicated security personnel is that they often provide operational flexibility and local/tacit knowledge of their working environment that automated systems simply do not possess (Hancock and Hart, 2002; Stedmon et al., 2013).

Through a unique understanding of their work contexts (and the ability to notice subtle patterns of behavior and underlying social norms in those environments) security personnel represent a key asset in identifying unusual behaviors or suspicious incidents that may pose a risk to public safety (Cooke and Winner, 2008). However, the same humans also present a potential systemic weakness if their requirements and limitations are not properly considered or fully understood in relation to other aspects of the total system in which they operate (Wilson et al., 2005).

From a similar perspective, cyber-security operates at a systemic level where users (e.g., the public), service providers (e.g., on-line social and business facilitators) and commercial or social outlets (e.g., specific banking, retail, social networks, and forums) come together in the virtual and shared interactions of cyber-space in order to process transactions. A key difference is that there are no formal policing agents present, no police or security guards that users can go to for assistance. Perhaps the closest analogy to any form of on-line policing would be moderators of social networks and forums but these are often volunteers with no formal training and ultimately no legal responsibility for cyber-security. Whilst there are requirements for secure transactions especially when people are providing their personal and banking details to retails sites, social media sites are particularly vulnerable to identity theft through the information people might freely and/or unsuspectingly provide to third parties. There is no common law of cyber-space as in the real-world and social norms are easily distorted and exploited creating vulnerabilities for security threats.

Another factor in cyber-security is the potential temporal distortions that can occur with cyber-media. Historic postings or blogs might propagate future security threats in ways that real-world artifacts may not. For example, cyber-ripples may develop from historic posts and blogs and may have more resonance following a particular event. Cyber poses a paradoxical perspective for security. Threats can emerge rapidly and dynamically in response to immediate activities (e.g., the UK riots of 2011), while in other ways the data are historical and can lie dormant for long periods of time. However, that data still possesses a presence that can be as hard hitting as an event that has just only happened. Understanding the ways in which users might draw significance from cyber-media is an important part of understanding cyber-influence.

From a cyber-security perspective, the traditional view of security poses a number of challenges:

- Who are the users (and where are they located at the time of their interaction)?
- Who is responsible for cyber-security?
- How do we identify user needs for cyber-security?
- What methods and tools might be available/appropriate for eliciting cyber-requirements?
- What might characterize suspicious behavior within cyber-interactions?
- What is the nature of the subject being observed (e.g., is it a behavior, a state, an action, and so on)?

Underlying these challenges are fundamental issues of security and user performance. Reducing the likelihood of human error in cyber-interactions is increasingly important. Human errors could not only hinder the correct use and operation of cyber technologies they can also compromise the integrity of such systems. There is a need for formal methods that allow investigators to analyze and verify the correctness of interactive systems, particularly with regards to human interaction (Cerone and Shaikh, 2008).

Only by considering these issues and understanding the underlying requirements that different users and stakeholders might have, can a more integrated approach to cyber-security be developed from a user-centered perspective. Indeed, for cyber-investigations, these issues pose important questions to consider in exploring the basis upon which cyber interactions might be based and where future efforts to develop solutions might be best placed.

USER REQUIREMENTS AND THE NEED FOR A USER-CENTERED APPROACH?

When investigating user needs, a fundamental issue is the correct identification of user requirements that are then revisited in an iterative manner throughout the design process. In many cases, user-requirements are not captured at the outset of a design process and they are sometimes only regarded when user-trials are developed to evaluate final concepts (often when it is too late to change things). This in itself is a major issue for developing successful products and process that specifically meet user needs. A further consideration in relation to user requirements for cyber-security is in the forensic examination techniques more commonly employed in accident investigations to provide an insight into the capabilities and limitations of users at a particular point when an error occurred.

More usually when writing requirement specifications, different domains are identified and analyzed (Figure 5.1).

For example, if a smart closed circuit television (CCTV) system was being designed it would be necessary to consider:

- **Inner domain**—product being developed and users (e.g., CCTV, operators) including different levels of system requirements to product level requirements.
- **Outer domain**—the client it is intended to serve (e.g., who the CCTV operator reports to).
- **Actors**—human or other system components that interact with the system (e.g., an operator using smart software, or camera sensors that need to interact with the software, etc.).
- **Data requirements**—data models and thresholds.
- **Functional requirements**—process descriptors (task flows and interactions), input/outputs, messages, etc.

This offers a useful way of conceptualizing requirements and understanding non-functional requirements such as quality assessment, robustness, system integrity (security), and resilience. However, a more detailed approach is often needed to map user requirements. User requirements are often bounded by specific "contexts of use" for investigations as this provides design boundaries as well as frames of reference for communicating issues back to end-users and other stakeholders. In order to achieve this, it is often necessary to prioritize potential solutions to ensure that expectations are managed appropriately (Lohse, 2011).

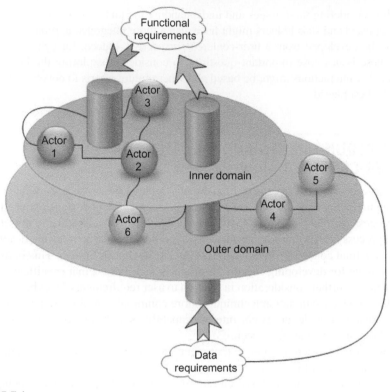

FIGURE 5.1

Domains for requirements specifications.

Seeking to understand the requirements of specific end-users and involving key stakeholders in the development of new systems or protocols is an essential part of any design process. In response to this, formal user requirements elicitation and participatory ergonomics have developed to support these areas of investigation, solution generation and ultimately solution ownership (Wilson, 1995). User requirements embody critical elements that end-users and stakeholders need and want from a product or process (Maiden, 2008). These requirements capture emergent behaviors and in order to achieve this some framework of understanding potential and plausible behavior is required (Cerone and Shaikh, 2008). Plausible behaviors encompass all possible behaviors that can occur. These are then mapped to system requirements that express how the interactive system should be designed, implemented, and used (Maiden, 2008). However, these two factors are not always balanced and solutions might emerge that are not fully exploited or used as intended. Participatory ergonomics approaches seek to incorporate end-users and wider stakeholders within work analysis, design processes and solution generation as their reactions, interactions, optimized use and acceptance of the solutions will ultimately dictate the effectiveness and success of the overall system performance (Wilson et al., 2005).

User-centered approaches have been applied in research areas as wide as health-care, product design, human-computer interaction and, more recently, security and counter-terrorism (Saikayasit et al., 2012; Stedmon et al., 2013). A common aim is the effective capture information from the user's perspective so that system requirements can then be designed to support what the user needs within specified contexts of use (Wilson, 1995). Requirements elicitation is characterized by extensive communication activities between a wide range of people from different backgrounds and knowledge areas, including end-users, stakeholders, project owners or champions, mediators (often the role of the human factors experts) and developers (Coughlan and Macredie, 2002). This is an interactive and participatory process that should allow users to express their own local knowledge and for designers to display their understanding, to ensure a common design base (McNeese et al., 1995; Wilson, 1995). End-users are often experts in their specific work areas and possess deep levels of knowledge gained over time that is often difficult to communicate to others (Blandford and Rugg, 2002; Friedrich and van der Pool, 2007). Users often do not realize what information is valuable to investigations and the development of solutions or the extent to which their knowledge and expertise might inform and influence the way they work (Nuseibeh and Easterbrook, 2000).

BALANCING TECHNOLOGICAL AND HUMAN CAPABILITIES

Within cyber-security it can be extremely difficult to capture user requirements. Bearing in mind the earlier cyber-security issues, it is often a challenge to identify and reach out to the users that are of key interest for any investigation. For example, where user trust has been breached (e.g., through a social networking site, or some form of phishing attack) users may feel embarrassed, guilty for paying funds to a bogus provider, and may not want to draw attention to themselves. In many ways this can be similar for larger corporations who may be targeted by fraudsters using identity theft tactics to pose as legitimate clients. Whilst safeguards are in place to support the user-interaction and enhance the user-experience, it is important to make sure these meet the expectations of the users for which they are intended.

In real world contexts, many aspects of security and threat identification in public spaces still rely upon the performance of frontline security personnel. However this responsibility often rests on the shoulder of workers who are low paid, poorly motivated and lack higher levels of education and training (Hancock and Hart, 2002). Real-world security solutions attempt to embody complex, user-centered, socio-technical systems in which many different users interact at different organizational levels to deliver technology focused security capabilities.

From a macro-ergonomics perspective it is possible to explore how the systemic factors contribute to the success of cyber-security initiatives and where gaps may exist. This approach takes a holistic view of security, by establishing the socio-technical entities that influence systemic performance in terms of integrity, credibility, and performance (Kleiner, 2006). Within this perspective it is also important to consider wider ethical issues of security research and in relation to cyber investigations, the balance between public safety and the need for security interventions (Iphofen, in print; Kavakli et al., 2005).

Aspects of privacy and confidentiality underpin many of the ethical challenges of user requirements elicitation, where investigators must ensure that:

- End-users and stakeholders are comfortable with the type of information they are sharing and how the information might be used.
- End-users are not required to breach any agreements and obligations with their employers or associated organizations.

In many ways these ethical concerns are governed by Codes of Conduct that are regulated by professional bodies such as the British Psychological Society (BPS) but it is important that investigators clearly identify the purpose of an investigation and set clear and legitimate boundaries for intended usage and communication of collected data.

The macro-approach is in contrast to micro-ergonomics, which traditionally focuses on the interaction of a single user and their immediate technology use (Reiman and Väyrynen, 2011). This has often been a starting point for traditional human factors approaches; however by understanding macro-level issues, the complexity of socio-technical factors can be translated into micro-level factors for more detailed analysis (Kleiner, 2006). For example, Kraemer et al. (2009) explored issues in security screening and inspection of cargo and passengers by taking a macro-ergonomics approach. A five-factor framework was proposed that contributes to the "stress load" of frontline security workers in order to assess and predict individual performance as part of the overall security system (Figure 5.2). This was achieved by identifying the interactions between: organizational factors (e.g., training, management support, and shift structure), user characteristics (i.e., the human operator's cognitive skills,

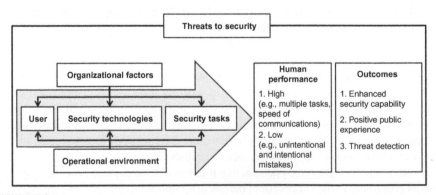

FIGURE 5.2

Macro-ergonomic conceptual framework for security.

Adapted from Kraemer et al., 2009.

training), security technologies (e.g., the performance and usability of technologies used), and security tasks (e.g., task loading and the operational environment).

The central factor of the framework is the user (e.g., the frontline security operator, screener, inspector) who has specific skills within the security system. The security operator is able to use technologies and tools to perform a variety of security screening tasks that support the overall security capability. However these are influenced by task and workload factors (e.g., overload/under load/task monotony/repetition). In addition, organizational factors (e.g., training, management support, culture and organizational structures) as well as the operational environment (e.g., noise, climate, and temperature) also contribute to the overall security capability. This approach helps identify the macro-ergonomic factors where the complexity of the task and resulting human performance within the security system may include errors (e.g., missed threat signals and false positives) or violations (e.g., compromised or adapted protocols in response to the dynamic demands of the operational environment) (Kraemer et al., 2009). This macro-ergonomic framework has been used to form a basis for understanding user requirements within counter-terrorism focusing on the interacting factors and their influence of overall performance of security systems including users and organizational processes (Saikayasit et al., 2012; Stedmon et al., 2013).

This framework provides a useful perspective on cyber-security and can be redrawn to embody a typical user and provides a basis for exploring user requirements (Figure 5.3).

In this way, cyber-security can be understood in terms of the user (e.g., adult or child) who has a range of skills but also presents vulnerabilities within the overall cyber-security security system (e.g., a child may not know the exact identity of someone who befriends them in a chat-room; an adult may not realize the significance of imparting details about a relative to friends on a social networking site; a lonely person may be susceptible to others people's approaches on the pretext of friendship). The user has a range of technologies and tools to perform a variety of tasks, some

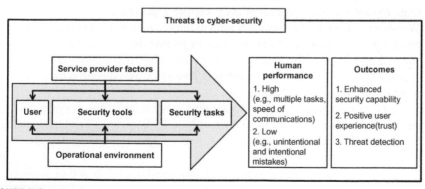

FIGURE 5.3

Macro-ergonomic conceptual framework for cyber-security.

Adapted from Kraemer et al., 2009.

of which will be focused either explicitly or implicitly on their own security or the wider security of the network (e.g., login/password protocols, user identity checks) and in a similar way to the security framework, performance is shaped by task and workload factors (e.g., overload/underload/task monotony/repetition). Within cyber-security, a key difference to the establish security framework is that organizational factors are supplanted by service provider factors. In this way cyber policies may dictate specific security measures but in terms of a formal security capability (policing the web in a similar way that security personnel police public spaces—supported by formal training, management support, culture and organizational structures) there is no such provision. Indeed, individual user training is at best very ad-hoc and in most cases nonexistent. The operational environment is only constrained by a user with access to the web. The user is just as capable of performing their tasks sitting on a busy train (where others can view their interaction or video them inputting login/password data) or in the comfort and privacy of their own home.

A particularly interesting area of cyber-security is that of user trust. From a more traditional perspective, as with any form of technology or automated process there must be trust in the system, specific functionality of system components, communication within the system and a clear distinction of where authority lies in the system (Taylor and Selcon, 1990). Applying this to cyber-trust a range of issues present themselves:

- User acceptance of on-line transactions are balanced against the risks and estimated benefits.
- Trust is generated from the technology used for interactions (e.g., the perception of secure protocols against the vulnerability of open networks) and also in the credibility of the individuals or organizations that are part of the interaction process (Beldad et al., 2010).
- To develop on-line trust, the emphasis is on individuals and organizations to present themselves as trustworthy (Haas and Deseran, 1981). In order to achieve this, it is important, to communicate trust in a way that users will identify with (e.g., reputation, performance, or even website appearance).
- Web-based interactions offer users with multiple "first-time" experiences (e.g., buying products from different websites, or joining different chat-rooms). This suggests that people who lack experience with online transactions and with online organizations might have different levels of trust compared to those with more experience (Boyd, 2003).
- Security violations in human-computer interaction may be due to systematic causes such as cognitive overload, lack of security knowledge, and mismatches between the behavior of the computer system and the user's mental model (Cerone and Shaikh, 2008).
- To some extent users will develop their own mental models and of such interactions by which to gauge subsequent procedures. Understanding the constructs and evolution of these mental models and how they evolve is a key factor in understanding the expectations of users for new cyber-interactions.

Table 5.1 Using the Cyber-Security Framework to Map Issues of Cyber-Trust

Factors	System Characteristics
Service provider factors	• Privacy, assurance and security features • Robustness • Fail safe characteristics (or redundancy)
User characteristics	• Propensity to trust/confidence • Experience and proficiency in internet usage • Expectation of what is being provided • Levels of awareness about cyber-security threats
Security tools	• Social presence cues • Customization and personalization capacity • Constrained interfaces that allow free use (e.g., ability to convey details over a secure network) • Dynamic nature should be seamless (and pervasive)
Security tasks	• User interface has high degree of usability • Explicit security characteristics • Information quality/quantity/timeliness • Graphical characteristics
Operational environment	• Experience and familiarity with the online company • Ease of use in different contexts of use • Communicating different threat levels

These factors can be related back to the cyber-security framework in order to highlight key issues for user requirements investigations (Table 5.1).

Using the cyber-security framework to identify potential user requirements issues is an important part of specifying cyber-specifications. However, in order to capture meaningful data it is also important to consider the range of methods that are available. The use of formal methods in verifying the correctness of interactive systems should also include analysis of human behavior in interacting with the interface and must take into account all relationships between user's actions, user's goals, and the environment (Cerone and Shaikh, 2008).

CONDUCTING USER REQUIREMENTS ELICITATION

As previously discussed, whilst methods exist for identifying and gathering user needs in the security domain, they are relatively underdeveloped. It is only in the last decade that security aspects of interactive systems have been started to be systematically analyzed (Cerone and Shaikh, 2008); however, little research has been published on understanding the work of security personnel and systems which leads to the lack of case studies or guidance on how methods can be adopted or have been used in different security settings (Hancock and Hart, 2002; Kraemer et al., 2009). As a result it is necessary to revisit the fundamental issues of conducting user requirements elicitation that can then be applied to security research.

User requirements elicitation presents several challenges to investigators, not least in recruiting representative end-users and other stakeholders upon which the whole process depends (Lawson and D'Cruz, 2011). Equally important, it is necessary to elicit and categorize/prioritize the relevant expertise and knowledge and communicate these forward to designers and policy makers, as well as back to the end-users and other stakeholders.

One of the first steps in conducting a user requirements elicitation is to understand that there can be different levels of end-users or stakeholders. Whilst the term "end-user" and "stakeholder" are often confused, stakeholders are not always the end-users of a product or process, but have a particular investment or interest in the outcome and its effect on users or wider community (Mitchell et al., 1997). The term "end-user" or "primary user" is commonly defined as someone who will make use of a particular product or process (Eason, 1987). In many cases, users and stakeholders will have different needs and often their goals or expectations of the product or process can be conflicting (Nuseibeh and Easterbrook, 2000). These distinctions and background information about users, stakeholders and specific contexts of use allow designers and system developers to arrive at informed outcomes (Maguire and Bevan, 2002).

Within the security domain and more specifically within cyber-security, a key challenge in the initial stages of user requirements elicitation is gaining access and selecting appropriate users and stakeholders. In "sensitive domains," snowball or chain referral sampling are particularly successful methods of engaging with a target audience often fostered through cumulative referrals made by those who share knowledge or interact with others at an operational level or share specific interests for the investigation (Biernacki and Waldorf, 1981). This sampling method is useful where security agencies and organizations might be reluctant to share confidential and sensitive information with those they perceive to be "outsiders." This method has been used in the areas of drug use and addiction research where information is limited and where the snowball approach can be initiated with a personal contact or through an informant (Biernacki and Waldorf, 1981). However, one of the problems with such a method of sampling is that the eligibility of participants can be difficult to verify as investigators rely on the referral process, and the sample includes only one subset of the relevant user population. More specifically within cyber-security, end-users may not know each other well enough to enable such approaches to gather momentum.

While user requirements elicitation tends to be conducted amongst a wide range of users and stakeholders, some of these domains are more restricted and challenging than others in terms of confidentiality, anonymity, and privacy. These sensitive domains can include those involving children, elderly or disabled users, healthcare systems, staff/patient environments, commerce, and other domains where information is often beyond public access (Gaver et al., 1999). In addition, some organizations restrict how much information employees can share with regard to their tasks, roles, strategies, technology use and future visions with external parties to protect commercial or competitive standpoints. Within cyber-security, organizations are very sensitive of broadcasting any systemic vulnerabilities which may be perceived by the public as a lack of security awareness or exploited by competitors looking for marketplace leverage. Such domains add further complications to ultimately reporting findings to support the wider understanding of user needs in these domains (Crabtree et al., 2003; Lawson et al., 2009).

CAPTURING AND COMMUNICATING USER REQUIREMENTS

There are a number of human factors methods such as questionnaires, surveys, interviews, focus groups, observations and ethnographic reviews, and formal task or link analyses that can be used as the foundations to user requirements elicitation (Crabtree et al., 2003; Preece et al., 2007). These methods provide different opportunities for interaction between the investigator and target audience, and hence provide different types and levels of data (Saikayasit et al., 2012). A range of complementary methods are often selected to enhance the detail of the issues explored. For example, interviews and focus groups might be employed to gain further insights or highlight problems that have been initially identified in questionnaires or surveys. In comparison to direct interaction between the investigator and participant (e.g., interviews) indirect methods (e.g., questionnaires) can reach a larger number of respondents and are cheaper to administer, but are not efficient for probing complicated issues or tacit knowledge (Sinclair, 2005).

Focus groups can also be used, where the interviewer acts as a group organizer, facilitator and prompter, to encourage discussion across several issues around predefined themes (Sinclair, 2005). However, focus groups can be costly and difficult to arrange depending on the degree of anonymity required by each of the participants. They are also notoriously "hit and miss" depending on the availability of participants for particular sessions. In addition, they need effective management so that all participants have an opportunity to contribute without specific individuals dominating the interaction or people being affected by peer pressure not to voice particular issues (Friedrich and van der Poll, 2007). As with many qualitative analyses, care also needs to be taken in how results are fed into the requirements capture. When using interactive methods, it is important that opportunities are provided for participants to express their knowledge spontaneously, rather than only responding to directed questions from the investigator. This is because there is a danger that direct questions are biased by preconceptions that may prevent investigators exploring issues they have not already identified. On this basis, investigators should assume the role of "learners" rather than "hypothesis testers" (McNeese et al., 1995).

Observational and ethnographic methods can also be used to allow investigators to gather insights into socio-technical factors such as the impact of gate-keepers, moderators or more formal mechanisms in cyber-security. However, observation and ethnographic reviews can be intrusive, especially in sensitive domains where privacy and confidentially is crucial. In addition, the presence of observers can elicit behaviors that are not normal for the individual or group being viewed as they purposely follow formal procedures or act in a socially desirable manner (Crabtree et al., 2003; Stanton et al., 2005). Furthermore, this method provides a large amount of rich data, which can be time consuming to analyze. However, when used correctly, and when the investigator has a clear understanding of the domain being observed, this method can provide rich qualitative and quantitative real world data (Sinclair, 2005).

Investigators often focus on the tasks that users perform in order to elicit tacit information or to understand the context of work (Nuseibeh and Easterbrook, 2000). Thus the use of task analysis methods to identify problems and the influence of user interaction on system performance is a major approach within human factors (Kirwan and Ainsworth, 1992). A task analysis is defined as a study of what the user/ system operation is required to do, including physical activities and cognitive processes, in order to achieve a specified goal (Kirwan and Ainsworth, 1992). Scenarios are often used to illustrate or describe typical tasks or roles in a particular context (Sutcliffe, 1998). There are generally two types of scenarios: those that represent and capture aspects of real work settings so that investigators and users can communicate their understanding of tasks to aid the development process; and those used to portray how users might envisage using a future system that is being developed (Sutcliffe, 1998). In the latter case, investigators often develop "user personas" that represent how different classes of user might interact with the future system and/or how the system will fit into an intended context of use. This is sometimes communicated through story-board techniques either presented as scripts, link-diagrams or conceptual diagrams to illustrate processes and decision points of interest.

Whilst various methods assist investigators in eliciting user requirements, it is important to communicate the findings back to relevant users and stakeholders. Several techniques exist in user experience and user-centered design to communicate the vision between investigators and users. These generally include scenario-based modeling (e.g., tabular text narratives, user personas, sketches and informal media) and concept mapping (e.g., scripts, sequences of events, link and task analyses) including actions and objects during the design stage of user requirements (Sutcliffe, 1998). Scenario-based modeling can be used to represent the tasks, roles, systems, and how they interact and influence task goals, as well as identify connections and dependencies between the user, system and the environment (Sutcliffe, 1998). Concept mapping is a technique that represents the objects, actions, events (or even emotions and feelings) so that both the investigators and users form a common understanding in order to identify gaps in knowledge (Freeman and Jessup, 2004; McNeese et al., 1995). The visual representations of connections between events and objects in a concept map or link analysis can help identify conflicting needs, create mutual understandings and enhance recall and memory of critical events (Freeman and Jessup, 2004). Use-cases can also be used to represent typical interactions, including profiles, interests, job descriptions and skills as part of the user requirements representation (Lanfranchi and Ireson, 2009). Scenarios with personas can be used to describe how users might behave in specific situations in order to provide a richer understanding of the context of use. Personas typically provide a profile of a specific user, stakeholder or role based on information from a number of sources (e.g., a typical child using a chat-room; a parent trying to govern the safety of their child's on-line presence; a shopper; a person using a home-banking interface). What is then communicated is a composite and synthesis of key features within a single profile that can then be used as a single point of reference (e.g., Mary is an 8-year-old girl with no clear understanding of internet grooming techniques; Malcolm is a 60-year-oldman with no awareness of phishing tactics). In some cases personas are given names and background information such as age, education, recent training courses attended and even generic images/photos to make them more realistic or representative of a typical user. In other cases, personas are used anonymously in order to communicate generic characteristics that may be applicable to a wider demographic.

User requirements elicitation with users working in sensitive domains also presents issues of personal anonymity and data confidentiality (Kavali et al., 2005). In order to safeguard these, anonymity and pseudonymity can be used to disguise individuals, roles and relationships between roles (Pfitzmann and Hansen, 2005). In this way, identifying features of participants should not be associated with the data or approaches should be used that specifically use fictitious personas to illustrate and integrate observations across a number of participants. If done correctly, these personas can then be used as an effective communication tool without compromising the trust that has been built during the elicitation process.

Using a variety of human factors methods provides investigators with a clearer understanding how cyber-security, as a process, can operate based on the perspective of socio-technical systems. Without a range of methods to employ and without picking those most suitable for a specific inquiry, there is a danger that the best data will be missed. In addition, without using the tools for communicating the findings of user requirements activities, the overall process would be incomplete and end-users and other stakeholders will miss opportunities to learn about cyber-security and/or contribute further insights into their roles. Such approaches allow investigators to develop a much better understanding of the bigger picture such as the context and wider systems, as well as more detailed understandings of specific tasks and goals.

CONCLUSION

A user-centered approach is essential to understanding cyber-security from a human factors perspective. It is also important to understand the context of work and related factors contributing to the overall performance of a security system. The adaptation of the security framework goes some way in helping to focus attention. However, while there are many formal and established methodologies that are in use, it is essential that the practitioner considers the key contextual issues as outlined in this chapter before simply choosing a particular methodology. Whilst various methods and tools can indeed be helpful in gaining insight into particular aspects of requirements elicitation for cyber-security, caution must be at the forefront as a valid model for eliciting such data does not exist specifically for cyber-security at present. At the moment, investigations rely on the experience, understanding and skill of the investigator in deciding which approach is best to adopt in order to collect robust data that can then be fed back into the system process.

ACKNOWLEDGMENT

Aspects of the work presented in this chapter were supported by the Engineering and Physical Sciences Research Council (EPSRC) as part of the "Shades of Grey" project (EP/H02302X/1).

REFERENCES

Beldad, A., de Jong, M., Steehouder, M., 2010. How shall I trust the faceless and the intangible? A literature review on the antecedents of online trust. Comput. Hum. Behav. 26, 857–869.

Biernacki, P., Waldorf, D., 1981. Snowball sampling. Problems and techniques of chain referral sampling. Sociol. Methods Res. 10 (2), 141–163.

Blandford, A., Rugg, G., 2002. A case study on integrating contextual information with analytical usability evaluation. Int. J. Hum.-Comput. Stud. 57, 75–99.

Boyd, J., 2003. The rhetorical construction of trust online. Commun. Theory 13 (4), 392–410.

Cerone, A., Shaikh, S.A., 2008. Formal analysis of security in interactive systems. In: Gupta, M., Sharman, R. (Eds.), Handbook of Research on Social and Organizational Liabilities in Information Security. IGI-Global, pp. 415–432 (Chapter 25).

Cooke, N.J., Winner, J.L., 2008. Human factors of homeland security. In: Boehm-Davis, D.A. (Ed.), Reviews of Human Factors and Ergonomics, vol. 3. Human Factors and Ergonomics Society, Santa Monica, CA, pp. 79–110.

Coughlan, J., Macredie, R.D., 2002. Effective communication in requirements elicitation: a comparison of methodologies. Requirements Eng. 7, 47–60.

Crabtree, A., Hemmings, T., Rodden, T., Cheverst, K., Clarke, K., Dewsbury, G., Huges, J., Rouncefield, M., 2003. Designing with care: adapting cultural probes to inform design in sensitive settings. Proc. OzCHI 2003, 4–13.

Eason, K., 1987. Information Technology and Organizational Change. Taylor and Francis, London.

Freeman, L.A., Jessup, L.M., 2004. The power and benefits of concept mapping: measuring use, usefulness, ease of use, and satisfaction. Int. J. Sci. Educ. 26 (2), 151–169.

Friedrich, W.R., van der Poll, J.A., 2007. Towards a methodology to elicit tacit domain knowledge from users. Interdisciplinary J. Inf. Knowl. Manage. 2, 179–193.

Gaver, B., Dunne, T., Pacenti, E., 1999. Design: cultural probes. Interaction 6 (1), 21–29.

Haas, D.F., Deseran, F.A., 1981. Trust and symbolic exchange. Social Psychol. Q. 44 (1), 3–13.

Hancock, P.A., Hart, S.G., 2002. Defeating terrorism: what can human factors/ergonomics offer? Ergonomics Design 10, 6–16.

Iphofen, R., in print. Ethical issues in surveillance and privacy. In: Stedmon, A.W., Lawson, G. (Eds.), Hostile Intent and Counter-Terrorism: Human Factors Theory and Application. Ashgate, Aldershot.

Kavali, E., Kalloniatis, C., Gritzalis, S., 2005. Addressing privacy: matching user requirements to implementation techniques. In: 7th Hellenic European Research on Computer Mathematics & its Applications Conference (HERCMA 2005), Athens, Greece, 22–24 September 2005.

Kirwan, B., Ainsworth, L.K., 1992. A Guide to Task Analysis. CRC Press, Taylor & Francis Group, Boca Raton, FL.

Kleiner, B.M., 2006. Macroergonomics: analysis and design of work systems. Appl. Ergonomics 37, 81–89.

Kraemer, S., Carayon, P., Sanquist, T.F., 2009. Human and organisational factors in security screening and inspection systems: conceptual framework and key research needs. Cogn. Technol. Work 11 (1), 29–41.

Lanfranchi, V., Ireson, N., 2009. User requirements for a collective intelligence emergency response system. In: Proceedings of the 23rd British HCI Group Annual Conference on People and Computers: Celebrating People and Technology. pp. 198–203.

Lawson, G., Sharples, S., Cobb, S., Clarke, D., 2009. Predicting the human response to an emergency. In: Bust, P.D. (Ed.), Contemporary Ergonomics 2009. Taylor and Francis, London, pp. 525–532.

Lawson, G., D'Cruz, M., 2011. Ergonomics methods and the digital factory. In: Canetta, L., Redaelli, C., Flores, M. (Eds.), Intelligent Manufacturing System DiFac. Springer, London.

Lohse, M., 2011. Bridging the gap between users' expectations and system evaluations. In: 20th IEEE International Symposium on Robot and Human Interactive Communication, 31 July–3 August 2011, Atlanta, GA, USA. pp. 485–490.

Maguire, M., Bevan, N., 2002. User requirements analysis. A review of supporting methods. In: Proceedings of IFIP 17th World Computer Congress, 25–30 August, Montreal, Canada, Kluwer Academic Publishers. pp. 133–148.

Maiden, N., 2008. User requirements and system requirements. IEEE Softw. 25 (2), 90–91.

McNeese, M.C., Zaff, B.S., Citera, M., Brown, C.E., Whitaker, R., 1995. AKADAM: eliciting user knowledge to support participatory ergonomics. Int. J. Indust. Ergonomics 15, 345–363.

Mitchell, R.K., Agle, B., Wood, D.J., 1997. Toward a theory of stakeholder identification and salience: defining the principle of who and what really counts. Acad. Manage. Rev. 22 (4), 853–886.

Nuseibeh, B., Easterbrook, S., 2000. Requirements engineering: a roadmap. In: Proceedings of International Conference of Software Engineering (ICSE-2000), 4–11 July 2000. ACM Press, Limerick, Ireland, pp. 37–46.

Pfitzmann, A., Hansen, M., 2005. Anonymity, unlinkability, unobservability, pseudonymity and identify management: a consolidated proposal for terminology. http://dud.inf.tu-dresden.de/Anon_Terminology.shtml,versionv0.25,December6,2005 (accessed 11.11.13).

Preece, J., Rogers, Y., Sharp, H., 2007. Interaction Design: Beyond Human–Computer Interaction, second ed. John Wiley & Sons Ltd, Hoboken, NJ.

Reiman, A., Väyrynen, S., 2011. Review of regional workplace development cases: a holistic approach and proposals for evaluation and management. Int. J. Sociotech. Knowl. Dev. 3, 55–70.

Saikayasit, R., Stedmon, A., Lawson, G., in print. A macro-ergonomics perspective on security: a rail case study. In: Stedmon, A.W., Lawson, G. (Eds.). Hostile Intent and Counter-Terrorism: Human Factors Theory and Application. Ashgate, Aldershot.

Saikayasit, R., Stedmon, A.W., Lawson, G., Fussey, P., 2012. User requirements for security and counter-terrorism initiatives. In: Vink, P. (Ed.), Advances in Social and Organisational Factors. CRC Press, Boca Raton, FL, pp. 256–265.

Sinclair, M.A., 2005. Participative assessment. In: Wilson, J.R., Corlett, E.N. (Eds.), Evaluation of Human Work: A Practical Ergonomics Methodology. third ed. CRC Press, Taylor & Francis Group, Boca Raton, FL, pp. 83–112.

Stanton, N.A., Salmon, P.M., Walker, G.H., Baber, C., Jenkins, D.P., 2005. Human Factors Methods: A Practical Guide for Engineering and Design. Ashgate Publishing Limited, Aldershot pp. 21–44.

Stedmon, A.W., Saikayasit, R., Lawson, G., Fussey, P., 2013. User requirements and training needs within security applications: methods for capture and communication. In: Akhgar, B., Yates, S. (Eds.), Strategic Intelligence Management. Butterworth-Heinemann, Oxford, pp. 120–133.

Sutcliffe, A., 1998. Scenario-based requirements analysis. Requirements Eng. 3, 48–65.

Taylor, R.M., Selcon, S.J., 1990. Psychological principles of human-electronic crew teamwork. In: Emerson, T.J., Reinecke, M., Reising, J.M., Taylor, R.M. (Eds.), The Human Electronic Crew: Is the Team Maturing? Proceedings of the 2nd Joint GAF/USAF/RAF Workshop. RAF Institute of Aviation Medicine, PD-DR-P5.

Wilson, J.R., 1995. Ergonomics and participation. In: Wilson, J.R., Corlett, E.N. (Eds.), Evaluation of Human Work: A Practical Ergonomics Methodology. second and revised ed. Taylor & Francis, London.

Wilson, J.R., Haines, H., Morris, W., 2005. Participatory ergonomics. In: Wilson, J.R., Corlett, E.N. (Eds.), Evaluation of Human Work: A Practical Ergonomics Methodology. third ed. CRC Press, Taylor & Francis Group, Boca Raton, FL, pp. 933–962.

High-tech investigations of cyber crime

6

Emlyn Butterfield

INTRODUCTION

Digital information has become ubiquitous with the world of today; there is an increasing reliance on digital information to maintain a "normal" life, communication and general socialization. The prolific use of networked devices now allows anybody from any country to now attack, or utilize a digital device to attack, their next door neighbor or someone on the other-side of the world with only a few clicks of a button. People's ignorance, including criminals, of what information a device stores and the amount of data it generates means that a properly trained and equipped expert can recover and make use of information from almost any digital device. This same digital information can now provide evidence and intelligence that can be critical to criminal and civil investigations. Understanding the threat of cyber-crime and cyber-terrorism allows us to put into context the current technical situation, however identifying the potential for attack is only the start. Within this chapter we will be looking at defining high-tech investigations and evidential processes that are applicable to all investigations. The description and processes will aid in the investigation of a crime, or malicious action, after the event has occurred.

HIGH-TECH INVESTIGATIONS AND FORENSICS

The term "forensics" can bring to mind popular American television series. Television shows that glorify forensic analysis such as these have both helped and, to some extent, hindered forensic science. It has helped by bringing the concept of forensic capabilities to a wider audience so that a heightened level of awareness exists. Conversely, it has also hindered it by exaggerating the technical capabilities of forensic scientists: no matter what the television shows suggest it is entirely possible for data to be beyond recovery by even the most eminent experts. However, surprisingly, many users remain ignorant of the kind of data that can be scavenged from various digital sources that will underpin an investigation. Digital devices are essentially a part of any investigation in one way or another:

- **Used to conduct the activity under investigation**: the device is the main focus of the activity, such as the main storage and distribution device in a case of indecent images of children.

- **Target of the activity under investigation**: the device is the "victim," such as in an incident of hacking.
- **Supports the activity under investigation**: the device is used to facilitate the activity, such as mobile phones used for communication.

High-tech investigations relate to the analysis and interpretation of data from digital devices, often called upon when an incident (criminal or civil) has occurred. They are not purely about using the most advanced technology to perform the work. A good proportion of what is done is actually "low-tech" in the sense it is the investigator's mind doing the work and interpreting the data that is available. The primary objective of a high-tech investigations is to identify what happened and by whom.

CORE CONCEPTS OF HIGH-TECH INVESTIGATIONS

It is generally agreed that a high-tech investigation encompasses four main distinct components, all of which are important toward the successful completion of an investigation:

1. **Collection**: the implementation of a forensic process to preserve the data contained on the digital evidence while following accepted guidelines and procedures. If performed incorrectly any data produced at a later date may not stand up in a court of law.
2. **Examination**: systematic review of the data utilizing forensic methodologies and tools whilst maintaining its integrity
3. **Analysis**: evaluating the data to determine the relevance of the information to the requirements of the investigation, including that of any mitigating circumstances.
4. **Reporting**: applying appropriate methods of visualization and documentation to report on what was found on the digital evidence that is relevant to the investigation.

These four main components underpin the entire investigative process allowing high-tech investigators and reviewers of the final product to be confident of its authenticity, validity, and accuracy (also see Chapter 4).

An important consideration throughout a high-tech investigation is to maintain the "chain of custody" of the exhibit, so that it can be accounted for at all stages of an investigation and its integrity maintained. With a physical exhibit this is achieved, in part, through the use of an evidence bag and a tamper evident seal. The integrity of digital information is maintained in the form of one-way hash functions, such as MD5, SHA-1, and SHA-256. One-way hash functions can be used to create a unique digital fingerprint of the data; this means that, when implemented correctly, even a small change to the data will result in a completely different digital fingerprint. If the physical and digital integrity of an exhibit is maintained then it allows for a third party to verify the process performed. This is an important factor in improving the chances of evidence acceptance within the legal proceedings.

Whilst each country may have their own guidelines or best practice in relation to handling digital evidence the general essence is almost always the same. The UK has the Association of Chief Police Officers (ACPO) Good Practice Guide for Digital Evidence (Williams, 2012) and in the US there is the Forensic Examination of Digital Evidence: A Guide for Law Enforcement (National Institute of Justice, 2004). These documents do not go into technical detail on how to perform analysis of the digital data, they are more focused toward the best practices involved in the seizure and preservation of evidence. The ability to correctly acquire or process digital evidence is extremely important for anyone working in high-tech investigations. The acquisition of exhibits provides the basis for a solid investigation. If the acquisition is not done correctly and the integrity, or the continuity, of the exhibit is questionable then an entire case may fail. The salient points will be discussed in the next sections.

DIGITAL LANDSCAPES

Traditionally digital forensics focused on the single home computer or a business' local area network (LAN). But in a world where networks are prolific, with the advent of the Internet and the mass market of portable devices, digital evidence can come from almost any device used on a daily basis. It is therefore important to consider different technical routes and peculiarities when dealing with the digital evidence.

The advent of advanced technology within business and at home now means that more advanced techniques of data capture are required. This has led to the development of live, online and offline data capture techniques. The remit of the investigation and the technology to be investigated will determine the data capture technique performed. However, the key to the data capture phase is that the captured data's integrity can be confirmed and verified.

THE "CRIME SCENE"

As with any kind of investigation it is important to plan prior to performing an investigation, in particular where physical attendance is required at a "crime scene," this will not always be possible, or required. Digital devices can appear within any investigation and it is easy to overlook the significance of a digital device to a particular investigation type.

Before attending a "crime scene" pre-search intelligence is key in identifying the layout of the scene, the potential number of people or devices, and the type of digital information relevant to the investigation. This information allows the organization of equipment and resources that may be required to seize or capture the data. Early consideration should be made as to whether digital devices can be removed from the "crime scene" or whether data needs to be captured and then brought back to the laboratory for analysis.

If attendance at a "crime scene" is required then the overarching rule is to preserve the evidence. This, however, cannot come before the safety of those on site. Once personal safety is assured then evidential preservation can commence. At the first opportunity everyone not involved in the investigation should be removed from the vicinity of all keyboards or mice (or other input device) so that no interaction can be made with any digital device. If left, people can cause untold damage to the digital data making the later stage of the investigation much harder, if not impossible.

The physical "crime scene" should be recorded using photographs, video recordings, and sketches. This makes it possible to identify the location of devices at a later date, and also allows a third party to see the layout and the devices *in situ*. It may be that these images are reviewed at a later date and, following analysis, important points found in the digital data allow inferences to be drawn from what was physically present; such as the connection of a USB DVD writer.

With the sheer number of digital devices that may be present at a "crime scene" consideration must be made to the likelihood that a device contains information in relation to the investigation. It is no longer feasible to go on site and seize every single digital item, budgets and time constraints will not allow this. Consideration must be made as to the investigation type, the owner of the device and any intelligence and background information available to determine whether the device is suitable for seizure. Such a decision should be made in conjunction with the lead investigator and legal and procedural restrictions.

If a device requires seizing, it should first be determined if the device is on or off. If on, then consideration should be made of live data capture and a record made of all visible running programs and processes. Once a decision has been made and any live data captured, the power should then be removed from the device. If the device is a server, or similar device, running critical systems and databases, then the correct shutdown procedure should be followed. It is possible that an unscrupulous individual has "rigged" a system to run certain programs, or scripts, when it is shutdown, such as wiping data or modifying certain information; however, the risk of losing critical business information through a corrupted database or system needs to be considered fully. Generally a normal home laptop or computer can simply have the power removed. Once taken offline, or if it is already off, the device should be placed into an evidence bag with a tamper evidence seal and the chain of custody maintained. Each device should be given a unique reference number to aid identification - and these should be unique to each high-tech investigation.

Once the crime scene is physically secure attention needs to be made of the devices to be seized and how technically to achieve that - this is detailed in the following sections.

LIVE AND ONLINE DATA CAPTURE

Live data capture is utilized when the device is not taken offline: that is, it is decided not to turn it off. For example if a critical business server is taken offline it may cause disruption or loss of revenue for the business. If a program is running, it may mean critical data will be lost or it will not be possible to recover that information if the power is removed. This can also be the case when dealing with encryption: if the power is turned off, the data is no longer in a format that is accessible without the correct password.

A high-tech investigation should enable someone to follow the steps performed and produce exactly the same results. However, the problem with live data is that it is in a constant state of change, therefore it can never be fully replicated. Although, these issues exist, it is now accepted practice to perform some well-defined and documented live analysis as part of an investigation, and the captured data can be protected from further volatility by generating hashes of the evidence at the time that it is collected.

Traditionally, when looking for evidence in relation to website access, data would be captured from the local machine in the form of temporary internet files. However, as advanced Internet coding technologies leave fewer scattered remnants on a local machine, techniques must now be used to log onto an actual webpage and grab the contents that can be seen by a user. Alternatively, requests can be made of the service provider to produce the information. This process requires detailed recording of the actions performed and a hash of the file at the conclusion. An example of online data capture is the capture of evidence from Social Networks, which is now becoming progressively prominent in high-tech investigations, including those related to cyberbullying.

With live data, even with the securing of a physical crime scene, it is still possible that an outside influence can be applied to the digital data, such as remote access. It is very important therefore that this information is seized digitally as soon as possible. If possible the data on the device should be reviewed and once satisfied that data will not be lost, the device should be isolated from network communication, mobile signals or any other form of communication that could allow data to be removed or accessed remotely. In large organizations support should be sought from the system administrators to help in the identification and isolation of digital devices, to prevent unwanted corruption of important data. The devices can then be removed or the data captured using appropriate tools.

OFFLINE (DEAD) DATA CAPTURE

This is the traditional method of data capture, through the removal of the main storage unit, typically a hard drive: an exact replica is made of the data on the device and later analyzed.

An essential principle of forensics is that the original data, which might be used as evidence, is not modified. Therefore, when processing physical evidence, it is imperative that a write-blocker is used; a write-blocker captures and stops any requests to write to the evidence. This device sits in line with the device and the analysis machine. There are numerous write-blockers available that can protect various kinds of physical devices from being modified by the investigator. There are physical write-blockers, which are physically connected to the digital evidence and the analysis machine. There are also software-based write-blockers which interrupt the driver behavior in the operating system.

VERIFICATION OF THE DATA

Having captured the data the first step, as a high-tech investigator, is to confirm that the data has not been altered. To facilitate this, the data capture has its hash value recalculated; this is then compared against the original hash. If these do not match then no further steps are performed until the senior investigating officer, or manager, is contacted and the situation discussed. Such an error may undermine even the most concrete evidence found on the exhibit. Hash mismatches can occur if the data was not copied correctly or there may have been a fault with the original device. The original exhibit may need to be revisited and a new image created. This may not be possible if an online, or live data capture, was performed as the data may no longer be available. The second the capture is made, new data may be added to the device and any old data may be overwritten, meaning the device will never be in the same state again.

REVIEWING THE REQUIREMENTS

The requirements of the investigation, or remit, provide the specific questions that need to be answered. This can be used to identify possible routes for analysis. It is important to ensure a thorough analysis of the requirements is made early on in the investigation to ensure that time and money are not wasted. From the remit, alongside any background information provided, the following need to be identified as a minimum:

1. **Number and type of exhibits**: so it is known what data is to be investigated
2. **Individuals/business involved**: so it is known who is to be investigated
3. **Date and times**: so it is known when the incident occurred, which will provide a time window to be investigated
4. **Keywords**: what may be of interest during the investigation if it is found, this could be names or bank account numbers for example
5. **Supplied data**: if a particular file or document on the data is to be looked for—it is useful if a copy of this is provided

STARTING THE ANALYSIS

There may be a wealth of information gleaned from the captured evidence some of which may not be relevant. No one process or method will necessarily answer all the questions posed. It is important to remember the following points when reviewing information to ensure nothing is missed or misinterpreted:

1. **False Positives**: files that are not relevant to an investigation but they may contain a keyword that is important
2. **Positives**: files/data that are relevant to the investigation
3. **False Negatives**: files that are not picked up but are relevant—they may be in an unreadable format (for example, compressed or encrypted)

The actual analysis of the data will vary depending on the type of investigation that needs to be carried out. Therefore at the beginning of the investigation consideration and a careful analysis must be made of the actual questions that are being asked.

The analysis of data can be broken up into two stages:

1. **Pre-Analysis**: if this is done incorrectly it can have a major impact on the rest of the investigation. It is the process of getting the data ready to make the actual analysis as smooth as possible. This process is all about preparing the data through the recovery of deleted files and partitions, and the mounting of compressed file and folders and encrypted files (so they then become searchable and have context)
2. **Analysis**: this is the review of the data to find information that will assist in the investigation, through the identification of evidence that proves, or disproves, a point

A high-tech investigation should not be dependent upon the tool used; a tool is simply a means to an end. However, it is important that the investigator is comfortable and sufficiently qualified and experienced in using the chosen digital analysis tool. The ability to click a button in a forensic tool or to follow a predefined process is not forensics—this is evidential data recovery. A high-tech investigator must be able to review what is in front of them and interpret that information to form a conclusion, and if appropriate, an opinion. The location of evidence can be as important as the evidence itself; therefore careful consideration must be made as to the context of what is seen. If a file resides in a user's personal documents folder, it does not mean that they put it there. It is the investigator's role to identify its provenance and provide context as to how it got there, when, and whether it has been opened. The interpretation and production of such information may help in proving, or disproving, an avenue of investigation.

There is no correct way to begin the actual analysis of the data; there is no rule book which will state exactly what to do and what to look at. Depending on any legal restrictions, the investigator may be limited to only reviewing certain files and data. If there is any uncertainty on this issue the investigator must discuss this with their manager or the senior investigator. If all data can be accessed then the investigator can browse through the folders and files. If anything stands out as "unusual" or of interest it may provide direction and focus to the technical analysis steps. To some extent this may depend on the operating system under review.

At the start of an investigation a check should be made to ensure that all the expected data in the capture is accounted for. It is very easy for partitions on a disc to be modified so that they are not seen straight away or for a partition to be deleted and a new one created. In terms of a physical disc this may involve the review of the number of sectors available on the disc compared to those currently used.

SIGNATURE ANALYSIS

It is easy to obscure a files' true meaning, and it useful to identify whether all the files are what they purport to be; this can be a simple way of highlighting notable files. Operating systems use a process of application binding to link a file type to an application. Windows, for example, uses file extensions and maintains a record of which application should open which file: for example .doc files are opened in Microsoft Word. The fact that Windows uses file extensions gives rise to a data-hiding technique whereby a user can change the extension of the file to obscure its contents. If a file named **MyContraband.jpg** was changed to **lansys.dll** and moved to a system folder, the casual observer would probably never find it.

Linux uses a files header (or signature) to identify which application should open the file (the file can be viewed in hex to see this). It is therefore harder to obscure a files' contents/true type as with a broken header the file will often not open. Linux (and Mac) have a built-in Terminal command that allows you to identify a file's signature, simply using the command *file –i* [where *–i* represents the input file].

Most Forensic tools have the capability to check a file's signature and report whether this is different from that expected from the extension. The file's signature can be checked against a precompiled database. If the signature exists it will then check the extension associated with it. One of the following results for each file will then be obtained (certain forensic tools may give more specific results but all align to the same two concepts):

- **Match** - the signature and extension match with what is stored
- **Mismatch** - the signature and extension do not match and therefore the file should be checked to identify evidence of manipulation

FILTERING EVIDENCE

It is well known that a hash value is an important tool within any high-tech investigation. Hash values are intrinsic to a forensic investigation; they are initially utilized to verify and confirm the integrity of the evidence received. They can then be used to confirm the integrity of any, and all, evidence produced. An investigator can also use hash values to reduce the amount of data under review - through the use of what is referred to as hash sets, which are simply a grouping of known hash values. An investigator can maintain a vast hash set which can significantly cut down on the files to be reviewed; removing what is "known good" can vastly reduce what needs to be investigated, thus speeding up the entire investigation.

It is also possible to create custom hash sets of notable files which can be run against a case to quickly identify what is present. If a file or data are provided at the start of the investigation, for example an image that is of interest, a hash can be created of the image and then searched for across the exhibit - based purely on the hash value. This is a quick way to identify notable files and will allow the investigator to focus on data that contains information definitely related to the investigation.

KEYWORD SEARCHING

Keyword searching allows the quick identification of notable terms and information, typically retrieved from the remit or the background information. An ability to identify keywords that are relevant to an investigation is an extremely important skill. The wrong keyword choice may take several days to run and months to review. There are generally two ways to conduct a search:

1. **An index search**: the tool used may be able to index all data, essentially recording every word present, so that it can be searched. This type of search is comprehensive as it does not generally care about the compression used, such as in PDF's or ZIP's, where a real-time search would not be able to identify all relevant keywords. Whilst this search is generally very slow to setup, once completed all results are almost instantaneous (Windows performs a similar action on your local computer).
2. **A real-time search**: a keyword can be created and run at any point in an investigation—the search can take some time to complete. Typically a real-time search is unable to search files that are compressed or in unusual formats, unless they are first uncompressed.

Regular expressions (regexp) can be utilized to make a more specific keyword search. Regexp is a way of defining a search pattern that utilizes wildcards and special characters to offer more flexibility and power than a simple keyword search. If **1234-1234** was provided as a serial number of a device, but it was not known if it included a hyphen; if it could be replaced by another special character; or if it existed at all then multiple search terms would need to be created (also see Chapter 7).

Rather than attempt to write every possible search term a simple regexp search could be created that covered this: for example **1234[.]?1234**.

The expression states that the characters in the brackets can be found zero or one time (this is denoted with a **?**). Within the bracket is a . (dot), this is a regexp character that denotes anything can be between the two numbers. It is good practice to test a regexp before launching it on a case, as it is a more complex string than a simple keyword search it can take more time to complete.

CORE EVIDENCE

It is impossible to detail the core evidence available on the various operating and file systems available within a single chapter; however there are several core evidential areas that are typically applicable in a high-tech investigation:

- **File Slack**: the way that files are stored on a device means that there is a significant amount of storage space that is unused but is allocated to a file. This is referred to as file slack and is simply the space between the end of a file and the space it was allocated on a device. This slack space can contain information from old files, which may be fragments of important data related to the investigation. It is also possible for a user to hide information in this space so that it is not easily recoverable.

- **Temporary Files**: many applications utilize temporary files when performing a function, such as when a user is working on a document or printing file. These files are typically deleted when the task is complete. However if there is an improper shutdown of the device, or it loses power, it is possible to recover and identify user actions.
- **Deleted Files**: the way in which digital data is deleted means that in a lot of instances it is possible to recover the data. In most cases of deletion all that is actually done is the pointer to the file is removed, the actual data is still resident on the exhibit and can be recovered in a relatively easy manner.

As Windows is still the most common operating system, the following sections will briefly describe some of the core artifacts that may be of use during an investigation: including the significance of this information (also see Chapter 7).

WINDOWS LNK FILES

Windows uses shortcuts to provide links to files in other locations. This could be to an application on a desktop or to a document on a network store. These files are referred to as LNK (or link) as they have the file extension .lnk. Of particular interest to a high-tech investigator are the LNK files found within a user's "**Recent**" folder. These files are created when a user opens a document and is the reference to the original document. LNK files are persistent which means they are there even after the target file is removed or no longer available. The "**Recent**" folder and LNK files are one of the first places an investigator will check when looking for user activity on a Windows-based system. These will provide information related to user activity; whether any external/remote drives are in use; and if any notable filenames can be found. LNK files include:

- The complete path to the original file
- Volume serial number: this is a unique reference to a partition (or volume)
- The size of the file that the LNK is pointing to
- MAC time stamps of the file the LNK is pointing to

WINDOWS PREFETCH FILES

Windows Prefetch files are designed to speed up the application start-up process and contain the name of the application; the number of times it has been run; and a timestamp indicating the last time it was run. This can give a solid indication as to the applications a user has run, and even malware that was run. These can be found within the folder **%SystemRoot%\Prefetch**.

WINDOWS EVENT LOGS

Windows maintains a record of all application and system activities within event logs. These are entries created automatically by the operating system and can provide significant information about chronological actions performed by users and the system. This will include user logons and offs; file access; account creation; services that are running; and the installation of drivers. They are typically used to perform troubleshooting activities on the computer: these can be found in **%SystemRoot%\Windows\system32\config**.

WINDOWS REGISTRY

The Windows registry is a database storing settings for a computer defining all the users; applications; and hardware installed on the system; and any associated settings, allowing the system to be configured correctly at boot-up. The registry is stored in a format that requires decoding to be read; there are numerous tools that can do this. Once opened it provides a wealth of information including, but is in no way limited to, evidence of the applications and files a user has opened; what devices were connected; and the IP addresses used.

RESTORE POINTS

Microsoft Windows provides a service known as restore points, the version of Windows determines what these actually contain. The simple purpose of restore points is to snapshot the computer, at a predefined date and time, or when an event occurs (such as the installation of software), so that it can be restored by the user if an error occurs. The restore points contain snapshots of the Windows Registry; system files; LNK files and with later versions of Windows they can also include incremental backups of user files. This can provide an invaluable resource for an investigation, as it will provide historic information such as applications that are no longer installed. Windows XP has a default retention period of 90 days for restore points, whereas later versions are only limited by the amount of disk space permitted to be used by them.

CASE STUDY

Following reports of customers being mis-sold legal-based documentation, a high-tech investigation was requested by a legal practice. Arrangements were made to attend the premises of the organization under investigation, legal proceedings meant that the organization had no idea that this was to happen—preventing malicious data destruction. A legal stipulation was enforced, intended to reduce loss of revenue for the business, which meant that digital devices could not be removed from the premises. Pre-search intelligence identified that up to 20 staff worked at the premises at any one time, and the access that was available for the building; including vehicle access routes. No information was available, nor time available, to identify what digital devices may be present.

The following day the premises were attended by both a legal team and a team of high-tech investigators. The scene was initially secured by removing all occupants from the vicinity of all digital devices. A full recording of the site was conducted using digital cameras and sketches and each digital device was identified. A review was made of the potential digital sources to determine their current state: in the main the devices were computers or laptops which had nothing significant running, and were therefore disconnected from power. A server was identified that was currently running, a capture was made of the memory to ensure running processes and connections were recorded, and then the server was shutdown.

Forensic data captures were made of all devices onsite, which in itself took over 12 hours. These captures were then placed into tamper proof evidence bags and returned to the laboratory and analyzed. The background to the investigation provided relevant keywords and file types. These were used to analyze the data which subsequently identified a number of files, emails and documents that were relevant to the investigation, these allowed the legal team to progress their legal proceedings.

SUMMARY

This chapter looked at the technical side of a high-tech investigation and how they are conducted. Included were key concepts associated with investigations of digital data as well as the tools; processes; and techniques pertinent to the process from collecting the evidence through to its analysis. These concepts are important for any investigator to know so that the correct procedures and processes can be implemented and the decisions made by others are also understood. It is important to remember that no two investigations will be the same; there is simply too much variation in the types of data storage and capabilities of devices for this ever to be the case. An investigation will almost always come down to the investigator and their ability to interpret and understand what they are seeing. It is important that even those who are not involved with the high-tech investigation are aware of the processes involved, as it has such a significant impact on any investigation into cyber-crime and cyber-terrorism. Such knowledge may assist in the identification of previously unthought-of digital devices or areas of investigation.

REFERENCES

National Institute of Justice, 2004. Forensic Examination of Digital Evidence: A Guide for Law Enforcement. Available: https://www.ncjrs.gov/pdffiles1/nij/199408.pdf (accessed 19.02.14).

Williams, J., 2012. ACPO Good Practice Guide for Digital Evidence. http://www.acpo.police.uk/documents/crime/2011/201110-cba-digital-evidence-v5.pdf (accessed 19.02.14).

Seizing, imaging, and analyzing digital evidence: step-by-step guidelines

7

David Day

INTRODUCTION

There are a number of approaches that can be taken when creating and subsequently executing a plan for a forensic investigation. Those that are selected, or created, are done so largely subjectively. However, there are certain criteria which should be followed both in terms of meeting best practice, complying with laws and regulations, and also ensuring any evidence discovered remains admissible in court. It is the purpose of this chapter to offer guidance in how to meet these aims, and in addition to discuss some of the more insightful methods used when searching for incriminating evidence. Further, it is intended to provide the examiner with an overall view of the processes. From what needs to be considered when applying for a search warrant, through to how to seize and acquire evidence appropriately. Finally it is discussed how to apply inventive methods to uncover crucial evidence via forensic analysis, including evidence that may have been obfuscated via anti-forensic techniques.

ESTABLISHING CRIME

Forensic evidence is usually gathered by a search of a suspect's premises and seizure of the relevant equipment. To do this legally it is typically necessary to obtain a search warrant. The details of this process differ depending on the laws of the country and the jurisdiction in which the alleged offence took place; however, in most instances warrants are supplied by a judge who has been convinced that enough evidence exists to justify its issue. For example, in the UK a judge needs to be satisfied that there are "reasonable grounds" for believing that an offence has occurred (Crown, 1984). Normally this offence would be listed under the computer misuse act. In the United States, the process is similar with the fourth amendment's inclusion of the term "probable cause" being cited (FindLaw, 2014). It is beyond the scope of this work to fully explore what is meant by both "reasonable grounds" and "probable cause" but in either case it is clear that significant evidence is need, and that the request to search a premises is not based on simply a suspicion or a hunch. Further, the evidence must support the assumption that a crime has been, is being, or will be committed or orchestrated from the premises.

COLLECTING EVIDENCE FOR A SEARCH WARRANT

Evidence that cybercrime has been committed can be collected in various ways dependent upon the crime being committed, with the crimes usually falling into one of the following four broad categories:

- Piracy: The reproduction and dissemination of copyrighted material.
- Malicious Hacking: The act of gaining illegal, unauthorized access to a computer system. This includes Phishing and identity theft.
- Child Pornography: The distribution, owning or viewing of child pornography.
- Financial: The purposeful disruption of a company's ability to conduct electronic commerce.

Regardless of the type of cybercrime committed, it is necessary to associate the suspect with the crime. The following sections discuss the techniques, tools, and methods for performing this.

REPORTED BY A THIRD PARTY

Parties who are suspected by a member of the public of having committed cybercrime can be reported to law enforcement. The criminal act could be discovered as a result of a work place audit or security monitoring program. Alternatively, it could be made by an individual who has become aware of criminal activity in a social context, either online via social media or in person.

IDENTIFICATION OF A SUSPECTS INTERNET PROTOCOL ADDRESS

A public Internet Protocol (IP) address uniquely identifies every device directly connected to the Internet. IP addressing employs a 32 bit (IPv4) or 128 bit (IPv6) hierarchical addressing scheme. The IP address is used by intermediary routers to make a decision on which path data packets should take from source to destination. When an IP address is used to potentially identify a suspect it has usually been assigned to the suspect by their Internet Service Provider (ISP) to their perimeter router. For a home user this would typically be housed on their premises. Their IP address remains encapsulated within the packets of data that constitute a communication session, and it uniquely identifies the public facing interface of that router. Identifying an IP address in a malicious communication is sufficient evidence to govern the issuing of a search warrant and arrest. However, there are some issues with this method of identification, the most notable being the use of IP spoofing and anonymizing proxy relay services. These are discussed in the following.

IP SPOOFING

IP spoofing is a process whereby a malicious hacker manually crafts data packets with a false source IP address. This not only hides their true IP address but also allows them to impersonate another system. The limitation is that it cannot be used in an attack which relies on a return communication from the victim to the attacker, for example, to take control of or view data from, the victim's machine. As a result it is a popular attack method for denial of service attacks which render a system inoperable by either overwhelming the system with a large quantity of packets, or by specifically crafting a packet which causes the service to terminate.

ANONYMIZING PROXY RELAY SERVICES

Anonymizing proxy relay services, such as Tor (2014), offer privacy and anonymity of origination. This is achieved by a using encryption and a relaying algorithm respectively. The Tor algorithm selects a random path from the source to destination via specific network nodes that have chosen by a supporting community to form part of the relay service. The connections between these nodes are encrypted in such a way that each node only has the IP address of the nodes it is immediately connected to. While the communication between the exit node and the final destination is not encrypted the original source IP address is still guarded behind multiple layers of encryption, one for each node. The final destination will only be aware of the IP address of the exit or final node used by the service, not the originating host of the message. This means if the logs of a server which has been compromised are examined; they will not reveal the details of an attacker using Tor, but rather the exit node of the Tor relay.

While proxy relay services such as Tor offer malicious hackers anti-surveillance and anonymity of origination, they also carry some drawbacks. Firstly they are slower than using the Internet conventionally; this is due to the additional nodes traversed (three in the case of Tor). These nodes can be in different countries and of poor quality and thus both the route and throughput becomes suboptimal. Second they can be difficult to configure, this is especially true if connectivity is not required through a web browser, as is the case with Internet Relay Chat (IRC), which although becoming less popular with the general public continues to remain a communication channel for malicious hackers. Lastly, they rely on the malicious party remembering to engage the service before each and every malicious operation, they only to need to forget on one occasion for their identity to be compromised. This is widely believed to have been the principal method by which Hector Xavier Monsegur, otherwise known as Sabu, from the hacking fraternity LulzSec was identified in 2011. He allegedly logged into an IRC channel just once without using an anonymizing service. It is reported that the FBI then requested records from the ISP responsible for that IP address, which revealed his home address (Olson, 2012).

INTRUSION DETECTION SYSTEMS, NETWORK TRAFFIC AND FIREWALL LOGS

Intrusion Detection Systems (IDS) are employed to monitor network traffic and detect malicious activity. This is usually achieved by matching the contents of the network traffic to already known malicious activity (the signature), if a match is discovered an alert is generated. It is common to perform network traffic capture in parallel with the network intrusion detection; this allows for subsequent investigation of the traffic which caused the alert, with the view to discovering more detail concerning the attack, including the IP addresses involved. Firewall and system logs too capture IP addresses and can hold information regarding malicious activity. Thus the information supplied by these systems can offer incriminating evidence relating to both the source of the breach and the severity of the crime, which could be sufficient to issue a warrant for search or arrest.

INTERVIEWS WITH SUSPECTS

Interviews of suspects following arrest can also be used to gain sufficient grounds for a search warrant where other involved parties are identified. For example, it is widely documented that subsequent to his arrest Sabu turned informer for the FBI, supplying information which subsequently led to the arrest and seizure of equipment from other members of LulzSec (Olson, 2012).

ANALYSIS OF SUSPECTS MEDIA

Evidence that incriminates a suspects allies in cybercrime can sometimes be found through the process of forensic investigation of their media storage, or via access to Virtual Private Servers (VPS) being used. Again this evidence may be sufficient to lead to a warrant for seizing the equipment of collaborating parties (see Chapters 6 and 8).

DOXING

To allow for group collaboration certain black hat hacking fraternities organize their attacks publically via online communication channels such as IRC and Twitter. This information is often deeply self-incriminating; however, as long as the true identification of the author is hidden behind an alias, they remain anonymous and thus safe. Hence one of the principle objectives in identifying a malicious party is often to associate them with their online persona, e.g., IRC handle, nickname, or twitter username. In digital forensic and hacking communities there is a term "doxing" which discusses how this can be achieved. Doxing is a term derived from the words document and tracing and essentially is the process of collecting information about Internet users which they would rather not be known, and of which they are probably not aware they have made available publically. Performing a successful "dox" involves gathering information such as, full name, date of birth, usernames, email accounts, home addresses, phone numbers, personal images and of course the online nicknames and handles of an individual. The techniques and practices necessary to perfect doxing involve a deep understanding of search engine operators, and how to collect together information from online sources such as social media, online advertising or anywhere else where information may have been published or leaked. They involve intelligent methods of cross referencing information between sources to build a profile of the suspect. Again, for the cyber investigator the aim here is to associate the incriminating evidence published via an alias with the suspect true identify with a view to gain a search and/or arrest warrant.

COLLECTING EVIDENCE

Once a search warrant has been granted, evidence of the suspected crime needs to be obtained; there are strict guidelines for how equipment should be seized, digital images acquired and evidence stored. These guidelines can vary dependent upon the jurisdiction of where the suspected crime took place, however, they all share processes related to the physical requirements, e.g., preservation of evidence. These will be discussed in the following sections.

SEIZING EQUIPMENT

It is essential that strict guidelines surrounding the seizure of equipment are adhered to. Data on computer equipment is both dynamic and volatile and seizing equipment incorrectly can lead to accidental deletion, modification or contamination of the evidence. The following section offering guidance in this process has been created in part from the Association of Chief Police Officers (ACPO) reference "Good Practice Guide for Computer-Based Electronic Evidence" (7Safe, 2007).

Initially, the area needs to be secured, meaning only law enforcement agents should be present in the area surrounding the equipment. All people unfamiliar with the process should be kept back from the equipment to reduce the risk of accidentally compromising the evidence. The area should be photographed and video recorded accurately, ensuring as much detail as possible is captured regarding how the equipment is connected. In addition all connections should be labeled to ensure the equipment can be successfully reconnected as it was, at a later time.

If the computer system appears powered off, this should be first confirmed. The unit could be in sleep mode, or a blank screen saver could be giving the impression that it is powered down. All lights should be examined to see that they are not lit, for example, hard drive monitoring lights. If after careful examination it is considered to be in sleep mode then it should be treated as powered on, see the following paragraph. If it is confirmed as switched off it should not be powered on as doing so will immediately compromise the validity of the evidence and allow the suspect repudiation on the grounds that there has been interaction with the media by law enforcement. After ensuring that all cables, connections and system equipment has been labeled and recorded as previously discussed, the system and all the peripherals and surrounding equipment can be disconnected and seized. If the system is a laptop then the battery should be removed to ensure that it is entirely powered down, and cannot be accidently turned on.

If the computer is powered on it is considered to be "live." Images on the screen should be photographed, once this has been done there are then two possible paths available. The computer can be turned off, to prevent any contamination of the evidence. If this option is chosen then it is advisable to unplug the system, or disconnect the battery if it is a laptop, rather than take the usual actions of shutting down the system from within the operating system. This is intended to not only limit the interaction with the live system, but also to address the possibility that the malicious party has set the machine to delete files on shutdown. However, turning off a live system can result in losing crucial ephemeral evidence stored in volatile RAM, for example decryption keys and remnants of conversations in chat rooms and on social media. The alternate approach is to acquire the contents of RAM from the live system by extracting a memory dump. The details of when and how this should be done are discussed in the RAM acquisition section which follows. With the RAM acquisition complete the system can be powered down in the manor previously described.

Finally, all equipment seized must be recorded using unique identifiers and have exhibit tags attached. All actions taken in the area at the time of the seizure should be documented. All reasonable efforts should be taken to prevent inadvertent operation of equipment, e.g., placing tamper proof tape over USB ports, and as previously discussed ensuring the batteries are removed from laptops. Tamper-proof tape should also be used on containers to ensure that the evidence is not modified or damaged during transport. Any subsequent movement of this evidence must be check-in, check-out documented to preserve the chain of custody.

SEARCH FOR WRITTEN PASSWORDS

The nondisclosure of passwords for both encryption and authentication can be a source of frustration for forensic analysts. 256-bit encrypted files using complex passwords cannot be cracked in a meaningful timeframe. Understandably, suspects are often not obliging in giving up these passwords. In the UK "The

Regulation of Investigatory Powers Act 2000" makes it a criminal offence to "fail to disclose when requested a key to any encrypted information." However, the usual defense against this is for the suspect to claim to have forgotten their password. In these circumstances there is little that can be done by law enforcement. Ironically, if the suspect later admits to knowing the password and reveals it, they can be charged with the offence of originally withholding it. However, as most malicious hackers understand the need for independent, unique and complex passwords to ensure privacy, then it is possible that the password is too difficult for them to remember; hence it could be written down. All papers in the area should be seized as these may contain passwords. Books should be seized too, as one common practice is to insert written passwords within their pages. Other common hiding places should also be considered, e.g., under the mattress of a bed. Finding hard copies of passwords is sometimes the only method of deciphering encrypted data from the media.

FORENSIC ACQUISITION

The most fundamental stage to ensuring the evidence remains omissible is to ensure the original image does not get altered during the process. This section discusses how to maintain the integrity of the evidence during the creation of an image from the media.

RAM

There is an inherent risk involved in acquiring a memory dump, thus a risk assessment should be performed to establish the potential benefit against the risk for the given situation. If it is both required and relatively safe then it may be performed, however, extreme care should be taken to both limit, and explain, the acquisition footprint which will be left on system. While courts are beginning to accept that a footprint will be introduced (Wade, 2011), it is essential that the correct tools and methods are used and that the entire process is documented, preferably video recorded, to reduce the likelihood that the acquisition footprint becomes the undoing of a case. Some applications such as chat room, malware and cryptography programs may employ anti-memory dumping technologies designed to prevent data being read from protected areas of RAM. These protection mechanisms data dump garbage, e.g., random values or zeroes instead of the valid contents of memory. Other applications utilize anti-debugging protection that can cause a system to lock or reboot on an attempt to read protected RAM. Due to the development of these anti-forensic methods it is desirable to use a memory-capturing tool that operates in "kernel" rather than "user" mode. Kernel mode allows unrestricted accesses to the underlying hardware, e.g., RAM, and is less likely to compromise the evidence through a system crash, nor will it provide false evidence

(Anson, et al. 2012). The tools selected should also leave as small a footprint as possible, and operate in read only mode. Most RAM acquisition tools are portable, usually taking the form or a USB device and require no installation, again, to limit the footprint. Once the memory dump has been taken the computer should be shut down using the methods previously discussed.

IMAGE

It is essential that the process of forensically analyzing the media does not introduce any contaminants from the investigator. Interacting with storage media without appropriate precautions will cause data to be written to the media and potentially invalidate the evidence. In order to reduce the likelihood of this happening forensic analysis should not be performed on the actual media storage device seized but should instead be performed on an image, that is a sector-by-sector replica of the media. There are many software tools to allow an image to be acquired from the media, and it is not within the scope of this work to discuss them individually. However, it is recommend that the selected tool should boot from a live CD/DVD and that the evidence is mounted by the tool in "read only" mode to reduce the likelihood of accidently writing to it. Further re-assurance that the evidence has not been contaminated can be provided through the use of write blockers. Write blockers are devices which are placed in line between the system being used to analyze the media and the media storage device itself. They allow read commands to be passed through to the media storage device, but block write commands. Write blockers are readily available and allow for the attachment to and from a variety of different interfaces, e.g., USB, Firewire, SCSI, and SATA controllers. Finally when an image has been acquired it should be verified as an exact copy by comparing the hash values of the two images. Hash values are a fixed sized bit string created by passing data through a cryptographic hash function. Any modification of the evidence, however small, will change its hash value. If the hash files of the acquired image and that of the media being investigated are different then either the image is invalid, or the evidence itself has been compromised.

FORENSIC ANALYSIS

A forensic investigator is usually given some remit into the purpose of the investigation, for example, what crime the suspect may be responsible for. Often though, the information shared may not be so specific. The reason for an investigator being given a narrow remit is to prevent the potential for prior knowledge bias. For example, an investigator may simply be asked to supply evidence that the profile of a machine is one which is setup up for malicious hacking, or they may be asked to find evidence to support the supposition that a particular online persona and the suspect are one and the same. In such circumstances it is often desirable to ensure

Table 7.1 Digital Evidence Categories

Address Books and Contact Lists	Configuration Files	Databases
Audio files and voice recordings	Process	Documents
Backups to various programs	Log files	Email and attachments files
Bookmarks and favorites	Organizer items	Registry keys
Browser history	Page files	Events
Chatting log	Network configuration	Hidden and system files
Calendars	Digital images	Videos
Compressed archives	Cookies	Virtual machines
Kernel statistic and modules	System files	Temporary files
Videos	Printer spooler files	Type of used applications

that the evidence found is without bias, and that it is found independently of case specifics (see Chapter 8).

While the focus of the forensic investigation will be governed by the remit presented, in most cases the digital evidence collected will be composed of one or more of the artifacts listed in Table 7.1.

The methods for how these artifacts are discovered will be discussed in the following sections.

ANTI-FORENSICS

Malicious hackers are becoming increasingly aware of forensic analysis methods. As a result they often implement counter measures to prevent an investigator harvesting useful evidence. This practice is referred to as anti-forensics, or sometimes counter forensics. In essence the practice involves eliminating or obfuscating evidence relating to criminal activity or malicious intent. With this in mind, the primary focus of this section is to discuss hard disk media storage forensics, with a focus on identifying where to uncover evidence stored in obscurely formatted areas of the media; areas which are either immune to anti-forensics or which simply may not have been considered by the suspect. Typical forensic analysis techniques are also discussed briefly in this section, and due to the increasing tolerance of courts in accepting RAM analysis as admissible, this too is discussed (see Chapter 8).

RAM ANALYSIS

If a RAM dump was taken from the image then it should be analyzed on a separate machine to avoid evidence contamination. There are many tools which can be used for RAM analysis; worthy of note is the tool Volatility, which is gaining a reputation as the principle open source command line tool for this purpose (Ligh, et al. 2014). Tools such as Volatility allow for the analysis of data such as:

- Running and recently terminated processes
- Memory mapped files
- Open and recently closed network connections
- Decrypted versions of programs, data, and information
- Cryptographic key passphrases
- Malware

DATA CARVING AND MAGIC VALUES

One of the principle methods of RAM analysis is achieved via a method referred to as "data carving." Carving is the process of looking for patterns in the data, sometimes referred to as "magic values." These values are indicative of a certain type of data being in memory. For example Skype v3 messages start with the data "1331," so any area of RAM with these characters has a likelihood that a Skype message follows. Similarly TrueCrypt (2014) passphrases contain the magic value "0x7d0." File types existing in RAM (as well as in media storage, or traversing a network) can be identified by their magic values too. On finding the data of a particular type the data carving process may continue, depending on the type of data discovered, to extract and present the data in a way that it becomes more intelligible to forensic analyst. For example, it may be necessary to organize the data based on field boundaries, to separate these out and identify them. In most instances, the forensic examiner can be abstracted from the detail of these processes by the forensic tools. However, one of the principle benefits of open tools such as Volatility is they allow the forensic examiner to code their own modules, allowing the freedom to carve out data of a certain type not available natively. This can then be made available for the benefit of the open source community (see Chapter 6).

MEDIA STORAGE FORENSICS

This section focuses on both the known and obscure practices and processes of analyzing media storage devices for forensic evidence. Included here is brief synopsis into the structure and format of a hard disk, to give some background context to the subsequent sections.

THE STRUCTURE AND FORMAT OF A HARD DRIVE

Hard disks are composed of one or more spinning magnetic film coated disks called platters. Each platter is divided into concentric bands called tracks; tracks located at the same area of each platter are collectively referred to as a cylinder. Each track is dived into sectors with each track having an identical amount of sectors regardless of its position on the platter, thus sectors are more densely populated at the center of the platter. A sector is the smallest possible area of storage available on a disk and is typically 512 bytes in size. Information is read and written onto the sectors using heads which generate magnetic fields as instructed by the disk controller, which in turn receives its instructions from the file and operating systems. Although both sides of the platter are used to store information, one side of one of the platters is used for track positioning information; this information is coded at the factory and it used to align the heads when moving between tracks and sectors. The number of sectors and tracks and their positioning is set at the factory using a process referred to low level formatting. Low level formatting is only performed once and is not performed by the user of the hard disk after purchasing, although the term low level format (LLF) is sometimes erroneously used to describe the process of re-initializing a disk to its factory state.

The way in which the computer communicates with a hard disk is set via the computer's Basic Input Output System (BIOS). It is within the BIOS that the addressing scheme, e.g., logical block addressing (LBA), is set for the drive. A logical block address is a 28-bit address which maps to a specific sector of a disk. It should be noted that while LBA is the most widespread addressing scheme, others are common, e.g., the older cylinder, head, sector (CHS), or the up and coming globally unique identifier (GUID) addressing scheme.

PARTITIONS

Partitions are the divisions of a hard drive; each partition can be formatted for use by a particular file system. Within current IBM PC architecture it is possible to have up to four partitions, one of which can be an extended primary partition. An extended partition can be subdivided further allowing for the creation of an additional 24 logical partitions as shown:

Primary partition #1
Primary partition #2
Primary partition #3
Primary partition #4
    Logical partition #1
    Logical partition #2
    Logical partition #3
    ...
    ...
    Logical partition #24

One of the primary partitions will be flagged as the active partition and this is the one which will be used to boot the computer into an operating system. Creating the first partition on the drive will result in the creation of the master boot record (MBR) which, amongst other responsibilities, holds information concerning the partitions.

MASTER BOOT RECORD

The MBR is stored on the first sector of the hard disk and is created along with the first partition on the drive. It is loaded into memory as one of the first actions during system start up. The MBR is comprised of a small section of operating system independent code, a disk signature, the partition table and an MBR signature. The disk signature is a unique four byte identifier for the hard drive, that is to say it should be unique for each drive attached to a system. It is used for purposes such as identifying the boot volume, and associating partitions and volumes with a specific drive. The MBR signature, sometimes referred to as the magic number, is set to value 0xAA55, which simply identifies it as a valid MBR. The partition table informs of the start position and length of each partition on the hard disk. During system start up the MBR code is executed first, and is responsible for parsing the partition table and identifying which partition is marked as active. Once the active partition is identified control is passed to that partitions boot sector, sometimes referred to as the volume boot record (VBR). The VBR is created when the drive is high level formatted for the use with a particular operating system.

THE VBR AND BIOS PARAMETER BLOCK

The VBR contains the operating system specific code necessary to load the operating system, along with a BIOS parameter block (BPB) which describes the partitions file system format, e.g., the number of tracks per sector and the number of sectors per cluster. Clusters, often referred to as allocation units or AUs, are the smallest storage area accessible by the operating system. The file system allocates multiple sectors, e.g., eight, to an individual cluster to reduce the overhead of disk management, this results in faster read and write speeds but also results in some disk space being wasted when storing files, or parts of files, which are smaller than the cluster size. This wasted space in the clusters is referred to as slack space.

FILE SYSTEM

Numerous file systems exist which support numerous different operating systems, each works differently yet all have the same primary aim; namely to manage how files and directories are stored, indexed, written and read. Along with the VBR they are created at the point at which the drive is formatted, and are loaded during the boot process from the VBR. Examples of file systems are NTFS, FAT32, ext4, XFS, and btrfs. Detailed discussion of file systems is beyond the scope of this chapter.

FILE TABLE

File tables hold information about each and every file, including its location, size, permissions, time stamps and whether it has been deleted, i.e., has the space been marked for re-use. This information itself is recorded in special files used by the file system, and therefore the file table itself will have a self-referencing entry. With NTFS the two files used to store this information are $MFT and $Bitmap, the former holds the information concerning the files and later concerning which clusters are used and unused.

SEARCHING FOR EVIDENCE

There are many forensic tools available to allow forensic analysis, some are proprietary, and others are on free or open source licenses. Proprietary tools such as Encase (Guidance Software, 2014) and FTK (Access Data, 2014) are used extensively by law enforcement, with freeware open source tools such as Autopsy (Carrier, 2013) gaining popularity with independent investigators and consultants. Individual tools have their own sets of strengths and weaknesses and it is not the intention to compare them here. However, they do carry some similarities in terms of functionality and operation, and the objectives of the investigation are the same regardless of the tool or tools selected. Thus the discussion in this section then will cover how artifacts are discovered and uncovered from hard drives and will not focus on the practicalities of how the tools are used to achieve this (also see Chapters 6 and 8).

KEYWORD AND PHRASES SEARCH

The primary tool of most investigative forensic software is its search facility. Searching can be performed for a word or phrase which is pertinent to the investigation. The word or phrase could match on the hard drive as ASCII text or may form part of a composite file. Composite files are those which rely on an application to render its information, for example, zip files, email files, Microsoft Office and Adobe documents; most investigative tools can render the formats for most common composite files. Searches can also be used to find files themselves by matching keywords against their file names. Particular composite file types can be identified and catalogued too, for instance, image files such as jpeg, bmp, and png files. These searches should be performed using the files magic numbers which were discussed earlier. This prevents malicious parties hiding a files true purpose by changing its extension. Most forensic tools offer a facility to mark any evidence you find of consequence and associate it with a case. Some also allow the ability to view files using inbuilt native applications which would not write to the evidence, thus maintaining its integrity (see Chapter 6).

RECOVERING DELETED INFORMATION

The deletion of files, folders, and partitions is not necessarily permanent and can often be recovered. Recovery of files, folders, and partitions is briefly discussed here.

RECOVERING DELETED FILES AND FOLDERS

The deletion process for files and folders involves simply marking the clusters used by the deleted file or folder as unallocated in the file table. Until the clusters are physically overwritten the data in the file or folder remains accessible in the unallocated clusters. Most forensic tools will allow for identification and recovery of deleted files where the clusters have not yet been overwritten.

RECOVERING DELETED PARTITIONS

Deleting partitions makes the data inside them unavailable to the operating system; however the data itself is not destroyed at the point of deletion and can often be recovered. Information concerning which sectors the deleted partition used to occupy are recorded in the partition table held in the MBR. Most tools will parse the information in the partition table, allowing the examiner to see the names of partitions, deleted or otherwise, and which sector they start and end at. Using this information the VBR, or backup VBR, for any individual partition can be located. The location differs depending on the file system used, but is well documented for all common file systems. Once located, most tools will parse the information in a VBR allowing the examiner to rebuild the deleted partition.

WHERE EVIDENCE HIDES

The following sections will discuss some of the more intricate hiding places that exist within Microsoft Windows operating systems. Some of these places may get overlooked in a forensic examination, and yet they frequently hold much sort after forensic evidence.

REGISTRY

The registry is responsible for holding system settings and configuration information for all aspects of the Windows operating system and installed software. In modern Windows operating systems the registry is composed of five files stored in the folder `Winnt\system32\config\`, namely Default, System, Security, Software and Sam, with another file Ntuser.dat being present for each user of the system (Nelson, et al. 2010). Their purpose is shown in Table 7.2.

On a live system the registry can be examined and modified using the registry editor regedit. Regedit combines the information stored in the files into hives, a format designed to make their information more accessible to the user. This information is organized within handle keys, referred to as HKEY's which in turn contain sub-keys and associated values (name, type, and data). These keys are HKEY_LOCAL_MACHINE

Table 7.2 Registry Files

Registry File	Registry Files Purpose
Default	Holds the computers system settings
System	Holds additional system settings
Security	Holds the computers security settings
Software	Holds settings for installed software and related usernames and passwords
Sam	Holds user account information
Ntuser.dat	Holds user specific data, e.g., desktop and recently used files

(HKLM), HKEY_USERS (HKU), HKEY_CURRENT_USER (HKCU), HKEY_CLASSES_ROOT (HKCR), and HKEY_CURRENT_CONFIG (HKCC). The function of each of these keys is shown in Table 7.3 (Nelson, et al. 2010).

Most investigators will use a tool which allows them to carve data from registry files and present it in a view adapted for investigation. Although the registry of most Windows systems is large and complex and a full discussion of it would be beyond the scope of this work, some key areas which could be of interest to forensic examiners are shown in the following table which has been summarized from Access Data's quick find registry chart (AccessDataGroup, 2010):

NTUser.data	SAM	SYSTEM
Chat rooms visited	Installed application list	Pagefile
IE-Auto logon, passwords, typed URLs	Last access of applications	Systems IP address, default gateway
Start-up programs[a]	System boot programs	Mounted devices[b]
EFS certificate thumbprint	Wired/Wireless connections	Storage media information
Outlook and POP3 passwords	Shared folders list	Removable media information#
Most recently used lists (see following)	Last logon time for user	Computers name
FTP access	Registered owner	System's configuration settings

[a] Particularly useful for detecting Trojans.
[b] Use to associate any discovered evidence on removal storage with the PC.

MOST RECENTLY USED LISTS

Most recently used (MRUs) are designed as a convenience for the user. When certain user input fields are revisited then users can either see the previous entered information in a list, or it may be autocompleted while typing. These lists are mostly extracted from the NTUSER.DAT. Examples of MRU lists include: mapped network

Table 7.3 HKEY Functions

HKEY	HKEY Function
HKLM	Contains the systems installed hardware, software and boot information
HKU	Contains the settings for all currently active user profile of the system
HKCU	A symbolic link to HKU for your user id, i.e., the account you are logged in with
HKCR	A symbolic link to an HKLM key containing file type and extension information
HKCC	A link to HKLM for the hardware profile is use

drives, media player, windows which have been opened saved or copied, applications opened in run box, Google history, recently accessed documents, and search terms used in search box.

LASTWRITE TIME

Every time a key is accessed, created, deleted, or modified the time is recorded. This is referred to as the "LastWrite" time. This allows an investigator to create a timeline of activity, for example, when a USB hard drive was last inserted, when a piece of software was installed, and so on.

HIBERFIL.SYS

Hibernation is a feature employed by modern Windows operating systems to allow the system to be entirely shutdown and yet maintain its last working state when powered back up. This is performed by copying the systems RAM into a file at the time when the system is put into hibernate, and restoring it from the file when the machine is restarted. This file is called hiberfil.sys and is located in the root of the drive, usually labeled C:\, and its size reflects the amount of system RAM available. As you would expect it is possible to extract potentially vital evidence from this file, in much the same way as it can be with RAM analysis. The structure of the file is not well documented at the time of writing; with only a limited number of tools which can carve the file. Worthy of note again however, is the volatility tool which includes a plugin, imagecopy, allowing `hiberfil.sys` to be converted into a raw image. This image can then be analyzed using Volatility, or other tools, to find evidence, e.g., passwords, digital certificates, and malware.

PAGEFIL.SYS

In order to allow the operating system access to larger amounts of RAM than is physically available to it, a paging file is employed. When the Windows operating system needs more RAM than is available, some of it can be written to a page file before being released and freeing physical memory. When the information in the page file is required by a running process, it is retrieved back into memory from the file. Since the file contains data which has been held in RAM, it can be an invaluable source of evidence for the examiner, e.g., contraband images, passwords, digital signatures, and so forth. All of the previously mentioned forensic tools, e.g., Encase, FTK and Autopsy are capable of carving the `pagefil.sys` file to allow viewing and extracting of evidence from it.

SYSTEM VOLUME INFORMATION FOLDERS

Operating systems from XP onwards have a feature call system restore. System restore holds a "snapshot" of the state of important operating system e.g., Windows, files on a hard drive at any given time. If something goes wrong with the PC, a failed installation of some software for instance, which causes the PC to become inoperable or unstable, it can be "rolled back," that is to say restored to this snap shot. The previous versions of the files would be recovered and the PC should become functional again. The native default behavior is that these snapshots are created on Windows 7 once a week and at the start of a software installation process. Alternatively they can be set manually. System restore has a fixed amount of space which is used for storing the restore points and will save as many as it can into that space on a round robin basis, with the oldest restore points being overwritten with the latest ones. The amount of space is configurable, but is 15% as a default in Windows Vista and 7.

From a forensic perspective these snapshots may contain copies of files which have subsequently been deleted or modified. Of significance when considering this is that copies of files which have become encrypted may still exist in system volume information folders in an unencrypted state. Thus, while it is often infeasible to decrypt certain files, it may be possible to find a copy of them unencrypted in the system volume information folders. The snapshots include backups of the registry, Windows system files (in the `\Windows` folder) and the local users profile. The users profile contains artifacts including any files stored in the "My Documents" area, application settings, internet favorites, the user's desktop (including any files saved to it), internet cookies, links to shared folders, and the recycle bin. The later can be particularly lucrative as the suspect may have emptied the live system's recycle bin yet be unaware that the files are still captured in recycle bin in the system volume information folders. System volume information folders sit on the root of the hard drive within a folder named "System Volume Information." Within this folder a separate volume copy set exists for each of the restore points created. Many forensic tools are capable of parsing the information in system volume information folders natively. Alternatively, the folders can be mounted as drives manually. The process for doing this is well recognized, with a step-by-step procedure documented in Microsoft's knowledge base article kb309531 (Microsoft, 2013). Once the volume has been mounted it can be captured and analyzed in the same way as physical drive, as previously discussed.

CHAPTER SUMMARY

This chapter offered guidelines and direction for forensic examiners. It discussed considerations necessary when forming the case for a search warrant, i.e., that it is necessary to show that there is either "reasonable grounds" or "probable cause" that an offence has, is or will be taking place. Methods of how to do this such as associating the alleged crime with the suspects IP address, social media accounts or IRC handle are discussed; as are the difficulties that can be encountered when attempting to do so. Following on from this best practice in seizing of evidence is proffered; this includes how to avoid contaminating digital evidence and minimizing the acquisition footprint. The use of write blockers is discussed for media storage devices and the need for a risk reward analysis prior to RAM forensics is highlighted. In order to offer context, the structure and format of hard drives is documented; including the physical structures, e.g., platters and heads, along with the logical structures such as sectors and clusters. How file systems and operating systems make use of the media is also described, e.g., file tables and master and volume boot records. In the final section some of the more fertile search areas for forensic evidence are emphasized along with how the data in these areas are formatted, and how it can be rendered. The Windows registry, `hiberfil.sys`, `pagefile.sys`, and the system volume information folders are discussed to this end.

REFERENCES

7Safe, 2007. Good Practice Guide for Computer-Based Electronic Evidence. 7Safe, London.

Access Data, 2014. Access Data. FTK. [Online] Available at: http://www.accessdata.com/products/digital-forensics/ftk (accessed 23.02.14).

AccessDataGroup, 2010. Registry Quick Find Chart. AccessDataGroup, London.

Anson, S., Bunting, S., Johnson, R., Pearson, S., 2012. Mastering Windows Networks and Forensic Investigations, second ed. John Wiley & Sons, Inc., Indianapolis.

Carrier, B., 2013. Autopsy. [Online] Available at: http://www.sleuthkit.org/autopsy/ (accessed 2014 February 2014).

Crown, 1984. Police and Criminal Evidence Act (1984). Her Majesty's Stationery Office (HMSO), London.

FindLaw, 2014. Find Law. Proabable Cause. [Online] Available at: http://criminal.findlaw.com/criminal-rights/probable-cause.html (accessed 22.02.14).

Guidance Software, 2014. Guidance Software. [Online] Available at: http://www.guidancesoftware.com/ (accessed 24.02.14).

Ligh, M., Case, A., Levy, J., Walters, A., 2014. Volatility an advanced memory forensic framework. [Online] Available at: http://code.google.com/p/volatility/ (accessed 22.02.14).

Microsoft, 2013. How to gain access to the System Volume Information folder. [Online] Available at: http://support.microsoft.com/kb/309531 (accessed 23.02.14).

Nelson, B., Phillips, A., Steuart, C., 2010. Guide To Computer Forensics and Investigations, fourth ed. Cengage Learning, Boston.

Olson, P., 2012. We Are Anonymous: Inside the Hacker World of LulzSec, Anonymous, and the Global Cyber Insurgency. Little, Brown and Company, Boston.

Tor, 2014. Tor. [Online] Available at: https://www.torproject.org/ (accessed 23.02.14).

TrueCrypt, 2014. TrueCrypt. [Online] Available at: http://www.truecrypt.org/ (accessed 2014 February 2014).

Wade, M., 2011. DFI News. [Online] Available at: http://www.dfinews.com/articles/2011/06/memory-forensics-where-start (accessed 22.02.14).

Digital forensics education, training and awareness

8

Hamid Jahankhani, Amin Hosseinian-far

INTRODUCTION

In a fully connected truly globalized world of networks, most notably the internet, mobile technologies, distributed databases, electronic commerce and e-governance e-crime manifests itself as Money Laundering; Intellectual Property Theft; Identity Fraud/Theft; Unauthorized access to confidential information; Destruction of information; Exposure to Obscene Material; Spoofing and Phishing; Viruses and Worms and Cyber-stalking, Economic Espionage to name a few.

According to the House of Commons, Home Affairs Committee, Fifth Report of Session 2013–14, on E-Crime, "Norton has calculated its global cost to be $388bn dollars a year in terms of financial losses and time lost. This is significantly more than the combined annual value of $288bn of the global black market trade in heroin, cocaine and marijuana" (E-crime, House of Commons, 2013).

Since the launch of the UK's first Cyber Security Strategy in June 2009 and the National Cyber Security Programme (NCSP) in November 2011, UK governments have had a centralized approach to cybercrime and wider cyber threats.

Until recently E-crimes had to be dealt with under legal provisions meant for old crimes such as conspiracy to commit fraud, theft, harassment, and identity theft. Matters changed slightly in 1990 when the Computer Misuse Act was passed but even then it was far from sufficient and mainly covered crimes involving hacking.

There were no new laws specific to computer crime since the Computer Misuse Act 1990, until The Fraud Act of 2006 to deal with e-crimes. The laws relied upon are as follows:

- Theft Act 1968 & 1978, (Amendment) 1996
- Criminal Attempts Act 1981
- Telecommunications Act 1984
- Public Order Act 1986
- Protection of Children Act 1978
- Obscene Publications Act 1959 & 1964
- Data Protection Act 1998
- Human Rights Act 1998
- Defamation Act 1952 & 1996

- Criminal Attempt Act 1981
- Freedom of Information Act 2000
- Protection from Harassment Act 1997

Despite all these lawsuit is still not adequate to tackle e-crime, because of the fast pace of information technology and information systems proliferation. In 2006 two new laws were passed to tackle e-crime namely the Fraud Act 2006 which came into force in 2007 which "the new law aims to close a number of loopholes in proceeding anti-fraud legislation, because, the Government said was unsuited to modern fraud," and the Police and Justice Act 2006 (part 5) which prohibits "unauthorized access to computer material; unauthorized acts with intent to impair operation of computer and the supply of tools that can be used for hacking" (Police and Justice Act, 2006).

Documented guidance, practices and procedures were outdated and wholly inadequate to help tackle electronic evidence in a forensic manner, until first e-crime publication by ACPO in July 2007 and subsequently revised in November 2009 and 2012. This is recognized as the best guidelines ever produced to assist law enforcement in handling digital evidence (ACPO Guidelines, 2009).

Digital evidence is the evidence that is collected from the suspect's workstations or electronic medium that could be used in order to assist computer forensics investigations.

There are basically two types of evidences that could support a digital forensic investigation, which are physical evidence and digital evidence. Physical evidences are categorized as touchable and substantial items that could be brought to court and shown physically. Examples of physical evidence that could assist in the investigations are computers, external hard disk drives and data storage (memory sticks and memory cards) handheld devices including mobile phones/smart phones, PDA's, networking devices, optical media, dongles and music players. Digital evidence would be the data that is extracted from the physical evidence, or the computer system.

In order to perceive a bit of information or data as evidence, it needs to satisfy the five rules which are:

1. the evidence should be admissible and excepted in the court of law
2. the evidence needs to be authentic and not contaminated
3. the evidence needs to the whole piece, not just indicative parts
4. the evidence has to be reliable, dependable
5. the evidence needs to be believable

Digital evidence, as compared to hard evidence, are difficult to find, in terms of defining the nature of the data, and classifying it as a digital evidence that is worthy to be presented in court.

Proving evidence which is reliable has been proven to be a difficult task, not just because the nature of evidence, but also the wide scope and environment in which the evidence are extracted from.

In a corporate environment, the forensic investigator team will need to identify, contain and maintain the integrity of the evidence, and differentiate whether the piece of evidence is relevant or not to the current crime being investigated, and whether it would stand a chance in finding the culprit and charging them through legal proceedings.

Among the considerations that needs to be evaluated by the investigator when dealing with collecting digital evidence are the expenses, cost and lost incurred and the availability of the service during and after the incident.

The lack of expertise by law enforcement to understand the intricacies of e-crime, the wide demographics it covered and most of all jurisdiction issues was an excellent opportunity for those in the private sector, by presenting a niche and a need in the market for private individuals to offer the service of computer forensics. A lot of private companies emerged offering initially data recovery services and eventually computer forensic services.

At the same time a variety of computer tools came onto the market such as, Encase, FTK, Helix, Paraben Cell Seizure, MOBILedit, BitPim, etc. The tools both software and hardware automated the processing of computer evidence and did not require an in-depth thought process or knowledge of computer science in order to operate them. This made life easy for those who had to process computer evidence but also gave a false sense of security and the belief that if one could use these tools adequately it validated their claim of being an expert.

These tools and services have become heavily relied upon by law enforcement and with the lack of proper evaluating processes in place for tools and services, individuals and companies without the appropriate qualifications, understanding or enough experience are unfortunately being relied upon as experts in the field of computer forensics.

DIGITAL FORENSICS LABORATORY PREPARATION AND TRAINING

To set up a forensic laboratory there are number of processes and procedures that are required to be followed. If the laboratory requires accreditation then further requirements are set by the accreditation bodies such as International Standards Organizations, or American Society of Crime Laboratory Directors (Jones and Valli, 2004; Watson and Jones, 2013).

There are many standards that are relevant when creating a digital forensics laboratory, including: Environmental management systems (ISO 14000), occupational health and safety (OHSAS 18000), Risk Management (ISO 31000), Information security management (ISO 27000), etc.

Any forensics laboratory needs to be protected against external and environmental threats such as: fire, flood, backup systems, etc. and on-site secure evidence storage for the purpose of only storing the evidences. Chain of custody requires that the robust procedures of management of evidences are followed.

All these and many more require that all employees are regularly trained on forensics laboratory information security awareness, specialist hardware and software, risk management and much more.

It is no secret that setting up a forensic laboratories are very resource intense and require variety of expensive tools that are needed to address different threats and different platforms/systems.

DIGITAL ANTI FORENSICS TOOLS AND APPROACHES

Anti-forensics as a concept is as old as the traditional computer forensics. Someone that commit a punishable action use any possible way to get rid of any evidence connected with the prohibited action. The traditional forensics can have a range of anti-forensics that start from a trivial level (e.g., wiping fingerprints from a gun) and to a level where our fantasy can meet the implementation of an anti-forensic idea (e.g., alteration of DNA left behind in a crime). In digital anti-forensics the same rules exist, with the difference that they are fairly new with little research and development (Jahankhani et al., 2007).

There are number of techniques that are used to apply anti-forensics. These techniques are not necessarily designed with anti-forensics dimension in mind. For instance, folder shielders have been designed in order to primarily provide a level of security and privacy, but they can be used as an anti-forensic tool since they can hide data. The others are:

- **Digital Media Wiping:** A proper wiping of the media that contain the digital evidence, will simply disappear the evidence.
- **Steganography:** Someone can use Steganography to hide a file inside another and make the investigator unable to take advantage of the evidence, since the last might not find a way to extract it.
- **Privacy Wipers:** These are tools aim to delete any privacy traces from operating systems, applications or both. If properly used the investigator might find no evidence at all inside the digital media.
- **Rootkits:** Rootkits can subvert the operating system kernel and even react to forensic acquisition processes by hijacking the way the operating system uses areas like process management or memory management to extract the evidence.
- **S.M.A.R.T. Anti-Forensics:** This kind of technology can be used by an attacker to suspect if a hard drive has been taken out for a forensic duplication process.
- **Homographic Attacks:** Such an attack can mislead an investigator since some letters that look similar to the human eye can be replaced with others in such a way to make a malicious file look legitimate.
- **File Signature Modification Attacks:** Someone can purposefully change the file signature of a file to make it look something else.
- **Encryption:** This can be used almost in every anti-forensic stage in order to obscure and make unreadable and unusable the evidence.
- **Metadata Anti-Forensics:** Information about data (metadata) can be altered in order to hide user actions.

- **Slack Space Anti-Forensics:** Someone can hide malicious software in areas that operating system might not use, like slack space, because they might be considered as reserved or empty.
- **Secure Digest Functions (MD4, MD5, etc.) Collision Generation:** Someone can alter a file and then use Anti-Forensic software to make this file having the same MD4 or MD5 value like before the alteration, thus bypass a forensic integrity check.
- **Digital Memory Anti-Forensics:** There are programs that are able to hide processes or other evidence from memory.
- **Misleading Evidence:** Someone can leave evidence in such a way to mislead the forensic investigation.
- **Packers/Binders:** Someone can use such a program in order to transform a file by changing its structure, thus it can bypass security mechanisms that searches for malicious behavior patterns inside files.
- **Forensic Tools Vulnerabilities/Exploits:** There are already implementations available to show that some of the computer current Forensic Tools can be bypassed or exploited.
- **Resource Waste:** To purposefully leave traces in a big network in order to make the forensic investigator waste valuable resources and time.
- **Forensic Detection:** Someone can install a mechanism to be triggered after any computer forensic-related presence.
- **Anonymous Actions:** It includes every action that can be done by a fake or unknown identity. The result from the investigator is to fail to trace back the malicious activities.
- **Anti-Forensics In Flushable Devices:** Someone can take advantage of devices that can be flashed (like PCI cards or BIOS) and install malicious code inside them, thus they can remain unnoticed.

From a forensic scope, anonymity can be considered as a major anti-forensic approach. For example, below are top Free Anonymous Web Proxy Servers (Mitchell, 2013):

- Proxify: this web proxy support encryption via Secure socket Layer (SSL), HTTPS network protocols and hides IP address and cookies filtering cookies.
- Anonymouse: has been around for many years and supports Web, email and Usenet (news) proxies.
- Anonymizer: is the most known name in the anonymous web proxy services.
- Ninja Cloak: from their homepage you can insert the URL of the site to be visited. This web-based proxy uses CGI.

Today WiFi networks are used widely; therefore, it would make it very easy for malicious network users to hide their true identities by stepping randomly on these wireless networks in order to conduct their attacks.

While in theory the forensics investigator should monitor everything available around the suspect, in reality the post incident response could end up quite dramatically. This could be due to: ignorance regarding the network activity logs, legal barriers between the access point and the forensics acquisition, noncooperative ISPs, etc.

The forensic process should be enhanced with security mechanisms which would upgrade the post-incident reaction to real time. The real-time acquisition tools should have capabilities of capturing activity of all the wireless point within a respectable distance.

Anti-forensics is a reality that comes with every serious crime and involves tactics for "safe hacking" and keeps the crime sophistication in a high level. Computer forensic investigators along with the forensic software developers should start paying more attention to anti-forensics tools and approaches.

If we consider the computer forensics as the actions of collection, preservation, identification and presentation of evidence, anti-forensics can affect the first three stages. Because these stages can be characterized as "finish to start" between them from a project management point of view, the failure of one of them could end up as a failure of the lot. Thus, there is a high impact of anti-forensics to the forensics investigations.

Officially there is no such thing as anti-forensic investigations because the anti-forensic countermeasures are still part of the investigator's skills.

THE MAIN DIFFICULTIES FACED BY LAW ENFORCEMENT OFFICERS FIGHTING CYBER-CRIME

It is evident that cybercrime is no longer in its infancy. It is "big business" for the criminal entrepreneur with potentially lots of money to be made with minimal risks. At the same time the main areas which have been recognized as the contributory elements in the failing by law enforcement officers are as follows:

- Lack of up-to-date guidelines
- Lack of proper training
- Lack of funding

The UK law enforcement cannot investigate all alleged offences, which then raises a question as to how decisions are made, as to which cases to investigate and which not to investigate, because of the scale and the international nature of these crimes. How much of the public interest is taken into consideration and is it another way of dealing with e-crime irrespective of how ineffective and discouraging it appears?

From law enforcement point of view the task of fighting cyber-crime is a difficult one. Although crime is irrespective of how big or small it is, a decision has to be made on the merits of each case as to whether investigating and prosecuting is in the public's interest. In April 2007, a decision was made that all credit card fraud should be reported to the banks and not directly to the police. The banks can then decide which ones to refer to the police for investigation. It is recognized that not all cases will have sufficient evidence and with the limited resources available to law enforcement this ensures that resources are allocated where they are required the most (ACPO Guidelines, 2009). This is not seen as a very good decision especially by politicians and one of the reasons given for this is that it prevents the acquisition of accurate statistics on e-crime. This was indeed never possible due to the fact that not all e-crimes are reported.

It is no longer adequate to depend on individuals as governments own and control vast databases with sensitive information both private to individuals and relevant to national security in general. It is becoming necessary to understand and manage the computer forensics process.

Some research (EURIM-IPPR, 2004; Taal, 2007) has formulated a set of principles and has suggested a high level methodology for this purpose. All procedures and guidelines for the collection and handling of computer evidence are based on the Association of Chief Police Officers (ACPO) guidelines; many follow the ACPO Guidelines including those in the private sector. ACPO is an independent, professionally led strategic body, they lead and coordinate the direction and development of the police service in England, Wales and Northern Ireland.

This guidance was created to assist law enforcement in dealing with computer evidence (ACPO Guidelines, 2009). This came in the form of four principles as follows:

Principle 1: No action taken by law enforcement agencies or their agents should change data held on a computer or storage media which may subsequently be relied upon in court.

Principle 2: In exceptional circumstances, where a person finds it necessary to access original data held on a computer or on storage media, that person must be competent to do so and be able to give evidence explaining the relevance and the implications of their actions.

Principle 3: An audit trail or other record of all processes applied to computer-based electronic evidence should be created and preserved. An independent third party should be able to examine those processes and achieve the same result.

Principle 4: The person in charge of the investigation (the case officer) has overall responsibility for ensuring that the law and these principles are adhered to.

In the private sector, the guidelines are usually incorporated into their internal procedures as most computer forensic companies in the private sector deal with defense work and civil matters where the guidelines may not always apply. Only a few may have contracts with the Metropolitan Police, Scotland Yard and other prosecution authorities in which case their procedures have to be followed and not that of the private sector.

From the above it is clear that the guidelines are necessary but without the successful use of the guidelines requires proper training and understanding of the guidelines. Most law enforcement agents found themselves in this field somewhat reluctantly, because of the heavy demand to tackle e-crime.

EDUCATIONAL PROVISION FOR THE STUDY OF COMPUTER FORENSICS

Computer forensics is no longer a new field as some would like to believe and a lot needs to be done to train and encourage new entrants to the field as well as unifying skills and experience acquired by those already in the field. The need to train not just on the technical side but also the legal aspects has been fully recognized by government, training companies and universities, and most universities are now offering courses specifically tailored to law enforcement officers, yet training is only embarked upon by most in law enforcement as a backup plan for post-retirement.

Those joining the profession will have to understand the importance of an academic qualification especially if they have no experience in the field at all.

Computer forensics is no longer a profession where training on the job to get experience is sufficient. Most other professions require one to have a degree before one can progress to train in their vocation, i.e. teachers, lawyers, forensic scientist and doctors, etc., the same should be with computer forensic as the work we do is as important as those in other fields and be it positive or negative does affect people's lives.

Numerous universities in this country and abroad are offering Computer Forensic and Information Security courses to graduate and post-graduate level which will help those taking on the courses to have a good grounding in computer science, a better understanding of computer forensic theories and most of all help them develop to be more innovative in coming up with new forensically sound ways of fighting e-crime and to "think outside the box."

It is time for the government to actively work in partnership with universities to encourage people to take on these courses especially those already working in the field in the public sector.

A degree is now a prerequisite in the private sector as well as experience, as it is becoming a lot more difficult for one to claim to be an expert in the field of computer forensics and an expert witness in a court of law. Gone are the days where do-it-yourself forensics will be accepted.

This leads us to another area a lot of experts in the field of computer forensics have been reserved about and that is the idea of accreditation. It is an area that is very difficult to make decisions on. Most agree and recognize that a board should be set up, but what cannot be agreed upon is who should lead it. Some have suggested that it should be led by universities, by government, by their peers or jointly by universities, government and businesses.

If it is university led, the concern is that those who have worked in the field for many years without academic qualifications may find that in order to be recognized as experts in the field and fully accredited they may have to get some recognized academic qualification in addition to their experience, which most are against.

If it is government led, without set standards the situation will be no different from what we have at present. It will also involve those working in the profession to give it some direction and it is still doubtful as to whether those people are in a position to decide what form of accreditation to be embarked upon.

This brings us to the last option, a joint partnership with government, universities and businesses. This is the most feasible option but a lot of joint effort will be required to come up with a credible accreditation that will be accepted by all.

The March 2007 an article written by a Peter Warren appeared in the Guardian newspaper, the incident has been of great concern to those in the profession. "Last month saw the downfall of Gene Morrison." A conman who masqueraded as a forensic scientist and gave evidence in more than 700 police cases, some of them involving rape and drink-driving, Morrison, 48, of Hyde, Tameside, was found guilty of 22 counts of perjury at Minshull Street Crown Court in Manchester and given a 5-year jail sentence. His claims to be a forensic scientist were bogus, and the BSc and PhD qualifications he claimed were in fact bought from a university that existed only on the internet.

One thing is for sure having a form of accreditations will force government, academics, researches and those working in the field of computer forensics to set more appropriate standards and controls for those who handle, analyze and investigate computer evidence.

THE CFM METHODOLOGY

The CFM consists of four phases namely Identify, Acquire, Preserve and Report:

1. **Identify:** Source of digital evidence.
2. **Acquire:** Taking an image of the media as it was found.
3. **Preserve:** Chain of custody as well as the integrity of the data itself making sure no information has been added or altered.
4. **Report:** To report all findings and processes used.

The persons carrying out the above must adhere to standard evidence rules, i.e., Police and Criminal Evidence Act (PACE) 1984 in criminal matters, that are admissible in a court of law. The Home Office current PACE codes came into effect on 27th of October 2013 (The Police and Criminal Act, 1984).

Stage 4 requires more detailed decomposition into the necessary methods for the analysis and classification of the data for use as evidence and as a historical record. In the field of computer forensics there is still a lot to be done, i.e., standardizing procedures, etc. The field in itself has various branches of digital forensics, for example, Internet Forensics, Network Forensics and Mobile phone Forensics to name but a few. Customized guidelines for these branches will enable the scientists to ensure the quality of both the process and the data collected.

It is also important to extend the CFM to include a fifth phase that of Review and Improve in the light of empirical data which can be classified, organized and mined for maximizing the effectiveness of the processes.

CONCLUSIONS

With all the above the most important thing people forget and this is by all, is that in this field the practical experience and the theoretical skills you acquire from academic institutes go hand-in-hand. You cannot call yourself an expert if you have all the experience in the world and lack the basic understanding of computer science.

There is concern within law enforcement, government and the private sector as to the lack of consensus to a standardize approach to training courses and lack of funds for research.

Defense lawyers have not been confident enough to challenge computer forensic findings, the lack of understanding and basic knowledge of computers and lastly the benefits of instructing computer forensic experts when defending individuals charged with crimes involving computers.

As defense lawyers become even more confident to challenge computer forensic findings, then, the prosecution success rate will be different and those of us working in the field of computer forensics are beginning to see the changes both within civil matters such as tort, breach of contracts, defamation, employee disputes, etc., to criminal matters theft, criminal damage, drugs related offence and criminal offences concerning copyright and theft of intellectual property. The key issue here is the lack of understanding and basic knowledge of computers and lastly the benefits of instructing computer forensic experts when defending individuals charged with crimes involving computers.

The development of one or more major multi-disciplinary research centers, following the model of Centre for Information Technology Research for the Interest of Society (CITRIS), is necessary to attract private funding and bring together experts from different academic departments and industry in a more integrated, multi-disciplinary research effort. It is recommended that the Research Councils take the lead in initiating discussions with Government, universities and industry with a view to the prompt establishment of an initial centre in UK.

REFERENCES

ACPO Guidelines, 2009. http://www.acpo.police.uk/documents/crime/2009/200908CRIECS01. pdf (accessed January 2014).

E-crime, House of Commons, Home Affairs Committee, Fifth Report of Session, 2013–14, http://www.publications.parliament.uk/pa/cm201314/cmselect/cmhaff/70/70.pdf (accessed January 2014).

EURIM-IPPR E-Crime study. Supplying the Skills for Justice, 18 May 2004.

Jahankhani, H., Anastasios, B., Revett, K., 2007. Digital Anti Forensics: Tools and Approaches. In: 6th European Conference on Information Warfare and Security Defence College of Management and Technology, Shrivenham, UK, 2–3 July 2007.

Jones, A., Valli, C., 2004. Building a Digital Forensic Laboratory: Establishing and Managing a Successful Facility. Publisher Syngress, ISBN 978-1856175104.

Mitchell, B., 2013. Top Free Anonymous Web Proxy Servers. http://compnetworking.about. com/od/proxyserversandlists/tp/anonymousproxy.htm (accessed January 2014).

Police and Justice Act, 2006. http://www.legislation.gov.uk/ukpga/2006/48/contents (accessed January 2014).

Taal, A., 2007. Report examining the weaknesses in the fight against cyber-crime from within. Int. J. Electronic Security Digital Forensics 1 (2), Interscience Publishers.

The Police and Criminal Act (PACE), 1984. http://police.homeoffice.gov.uk/operational-policing/powers-pace-codes/pace-code-intro/ (accessed January 2014).

Watson, D., Jones, A., 2013. Digital Forensics Processing and procedures, meeting the requirements of ISO 17020, ISO 17025, ISO 27001 and Best practice requirements. Publisher Syngress, ISBN 978-1-59749-742-8.

Understanding the situational awareness in cybercrimes: case studies

9

Eleanor Lockley, Babak Akhgar

INTRODUCTION

As already mentioned in chapters throughout this book (see Chapters 1, 3, 5, and 13) cybercrime and cyber terrorism are increasingly important concerns not only for policy makers, but also businesses and citizens. In many countries, societies have come to rely on cyberspace to do business, consume products and services or exchange information with others online. Between 2000 and 2012, the growth of Internet users has been estimated at 393.4% (World Internet Usage and Population Statistics, 2012). Yet, Khoo Boon Hui, former President of Interpol, announced in May 2012 a figure of €750 billion is lost globally per year due to cybercrime. Cybercrime not only costs money, it also jeopardizes critical infrastructures, citizens and businesses, as well as security, identity and privacy.

This chapter shows that a clearer understanding of the motivations and intentions behind cybercrimes/cyber terrorism can lead to clearer situational understanding. Furthermore, it provides frontline agencies (LEAs) with the capability to recognize and act on cybercrime and cyber terrorism situations through the design of a taxonomy model. Situational understanding and attack attribution of cybercrimes is one of the key problems defined by the U.S. Department of Homeland Security (2009) for cyber security research. In particular, situational understanding is critical for a number of reasons:

- Improved systems security
- Improved defense against future attacks
- Attack attribution
- Identification of potential threats
- Improved situational awareness

This chapter proposes that the lessons learnt from real-life scenarios can be used to create a knowledge repository which can support a clearer understanding and knowledge framework for cybercrime. The prerequisite for a knowledge repository is the development of a taxonomy which will help to develop the situational understanding behind the cybercrimes.

Leaning toward a sociological perspective, this chapter considers five pertinent cyber-crime cases and makes use of a taxonomical classification method to cluster these based on perceived intention/motivation of the attack. This chapter also makes use of Akhgar's (1999) concept of knowledge management—where knowledge is built upon a continuum of data which is first turned into information through an interpretation of the context using domain intelligence and then information into knowledge (which is an abstraction of the learning process).

To further support the need for a taxonomy for the situational understanding of cybercrime, the U.S. Department of Homeland Security (2009) stresses a need for a "people layer knowledge" which consists of data outside networks and hosts (p. 68). The taxonomy is developed with this in mind. The Department for Homeland Security roadmap for cyber security research report also highlights a need for analysis on:

> *repeated patterns of interaction that arise over the course of months or years, and unexpected connections between companies and individuals. These derived quantities should themselves be archived or, alternatively, be able to be easily reconstructed (US Department of Homeland Security, 2009, p. 70). Whilst also stressing that "situational understanding requires collection or derivation of relevant data on a diverse set of attributes"*

> **(US Department of Homeland Security, 2009, p. 73).**

As it has been noted through this book, cybercrime has become an everyday problem for internet users. In 2012 in the US the Internet Crime Complaint Center (IC3) who partners with the FBI received 289,874 consumer complaints resulting in a total loss of over $500 million dollars. Clearly as well as companies, individuals across the globe are subject to cyber-related crime. There are multiple motivations for carrying out cybercrime: Moral, financial, political, for exploitation, self-actualization, and promotion, and these are outlined below.

However before outlining the case studies it is important to define cybercrime. For the purposes of this work, the Association of Chief Police Officer e-Crime Strategy definition of E-crime (2012) will be used: "The use of networked computers or internet technology to commit or facilitate the commission of crime."

According to ACPO (2012):

> *The internet allows criminals to target potential victims from anywhere in the world, and enables mass victimization to be attempted with relative ease...The internet provides the criminal with a high degree of perceived anonymity, as well as creating jurisdictional issues that may impede rapid pursuit and prosecution of offenders. In addition there is not yet a clear distinction between issues that are best dealt with through better regulation and those that require law enforcement action.*

> **(APCO, 2012, p. 6).**

This statement is particularly applicable to the case studies outlined below. The very fact that the hacking is happening across times zones and jurisdictions means that is it easier for hackers, hacktivists, cyber criminals, etc. to continue their attacks. It also helps to emphasize a need for clear communication strategies and intelligence about the attacks to be shared between not only by affected countries/governments, but also networks across the globe to strengthen security networks against future attacks and risks.

It is also important to make clear that the following chapter outlines some of the activities in cyber space—without prejudice. The authors are neither in support nor against the activities summarized below. The outlined cases show the variation in the motivation behind cybercrimes and terrorist use of the internet, and also show the potential difficulties for taxonomizing motivations behind attacks. It is also important to highlight the difference in jurisdiction across the world in relation to the definition of cybercrime (see Chapters 1 and 3). There is for instance a fine line between covert operations and terrorist attacks depending on where in the world the activity is occurring. Therefore, this chapter does not intend to address the issues of law and legislation behind the activity. The cases that have been used are summarized by outlining the information that is publicly available about them. They are followed by an overview of the strategic responses from the UK, US and EU and then a threat assessment is discussed.

TAXONOMICAL CLASSIFICATION OF CYBERCRIME/ CYBERTERRORISM

There are a number of taxonomies developed in relation to cybercrime and activity. Other taxonomies for cybercrime concentrate on the characteristics of attacks (Lough, 2001) whilst Howard and Longstaff (1998) taxonomy accounts for motivations and objectives and consists of five process stages. However, a key problem in the area of cyber security is the lack of agreed terminology across different organizations, research disciplines and approaches, and stakeholders. This taxonomy therefore attempts to overcome linguistic barriers by using nontechnical language. Taking a human-centric approach this taxonomy focuses on the situational understanding of cybercrime and helps to foster the practical implementations of countermeasures by focusing on intentions (and circumstances) surrounding the cybercrimes.

The proposed taxonomy below relates to the perceived motivations/intentions for cybercrime and attacks and therefore does not focus on the technical considerations of cybercrime. The taxonomy needs to be elaborated, not only as a list of words but also to reflect the attributes (and their inter-relationships) that are key to all the target user communities—for example law enforcement agencies, especially investigative officers.

Whilst this is a starting point for a categorization process there is room for development as cyber security demands change and develop. Currently it is not exhaustive and a limitation could be the lack of room for technical detail, however in its current form it helps to establish the perceived motivations behind cyber-attacks which in turn provides basis for situational understanding (Table 9.1).

Table 9.1 A Taxonomy for Perceived Motivation of Cybercrime

Motivations/ intent	Primary	Secondary	Tertiary	Context	Major website has gone down— affected users include public
Financial				Who	British electronic army
Political	✓			What	DDoS attacks
Moral		✓		Where	Website/card system failure
Self-actualization			✓	When	2pm-4pm Thursday 21st
Exploitation				How	No technical detail currently known
Promotional		✓		Other	Second attack of its type in 2 days

For operational use and in order to create a repository—the grid above can be used for each cybercrime incident. A mock example has been included to show how it could be used. The first section of the grid enables a tick box system where multiple motivations may be ticked. For instance a decision may be made that the case is primarily politically motivated but has moral and promotional motivations (see example above). Different investigative officers may have different opinions or evidence about the motivations—there is no limit on how many boxes can be ticked—especially given that some cases may be complex in nature—although it is recommended that decisions are made about the primary, secondary and tertiary motivations rather than clustering motivations into one category. It is possible that there are no secondary or tertiary motivations—in these cases the boxes can be left blank. Information relating to the cybercrime case can be included to the right of the table and can be as detailed as is necessary. The "context" and "other" boxes allow for any field notes or important information relating to the case to be included. The "who" box relates to potential suspects and can also include potential victims. If information is not known, again these boxes can be left blank. This design has purposefully been created to be flexible given that each case will be made up of different characteristics.

The financial motives for cybercrimes can be fraudulent and for financial gain however financial motivations can also relate to disruption of financial systems. Political motives link to the support or countering governmental policies or actions and can include state sponsored attacks, espionage and propaganda.

Moral motives can be associated with fighting for freedom, rights, and ethics, or against exploitation and oppression. Religious systems could fall into this category and are twofold: attacks by religious groups against other religious systems/beliefs; attacks toward religious groups against their belief systems/exploitation/religion as oppression. Moral motivations for cyber-attacks can be complex in nature—this taxonomy allows for general categorization and a limitation is that it could be seen as too simplistic.

Self-actualization relates to individuals or groups who carry out attacks out of curiosity—they could be testing their own knowledge and skill or testing the security systems—again for knowledge rather than for purposeful corruption or disruption. They may also hack for kudos or notoriety.

Whilst exploitation could fall in line with moral motivations it is a separate category which relates to the exploitation of human beings (for example, in cases of human trafficking and child abuse). Cases involving cyber bullying and/or cyber harassment could also fall under this category. In this chapter there is no case study which relates to this category however Chapter 11 discusses issues surrounding child exploitation.

The final motivation listed in this taxonomy is promotional which relates to publicity and for this taxonomy it means to gather awareness through news media, social media and in some cases develop and maintain an online presence. These definitions are not exhaustive but provide concepts for operators using the grid to create a repository.

In cases where cybercrimes have been conducted anonymously, it is difficult to categorize the agent's motivations unless they have released a statement to the press, or publicly laid claim to the attack outlining their reasons for conducting it. Whilst some hackers overtly state their reasons behind the attack, it is important to acknowledge that covert motivations may also be present but not publically acknowledged. This taxonomy works by being able to interchange the categories. The cyber-attack or crime may appear to have a primary motivation but then may also have a secondary motivation (which in some cases may be underlying). In more complicated contexts there may be multiple motivations where "tertiary" motivations can be applied. So for instance a DDoS attack on a bank may primarily be moral (against the fact the banking system is corrupt and has caused an economic crisis) but the secondary motivation may be publicity, whilst a tertiary may be self-actualization. Each case should be assessed individually and may even have multiple primary and secondary motivations.

CASE STUDIES

The following case studies demonstrate each of the taxonomical motivations for conducting cybercrime. The Syrian Electronic army has "moral" motivates but is heavily driven by the need for publicity and is linked to the political motive category. This group of hackers claims to be conducting attacks in order to get their voices heard. The Stuxnet attack is linked to potential political motivation: to prevent the development of nuclear weapons. The attacks on the banking systems are linked to financial and moral motives whilst also linking to publicity. The Mafiaboy case relates to "self-actualization." A case study for exploitation has not been included in this chapter but further information relating to exploitation can be found in Chapter 11.

POLITICAL/PUBLICITY/SELF-ACTUALIZATION: THE CASE OF THE SYRIAN ELECTRONIC ARMY

The SEA were officially placed on the FBI's advisory list following a number of attacks in 2011. The FBI refers to the SEA as a "pro-regime hacker group" that emerged during Syrian anti-government protests in 2011 (Federal Bureau of Investigation, 2013). Information accompanying the advice says that the SEAs primary capabilities are spearphizing; web defacement and hijacking social media with an aim of spreading propaganda.

WHO ARE THEY?

A team of eight people—thought to be young Syrians (five of whom had their own pseudonyms when their website was available to access)—who are in no way affiliated with any political party. They claim to have set up SEA in 2011 in response to Western and Arab media who they believe biasedly reported in favor of terrorist groups that have killed civilians, and are in favor of the Syrian Army. Currently, the group believes that they are protecting their homeland and strongly support the reforms of President Bashar-Al Assad.

Schneier (2013) speculates how much of an actual army the SEA are, and suggests that we do not actually know much about their age or whether they are even Syrian. What we do not definitely know is to what extent this group are backed by the Syrian government, so it is possible that the SEA are a group of amateur geo-Politian's.

In January 2014 their website was removed from Google Searches and their existing online profiles for twitter, Facebook and Instagram were removed although on 29th January 2014 they had re-set up accounts. Presumably this is something they will continually have to do if they are fighting against large-scale organizations like Microsoft (Hanley Frank, 2014).

The Facebook and twitter pages allow the group to publically lay claim to the attacks but also to voice their political viewpoints. They are particularly critical of organizations who deny users their rights to privacy.

POLITICAL OR MORAL HACKERS?

It goes without saying that the more this group hacks and takes ownership for the hacking and phishing attacks, the more the media start covering stories about them and the more well-known they become. It is generally thought that they are not doing anything new or unusual in relation to the technical side of the attacks (basic phishing attacks and DOS attacks). However, these have been effective enough to cause inconvenience for companies such as Microsoft (who believes it is possible that their staff's social media accounts have been compromised—see Chapter 3).

It is clear from the closing down of SEAs social media sites and the re-opening of them hours later that this group understands the need to have an online social media presence in order to be a continued and renowned threat. On their current Facebook page they claim to be a Non-Governmental Organization (NGO) and three hours after re-instating a profile page they had 1600 "likes" whilst their twitter followers jumped from 10,000 in the first weeks of January to 12,500. They undoubtedly have some public backing although without conducting an analysis of the Facebook users who have liked the page and an analysis of their twitter followers it is difficult to categorically know who is backing them (see Chapter 10 for further discussion).

Before the SEA website (www.SEA.sy) was removed from Google searches it contained detailed information about the attacks they have instigated and also detailed why they had carried them out. They referred to hacks as achievements once again re-enforcing the argument that to be affective they need to hack high-profile organizations—and ensure that there is media coverage in order for them to re-enforce their notoriety—but also ensure their voice is being heard.

METHODS: PHISHING AND DDoS

The media report on two main methods that the SEA makes use of: Phishing and DDoS attacks.

Phishing can involve sending out large numbers of e-mails, which contain a message that appears to originate from a legitimate source (i.e., a well-known company such as PayPal or Twitter). The aim of the e-mail is to convince the potential victim to provide their personal details. Some e-mails can direct readers to an external hoax website, which is made to look authentic. The website can also encourage the victim to provide their confidential information (bank account details, identifying details, social security numbers, passwords, etc.)—which can then be used by the Phisher to commit an array of subsequent fraudulent acts. Some more complicated phishing campaigns can include harmful malware in the email itself, or on the hoax website—which can directly extract the information it needs from the target's computer, without requiring the victim to provide the confidential information directly (see Chapter 12 for more detail about Phishing).

DDoS (Distributed Denial of Service) or a denial-of-service (DoS) usually involves a system being overwhelmed by simultaneous online requests. This can result in the service becoming unavailable to its users. Distributed denial of service attacks are sent by two or more people or bots whereas denial of service attacks are sent by one system or person (see Chapter 17 for further information).

WHO HAVE THEY HACKED TO DATE?

The following information is a summary of the information available from media sources. The SEA have infiltrated the media across the world however it is not clear exactly how many attacks and who have been affected. The following are a number of examples which have occurred in 2013 and 2014.

Schneier claimed in August 2013 that the SEA had attacked the websites of the New York Times, Twitter, the Huffington Post amongst others although they had not done this directly but had gone through an Australian domain name called Melbourne IT. However, in January 2014, they made a number of "attacks" on the following organizations:

CNN

The SEA targeted the twitter and Facebook accounts of CNN. They laid claim to an attack on CNN (January 2014) advising on their twitter feed that

> *Tonight, the #SEA decided to retaliate against #CNN's viciously lying reporting aimed at prolonging the suffering in #Syria…#CNN used its usual formula of present unverifiable information as truth, adopting a report by Qataris against #Syria…Instead of any actual journalism, #CNN turned into a loud horn calling for the destruction of the #Syria-n state…US media strategy is now to hide the fact that the CIA controls and funds Al Qaeda by blaming #Syria instead for their terror #SEA…The #SEA will not stop to pursue these liars and will expose them and their methods for the world to see.*

Given that their one of their main motivations is deemed to be political mobilization it is not surprising to see that the justification for the attack by SEA relates to the supposed misreporting about what is happening in Syria by CNN.

The SEA sent out five tweets before the CNN twitter feed was re-instated:

> Syrian Electronics Army was here…Stop lying…All your reports are fake! via @Official_SEA16 #SEA
> Long live #Syria via @Official_SEA16 #SEA ow.ly/i/4nt9l
> Obama Bin Laden the lord of terror is brewing lies that the Syrian state controls Al Qaeda
> For 3 years Al Qaeda has been destroyed the Syrian state but they think you're stupid enough to believe it
> DON'T FORGET: Al Qaeda is Al CIA da. Funded, armed and controlled. (http://www.buzzfeed.com/michaelrusch/syrian-electronic-army-hacks-cnns-twitter-account)

Of course the content of these tweets can neither be confirmed nor denied: they are simply recorded for information. A CNN statement advised that the tweets were removed immediately and the affected accounts secured (Shoichet, 2014).

ANGRY BIRDS

In January 2014 the AngryBirds website was defaced. The angry birds logo was changed to "spying birds" with an NSA logo placed over one of the apps logos. This was thought to be carried out by a friend of SEA. Their twitter account said the following:

A friend hacked and defaced @Angrybirds website after reports confirms its spying on people. The attack was by "Anti-NSA" Hacker, He sent an email to our official email with the link of the hacked website.

(www.twitter com/offcial_SEA16)

The attack was in connection to a supposed NSA report which claimed that US and UK spy agencies (i.e., GCHQ) could access personal information—such as age and date of birth from the mobile app third-party advertising companies. Rovio (the app makers company) released a statement which said that they have not collaborated or colluded with any government spy agencies anywhere in the world (Rovio, 2014). Such a small defacement to a website by an outside source demonstrates a weakness in the sites security whilst also helping to publicize the supposed compromise of the personal data of its users.

MICROSOFT (JANUARY 2014)

January 2014 saw several attacks by the SEA on Microsoft. Reportedly through Phishing tactics the SEA gained access to employee social media and email accounts being impacted. They tweeted the following from @MSFTnews account: "Syrian Electronic Army Was Here via @Official_SEA16 #sea" which was removed quickly. Another tweet said: "Don't use Microsoft emails (hotmail, outlook), They are monitoring your accounts and selling the data to the governments #SEA @Official_SEA16."

Berkman (2014) has reportedly contacted the SEA and received the following response when asked why they targeted Microsoft:

Microsoft is monitoring emails accounts and selling the data for the American intelligence and other governments.
And we will publish more details and documents that prove it.
Microsoft is not our enemy but what they are doing affected the SEA.

SAUDI ARABIAN GOVERNMENT WEBSITES (JANUARY 2014)

Neal (2014) reports that the SEA was also responsible for targeting the Saudi Arabian government website and seized control of a number of their domains. SEA were attacking in protest of the Al Saud regime which they believe makes use of a terrorist group. Their twitter feed once again allowed them to take credit and advertise their efforts. Each of the 16 principles of Saudi Arabia were mentioned individuality followed by a hashtag: #ActAgainstSaudiArabiaTerrorism #SaudiArabia. It is worth noting that there is less media coverage about this incident than other attacks on large companies (see Chapter 13 for further information).

SOCIAL MEDIA PRESENCE

Given that they are aware of their need for social media presence members of the SEA have reportedly spoken to a number of press sources. However one interview in particular was tweeted via a link refers to a text-based conversation that they had with Matthew Keys in December 2013. In their exchange they advise that they are students and highlight that SEA chooses its targets based on media reporting bias—they particularly refer to a times article which they believe reports on only one side, i.e., against Bashar Assad. In the interview they highlight that they do not trust media in general but particularly that some media are not agenda driven when it comes to Syria. They also believe that their identities must be kept unknown or they will be subject to threats from the US. In the interview they stress that they are only doing what they do to ensure that the media report the truth to the world after witnessing terrorist attacks on their countries police. It is difficult to know definitively how much of what they say in the interview is propaganda and how much is truth. Ultimately the SEA advise that they want to stop the fourth generation war on their country but their counter message is that they want to reveal the real hand behind terrorism. They also categorically deny any ties to the Syrian, Russian or Iranian governments. The full interview transcript can be accessed at http://thedesk.matthewkeys.net/2013/12/11/a-live-conversation-with-the-syrian-electronic-army/ (Keys, 2013) (see Chapter 15 for further detail about social media).

Masi (2013a) claimed to speak to a SEA member named "Richie" in September 2013 but she herself admits that there is no way of confirming this. The transcript reiterates similar main messages from the Key's interview in December 2013: "Hacking will drive attention, opinions and a well delivered message to whatever the issue is." In a second interview with a SEA leader Masi (2013b) highlights the possibility that some of the media presence is being conducted by others who claim to be SEA but are not.

The SEA claim to not be linked to the Syrian government however some of their attacks have been to an extent politically motivated. For the purposes of this taxonomy the cases listed could primarily fall under the "moral" category—and the SEA often make public statements about why they are carrying out their acts—linking their actions to ethical causes. However, the fact that they heavily rely on social media and lay claim to attacks that occur globally leads to a secondary motivation as potentially being publicity. Some of their actions could also be linked to self-actualization.

THE CASE OF STUXNET

In June 2010, a computer virus Stuxnet was believed to be created to attack Iran's nuclear facilities. It is widely speculated by media sources that the United States and Israel collaborated to facilitate this attack although it has never been officially confirmed by either country. This is the first case of publicly known intent of cyber warfare. A NATO research team in 2013 agreed that the Stuxnet attack on Iran was an "act of force" (Schmitt, 2013). The virus included a special malware that specifically monitors industrial systems whilst doing little harm to computers and networks that do not meet its configuration requirements. It is thought that it was designed to destroy nuclear plant machinery and as a result slow or halt the production of Low Enriched Uranium.

It is believed that different variations of the virus targeted five Iranian organizations including the Natanz nuclear facility (Zetter, 2010). Security specialists (Kaspersky, Sysmantic, Cherry, 2010; Langner, 2011) believe that due to the complexity of the virus implementation and its sophisticated nature, it was more than likely conducted with "nation state support." UK and US media sources (The Guardian, the BBC and The New York Times) also claimed that (unnamed) experts studying Stuxnet believe that only a nation-state would have the capabilities to produce it due to the complexity of the code (Halliday, 2010; Markoff, 2010; Fildes, 2010).

Borg (2010) of the United States Cyber-Consequences Unit stated,

> *Israel certainly has the ability to create Stuxnet and there is little downside to such an attack, because it would be virtually impossible to prove who did it. So a tool like Stuxnet is Israel's obvious weapon of choice.*
>
> **(Marris, 2010)**

To date, Israel has not publicly commented on the Stuxnet attack but has confirmed that cyber warfare is now at the forefront of their defense doctrine, with a military intelligence unit set up specifically to pursue both cyber-related defensive and offensive options (Williams, 2009). American officials have indicated that the virus originated abroad.

Either way the nature of cyberspace means that it is challenging to find out exactly who is responsible for the activities conducted, the actions taken, and the origin of an activity. It is especially difficult to prove who is behind Stuxnet. Although it does seem that Stuxnet was designed to be destructive and is the first attack of its kind. Given the facts available about this incidence, it would more than likely fall under the political category although it could fall under moral or financial categories if further information surrounding the attack was made public (Chapters 3 and 13 also make use of this example).

THE CYBER-ATTACKS ON BANKS
ON A GLOBAL SCALE

Operation High Roller consisted of a series of fraud activities targeted at the banking system across the world. It made use of multifaceted automation to collect data in order to raid bank accounts including commercial accounts and institutions of all sizes. This sophisticated method for data collection allowed the operation to run faster. A review in 2012 of the operation led McAfee and Guardian Analytics found that nearly $78 million was removed from bank accounts due to this attack. The operations servers were based in Russia, Albania and China, but the attacks started in Europe, moved to Latin America and then targeted the US. Whilst there are no concrete figures for how much cybercrimes cost the world economy estimated figures range from $100 to $500 billion per year.

IN THE UK

In November 2013 the Bank of England released a financial stability report which detailed a number of attacks across the UK banking sector—the report states:

> *Cyber attack has continued to threaten to disrupt the financial system. In the past six months, several UK banks and financial market infrastructures have experienced cyber attacks, some of which have disrupted services.*
>
> **(Bank of England, 2013, p. 25)**

The report also accepts that the banking sector is susceptible to cyber-attacks as it has a "high degree of interconnectedness, its reliance on centralised market infrastructure and its sometimes complex legacy IT systems" (Bank of England, 2013, p. 54).

The "systemic" threat to the UK banking and payments system is recognized in the report: "While losses have been small relative to UK banks' operational risk capital requirements, they have revealed vulnerabilities. If these vulnerabilities were exploited to disrupt services, then the cost to the financial system could be significant and borne by a large number of institutions" (p. 25).

The report was published as the UK banks took part in a one day cyber threat exercise called Operation Waking shark II which aimed to test the financial systems ability to withstand major cyber-attacks. These types of operations require competitors across the sector to share information about the potential threats and this type of co-operation is not yet believed to be present.

In December 2013 Natwest and Royal Bank of Scotland, UK-based banks were subject to a number of DDoS attacks which reportedly cost them millions in compensation. The DDoS impacted on the bank's websites and directly affected the bank's customer's ability to use their services. Currently, there is no conclusive information about who was responsible for the attack or motivation for the attack. Had a notorious hacking group been behind the attack they would more than likely to have laid claim to it (Tadeo, 2013).

In October 2012, a group of hacktivists did lay claim to the DDoS attack on HSBC which impacted millions of user's ability to access their online accounts around the world. Following these kinds of attacks it is commonplace to see banks defending customer data—usually insisting that the attacks did not compromise personal information. A hacking group who call themselves fawkes security on Twitter and who act in association with the "Anonymous" ideology (see section below) laid claim to the DDoS attack on HSBC their justification being that the banks are corrupt and have caused the global economic crisis. The group tweeted counter information suggesting that personal data were affected:

> *When HSBC said "user data had not been compromised" This isn't entirely correct. We also managed to log 20,000 debit card details. #OpHSBC*

There is no evidence to back these claims. There is also no evidence to suggest that it was related to fraudulent activity. Although DDoS attacks can be used in conjunction with takeovers of bank's systems to commit fraud or steal intellectual property.

Disruptive DDoS attacks are becoming larger with volumetric flooding of servers with jumbled or incomplete data. Meaning there is an increasing need to gather and share intelligence and strategies amongst networks and across the financial sector in relation to attacks of this nature (Ashford, 2013; Rashid, 2013).

Whilst the context for this case study is financial—the primary motivation may not fall under "financial" as the Anonymous attack on HSBC demonstrates and thus could fall into the "moral" category. However, publicity could also motivate the attacks for notorious groups. DDoS attacks are usually highly disruptive and can be used to mask other fraudulent activities—in these cases then "financial" would be the primary motivation.

THE CASE OF THE ANONYMOUS ATTACKS ON SCIENTOLOGY

Anonymous is an international network of activists who originated on an image-based bulletin board (B) 4Chan in 2003. Over the past ten years they have become known for a large number of DDoS attacks on corporate, government, religious websites. Anonymous (Anonymous, 2014a) describe themselves as "a decentralized network of individuals focused on promoting access to information, free speech, and transparency" (http:www.anonanalytics.com). According to Kelly (2009) "even under the discrete umbrella of hacktivism, however, Anonymous has a distinct make-up: a decentralized (almost non-existent) structure, unabashed moralistic/political motivations, and a proclivity to couple online cyberattacks with offline protests" (p. 1668). A website associated with the group describes it as "an internet gathering" with "a very loose and decentralized command structure that operates on ideas rather than directives" (http://anonnews.org/static/faq) (Anonymous, 2014b).

Internet censorship and control is at the heart of the group's philosophy and they have orchestrated a number of well publicized stunts. This case study will focus on Project Chanology—a protest against the practices of the Church of Scientology (2008).

Project Chanology started after the Church of Scientology tried to remove a mock-up of an interview conducted by Tom Cruise talking about Scientology from Youtube. Anonymous stated that they believed that the Church of Scientology were committing acts of Internet Censorship and started a number of DDoS attacks which were followed by a series of prank calls designed to cause the Church of Scientology as much disruption as possible.

Following the DDOs attacks, in February 2008 people across the world who associated themselves with the Anonymous philosophy took direct action by protesting against the church on the streets. It is estimated that about 7,000 people protested in at least 100 cities worldwide—with thousands of photos of the events uploaded onto websites like flickr. Further protests were carried out in March and then April 2008.

The DDoS attacks impacted on the Church of Scientology's website which went down on a number of occasions in late January (Kaplan, 2008; Vamosi, 2008). As a result the scientology.org website was moved to a safeguarding company to prevent further DDoS, however the attacks against the site increased and consequently was once again inaccessible (Kaplan, 2008). Anonymous in a press release and video declared "war on scientology" advising that it would continue its attacks in order to protect freedom of speech (see Youtube Anonymous 2008 Message to Scientology).

Whilst this case could fall under the categorization of "religion" the underlying reasons for the attacks are much more complicated. Whilst publicity does play a part in the campaign, claims relating to morals are a key justification for the attacks. This case is also interesting because it is not restricted to online attacks but also direct action. Ethical hacktivists such as Anonymous maintain that they are fighting for the moral high ground aiming to seek quality of life for others as well as world improvement.

SELF-ACTUALIZATION: THE CASE OF "MAFIABOY"

Michael Calce (Mafiaboy) was a 15-year-old Canadian school student when he carried out a series of DDoS attack on several major corporations including Yahoo, eBay, CNN, Dell and Amazon in 2000. Calce started by targeting Yahoo in an operation he called Project Rivolta (meaning Riot in Italian) his goal being to establish dominance for himself and TNT, his cyber group (Calce, 2008).

Genosko (2006) said of the case:

> He wasn't a programmer. He acquired an automated "rootkit" written by somebody else and then set it to work "anonymously." Mafiaboy executed a Distributed Denial of Service Attack (DDoS) – a "flood" of messages (packets) that by volume alone disabled servers unable to cope with the demands placed upon them – with borrowed script, in this case, a denial-of-service program authored by "Sinkhole" (although early press reports fingered a creation by a "mixter" called Tribal Flood Network). He planted a number of DOS agents on "zombies" – hijacked computer systems at universities, and remote-controlled the operation with his automated software, using the captured computers to inundate selected Web sites with data packets (numbered chunks of files).

This was a groundbreaking case of cybercrime at the time and proved that internet security needed to be drastically improved given that the largest website in the world (Yahoo in 2000) could be shut down by a 15-year-old. The hacks provided evidence that there were major holes in internet security and this was used as a part of his argument for defense: he wanted to expose such faults and become a computer security specialist.

Calce admitted that he committed the attacks out of curiosity. "At that point in time, everyone was running tests and seeing what they could do and what they could infiltrate" (Infosecurity, 2013). Whether this was motivated by self-actualization, curiosity or a method for testing weaknesses in security systems, Calce' DDoS attacks are thought to have costs companies in excess of $1 billion (CAD) according to various media sources (Niccolai, 2000).

STRATEGIC RESPONSES TO CYBER ATTACKS

Having explored the different cyber cases above it is also important to highlight that different countries use different strategies for dealing with these attacks. Below is a brief overview of the UK, USA's, and EUs strategies for dealing with cybercrime.

The Comprehensive National Cyber security Initiative set up by the US government in 2008 consists of the following goals which are designed to help secure the US:

- To establish a front line of defense against today's immediate threats
- To defend against the full spectrum of threats
- To strengthen the future cyber security environment

The document also lists 12 key initiatives:

- Manage the Federal Enterprise Network as a single network enterprise with trusted internet connections
- Deploy an intrusion detection system of sensors across the Federal enterprise
- Pursue deployment of intrusion prevention systems across the Federal enterprise
- Co-ordinate and redirect research and development (R&D) efforts.
- Connect current cyber ops centers to enhance situational awareness
- Develop and implement a government-wide cyber counterintelligence (CI) plan
- Increase the security of our classified networks
- Expand cyber education
- Define and develop enduring "leap-ahead" technology, strategies, and programs
- Define and develop enduring deterrence strategics and programs
- Develop a multi-pronged approach for global supply chain risk management
- Define the Federal role for extending cyber security into critical infrastructure domains (The White House, 2009).

The Department of Defense Strategy for Operating in Cybercrime (2011) has Five Strategic Initiatives:

1. Treat cyberspace as an operational domain to organize, train, and equip so that DoD can take full advantage of cyberspace's potential
2. Employ new defense operating concepts to protect DoD networks and systems
3. Partner with other U.S. government departments and agencies and the private sector to enable a whole-of-government cybersecurity strategy
4. Build robust relationships with U.S. allies and international partners to strengthen collective cybersecurity
5. Leverage the nation's ingenuity through an exceptional cyber workforce and rapid technological innovation

The UKs Cyber Security Strategy (2011) consists of four main objectives:

- Tackling cyber-crime and making the UK one of the most secure places in the world to do business in cyberspace.
- Making the UK more resilient to cyber-attack and better able to protect our interests in cyberspace.
- Helping to shape an open, vibrant and stable cyberspace which the UK public can use safely and that supports open societies.
- Building the UKs cross-cutting knowledge, skills and capability to underpin all our cyber security objectives.

The UK strategy involves focusing on individuals and businesses. The UK strategy admits that the threats are changing but details the following as being current threats in cyberspace:

- Criminals (fraud/identity theft)
- Other States (espionage/propaganda)
- Terrorists (propaganda/radicalize potential supporters/communicate/plan)
- Hacktivists (disruption/reputation management/financial damage/gaining publicity)

The UK strategy also highlights the difficulty in targeting the perpetrators of cybercrimes: "But with the borderless and anonymous nature of the internet, precise attribution is often difficult and the distinction between adversaries is increasingly blurred" (2011, p. 16).

The EU Cybersecurity-Strategy of the Europe Union: An Open, Safe and Secure Cyberspace (2013) understandably considers the concerns of a number of countries as opposed to one, and therefore stresses the borderless multi-layered nature of the internet. It has five key strategic priorities:

- Achieving cyber resilience
- Drastically reducing cybercrime
- Developing cyberdefence policy and capabilities related to the Common Security and Defence Policy (CSDP)
- Develop the industrial and technological resources for cybersecurity
- Establish a coherent international cyberspace policy for the European Union and promote core EU values.

The different strategies highlight a need for a strong global network of shared intelligence and communication about cybercrimes. The networks are not only the responsibility of governments and experts but also industry and the wider society. Strong partnerships, along with shared knowledge and information could strengthen the plight against cybercrime and attacks which cost the global economy billions each year (McAfee, 2013).

There are three different strategies for managing cybercrime presented above; however there are many more initiatives globally (for example see Australia's 2009 or see Canada's 2010 strategy). To create a strategy which extends across many different domains, the appropriate knowledge can be extracted from these strategies (and others), and used to recommend an increasingly consolidated viewpoint. The applicable gaps and overlaps would help to provide efficient and integrated solutions (be they regulatory, technical, ethical, legal or societal) to existing threats and could also help to anticipate (and therefore prevent) future ones.

CONCLUDING REMARKS

This chapter has reviewed a number of examples of cyber-attacks. Based on different legal and political jurisdictions they may constitute as a criminal offence. For example in the case of the SEA conducting "hacktivism" is claimed to be a method for making the voices of people who would not normally have a voice, be heard. Carrying out phishing attacks and DDoS for this group seems to be a form of political mobilization but in many instances—government websites are not at the forefront of these attacks—businesses are. It drums up publicity for their cause—whilst highlighting that there are security breaches in even in the largest organizations that are supposed to be leaders of security—thus increasing their notoriety. Without condoning or condemning their actions, this seems to be a simple way of causing disruption for companies—and is one which replaces protesting on the streets. Key to their voice being heard is the fact that they know there is a need for them to have a social media presence—to the point where they have to create a new social media pages sometimes daily. With a constant social presence and continued phishing attacks and DDOS attacks aimed at various outlets they manage to create not just a social media presence but a presence in the media and, consequently, to some extent an awareness of their cause. On the other hand, the SEA may be targeting nonpolitical websites because they are vulnerable opportunities and may be claiming moral significance to obtain publicity. Either way it is slightly incongruous that they claim to not trust media in general but make use of it for their own means.

Stuxnet is thought to be the first case of publicly known cyber warfare and whilst it is politically driven, it may also have moral and financial motives. The case is shrouded in speculation—experts have guessed that it was the work of a nation state and if there was hard evidence to support these assertions this case would be categorized as political. Whilst legally it remains unclear who carried out the attack, moral motivates can be applied (in relation to the point of the attack: to disrupt the production of nuclear outputs) whilst also disrupting the finances of the country through damaging industrial systems.

Operation High Roller directly points to financial motivations since fraud activities were committed during the attacks. Whilst DDoS attacks disrupt banking services they can also cover up fraudulent activity, and can be classed as financial, they can also be classed as moral since hackers also claim that banks are corrupt. The threat here remains with the banking sector but can have a direct impact upon individuals.

In cases where self-actualization occurs—i.e. the hackers attack to test systems or do it because they can—like in the Mafiaboy case—the threat can be classed as high impact.

Operationally, to start making assessments about threats, a method for collecting information and data using a taxonomy system for situational understanding has been presented. This model focuses on the intent and motivation behind cybercrimes and rather than taking a technical approach focuses on human factors. The five real-life cases not only show the diversity and sometimes complexity of individual crimes but also show the difference in motivations for the crimes. The proposed taxonomy for creating a knowledge repository therefore particularly focuses on the perceived motivations and intent of potential suspects and perpetrators. Using the taxonomy model above provides a starting point toward gaining a clearer situational understanding of cybercrimes. Currently with a number of cybercrime strategies across the globe, and with no agreed definitions or legislation—gathering knowledge about the cybercrimes—including situational knowledge will help to foster the practical implications for countermeasures. This is especially true when considering our earlier definition of knowledge. Given the lack of agreed definitions and numerous strategies for cybercrime, the model has been designed to be flexible for front line officers especially in light of the fact that cases vary in nature. The model also makes use of simple language since a Universal linguistic system for cybercrime has not yet been agreed.

REFERENCES

Akghar, B., 1999. Strategic information systems beyond technology: a knowledge management perspective, SHU presentation.

Anonymous, 2008. Message to scientology, Youtube 21st January 2008 [online], http://www.youtube.com/watch?v=JCbKv9yiLiQ (accessed 13.12.13).

Anonymous, 2014a. About Us. http://www.anonymusanalytics.com (accessed 13.02.14).

Anonymous, 2014b. Anon New: Everything Anonymous. [online], http://anonnews.org/static/faq (accessed 12.02.14).

Ashford, W., 2013. More than one-fifth of UK firms hit by DDoS attacks in 2012. 16th July 2013, Computer weekly. [online], http://www.computerweekly.com/news/2240188089/More-than-one-fifth-of-UK-firms-hit-by-DDoS-attacks-in-2012 (accessed 03.01.14).

Association of Chief Police Officer of England, Wales and Northern Ireland, 2012. ACPO e-Crime Strategy. http://www.acpo.police.uk/documents/crime/2009/200908CRIECS01.pdf (accessed 01.02.14).

Australian Government, 2009. Cyber security strategy. [online], http://www.ag.gov.au/RightsAndProtections/CyberSecurity/Documents/AG%20Cyber%20Security%20Strategy%20-%20for%20website.pdf (accessed 02.02.14).

Bank of England, 2013. Financial Stability report. November 2013 Issue No 34. [online], http://www.bankofengland.co.uk/publications/Documents/fsr/2013/fsrfull1311.pdf (accessed 13.12.13).

Berkman, F., 2014. Syrian Electronic army hacks microsofts twitter accounts and blog. 11th January 2014. Mashable, [online], http://mashable.com/2014/01/11/syrian-electronic-army-hack-microsoft/ (accessed 28.01.14).

Calce, M., 2008. Mafiaboy: How I Cracked the Internet and why it's Still Broken. Penguin Group, Toronto.

Cherry, S., 2010. How Stuxnet is rewriting the terrorism playbook. IEEE Spectrum. [online], http://spectrum.ieee.org/podcast/telecom/security/how-stuxnet-is-rewriting-the-cyberterrorism-playbook (accessed 13.12.13).

Federal Bureau of Investigation, 2013. FBI Cyber Division advisory: Syrian Electronic Army targeting social media. 5th September 2013. [online], http://publicintelligence.net/fbi-sea/ (accessed 12.01.14).

Fildes, J., 2010. Stuxnet worm 'targeted high value Iranian assets' 23rd September 2010. BBC. [online], http://www.bbc.co.uk/news/technology-11388018 (accessed 02.02.14).

Genosko, G., 2006. The case of 'Mafiaboy' and the rhetorical limits of hacktivism. The fibreculture J. (Issue 9). [online], http://nine.fibreculturejournal.org/fcj-057/ (accessed 13.12.13).

Government of Canada, 2010. Canada's cyber security strategy: for a stronger and more prosperous Canada. [online], http://www.publicsafety.gc.ca/cnt/rsrcs/pblctns/cbr-scrt-strtgy/cbr-scrt-strtgy-eng.pdf (accessed 02.02.14).

Halliday, J., 2010. Stuxnet worm is the 'work of a national government agency' 24th September 2010. The Guardian. [online], http://www.theguardian.com/technology/2010/sep/24/stuxnet-worm-national-agency (accessed 13.12.13).

Hanley Frank, B., 2014. Syrian Electronic Army may have stolen government data requests Microsoft says. 26th January 2014 Geekwire. [online], http://www.geekwire.com/2014/syrian-electronic-army-may-stolen-govt-data-requests-microsoft-says/ (accessed 27.01.14).

Howard, J.D., Longstaff, T.A., 1998. A common language for computer security incidents. Technical report, Sandia National Laboratories.

Infosecurity, 2013. A Q&A with MafiaBoy. 3rd September 2013, Infosecurity magazine. [online], http://www.infosecurity-magazine.com/view/34309/a-qa-with-mafiaboy/ (accessed 13.12.13).

Internet Crime Complaint Centre, 2012. Internet crime report. [online], http://www.ic3.gov/media/annualreport/2012_IC3Report.pdf (accessed 03.01.14).

Kaplan, D., 2008. DDoS hack attack targets church of scientology. 25th January 2008 SC magazine. [online], http://www.scmagazine.com/ddos-hack-attack-targets-church-of-scientology/article/104588/ (accessed 13.12.13).

Kelly, B., 2009. Investing in a centralized cybersecurity infrastructure: why "hacktivism" can and should influence cybersecurity reform. PhD Boston University School of Law. [online], http://www.bu.edu/law/central/jd/organizations/journals/bulr/volume92n4/documents/KELLY.pdf (accessed 12.02.14).

Keys, M., 2013. A live conversation with the Syrian Electronic Army. 11th December 2013 The Desk: Journalism and Social Media by Matthew Keys. [online], http://thedesk.matthewkeys.net/2013/12/11/a-live-conversation-with-the-syrian-electronic-army/ (accessed 14.01.14).

Langner, R., 2011. Cracking Stuxnet, a 21st Century Cyber Weapon. Ted. [online], http://www.ted.com/talks/ralph_langner_cracking_stuxnet_a_21st_century_cyberweapon.html.

Lough, D.L., 2001. A taxonomy of computer attacks with applications to wireless networks. PhD thesis Virginia Polytechnic Institute and State University.

Marcus, D., Sherstobitoff, R., 2012. Dissecting Operation High Roller. White Paper. [online], http://www.mcafee.com/uk/resources/reports/rp-operation-high-roller.pdf (accessed 13.12.13).

Markoff, J., 2010. A silent attack but not a subtle one. 26th September 2010 New York Times. [online], http://www.nytimes.com/2010/09/27/technology/27virus.html?_r=2& (accessed 13.12.13).

Marris, T., 2010. A worm in the centrifuge: an unusually sophisticated cyber-weapon is mysterious but important. The Economist. [online], http://www.economist.com/node/17147818 (accessed 13.12.13).

Masi, A., 2013a. My Brief but Intriguing talk with the Syrian Electronic Army. 10th September 2013 Vocativ, [online], https://www.vocativ.com/09-2013/my-brief-but-intriguing-conversation-with-the-syrian-electronic-army/ (accessed 16.12.13).

Masi, A., 2013b. I think I pissed off a Syrian electronic army leader. Vocativ. [online], http://www.vocativ.com/09-2013/i-think-i-pissed-off-a-syrian-electronic-army-leader-by-asking-him-about-ice-cream/ (accessed 13.12.13).

McAfee Centre for Strategic and International Studies, 2013. The economic impact of cyber crime and cyber espionage. [online], http://www.mcafee.com/uk/resources/reports/rp-economic-impact-cybercrime.pdf (accessed 02.02.14).

Neal, D., 2014. Syrian Electronic Army Attacks Saudi Websites. 16th January 2014 The Inquirer. [online], http://www.theinquirer.net/inquirer/news/2323371/syrian-electronic-army-attacks-saudi-websites (accessed 01.02.14).

Niccolai, J., 2000. Analyst puts hacker damage to $1.2 billion and rising. 10th February 2000 Info world. [online], http://web.archive.org/web/20071112081103/http:/www.infoworld.com/articles/ic/xml/00/02/10/000210icyankees.html (accessed 13.12.13).

Rashid, F., 2013. Lessons learned from bank DDoS attacks. 9th September 2013 Bank Info Security. [online], http://www.bankinfosecurity.com/3-lessons-learned-from-bank-ddos-attacks-a-6049/op-1 (accessed 13.12.13).

Rovio, 2014. Rovio does not provide end user data to government surveillance agencies. 30th January 2014 Rovio. [online], http://www.rovio.com/en/news/press-releases/450 (accessed 02.02.14).

Schmitt, M. (Ed.), 2013. Tallin Manual on the International Law Applicable to Cyber Warfare. In: Cambridge University Press, Cambridge.

Schneier, B., 2013. Schneier on security: Syrian Electronic Army Cyberattacks. 3rd September 2013, [online], https://www.schneier.com/blog/archives/2013/09/syrian_electron.html (accessed 12.12.13).

Shoichet, C.E., 2014. Some CNN social media accounts hacked. 24th January 2014 CNN. [online], http://edition.cnn.com/2014/01/23/tech/cnn-accounts-hacked/ (accessed 12th February 2014).

Tadeo, M., 2013. NatWest victim of cyber attack after site crashes for a second time. 6th February 2013 The Independent. [online], http://www.independent.co.uk/news/business/news/natwest-victim-of-cyber-attack-after-site-crashes-for-the-second-time-8988811.html.

The EU Cybersecurity – Strategy of the Europe Union: An Open, Safe and Secure Cyberspace, 2013. http://eeas.europa.eu/policies/eu-cyber-security/cybsec_comm_en.pdf (accessed 24.01.14).

The UK Cyber security strategy: Protecting and promoting the UK in a digital world, 2011. [online], https://www.gov.uk/government/uploads/system/uploads/attachment_data/file/60961/uk-cyber-security-strategy-final.pdf (accessed 02.02.14).

The White House, 2009. The comprehensive National cyber security initiative. [online], Foreign Policy. [online], http://www.whitehouse.gov/issues/foreign-policy/cybersecurity/national-initiative (accessed 02.02.14).

U.S Department of Homeland Security, 2009. A roadmap for Cyber Crime Research. [online], http://www.dhs.gov/sites/default/files/publications/CSD-DHS-Cybersecurity-Roadmap.pdf (accessed 02.02.14).

Vamosi, R., 2008. Anonymous hackers take on the church of scientology. 24th January 2008 CNET. [online], http://news.cnet.com/8301-10789_3-9857666-57.html (accessed 13.12.13).

Williams, D., 2009. Spymaster sees Israel as world cyberwar leader. 15th December 2009 Reuters. [online], http://www.reuters.com/article/2009/12/15/us-security-israel-cyberwarfare-idUSTRE5BE30920091215 (accessed 13.12.13).

World Internet Usage and Population Statistics, 2012. [online], http://www.internetworldstats.com/stats.htm (accessed 16.11.12).

Zetter, K., 2010. Blockbuster worm aimed for infrastructure, but no proof Iran nukes were target. 23rd September 2010 Wired. [online], http://www.wired.com/threatlevel/2010/09/stuxnet/ (accessed 02.02.14).

Terrorist use of the internet

10

Bruno Halopeau

TERRORIST USE OF THE INTERNET

This chapter is not only an attempt to describe how terrorist groups use the Internet but it also provides information on how the internet could be used in the near future taking into account the latest technological developments. Numerous articles have already been written on the subject but they have treated it partially, focusing on the propaganda side or on the hacking and "technical" side. In this chapter, the propaganda and the encryption techniques used by terrorists will be described.

PROPAGANDA—INDOCTRINATION—RECRUITMENT

The use of Internet by terrorists has been described for many years as a growing trend. In reality, this phenomenon is more limited than it seems to be. In the articles provided by news media and so-called experts, there has been an attempt to provide an estimate on the number of terrorist websites (Weimann, 2008). However these statistics do not mean anything on their own; they have to be compared with the total number of websites available on the web.

Terrorist organizations generally use the Internet for propaganda purposes. The worldwide web and steady developments of web 2.0 have given an opportunity to the public to easily access and publish information. High IT skills are no longer necessary to publish and post information, photos and videos online and it is also a very cost effective method of communication.

Terrorist propaganda on the Internet is disseminated through several types of platforms; video sharing websites such as YouTube; online Social Network services such as Facebook; and through traditional online forums and blogs.

THE ROLE OF THE VIDEO

Videos play a key role in the propaganda; they show the ability of a terrorist group to carry successful operations such as suicide attacks. They also act as evidence for funders and sponsors proving that the money they have donated is well used for instance for the "Jihadi cause" concerning al-qaeda type terrorism.

According to law enforcement open source monitoring of Syrian groups, within a year, most of the moderate Syrian fighting groups that aimed at democratic elections after the fall of Bashar al-Assad have now shifted toward the jihadi ideologies which target the establishment of the Sharia law. All these fighting groups have released statements on the Internet to publicize their change of ideology—most probably to get the attention (and funds) of sponsors who are in favor of a Syria ruled by Sharia law.

ONLINE FORUMS—BLOGS

Forums are the most common way of promoting terrorism on the Internet since they provide a platform where people with the same way of thinking gather together; nevertheless, these forums have also some inconvenience which needs to be clarified. In the past, each terrorist forum used to be controlled by only one administrator but the success of several Law Enforcement Authorities in arresting administrators brought down or disrupted the operation of several terrorist forums. Because of those arrests, a new trend has emerged which aims at sharing the administration of a terrorist forum between several administrators. They either all share the same login/passwords or have multiple administrators and they all know how to run the forum. If one of them is arrested, the forum can continue its usual activity. This is exactly what happened when the Spanish authorities arrested an administrator of the terrorist forum "Ansar al Mujahideen" few years ago.

The main advantages for those terrorist groups to own their own forum is to have a total control over censorship, namely the communications between its members: messages and threads can be modified, deleted. They also have total freedom over the choice of the running platform, hosting location, activity logs and user access control, so members can be banned or promoted based on the way they behave.

ONLINE SOCIAL NETWORK SERVICES

Online social network services used by terrorists are the latest growing trend; more and more supporters of terrorism appreciate the freedom to exchange or comment on any terrorist action without restriction from any forum administrator as described above.

The increasing number of terrorist sympathizers using Social Network services has already revealed that the terrorist community is not so united and supportive as it seemed to be. There are several disagreements about claims of attacks, or even the purpose of an attack; for instance, the dissention between the Islamic Army of Iraq who claimed that Syrian *Jabhat al-Nusra* is one of its affiliated groups, whilst *Jabhat al-Nusra* rejects this affiliation and claims that the Syrian conflict has nothing to do with Iraq is an example among many.

The increase in the number of terrorist accounts on Twitter raises the issue of identification of individuals or groups, for instance, several Twitter accounts claimed to be the official media entity of the Somali terrorist organization; *al-Shabab*, however it is difficult to determine who is genuine and who are impersonators. This is posing a serious issue about who to monitor for intelligence services.

In early 2012, several posts on the "Ansar al Mujahideen" forum discussed about the possibility of developing a Jihadi Social Network website (Levine, 2012). This "website" would replicate the mainstream services and functionalities offered by Facebook or Google+ in a hope to increase the number of sympathizers and as a consequence the terrorist community emulate in publishing more postings.

The initial idea does not cover the following issues: the amount of work required to develop and maintain such a website; hosting such a service; or the control over users' identity accessing this platform.

The emergence of an independent trustable Social Network service with no intrusion from Government Agencies or Law Enforcement is in reality unlikely to happen and quite difficult to materialize.

RADICALIZATION PROCESS ON THE INTERNET

Internet users or terrorist sympathizers are initially attracted to the terrorist environment through video sharing websites such as YouTube where videos showing terrorist attacks are displayed. The YouTube accounts refer to a URL of a terrorist forum where people can click to access the forum, and they can join the forum by sending an email to its administrators.

When the "junior member" joins the forum, they will be tested to fulfill basic tasks. They will be then assessed, and based on good results, will be granted a higher rank such as "member," "confirmed member," "senior member," etc. At the same time they will also be granted more privileges, for example they could be given the task to administrate new comers on the forum. After a certain time one of the top administrators will ask the "senior member" to meet physically in order to further assess and validate that person as a good candidate. Following this crucial meeting the "new recruit" is introduced to a very small network of much radicalized individuals via VoIP such as Skype or Paltalk. This is where the candidate is entrusted with sensitive information, including where attacks are planned or targets designated.

PARTICULAR CASE: LONE WOLF

By definition Lone Wolves are the most difficult individuals to detect since they act alone and do not use the Internet to communicate with peers. However, they use the Internet to prepare their attacks and also to advertise their claims in videos or emails for instance. They also use the Internet to interact with persons/groups which are having similar ideologies and sometimes express their discontent on Social Networks.

Lone Wolves can be investigated by detect browsing deviation and also the online purchase of products such as explosives, precursors in the view of building IED (Improvised Explosive Device) or weapons.

Also, some cases reported that the "insider" threat should not be neglected. Usually these are highly skilled or knowledgeable people who have access to an environment that deals with dangerous materials, or are well positioned in organization and are turned into Lone Wolves to perform a one-shot attack using their expert knowledge. The most known case to date is certainly the Ivins case and the bioterrorism Anthrax attacks in 2001 (named Amerithrax).

Motivation for the lone wolf can be twofold:

- Internal or self-motivator: Disgruntled and with the adoption of an ideology and involve a nervous breakdown or mental health issue.
- External influence: Target of social engineering and then indoctrinated.

INFORMATION SHARING

Initially, Al-Qaeda type groups were reported as using Steganography to hide messages in pictures and/or movies. Though Steganography is an obfuscation method and cannot be considered as an encryption technology, it serves the purpose of hiding a message from plain sight which in turn ensures relative privacy and is one of the aims of encryption. This Modus Operandi was highly probable but has never really been proven to be widely used. The size of the information that can be hidden in a picture is very limited as, for instance, it would be very suspicious to have a poor quality picture consisting of a high number of Mega Bites.

After the train bombings in Madrid on March 11th, 2006, the arrested suspects revealed that they were using a trick to avoid email surveillance detection. The concept was to have one single email account (such as Hotmail, Yahoo!) shared among the group members where they could write emails and then leave them in the Draft folder. In doing so, no traces were left since no emails where sent. Nowadays, this technique is less likely since the trick is now well known and having one single account accessed from several diverse locations at the same time or from very distant geographical locations within small amount of time will certainly raise alerts to the mail provider that a particular account is shared among several persons.

In the past, Al-Qaeda type terror groups have been attempting to use some encryption technologies too. However, mistrust in ready-to-use tools such as PGP which was privately developed or TrueCrypt which was a community-developed open-source tool and potential backdoors placed by governments, did not provide them total insurance of confidentiality protection. Hence, they decided to develop their own tool "Mujahideen Secrets" (or "Asrar al-Mujahedeen") and later on Mujahideen Secrets 2. The first release was made by the Global Islamic Media Front in 2007 and quickly followed by the second version in 2008.

Of course, having their own tool has some advantages like better trust in its use but certainly brought more disadvantages. As such having a proprietary tool not thoroughly tested by a wider community makes it more prone to vulnerabilities. Once known, this tool was also the main target for reverse engineering from the different counter terrorism intelligence and law enforcement departments across the globe. Lastly, the possession of such a tool gives additional indications that a person is potentially pertaining to a terrorist group or is linked to it in some way.

In February 2013, the Global Islamic Media Front released a new encryption tool "Asrar al-Dardashah" but this time as a plugin to instant messaging client Pidgin that can be used in conjunction with user accounts on popular platforms such as Google Talk, MSN, Yahoo, AOL Instant Messenger, and Jabber/XMPP.

Though it can be seen as a shift in strategy for the use of Internet by implementing an encryption layer on top of existing services, the main disadvantage is that Public Keys have a very explicit heading "#—Begin Al-Ekhlaas Network ASRAR El Moujahedeen V2.0 Public Key 2048 bit—" leading to increased difficulty to store keys on public server or exchange those keys without raising the attention of counter-terrorism units.

The very same group, Global Islamic Media Front, also released an Android application to send/receive encrypted SMS and files. Indeed, this tool cannot be downloaded directly from the official store but is available on their website and a tutorial is available for the would-be users.

Finally in December 2013, a new tool has been discovered and was released by Al-Fajr Media Centre. This encryption tool is the latest program available for Al-Qaeda-type terrorists and codenamed "Amn al-Mujahid" (secret of the Mujahid). It's a software like PGP giving the possibility for users to choose among a set of well know encryption algorithm and to generate key pairs.

FUTURE DEVELOPMENTS
CYBER TERRORISM

We can imagine in the near future that terrorist and/or associated type of groups will want to leverage their attacks to be able to attain an unprecedented scale of impact of fear and destruction. With this in mind, the Internet can clearly be used as a tool to directly sustain a major attack. The most obvious target will certainly be critical infrastructure systems where disruption can be life-threatening and/or having mass disruption whilst generating distrust from the wider population (e.g., a transportation system hack). It is quite difficult to assess if terrorist groups are close to performing such attacks. However, if traditional terrorist groups are willing to, it means that they will have to either recruit very knowledgeable individuals or ask for external help such as for purchasing particular skills via a platform such a CaaS (Crime as a Service) or individuals such as Hackers-for-Hire.

However, as previously mentioned, trust is the biggest issue and the amount of time requested to develop this type of attack can be quite significant. Also information leakage about an operation cannot be ignored. The attack would also need to be built (e.g., software development, etc.) and tested. The problem with testing is either it is performed "off-line" or out of the target system. In the "off-line" option, it requires reconnaissance/intelligence first but also enormous resources to reproduce the target system and most of the time this is impossible (e.g., SCADA systems). The second problem with testing, if done on the live system, is that it leaves noises (e.g., traces/logs) that can raise the attention of the targeted system monitoring capabilities. This option is too risky and very unlikely to be chosen by terrorist groups.

On the other hand, extremist or activist groups may have a different view of trust issues and may not hesitate to call for external help and purchase in the underground market the missing skills they need to perpetrate a cyber-attack.

Additionally, if we take the particular case of Hacktivism, it is groups gathering extremely skilled and IT savvy individuals who make them more likely to succeed in a cyber terrorism attack than the other type of groups mentioned so far.

Taking the example of a successful event, STUXNET, that occurred in 2010. It was a very sophisticated code that has been developed to target a SCADA system to damage centrifuge machines to slow down Iranian uranium enrichment program (see Chapter 3). After reverse engineering the code, it shows that the resources required and knowledge of the target needed to successfully complete such an operation were massive and seems not in the reach yet of terrorist, extremism, or activist groups and can only be coming from state-sponsored or state-run CyberTeams.

FINANCING

The main element for a terrorist group to be able to achieve its attacks is the need of funding by partners, sponsors, or peers. States and Law Enforcement communities have therefore pushed to have rules, regulations and techniques to detect suspicious financial transactions to identify potential individuals participating in terrorist activities. Considering this, we can take as an example, the US and Europe agreement, EU-US TFTP (2010) Terrorist Finance Tracking Programme, signed in August 2010 in order to deal with that issue. The European Commission is currently studying a European agreement, EU TFTS (Terrorist Finance Tracking System). Though, these agreements might be relevant and quite efficient, it does not address emerging technological issues such as the rise of Virtual currencies. Virtual currencies are alternative currencies neither endorsed nor produced by any government. They can be split into two main streams: electronic money from Internet Games like Second Life and crypto currencies (or open-source digital currency).

Internet Games-based electronic money could be used to transfer large amount of virtual money across individuals and cash them out into real money. However especially following Snowden's (2013) revelations, these kinds of games have been infiltrated by the NSA and GCHQ in search of terrorist activity (Leapman, 2007). Also, individuals playing these games are required to become acquainted with the game rules and also how to use the virtual money. For instance they need to know who is behind the character and where the money is sent to. Another disadvantage is that the type of money is of course tied to the success of the game and its future development.

The second alternative, crypto currency seems more probable and has developed quickly in the last 3 to 4 years. Among the multiple currencies available today, Bitcoin is leading the way. It consists of a system of payment organized as a peer-2-peer network based on public-key cryptography. This tool is increasingly interesting for criminals and also terrorists since wallets are to some extent anonymous and dependent of the currency provisions toward privacy and provide facilitated ways to cash-in and cash-out the virtual money into hard money without possible tracking through financial institutions and therefore current watchdogs developed are inefficient.

On the other hand, those currencies are still young in existence and regulation on the legality of use is uncertain (and future of cashing out real money). A second point, the concept of peer-2-peer networks, renders the anonymity of a wallet's owner fairly limited. In order to make the currency work, and since there is no central point of validation, all transactions are rendered public in order for each node to know what is the balance of a wallet at any time and which transactions have been performed by the wallet owner.

To receive and/or send virtual money a user has transaction address(es). So, as soon as a transaction address owner has been identified all transactions made by that person with that transaction address are known by the whole network. Obviously, to remain anonymous users tend to change transaction address frequently. Digital currencies are also highly volatile, so between the times a person injects money into the system and another individual cashes it out, the loss might be quite significant.

However, it seems that criminals find this type of currency extremely practical/attractive and are using it more and more. For instance, the take down of the underground criminal marketplace SilkRoad led to the seizure of 175.000 Bitcoins (valued $33 million at the time) by the FBI. In May 2013, the take down of Liberty Reserve, the oldest and largest digital currency service was proven to have benefited largely criminal activities by providing money laundering to an amount of 4.4 billon € ($6 billon).

Another advantage for terrorists is the possibility of switching between virtual currencies (such as Litecoin, Peercoin or Namecoin to name a few others) in order to better cover their tracks. The task of investigating and tracking transactions is becoming complex since today there are already around 70 crypto currencies (Coinmarketcap.com).

This type of currency is so attractive that criminals started to develop malware and botnets that are scanning target's computers for wallets in order to steal its content and also to use their targets' processing power to "mine" (namely generate) digital currency.

Despite those drawbacks, crypto currency will certainly be attractive to terrorist networks to transfer large amounts of money from one party to another whilst keeping a low profile. There are multiple ways of cashing-in (from real-to-virtual) and they can be done anonymously. For instance by using Western Union, MoneyGram via a platform like CoinMama (coinmarketcap.com) or by directly purchasing virtual money from person-to-person in a proximity area, for instance on LocalBitoins.com.

Similar to cashing-out, Localbitcoins.com also sell virtual money to a physical person directly in exchange of real money. It is the easiest way but not very convenient for large amounts. An alternative is to use a one-shot mule(s) to cash-out money from an official exchange such as VirCurEx. Either way, crypto currencies are opening new ground for criminals and terrorists to cash-out legal tender anonymously.

Lastly, undoubtedly after the Edward Snowden revelations (2013) and PRISM, it is very likely that the systems mentioned above will seek to evolve and implement even more privacy, and that in turn will obviously benefit its users—some of who are criminals and terrorist.

As a conclusion, crypto currencies will be very attractive to terrorist organizations when it will reach a combination of high anonymity or low traceability (to prevent identification of transaction senders/receivers), currency stability (to minimize the risk of loss of money invested into the crypto currency) and flexibility (variety of options to cash in/out the crypto currency into real money).

DARKNET

In the early 2000, some developments have seen emerging alternate networks running in parallel to the Internet. The original purpose of these was to help people under oppressive regimes and without free-speech to be able to communicate—giving them increased anonymity and the ability to bypass their national surveillance.

Such networks provide traffic anonymization between a client and a server but also permit to develop/host Hidden Services such as web services, file exchange, blogging, chatting hidden from the Internet. Consequently such an opportunity has attracted not only oppressed people but also criminals and terrorist that found through those networks a new way of exchanging information, and spreading knowledge, etc.

Today there are two main anonymous network: TOR (The Onion Router) the oldest, and I2P. Unlike social networks and forums/blogs where terrorist groups use to advertise, claim attack responsibilities and recruit on the Internet, the darknet networks are used to provide specific content such as videos and training materials that can be found on TOR Hidden Services.

3D PRINTING

Though not a direct use of the Internet, 3D printing is becoming available to the wider public. This technology has already been proven to produce weapons such as knives and guns. The Internet in these instances is generally used to find virtual objects or 3D blueprints. Singular or multiple objects can be created. Though the weapons created are quite primitive, the advantage is that they are undetectable through current airport security check controls. For instance an Israeli reporter made a test by printing a gun and went successfully through the security of the Knesset and was able to pull it out in front of the prime minister (Egozi, 2013).

In 2013, Police found gun parts while searching houses (DeZeen Magazine, 2013). It can be expected in the near future that there will be a steep progression in the quality and possibilities of 3D printing as well as the multiplication of available blueprints. Already, some websites are providing search engines and/or torrent search for 3D blueprints. For instance, DEFCAD, a website dedicated to hosting blueprint designs has clearly decided to restrict designs that can produce harmful products like guns. Though this website has been formally asked by the Department of State Office of Defense Trade Controls to withdraw those blueprints, it is already too late as the blueprints in question where downloaded thousands of time during the time frame it was available. And inevitably, those blueprints can now been found on peer-to-peer networks and on The Pirate Bay.

FULL VPN

As communication and exchange between members of a terrorist cell or organization is crucial, some existing devices can be leveraged to better enforce anonymity. For instance by having a full VPN service across the members and having all communications going through this VPN central point.

Nowadays devices such as NAS (Network Attached Storage) are now providing a number of additional services which are easy to install on top of providing storage. We can imagine having such a NAS installed in a safe or unsuspected location or in a nursing place with a broadband ADSL access. If sufficient trust is placed by a terrorist organization on the NAS device, this device can be configured to enable VPN only communications, and through this channel provide additional dedicated VoIP (Voice over IP) telephony, email servers, web server, video server, file sharing/storage, any other kind of application needed by the cell and/or group to function and prepare an attack.

This has the advantage of being accessible not only by laptops and workstations but also by smartphones that are all now supporting VPN functionalities. This allows the cell/group members to use the different services without having to actually do a real phone call or exchange of information outside the VPN and thus they remain undetectable.

From this perspective, it is quite difficult to identify that a particular VPN connection is used by a terrorist group/cell. In a case where it is identified, it would then be difficult to access the content of the exchange over the encryption implementation via electronic surveillance. Lastly, if the end-points are used solely for VPN communications, it adds a difficulty in identifying the people who are connecting to the NAS.

Unless, one or several of those members make some mistakes that can lead to identify them via electronic surveillance; Law Enforcement have to use more traditional investigation methods to identify the terrorist group.

CONCLUSION

As of today and seen in this chapter, terrorist organizations use the Internet mainly for spreading their ideas and communicating. However, as technology develops, the availability of a variety of offerings in the underground market, and the decreasing skills required to perform cyber-attacks will certainly attract those groups to leverage their traditional attacks into cyber ones.

We have seen that a CyberTerrorist-like attack is already possible but not yet in the reach of terrorist organizations which remains at the level of state-sponsored teams or capabilities. Though still very expansive and requiring a lot of expertise and resources, this will undoubtedly be in the reach of terrorists in a few years.

Also seen in this chapter, criminals are early adopters of new technologies not only to exploit those technologies to their advantages but also to keep ahead of law enforcement and regulations. Nevertheless, terrorist groups are more careful and will rather seek proven technologies or mimic existing one by developing their own.

Lastly, terrorist groups might not be the first in the reach of CyberTerrorist-like attack but rather extremism or activism (including Hacktivism) that are more inclined to use readily available resources in the underground market such as Crime-as-a-Service and Hacker-for-hire that can be purchased and coordinated to perform such attacks.

REFERENCES

http://coinmarketcap.com/ (accessed 20.02.14).

DeZeen Magazine, 2013. '3D-Printer gun parts' seized by police in Manchester. DeZeen Magazine, [online] http://www.dezeen.com/2013/10/25/3d-printed-gun-parts-seized-by-police-in-manchester/ (accessed 20.02.14).

Egozi, A., 2013. The 3D printer aviation security headache. Flightglobal. 5 August 2013. [online], http://www.flightglobal.com/blogs/ariel-view/2013/08/the-3-d-printer-aviation-security-headache/ (accessed 20.02.14).

Europa, E.U., 2010. The EU-US TFTP Agreement: main elements. European Commission MEMO/13/1060 27/11/2013, [online] http://europa.eu/rapid/press-release_MEMO-13-1060_en.htm (accessed 20.02.2014).

Leapman, B., 2007. Second Life World may be Haven for Terrorists. Telegraph 13 May. [online], http://www.telegraph.co.uk/news/uknews/1551423/Second-Life-world-may-be-haven-for-terrorists.html (accessed 20.02.14).

Levine, A., 2012. A social network for terrorists. CNN Security Clearance. http://security.blogs.cnn.com/2012/04/05/faqebook-dreams-of-a-jihadi-social-network/ (accessed 20.02.14).

Weimann, G., 2008. WWW.Al-Qaeda: the reliance of al-Qaeda on the internet. In: Responses to Cyber Terrorism (Edited the Centre of Excellence Defense Against Terrorism, The NATO Science for Peace and Security Program). IOS Press. 133, Amsterdam, pp. 61–69.

ICT as a protection tool against child exploitation

11

Mohammed Dastbaz, Edward Halpin

INTRODUCTION

Albert Einstein is quoted as saying: "It has become appallingly obvious that our technology has exceeded our humanity." Indeed 2013 has been a year of significant revelations about the dominance of Information Communication Technologies in our lives. The dominance of mobile communication technologies, the 24/7 constantly connected lives we live in, and the shifting patterns of how we socialize, shop, learn, entertain, communicate or indeed how we diet and are ever more conscious about our health and wellbeing, points to what some would like to term the "third industrial revolution" (Rifkin, 2011).

The phenomenal advance of technology has meant concepts such as privacy and private information, for those billions of people who have ventured into the web of technology is nothing but a mirage. Revelations about security agencies around the world monitoring every digital move we make (from text messaging to our tweets, Facebook conversations and even our shopping patterns) has confirmed that as individuals we have no right, and indeed very little if any protection, against these unwanted and unwarranted intrusions. The Guardian (16 January 2014) reported that: "The National Security Agency has collected almost 200 million text messages a day from across the globe, using them to extract data including location, contact networks and credit card details, according to top-secret documents...."

Another growing concern in recent years has been issues around children's safety on the global digital network. From "Cyber bullying" to children being exposed to violence and pornography, to the "net" being used as a channel for trafficking children and other criminal activities, there is growing concern and challenges around how we can provide a safe digital environment for children.

A report published by "Childhood Wellbeing Research Centre" in UK in 2011 stated that: "Ninety-nine percent of children 12-15 use the internet as 93% of 8-11 years old and 75% of 5-7 years old" (Munro, 2011).

The report further highlights that a US survey reported 42% of young people age 10-17 being exposed to on-line pornography in a one-year period and 66% of this was unwanted.

In a report by "E-Crime," The House of Commons Home Affair Committee we read: "We are deeply concerned that it is still too easy for people to access inappropriate online content, particularly indecent images of children... There is no excuse for complacency. We urge those responsible to take stronger action to remove such content. We reiterate our recommendation that the Government should draw up a mandatory code of conduct with internet companies to remove material which breaches acceptable behavioural standards... [it is] important that children learn about staying safe online as it is that they learn about crossing the road safely" (E-Crime House of Commons, 2013).

While there is much to do to develop the legal framework around what can be blocked, or not, and to put the necessary technologies in place, the Web itself is rapidly developing and new technological challenges emerge. Time magazine (November 2013) produced a special report about what has been termed as the "Deep Web." Like the story of the Internet the story of the "Deep Web" is also associated with the US military and research done by scientist associated with the US Naval Research Laboratory aimed at "Hiding Routing Information." The report states that what was being developed: "laid out the technical features of a system whereby users could access the Internet without divulging their identities to any Web server or routers they might interact with along the way."

The "Deep Web" as the report worryingly suggests is where organized crime or terror networks work with masked identities and it is also where drugs, false passports, sophisticated SPAM, child prosopography and other criminal activities are organized with untraceable currency like "Bitcoin" (also see Chapter 9).

So given the complexity of the legal frame work and the ever increasing technical challenges what are the key issues that we need to tackle not only to provide a safer digital world for the children but also use the technology itself to help us develop the solutions.

KEY ISSUES AND CHALLENGES

The key issues and challenges facing governments, child care organizations and parents alike can be broadly categorized into the following:

- Information and awareness about the issues
- Legal framework and difficulties dealing with cross border issues and globally agreed methods of working
- Technical challenges (information flow, access and processing)

It is perhaps worth considering what the overarching legal framework, applied to all countries, provides for when considering children, in relation to these key issues. The United Nations Conventions on the Rights of the Child (CRC) (UN, 1989), amongst other clauses provides the following:

- Article 3—on the best interests of the child—states that in all circumstances concerning the child, they should be the primary focus, whether this is within public or private institutions, legal or administrative settings. In each and every circumstance, in each and every decision affecting the child, the various possible solutions must be considered and due weight given to the child's best interests. "Best interests of the child" means that the legislative bodies must consider whether laws being adopted or amended will benefit children in the best possible way.

- Article 16 (Right to privacy): Children have a right to privacy. The law should protect them from attacks against their way of life, their good name, their families and their homes. 5 Article 17 (Access to information; mass media): Children have the right to get information that is important to their health and well-being. Governments should encourage mass media—radio, television, newspapers and internet content sources—to provide information that children can understand and to not promote materials that could harm children. Mass media should particularly be encouraged to supply information in languages that minority and indigenous children can understand. Children should also have access to children's books.

Hick and Halpin (2001), in considering the issue of children, child rights, and the advances of "Child Rights and the Internet" make the point that rights are balanced and not absolute and that technological advances will continue bringing the same need to review and reflect change to protect children and ensure that they benefit from technology.

INFORMATION AWARENESS AND BETTER EDUCATION

The extant literature points to the fact that lack of awareness and useful information around the risks involved as well as privacy and the implications of our behavior quite often leads to increased risk specially when it comes to children and teenagers. In a research carried out by Innocenti Research Centre (IRC) and published by UNICEF titled: "Child Safety Online Global challenges and strategies," in 2011 serious concerns are raised about lack of understanding of issues and risk associated with children using the Internet and making information about themselves so publically available. The report goes on to state:

> *Concern is often expressed among adults about the risks associated with posting information and images online. Hence, much research starts from the premise that posting information is in itself risk-taking behaviour. Young people are indeed posting information that adults may find disturbing. A wealth of evidence from across the globe shows that many young people, particularly in the age range of 12 to 16 years, are placing highly personal information online. In Brazil, for example, surveys indicate that 46 per cent of children and adolescents consider it normal to regularly publish personal photos online, while a study in Bahrain indicates that children commonly place personal information online, with little understanding of the concept of privacy.*

The report further notes that:

In addition, significant numbers of teenagers are uploading visual representations of themselves that are sexual in tone. This is sometimes in response to grooming that involves encouragement to place such images online, which may be followed by blackmail or threats of exposure to coerce teenagers to upload increasing numbers of explicit images. But in other cases, the initial placement is unsolicited, and may encourage and attract potentially abusive predators.

Clearly while the reach and use of social network grows and posting highly personalized information is viewed as "normal" there needs to be much better education as well as a more responsible social network protocols governing children use.

GOVERNMENT RESPONSIBILITIES AND LEGAL FRAMEWORK

Organization for Economic Co-operation and Development (OECD), in a report published in May 2011, acknowledges that the legal and policy framework for protecting children in the global digital network is extremely hazardous and complex. The complex policy challenges include: how to mitigate risks without reducing the opportunities and benefits for children online; how to prevent risks while preserving fundamental values for all Internet users; how to ensure that policies are proportionate to the problem and do not unsettle the framework conditions that have enabled the Internet economy to flourish?

Furthermore, governments have tended to tackle online-related sexual exploitation and abuse with an emphasis on building the "architecture" to protect or rescue children—establishing legislation, pursuing and prosecuting abusers, raising awareness, reducing access to harm and supporting children to recover from abuse or exploitation. These are essential components of a protection response.

It is also worth noting that despite various efforts we are far from a globally agreed set of guidelines and legal framework that protects children from serious risks they face on-line. Clearly this is a serious gap exploited by criminals and those who have vested interest in using the current "freedoms" for personal monitory benefit.

TECHNICAL ISSUES AND CHALLENGES
A CASE STUDY ON USE OF TECHNOLOGY AND PROPOSED METHODOLOGY

In a research conducted by Lannon and Halpin (2013), to investigate the development and delivery of a Missing Child Alert (MCA) program, an initiative instigated and led by Plan International (referred to as Plan) in 2012, the feasibility of developing a technology-enabled system that would act as a digital alert system providing support for relevant government and nongovernment agencies dealing with Child Trafficking in South East Asia was explored (Lannon and Halpin, 2013).

One of the key issues and challenges for the research was how we classify missing children. Children go missing for many reasons. In South Asia, many are abducted and put into forced labor. Others are persuaded to leave home by somebody they know, and are subsequently exploited in the sex trade or sold to work as domestic help. Some simply run away from home, or are forced to leave because of difficult circumstances such as domestic violence or the death of a parent.

The issue of missing children is also linked to, although not limited to, child trafficking. This is a highly secretive and clandestine trade, with root causes that are varied and often complex. Poverty is a major contributor but the phenomenon is also linked to a range of other "push" (supply side) and "pull" (demand side) factors. The push factors include poor socio-economic conditions; structural discrimination based on class, caste and gender; domestic violence; migration; illiteracy; natural disasters such as floods; and enhanced vulnerability due to lack of awareness. The pull factors include the effects of the free market economy, and in particular economic reforms that generate a demand for cheap labor; urbanization; and a demand for young girls for sexual exploitation and marriage. Trafficking is a complex phenomenon, but many of the children end up in the leisure industry that could include pornography, with an international market via technology.

A UNICEF report in 2008 noted that there is a lack of synergy and coordination between and among the action plans and the many actors involved in anti-trafficking initiatives in the region, including governments, UN agencies and NGOs. According to the report the diversity of their mandates and approaches makes coordination at national and international levels a challenge.

Attempts to address cross-border child trafficking have proved to be particularly problematic because of a lack of common definitions and understandings, and the existence of different perspectives on the issue. For a start there is no commonly agreed definition of trafficking (UNODC, 2011). Furthermore, the definition of a "child" can vary as has been noted already. This has an impact on how the police, courts and other stakeholders address a child's rights, needs, vulnerability and decision making.

Child trafficking is often seen in the context of labor or sexual exploitation, with the latter focusing primarily on women and girls, but increasingly can include boys. In some cases it is approached as a migration issue or as a sub-category of human trafficking. Furthermore, authorities often see it as a law enforcement issue, and their responses are thus primarily focused on criminal prosecution and tighter border controls.

Worldwide, the most widely accepted definition of trafficking is the one provided by the UN Protocol on Trafficking (Palermo Protocol). It defines "trafficking in persons" as

> *the recruitment, transportation, transfer, harbouring or receipt of persons, by means of the threat or use of force or other forms of coercion, of abduction, of fraud, of deception, of the abuse of power or of a position of vulnerability or of the giving or receiving of payments or benefits to achieve the consent of a person having control over another person, for the purpose of exploitation.*

As the UNODC (2011) report notes, domestic laws in the South Asia region lack a shared understanding of trafficking. The most commonly applied definition is the one adopted by the SAARC Trafficking Convention which, as was noted already, is limited to trafficking for sexual exploitation. Nonetheless, it is important to have a common understanding between governments and other MCA stakeholders in order to ensure the effectiveness of cooperation efforts and the development of future policy.

A "missing child" is generally understood to be a person under the age of 18 years whose whereabouts are unknown. This definition encapsulates a range of sub-categories of missing children. The International Centre for Missing & Exploited Children (ICMEC) has identified a number of these, including but not limited to: "Endangered Runaway," "Family Abduction," "Non-family Abduction," Lost, Injured, or otherwise missing and "Abandoned or Unaccompanied Minor."

The ICMEC highlight the importance of understanding what is meant by a missing child:

A common definition of a 'missing child' with clear categories facilitates coordination and communication across jurisdictions and ensures that policies and programs comprehensively address all aspects of missing children's issues. Although all missing child cases should receive immediate attention, investigative procedures following the initial report may vary based on the case circumstances.

Already a large body of knowledge exists in relation to the recording and alerting of missing children. At a regional level there are a myriad of formats in use to describing a missing child. Getting agreement on a shared, comprehensive data model, with coded typologies to describe the status of a missing child, the physical identification markings on him or her, etc. will ensure coherence and consistency of information and will facilitate faster searching across systems. This data model should also support the use of noncoded data, and in particular photographic and biometric data.

The use of coded typologies will ensure that the recording of missing and found children is consistent across all languages, and that matches can be found between records entered in different languages.

The MCA program should take a proactive role in efforts to develop coded typologies or thesauri to support consistent and standard reporting of missing children in South Asia, in line with child protection norms and best practice. This should be done in collaboration with ICMEC who are already working in a number of related research areas.

OBJECTIVITY, CONSISTENCY AND CREDIBILITY

Furthermore, in order to produce meaningful statistics a controlled vocabulary is a fundamental requirement. It transforms the data relating to child trafficking cases into a countable set of categories without discarding important information and without misrepresenting the collected information.

The development of a standard data model should be the basis for the design of any technologically enabled information systems implemented as part of the MCA initiative.

A SYSTEMS APPROACH TO CHILD PROTECTION

A system is a collection of components or parts organized around a common purpose or goal. As the MCA's goal is improved protection of children from trafficking and exploitation it can be described as a child protection system. System components can be best understood in the context of relationships with each other rather than in isolation. Several key elements of systems apply to child protection systems (Wulczyn et al., 2010). These include the following:

- Systems exist within other larger systems, in a nested structure. Children are embedded in families or kin, which live in communities, which exist within a wider societal system.
- Given the nested nature of systems, attention needs to be paid to coordinating the interaction of related systems so that their work is mutually reinforcing.
- Systems accomplish their work through a specific set of structures and capacities, the characteristics of which are determined by the context in which the system operates. In the case of cross-border child trafficking, the context varies between countries, government departments and in some cases even interventions.
- Changes to any system can potentially change the context, while changes to the context will change the system.
- Well-functioning systems pay particular attention to nurturing and sustaining acts of cooperation, coordination and collaboration among all levels of stakeholders.
- Systems achieve their desired outcomes when they design, implement, and sustain an effective and efficient process of care in which stakeholders are held accountable for both their individual performance and the performance of the overall system.
- Effective governance structures in any system must be flexible and robust in order to cope with uncertainty, change, and diversity.

The adoption of a systems approach means that the challenges presented by the MCA initiative are addressed holistically. The roles and assets of all the key actors, including governments, NGOs, community structures, families and caregivers, technology providers, and most importantly children themselves, are all taken into consideration.

CHILD-CENTERED INFORMATION FLOWS

A holistic approach to child protection dictates that a cross-border child Information Management and Child Protection trafficking response system should support the full range of activities triggered by the reporting of a missing child who is presumed to have been trafficked. Taking an event-based approach favored by human rights organizations, a series of high level events can be identified. These include but are not limited to: child is reported as missing; child is recovered; child's body has been found; child is referred for rehabilitation; child is safely integrated into a new environment in the country in which (s) he was rescued; repatriation process has been initiated; repatriation has been completed/process of reintegration has be set in train; and child is safely reintegrated into their family and community.

Each event triggers a set of child-centered actions and information flows that can be configured based on the details of the event and the context in which the event is occurring. Figure 11.1 describes the information flow that should take place in the source country for the first event in the process, which is that a child is reported as missing. It shows a series of six fundamental actions that should occur as follows:

> Intake of initial missing child report. This occurs when a family member approaches the police or other agency to report a missing child.

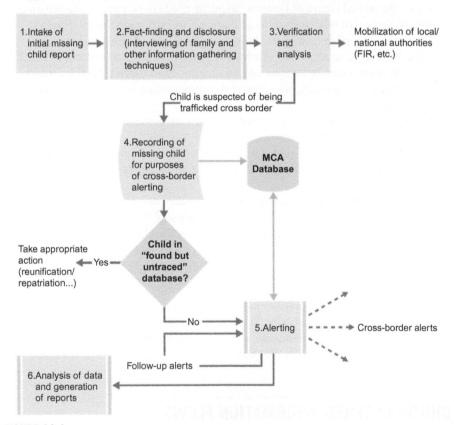

FIGURE 11.1

Flowchart showing information flows for reported missing child.

The analysis and verification of information relating to a missing child should be done by police in the source country, whereas the recording of a trafficked child, the sending of alert messages, and the subsequent analysis of data and generation of periodic reports can be handled by a regional cross-border response system. The processes of reporting and alerting could be implemented as one technological system with distinct functionality and user roles.

The functionality and user interfaces of the systems for reporting, recording and alerting must be done through discussion with key stakeholders, particularly the police who will record and initiate alerts for a missing child. While this will inevitably slow down the deployment process, failure to do so may result in a system that is not accepted by the authorities upon whom its success depends.

This means that State support for the concept and their involvement from the start are essential as well as NGOs along the likely transit routes. It must also schedule follow-up alerts if the child has not been found/rescued after a period of time. The configuration of the alerting schedule is a vital component of the system which requires expert understanding of.

One point that requires further discussion with stakeholders is the question of alerting for children who are reported as missing and may have been trafficked or abducted internally within the country. These cases could be handled by internal police systems. Alternatively, the cross-border response system could be designed to support responses to internal trafficking.

The proposed CBCT (Centralized Cross-Border Child Traffic) response system should limit its activities to those that require cross-border communication and collaboration. This means it should support information flows relating to trafficked children that may have been taken across a border, found children whose identity is not known (resulting in a search of existing databases, including the CBCT response database), and rescued children whose needs may be best addressed through repatriation and reunification. How the traffickers behave and their routes. Furthermore, it will benefit from a proactive approach whereby alert recipients are identified along with the most appropriate means of alerting them. A controlled database of alert recipients should be managed in support of this work.

It is widely accepted that the first hours after a child has been taken to provide the best opportunities for rescue. It is therefore vital that alert notifications are sent as quickly as possible to the authorities and NGOs along the likely trafficking route taken. However, the advantage of immediate alerting must be balanced with the need to ensure the veracity of a missing child report. Even more importantly, a decision to send an alert notification needs to take into account the safety, well-being, and dignity of the child. A basic principle adopted in missing child alert systems around the world is that there must be sufficient information for the recipients to be able to respond to an alert. While much of the alerting can be automated, the preceding activities can be assisted by technology but are primarily human-based. The decision-making process leading to the issuing of an alert must be clearly defined and understood. Many MCA stakeholders are of the view that a system to coordinate all activities relating to the rescue, rehabilitation, repatriation, and reintegration of

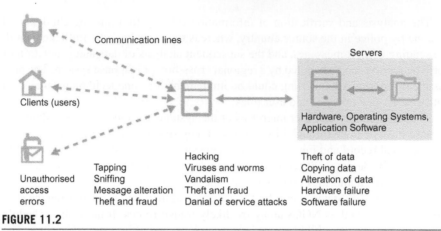

FIGURE 11.2

Security challenges and vulnerabilities in a typical MCA network.

victims of cross-border trafficking would be helpful. The research goes on to propose that the MCA would have a role in actively supporting prosecution. While these are all desirable, it is overly ambitious and unnecessary to try to coordinate all these activities in one technological system or database. Instead, in-country (national) systems need to be strengthened to address areas like child welfare and justice. Each case recorded in the cross-border response system should remain open until the child's rights and needs are known to have been fully met. This can take many years and may span a series of interventions including shelter home (Figure 11.2).

The report draws a conclusion that indicates the requirement for a technological solution, and provides a strategy for delivering this, but reiterates the complex social, economic, legal, and political setting in which such technology needs to, and will be, deployed.

This recognition leads us back to the three key issues identified at the outset.

- Information and awareness about the issues
- Legal framework and difficulties dealing with cross border issues and globally agreed methods of working
- Technical challenges (information flow, access and processing)

CBCT RESPONSE SYSTEM

One of the options considered by the research was a centralized CBCT response system dedicated to addressing the needs of children who have been trafficked across a border. For this, a regional database, with effective national alerting mechanisms, needs to be put in place. Members of the public, community centers, etc., can report missing children; these are initially investigated by the police in the source country, who can then activate in-country and cross-border alert requests through the centralized regional system, on the basis of their analysis of a missing child report. This model focuses specifically on cross-border trafficking of children.

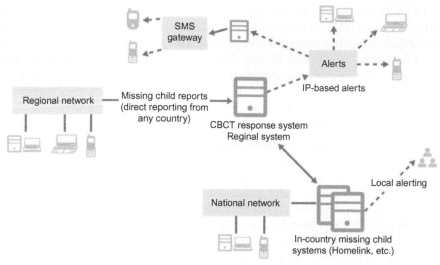

FIGURE 11.3

MCA centralized model architecture.

The MCA program would implement and operationalize a regional system to address the issue is a coordinated manner. This regional CBCT response system would manage each child's case from initial logging through to repatriation of a rescued child (Figure 11.3).

It is envisaged that this regional system would work as follows:

1. A secure, centralized server records missing (trafficked) children. Found children could also be recorded in this system. Alternatively, found children could be recorded in in-country systems which would be checked on an as-needed basis by the CBCT response system.
2. Web browser interfaces for the initial reporting, alert activation and management (by the police or other authorized agency), and the provision of updates relating to the initial search and to the status of the missing child. Even though a missing child may be reported via the web interface it must be reviewed (by the police) before it is confirmed and accepted as a valid record of a missing child.
3. Child records remain open on the system until such time as the child has been successfully repatriated (by which time the child may be over 18).
4. A database of alert recipients is maintained by a system coordinator, and for each missing child alert a schedule of alerts may be created by an authorized agent (for example, certain police officers who have the authority to issue an alert). In the first phase at least, alerting is IP-based, and may consist of:
   a. email notifications;
   b. RSS news feeds;
   c. XML-based data feeds to partner systems. These may include broadcast media outlets, national/local missing persons systems, and networks such as the police and railway police in India.

IP-based alerting can be done by the centralized regional system hosted in any part of the world. However, if alerting is done using voice or SMS messaging then it should be initiated in-country for cost reasons. This would necessitate either (a) the mirroring of the cross-border alerting database in each of the three countries, with notifications sent from the locally mirrored sites; or (b) local alerting done by local agents or nodes in each of the countries. These local alerting nodes could receive the alert information by email, etc., and respond by sending an SMS broadcast using their own gateway software or by making phone calls.

5. Links will be provided to national child tracking systems in Nepal and Bangladesh (if/when these exist), as well as to other partner systems such as Homelink and the AP-NIC missing persons system) so that:
   a. Data can be automatically transferred from these to the regional system if a missing child has already been recorded.
   b. National/local partner databases can be searched for a reported missing child. Missing child searches could be implemented from/to in-country systems (such as Homelink, for example).

The MCA program needs to actively encourage potential partners to receive and act on the alerts, starting with the proposed pilot project districts. It is important to recognize that the regional system is not replacing the case management systems used by the police, child welfare service providers, helplines, shelter homes or any of the other stakeholders, nor is it replacing the national missing child/persons systems. It is a separate system which focuses on cross-border child trafficking, and in particular on the coordination of rescue and repatriation. A typical scenario for when a child is reported missing is presented in Figure 11.4.

The advantages of the centralized option are:

1. It is not dependent on the implementation of national missing child systems. The intervention still needs the support and cooperation of the authorities to succeed, but the technological system can be deployed independently of them. This is likely to result in faster implementation as well as better coordination of activities across the three countries.
2. Since the alert notifications are controlled centrally, the response to a missing child report can be coordinated and have a broad reach. It is possible, for example, to configure a notifications database to send alerts according to a predetermined schedule (for example, immediately to BGB in Bangladesh, to railway police and others along known transit routes in India after a period of number of hours, and later to trusted organizations operating in the likely destination cities).
3. As with Option 1, this may require the drafting and implementation of SOPs to handle the information flows and collaboration between governments. However, the information exchange is more likely to succeed if it is being coordinated at regional level.
4. The system will, over time, provide accurate data in relation to cross-border trafficking of children.

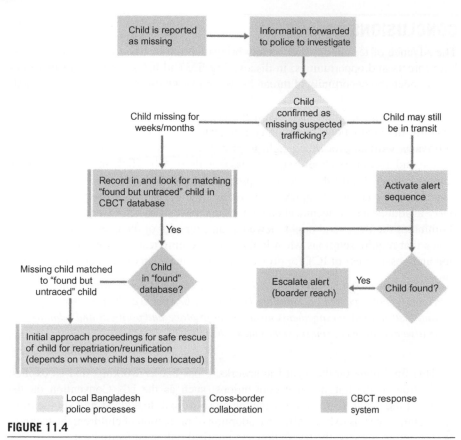

FIGURE 11.4

Centralized Option—High-Level Scenario: Child is reported as missing.

Some of the risks/disadvantages are:

1. Without in-country missing child systems or some mechanisms for effective, coordinated responses by the authorities in Nepal and Bangladesh, and without a national system in India, this model is limited in its capacity to distribute alerts amongst the police, border guards, railway police, etc.
2. The management and operation of the CBCT response system requires significant resources which the MCA program would have to provide.
3. There is a risk that the system is seen as a private initiative, which may inhibit the engagement by governments and participation by the State authorities.
4. The costs associated with the implementation of the regional CBCT response system are primarily dependent on the technological components used to build it, and where/how it is hosted. Taking the same approach as was taken for the national missing child tracking systems, it is expected that the TCO is in the order of $400,000 over the three years of the pilot phase.

CONCLUSIONS

The advance of technology and society brings with it, as has always been the case, both threats and opportunities; in discovering fire and using it to benefit there has always been the opportunity of threat, by use or malign use. We can extend this analogy to technology today, but there is clearly a need to address the ubiquity of access and mechanisms of application that technology provides. The United Nations, as a voice for the international community, articulates the rights to both information and to privacy, with an over-riding right to protection. This includes the right to information and awareness about issues, an issue addressed by Hick and Halpin (2001), amongst others. Whilst the case study presented earlier illustrates the technical challenges, and the equally complex social issues, that need to be addressed simultaneously in addressing the technical challenges that have to be addressed; the case study illuminates the issues and might viewed as an exemplar of the many other technical issues that require solutions when looking at emerging technologies child exploitation and possible use of ICT for protection. The conclusion of the study notes that

> *Technological systems to address the issue of cross-border trafficking must be viewed as only part of the solution. For them to be effective, the necessary legal and institutional arrangements must be put in place and political and administrative arrangements must exist to make them work.*
>
> **(Lannon and Halpin, 2013)**

This final point on the legal frameworks, cross-border working, and an explicit application of the international conventions, such as the UN Convention on the Rights of the Child, seem at this stage the most difficult to address and yet the most important, if there is to be an effective adoption of protection of children; the technology can offer answers, the legislation and political will must facilitate it.

REFERENCES

E-Crime, 2013. House of Commons Home Affair Committee, July 2013..

Hick, S., Halpin, E., 2001. Children's rights and the Internet. Ann. Am. Acad. Polit. Social Sci. 56–70, May.

Lannon, J., Halpin, E., 2013. Responding to Cross-Border Trafficking in South Asia: An Analysis of the Feasibility of a Technologically Enabled Missing Children Alert System. Plan International, Bangkok.

Munro, E.R., 2011. The Protection of Children On-line: A Brief Scoping Review to Identify Vulnerable Groups. Childhood Wellbeing Research Centre, Bedford Way, London, August 2011.

OECD—Directorate for Science, Technology and Industry—Committee for Information, Computer and Communications Policy, 2011. The Protection of Children Online—Risks Faced By Children Online and Policies to Protect Them, May 2011.

Rifkin, J., 2011. The Third Industrial Revolution; How Lateral Power is Transforming Energy, the Economy, and the World. Palgrave Macmillan, USA.

UN, Convention on the Rights of the Child, 1989.

UNICEF Innocenti Research Centre, 2008. South Asia in Action: Preventing and Responding to Child Trafficking. UNICEF.

UNICEF Innocenti Research Centre, 2011. Child Safety Online Global Challenges and Strategies. UNICEF.

Wulczyn, F., Daro, D., Fluke, J., Feldman, S., Glodek, C., Lifanda, K., 2010. Adapting a Systems Approach to Child Protection: Key Concepts and Considerations. UNICEF, New York.

Cybercrime classification and characteristics

12

Hamid Jahankhani, Ameer Al-Nemrat, Amin Hosseinian-Far

INTRODUCTION

The new features of crime brought about as a result of cyberspace have become known as cybercrime.

Cybercrime is growing and current technical models to tackle cybercrime are inefficient in stemming the increase in cybercrime. This serves to indicate that further preventive strategies are required in order to reduce cybercrime. Just as it is important to understand the characteristics of the criminals in order to understand the motivations behind the crime and subsequently develop and deploy crime prevention strategies, it is also important to understand victims, i.e., the characteristics of the users of computer systems in order to understand the way these users fall victim to cybercrime.

The term "cybercrime" has been used to describe a number of different concepts of varying levels of specificity. Occasionally, and at its absolute broadest, the term has been used to refer to any type of illegal activities which results in a pecuniary loss. This includes violent crimes against a person or their property such as armed robbery, vandalism, or blackmail. At its next broadest, the term has been used to refer only to nonviolent crimes that result in a pecuniary loss. This would include crimes where a financial loss was an unintended consequence of the perpetrator's actions, or where there was no intent by the perpetrator to realize a financial gain for himself or a related party. For example, when a perpetrator hacks into a bank's computer and either accidentally or intentionally deletes an unrelated depositor's account records.

Wall (2007) argues that in order to define cybercrime, we need to understand the impact of information and communication technologies on our society and how they have transformed our world. Cyberspace creates new opportunities for criminals to commit crimes through its unique features. These features are viewed by Wall (2005) as "transformative keys," and are as follows:

1. "Globalization," which provides offenders with new opportunities to exceed conventional boundaries.
2. "Distributed networks," which generate new opportunities for victimization.
3. "Synopticism and panopticism," which empower surveillance capability on victims remotely.
4. "Data trails," which create new opportunities for criminal to commit identity theft.

To fully grasp how the Internet generates new opportunities for criminals to commit new Cybercrimes, Wall (2005) has compiled a matrix of cybercrimes which illustrate the different levels of opportunity each type of crime enables.

In Table 12.1, Wall (2005) illustrates the impact of the Internet on criminal opportunity and criminal behaviour. There are three levels of the Internet's impact upon criminal opportunity, as shown on the Y-axis of the table.

Firstly, the Internet has created *more opportunities for traditional crime,* such as phreaking, chipping, fraud, and stalking. These types of crime already existed in the physical or "real" world, but the Internet has enabled an increase in the rate and prevalence of these crimes. Traditional crime gangs are using the Internet not only for communication but also as a tool to commit "classic" crimes, such as fraud and money laundering, more efficiently and with fewer risks. Secondly, the Internet's impact has enabled *new opportunities for traditional crime,* such as cracking/hacking, viruses, large-scale fraud, online gender trade (sex), and hate speech. Hacking is the traditional documented form of committing offences against CIA (Confidentiality, Integrity, and Availability). However, recent developments include parasitic computing, whereby criminals use a series of remote computers to perform operations, including storing illegal data, such as pornographic pictures or pirated software.

Thirdly, the Internet's impact is so great it has led to *new opportunities for new types of crime* arising, such as spam, denial of service, intellectual property piracy, and e-auction scams.

As for the impact of the Internet on criminal behaviour, the table shows on the X-axis that there are four types of crime: integrity-related (harmful trespass); computer-related (acquisition theft/deception); content-related (obscenity); and content-related (violence). As Wall argues, for each type of these crimes there are three levels of harm: least; middle; and most harmful. So, for example, within the integrity-related (harmful trespass) type, phreaking and chipping is least harmful, whereas denial of service and information warfare is most harmful.

WHAT IS CYBERCRIME?

In recent years there has been much discussion concerning the nature of computer crime and how to tackle it. There is confusion over the scope of computer crime, debate over its extent and severity, and concern over where our power to defeat it lies (Jahankhani and Al-Nemrat, 2011; Rowlingston, 2007). There are many available policy documents and studies that address how the nature of war is changing with the advent of widespread computer technology.

Wall in 2005, raised questions about what we understand by the term "Cybercrime," arguing that the term itself does not actually do much more than signify the occurrence of a harmful behaviour that is somehow related to a computer, and it has no specific reference in law. Over 10 years later, this argument is still true for many countries that still have very vague concepts in their constitutions regarding cybercrime.

Table 12.1 The Matrix of Cybercrime: Level of Opportunity by Type of Crime (Wall, 2005)

	Integrity-Related (Harmful Trespass)	Computer-Related (Acquisition Theft/ Deception)	Content-Related 1 (Obscenity)	Content-Related 2 (Violence)
More opportunities for traditional crime (e.g., through communications)	Phreaking Chipping	Frauds Pyramid schemes	Trading sexual materials	Stalking Personal Harassment
New opportunities for traditional crime (e.g., organization across boundaries)	Cracking/Hacking Viruses H Activism	Multiple large-scale frauds 419 scams, Trade secret theft, ID theft	Online Gender trade Camgirl sites	General hate speech Organized pedophile rings (child abuse)
New opportunities for new types of crime	Spams (List construction and content) Denial of Service, Information Warfare, Parasitic Computing	Intellectual Property Piracy Online Gambling E-auction scams Small-impact bulk fraud	Cyber-Sex, Cyber-Pimping	Online grooming, Organized bomb talk/ Drug talk Targeted hate speech

This lack of definitional clarity is problematic as it impacts upon every facet of prevention and remediation, while, number of people and businesses affected by various types of perceived cybercrime is "growing with no signs of declining."

The Commissioner of Metropolitan Police, Sir Bernard Hogan-Howe, in his commentary published in the Evening Standard in November 2013, highlighted that, in 2012-13 there has been a 60% rise in the number of reports of cybercrime. In the same financial year cybercrime and other types of fraud cost the British economy £81 billion. *"Criminals have realised there are huge rewards to be reaped from online fraud, while the risk of getting arrested falls way below that of armed robbers, for instance"* (Hogan-Howe, 2013).

Unlike traditional crime which is committed in one geographic location, cybercrime is committed online and it is often not clearly linked to any geographic location. Therefore, a coordinated global response to the problem of cybercrime is required. This is largely due to the fact that there are a number of problems, which pose a hindrance to the effective reduction in cybercrime. Some of the main problems arise as a result of the shortcomings of the technology, legislation, and cyber criminology.

Many criminological perspectives define crime on the social, cultural and material characteristics, and view crimes as taking place at a specific geographic location. This definition of crime has allowed for the characterization of crime, and the subsequent tailoring of crime prevention, mapping and measurement methods to the specific target audience. However, this characterization cannot be carried over to cybercrime, because the environment in which cybercrime is committed cannot be pinpointed to a geographic location, or distinctive social or cultural groups. For example, traditional crimes such as child abuse and rape allow for the characterization of the attacker based on the characteristics of the crime, including determination of the social status of the attacker, geographic location within country, state, district, urban or rural residential areas, and so on. However, in the case of cybercrime, this characterization of the attacker cannot be done, because the Internet is "anti-spatial." As a result, identifying location with distinctive crime inducing characteristics is almost impossible in cybercrimes. This, in turn, serves to render the criminological perspectives based on spatial distinctions useless.

Criminology allows for the understanding of the motivations of the criminals by analyzing the social characteristics of the criminals and their spatial locations (see Chapter 9). For example, poverty may be considered to be a cause of crime if poor areas exhibit high crimes, or a high percentage of criminals are found to come from poor backgrounds. Criminology helps in understanding the reasons behind the preponderance of crimes committed by people with particular characteristics, such as the over-representation of offenders from groups of people who are socially, economically or educationally marginalized. It was further explained that the association between geographic location and social characteristics had led to the association between crime and social exclusion in mainstream criminology.

However, in the case of cybercrime, such a correspondence appears to break down. One of the most important points to consider is that access to the Internet is disproportionately low among the marginalized sections of society who were considered to be socially excluded and therefore more likely to commit a crime. Furthermore, the execution of a cybercrime requires that the criminal have a degree of skill and knowledge that is greater than the level of skills and knowledge possessed by the average computer user. It can, then, be said that cyber criminals are those who are relatively more privileged and who have access to the Internet, knowledge and skills at a level above the average person. Therefore, the relationship between social exclusion and crime that had been widely accepted in traditional crime could not be true in the case of cybercrimes, and that cyber criminals are fairly "atypical" in terms of traditional criminological expectations. Hence, the current perspectives of criminology that link marginality and social exclusion to crime have no use in explaining the motivations behind cybercrimes. Without an understanding of motives, it is difficult for law enforcement agencies and government to take effective measures to tackle cybercrime.

The UK law enforcement agencies sort any crime involving computers into one of three categories. Firstly, a computer can be the target of criminal activity, for example, when a website is the victim of a denial-of-service attack, or a laptop is stolen. Secondly, computers can act as an intermediary medium, where the computer is used as a vehicle for crime against a business or individual, for example, hacking into a website to steal documents or funds. Thirdly, it can be an intermediary facilitator, for example, when criminals use the computer for activities that are related to the crime, but are not in themselves criminal, such as planning and research. As a medium, the computer can perform as the criminal's modus operandi, and as an intermediary, computer systems act as a buffer between offenders and their victims, affecting how an offence is undertaken or executed. As a facilitator, a computer can enable communications between offenders in a globally accessible space which is near relatively instantaneous. When the computer performs as an offending medium, the offender-victim/conspirator contact must be considered, whereas when it acts as an offending facilitator, it aids the contacts between offenders. The difference between these categories is often a matter of emphasis, and it is possible for a computer to play both roles in a single given offence, as an Internet e-commerce based fraud may also involve significant online communication between offenders.

In 2001 The Council of Europe (CoE), adopted its Convention on Cybercrime Treaty, known as Budapest Convention which identifies several activities to be cybercrime offences (CoE, 2001)

- *Intentional access without right to the whole part of any computer system.*
- *Intentional interception, without right, of non-public transmissions of computer data.*
- *Intentional damage, deletions, deterioration, alteration, or suppression of computer data without right.*
- *Intentional and serious hindering of the function of a computer system by inputting, transmitting, damaging, deleting, deterioration, altering, or suppressing computer data.*
- *The production, sale, procurement for use, importation, or distribution of devices designed to commit any of the above crimes, or of passwords or similar data used to access computer systems, with the intent of committing any of the above crimes.*

On March 1st, 2006 the Additional Protocol to the Convention on Cybercrime came into force. Those States that have ratified the additional protocol are required to criminalize the dissemination of racist and xenophobic material through computer systems, as well as threats and insults motivates by racism or xenophobia.

An additional definition has utilized existing criminological theory to clarify what is meant by computer crime. Gordon et al. adapted Cohen and Felson's Life-Style Routine Activity Theory (LRAT)—which states that crime occurs when there is a suitable target, a lack of capable guardians, and a motivated offender—to determine when computer crime takes place. In their interpretation, computer crime is the result of offenders "…perceiving opportunities to invade computer systems to achieve criminal ends or use computers as instruments of crime, betting that the 'guardians' do not possess the means or knowledge to prevent or detect criminal acts" (Gordon and Ford, 2006; Jahankhani and Al-Nemrat, 2010; Wilson and Kunz, 2004).

The definition should be designed to protect, and indicate violations of, the confidentiality, integrity and availability of computer systems. Any new technology stimulates a need for a community to determine what the norms of behaviour should be for the technology, and it is important to consider how these norms should be reflected, if at all, in our laws.

WHAT ARE THE CLASSIFICATIONS AND TYPES OF CYBERCRIME?

The other approach to defining cybercrime is to develop a classification scheme that links offences with similar characteristics into appropriate groups similar to the traditional crime classifications. Several schemes have been developed over the years. There are suggestions that there are only two general categories: *active* and *passive* computer crimes. An active crime is when someone uses a computer to commit the crime, for example, when a person obtains access to a secured computer environment or telecommunications device without authorization (hacking). A passive computer crime occurs when someone uses a computer to both support and advance an illegal activity. An example is when a narcotics suspect uses a computer to track drug shipments and profits.

Literature has widely categorizes four general types of cybercrime by the computer's relationship to the crime:

- *Computer as the Target: theft of intellectual property, theft of marketing information (e.g., customer list, pricing data, or marketing plan), and blackmail based on information gained from computerized files (e.g., medical information, personal history, or sexual preference).*
- *Computer as the Instrumentality of the Crime: fraudulent use of automated teller machine (ATM) cards and accounts, theft of money from accrual, conversion, or transfer accounts, credit card fraud, fraud from computer transaction (stock transfer, sales, or billing), and telecommunications fraud.*

- *Computer Is Incidental to Other Crimes: money laundering and unlawful banking transactions, organized crime records or books, and bookmaking.*
- *Crime Associated with the Prevalence of Computers: software piracy/ counterfeiting, copyright violation of computer programs, counterfeit equipment, black market computer equipment and programs, and theft of technological equipment.*

Yar (2006), who has subdivided cybercrime into four areas of harmful activity, illustrates a range of activities and behaviors rather than focusing on specific offences. This reflects not only the various bodies of law, but also specific courses of public debate. The four categories are as follows:

Cyber-trespass: the crossing of cyber boundaries into other people's computer systems into spaces where rights of ownership or title have already been established and causing damage, e.g., hacking and virus distribution.

Cyber-deceptions and thefts: the different types of acquisitive harm that can take place within cyberspace. At one level lie the more traditional patterns of theft, such as the fraudulent use of credit cards and (cyber) cash, but there is also a particular current concern regarding the increasing potential for the raiding of online bank accounts as e-banking become more popular.

Cyber-pornography: the breaching of laws on obscenity and decency.

Cyber-violence: the violent impact of the cyber activities of others upon individual, social or political grouping. Whilst such activities do not have to have a direct manifestation, the victim nevertheless feels the violence of the act and can bear long-term psychological scars as a consequence. The activities referred here range from cyber-stalking and hate-speech, to tech-talk.

In addition to the above, Yar (2006) has added a new type of activity which is "crime against the state," describing it as encompassing those activities that breach laws which protect the integrity of the nation's infrastructure, like terrorism, espionage and disclosure of official secrets.

Gordon and Ford (2006) attempted to create a conceptual framework which law makers can use when compiling legal definitions which are meaningful from both a technical and a societal perspective. Under their scheme, they categorize cybercrime into two types:

1. The first type has the following characteristics:
   - *It is generally a singular, or discrete, event from the perspective of the victim.*
   - *It is often facilitated by the introduction of crime-ware programs such as keystroke loggers, viruses, rootkits or Trojan horses into the user's computer system.*
   - *The introductions can (but not necessarily) be facilitated by vulnerabilities.*

2. At the other end of the spectrum is the second type of cybercrime, which includes, but is not limited to, activities such as cyber stalking and harassment, blackmail, stock market manipulation, complex corporate espionage, and planning or carrying out terrorist activities online. The characteristics of this type are as follows:

  • *It is generally facilitated by programs that do not fit under the classification of crime-ware. For example, conversations may take place using IM (Instant Messaging), and clients or files may be transferred using the FTP protocol.*
  • *There are generally repeated contacts or events from the perspective of the user.*

CYBERCRIME CATEGORIES
Phishing

Is the act of attempting to trick customers into disclosing their personal security information; their credit card numbers, bank account details, or other sensitive information by masquerading as trustworthy businesses in an e-mail. Their messages may ask the recipients to "update," "validate," or "confirm" their account information.

Phishing is a two time scam, first steals a company's identity and then use it to victimize consumers by stealing their credit identities. The term Phishing (also called spoofing) comes from the fact that Internet scammers are using increasingly sophisticated lures as they "fish" for user's financial information and password data.

Phishing becomes the most commonly used social engineering attack to date due to the fact that it is quite easy to be carried out, no direct communication between hacker and victim is required (i.e., hacker does not need to phone their prey, pretending that they are a technical support staff, etc.). Sending mass-mails to thousands of potential victims increases the chance of getting someone hooked. There are usually three separate steps in order for such attacks to work, these are:

1. Setting up a mimic web site.
2. Sending out a convincingly fake e-mail, luring the users to that mimic site.
3. Getting information then redirect users to the real site.

In step 1, the hacker steals an organization's identity and creates a look-alike web site. This can easily be done by viewing the targeted site's source code, then copying all graphics and HTML lines from that real web site. Due to this tactic, it would really be very hard for even an experienced user to spot the differences. On the mimic web site, usually there will be a log-in form, prompting the user to enter secret personal data. Once the data are entered here, a server-side script will handle the submission, collecting the data and send it to the hacker, then redirect users to the real web site so everything look unsuspicious.

The hardest part of phishing attack that challenges most hackers is in the second step. This does not mean it is technically hard, but grammatically it is! In this step, the hacker will make a convincingly fake e-mail which later will be sent by a "ghost" mailing program, enabling the hacker to fake the source address of the e-mail.

The main purpose of this fake e-mail is to urge the users going to the mimic web site and entering their data that hackers wanted to capture. Commonly employed tactics are asking users to response over emergency matters such as warning that customers need to log-in immediately or their accounts could be blocked; notifying that someone just sends the user some money and they need to log in now in order to get it (this usually is an effective trap to PayPal users), etc. Inside this fake e-mail, users often find a hyperlink, which once clicked, will open the mimic web site so they can "*log in.*" As discussed before, the easiest way to quickly identify a fake e-mail is not just by looking at the address source (since it can be altered to anything) but to check English grammar in the e-mail. You may find this sounds surprising, however, 8 out of 10 scam e-mails have obvious grammar mistakes. Regardless of this, the trick still works.

In the last step, once a user has opened the mimic web site and "*log in,*" their information will be handled by a server-side script. That information will later be sent to hacker via e-mail and user will be redirected to the real web site. However, the confidentiality of user's financial data or secret password has now been breached.

Due to the recent financial crises, mergers and takeovers, many changes have taken place in the financial marketplace. These changes have encouraged scam artists to phish for customers' details.

The key points are:

- Social engineering attacks have the highest success rate
- Prevention includes educating people about the value of information and training them to protect it
- Increasing people's awareness of how social engineers operate
- Do not click on links in the e-mail message
- It appears that phishing e-mail scam has been around in one form or another since February 2004 and it seems to be still evolving, similar to the way virus writers share and evolve code.

According to the global phishing survey carried out by the Anti-Phishing working group published in 2013 (APWG, 2013)

1. *Vulnerable hosting providers are inadvertently contributing to phishing. Mass compromises led to 27% of all phishing attacks.*
2. *Phishing continues to explode in China, where the expanding middle class is using e-commerce more often.*
3. *The number of phishing targets (brands) is up, indicating that e-criminals are spending time looking for new opportunities.*
4. *Phishers continue to take advantage of inattentive or indifferent domain name registrars, registries, and subdomain resellers. The number of top-level registries is poised to quintuple over the next 2 years.*
5. *The average and median uptimes of phishing attacks are climbing.*

According to Symantec Intelligence Report (2013) Fake offerings continue to dominate Social Media attacks, while disclosed vulnerability numbers are up 17% compared to the same period in 2012 (Symantec, 2013).

SPAM

Another form of Cybercrime is spam mail, which is arguably the most profound product of the Internet's ability to place unprecedented power into the hands of a single person. Spam mail is the distribution of bulk e-mails that advertise products, services or investment schemes, which may well turn out to be fraudulent. The purpose of spam mail is to trick or con customers into believing that they are going to receive a genuine product or service, usually at a reduced price. However, the spammer asks for money or sensible security information like credit card number or other personal information before the deal occur. After disclosing their security information the customer will never hear from the spammer.

Today, spammers who spread malicious code and phishing e-mails are still looking for the best way to reach computer users by using social engineering and technical advances, however, according to a Symantec Intelligence Report (Symantec, 2012), spam levels have continued to drop to 68% of global e-mail traffic in 2012 from 89% highest in 2010.

In April 2012, political spams were back in action targeting primarily US and French population. The complex situation in Syria has also become the subject of spam e-mails too.

In 2012, USA was in second place after India for spam origination with China ranked as number 5 (Kaspersky, 2012).

HACKING

Hacking is one of the most widely analyzed and debated forms of cyber-criminal activity, and serves as an intense focus for public concerns about the threat that such activity poses to society. The clear-cut definition of hacking is "the unauthorized access and subsequent use of other people's computer systems" (Yar, 2006).

The early hackers had a love of technology and a compelling need to know how it all worked, and their goal was to push programs beyond what they were designed to do. The word hacker did not have the negative connotation as it has today.

The attacks take place in several phases such as information gathering or reconnaissance, scanning and finally entering into the target system. Information gathering involves methods of obtaining information or to open security holes. It is just like the way in which the traditional type of robbery is carried out. The robber will find out the whole information about the place that wants to rob before making attempt. Just like this the computer attacker will try to find out information about the target. Social Engineering is one such method used by an attacker to get information.

There are two main categories under which all social engineering attempts could be classified, computer or technology-based deception and human-based deception. The technology-based approach is to deceive the user into believing that is interacting with the "real" computer system (such as popup window, informing the user that the computer application has had a problem) and get the user to provide confidential information. The human approach is done through deception, by taking advantage of the victim's ignorance, and the natural human inclination to be helpful and liked.

Organized criminals have the resources to acquire the services of the necessary people. The menace of organized crime and terrorist activity grows ever more sophisticated as the ability to enter, control and destroy our electronic and security systems grows at an equivalent rate. Today, certainly, e-mail and the Internet are the most commonly used forms of communication and information sharing. Just over 2 billion people use the Internet every day. Criminal gangs "buying" thrill-seeking hackers and "script kiddies" to provide the expertise and tools, this is called cyber child labor.

CYBER HARASSMENT OR BULLYING

Cyber-harassment or bullying is the use of electronic information and communication devices such as e-mail, instant messaging, text messages, blogs, mobile phones, pagers, instant messages and defamatory websites to bully or otherwise harass an individual or group through personal attacks or other means. "At least in a physical fight, there's a start and an end, but when the taunts and humiliation follow a child into their home, it's 'torture,' and it doesn't stop" (Early, 2010). Cyber-bullying, taunts, insults and harassment over the Internet or text messages sent from mobile phones has become rampant among young people, in some cases with tragic consequences. Derek Randel, a motivational speaker, former teacher and founder of StoppingSchoolViolence.com, believes that "cyber-bullying has become so prevalent with emerging social media, such as Facebook and text messaging, that it has affected every school in every community" (Early, 2010; StopCyberbullying, 2013).

IDENTITY THEFT

this is the fastest growing types of fraud in the UK. Identity theft is the act of obtaining sensitive information about another person without his or her knowledge, and using this information to commit theft or fraud. The Internet has given cyber criminals the opportunity to obtain such information from vulnerable companies' database. It has also enabled them to lead the victims to believe that they are disclosing sensitive personal information to a legitimate business; sometimes as a response to an e-mail asking to update billing or membership information; sometimes it takes the form of an application to a (fraudulent) Internet job posting. According to the All Party Parliamentary Group, the available research, both in the UK and globally, indicates that identity fraud is a major and growing problem because of the escalating and evolving methods of gaining and utilizing personal information. Subsequently, it is expected to increase further over the coming years.

This is an issue which is recognized in the highest levels of Government.

In 2012 alone CIFAS, the UK's Fraud Prevention Service, identified and protected over 150,000 victims of these identity crimes (CIFAS, 2012).

PLASTIC CARD FRAUD

Plastic Card Fraud is the unauthorized use of plastic or credit cards, or the theft of a plastic card number to obtain money or property. According to APACS (analysis of policing and community safety framework), the UK payments association, plastic card losses in 2011 was £341m, of which £80m was the result of fraud abroad (Financial fraud action UK, 2012). This typically involves criminals using stolen UK card details at cash machines and retailers in countries that have yet to upgrade to Chip and PIN.

The biggest fraud type in the UK is card-not-present (CNP) fraud. In 2011 65% of total losses was CNP, which was £220.9 Million (down by 3%) (Financial fraud action UK, 2012). CNP fraud encompasses any frauds which involve online, telephone or mail order payment. The problem in countering this type of fraud lies in the fact that neither the card nor the cardholder is present at a physical till point in a shop. There are a number of methods that fraudsters use for obtaining both cards and card details, such as phishing, sending spam e-mails, or hacking companies' database, as aforementioned.

INTERNET AUCTION FRAUD

Internet auction fraud is when items bought are fake or stolen goods, or when seller advertises nonexistent items for sale which means goods are paid for but never arrives. Fraudsters often use money transfer services as it is easier for them to receive money without revealing their true identity.

Auction fraud is a classic example of criminals relies on the anonymity of the internet. According to action fraud 2013, some of the most common complaints involve:

- *Buyers receiving goods late, or not at all*
- *Sellers not receiving payment*
- *Buyers receiving goods that are either less valuable than those advertised or significantly different from the original description*
- *Failure to disclose relevant information about a product or the terms of sale.*

These fraudulent "sellers" use stolen IDs when they register with the auction sites, therefore tracing them is generally a very difficult tasks.

CYBER-ATTACK METHODS AND TOOLS

Any Internet-based application is a potential carrier for worms and other malware; therefore Internet messaging is not exceptional. Criminals use these common chat methods for ID theft purposes by getting to know the individuals who they are communicating with or via the spreading of malware, spyware, and viruses.

E-mails are a critical tool in the hands of criminals. Not only is e-mail one of the fastest and cheapest mediums form spamming and phishing, but they are easily manipulated into carrying deadly virus attacks capable of destroying an entire corporate network within minutes. Some viruses are transmitted through harmless-looking e-mail messages and can run automatically without the need for user intervention (like the "I Love You" virus). Technically, attacks on "system security that can be carried out via electronic mail" can be categorized into the following:

- Active content attacks, which take advantage of various active HTML (hypertext markup language) and other scripting features and bugs.
- Buffer overflow attacks, where the attacker sends something that is too large to fit into the fixed-size memory buffer of the e-mail recipient, in the hopes that the part that does not fit will overwrite critical information rather than being safely discarded.
- Shell script attacks—where a fragment of a Unix shell script is included in the message headers in the hopes that an improperly configured Unix mail client will execute the commands.

Staged downloaders are threats which download and install other malicious codes onto a compromised computer. These threats allow attackers to change the downloadable component to any type of threat that suits their objectives, or to match the profile of the computer being targeted. For example, if the targeted computer contains no data of interest, attackers can install a Trojan that relays spam, rather than one that steals confidential information. As the attackers' objectives change, they can change any later components that will be downloaded to perform the requisite tasks.

A virus is a program or code that replicates itself onto other files with which it comes into contact. A virus can damage an infected computer by wiping out databases or files, damaging important computer parts, such as Bios, or forwarding a pornographic message to everyone listed in the e-mail address book of an infected computer.

2007 was the year when botnets were first used. A bot is shot from robot where cyber criminals take over control of their victim's computer without his or her knowledge. This occurs when cyber criminals or hackers install programs in the target's computer through a worm or a virus. Collections of these infected computers are called botnets. A hacker or spammer controlling these botnets might be renting them for cyber criminals or other hackers, which in turn make it very hard for authorities to trace back to the real offender.

In March 2009, BBC journalist investigated the world of Botnets. The BBC team investigated thousands of Trojan horse malware infected, mostly domestic PCs running Windows, connected via broadband Internet connections, which are used to send most of the world's spam e-mails and also for Distributed Denial of Service attacks, and blackmails against e-commerce websites. The BBC team managed to rent a botnet of over 21,000 malware-infected computers around the world. This botnet was said to be relatively cheap, as it was mostly infecting computers in less developed countries, which have less security measures installed on them.

A keylogger is a software program or hardware device that is used to monitor and log each of the keys a user types into a computer keyboard. The user who installed the program or hardware device can then view all keys typed in by that user. Because these programs and hardware devices monitor the keys entered, a hacker user can easily find user passwords and other information a user may wish and believe to be private.

Keyloggers, as a surveillance tool, are often used by employers to ensure employees use work computers for business purposes only. Unfortunately, keyloggers can also be embedded in spyware, allowing information to be transmitted to an unknown third party. Cyber criminals use these tools to deceive the potential target into releasing their personal sensitive data and restoring it for later access to the user's machine, if the data obtained contained the target ID and password. Furthermore, a keylogger will reveal the contents of all e-mails composed by the user and there are also other approaches to capturing information about user activity.

- Some *keyloggers* capture screens, rather than keystrokes.
- Other *keyloggers* will secretly turn on video or audio recorders, and transmit what they capture over your Internet connection.

CONCLUSION

All countries face the same dilemma of how to fight cybercrime and how to effectively promote security to their citizens and organizations.

Cybercrime, unlike traditional crime which is committed in one geographic location, is committed online and it is often not clearly linked to any geographic location. Therefore, a coordinated global response to the problem of cybercrime is required. This is largely due to the fact that there are a number of problems, which pose a hindrance to the effective reduction in cybercrime. Some of the main problems arise as a result of the shortcomings of the technology, legislation and cyber criminology.

Many criminological perspectives define crime on the social, cultural and material characteristics, and view crimes as taking place at a specific geographic location. This definition of crime has allowed for the characterization of crime, and the subsequent tailoring of crime prevention, mapping and measurement methods to the specific target audience. However, this characterization cannot be carried over to cybercrime, because the environment in which cybercrime is committed cannot be pinpointed to a geographic location, or distinctive social or cultural groups.

In 2014, a world-leading unit to counter online criminals will be established in UK in order to change the way police deals with cybercrime as was reported by the Commissioner of Metropolitan Police in November 2013.

The aims are fivefold:

1. To bring more fraudsters and cyber-criminals to justice;
2. To improve the service to their victims;
3. To step up prevention help and advice to individuals and businesses;

4. To dedicate more organized crime teams to stemming the harm caused by the most prolific cyber-criminals;

5. To invite business and industry to match the Metropolitan police determination and work with together to combat fraud and cybercrime.

Clearly, the traditional way of policing cybercrime has not been working despite, plethora of internet-related legislation. This is because of the high volume online nature of the crimes.

REFERENCES

Anti-Phishing Working Group (APWG), 2013. Global Phishing Survey: Trends and Domain Name Use in 1H2013. http://docs.apwg.org/reports/APWG_GlobalPhishingSurvey_1H2013.pdf (accessed December 2013).

CIFAS, The UK's Fraud Prevention Service, 2012. http://www.cifas.org.uk/ (accessed December 2013).

Council of Europe (CoE), 2001. Convention on Cybercrime. Budapest, 23.11.2001, http://conventions.coe.int/Treaty/en/Treaties/Html/185.htm (accessed December 2013).

Early, J.R., 2010. Cyber-bullying on increase. http://www.tmcnet.com/usubmit/2010/02/07/4609017.htm (accessed January 2014).

Financial fraud action UK, 2012. Fraud: The Facts 2012. The definitive overview of payment industry fraud and measures to prevent it, http://www.theukcardsassociation.org.uk/wm_documents/Fraud_The_Facts_2012.pdf (accessed January 2014).

Gordon, S., Ford, R., 2006. On the definition and classification of cybercrime. J. Comput. Virol. 2 (1), 13–20.

Hogan-Howe, Bernard, the Commissioner of Metropolitan Police, 2013. Met to Tackle the wave of cybercrime with 'world-leading unit' published in the Evening Standard, 21st November 2013. http://www.standard.co.uk/news/crime/commentary-sir-bernard-hoganhowe-on-new-cybercrime-push-8954716.html (accessed January 2014).

Jahankhani, H., Al-Nemrat, A., 2011. Cybercrime Profiling and trend analysis. In: Akhgar, B., Yates, S. (Eds.), Intelligence Management, Knowledge Driven Frameworks for Combating Terrorism and Organised Crime. Springer, London, ISBN 978-1-4471-2139-8.

Jahankhani, H., Al-Nemrat, A., 2010. Cybercrime. In: Jahankhani, et al. (Eds.), Handbook of Electronic Security and Digital Forensics. World Scientific, London, ISBN 9978-981-283-703-5.

Kaspersky, 2012. Spam in April 2012: Junk Mail Gathers Pace in the US, http://www.kaspersky.co.uk/about/news/spam/2012/Spam_in_April_2012_Junk_Mail_Gathers_Pace:in_the_US (accessed January 2014).

Rowlingston, R., 2007. Towards a strategy for E-crime prevention. In: ICGeS Global e Security, Proceedings of the 3rd Annual International Conference, London, England, 18–20 April 2007, ISBN 978-0-9550008-4-3.

StopCyberbullying, 2013. http://stopcyberbullying.org/index2.html (accessed January 2014).

Symantec, 2012. Intelligence Report: October 2012, http://www.symantec.com/connect/blogs/symantec-intelligence-report-october-2012 (accessed January 2014).

Symantec, 2013. Intelligence Report: October 2013, http://www.symantec.com/connect/blogs/symantec-intelligence-report-october-2013 (accessed January 2014).

Wall, D., 2007. Hunting Shooting, and Phishing: New Cybercrime Challenges for Cybercanadians in The 21st Century. The ECCLES Centre for American Studies. http://bl.uk/ecclescentre,2009.

Wall, D.S., 2005. The internet as a conduit for criminal activity. In: Pattavina, A. (Ed.), Information Technology and the Criminal Justice System. Sage Publications, USA, ISBN 0-7619-3019-1.

Wilson, P., Kunz, M., 2004. Computer crime and computer fraud. Report to Montegmery County Criminal Justice Coordination Commission, http://www.mongomerycountymd.gov (accessed September 2007).

Yar, M., 2006. Cybercrime and Society. Sage Publication Ltd, London.

Cyber terrorism: Case studies

13

Daniel Cohen

INTRODUCTION

If we examine one of the key concepts in cyberspace—namely, dealing with terrorist threats—we find the rationale underlying the concept (which emerged, among others, after the formative events at the beginning of the twenty-first century, such as the Y2K bug and the September 11, 2001 terrorist attacks) in the world appears to be at the peak of a process belonging to the post-modern and post-technology era, an era with no defensible borders, in which countries are vulnerable to invasion via information, ideas, people, and materials—in short, an open world. In this world, the threat of terrorism takes a new form: a terrorist in a remote, faraway basement having the potential ability to cause damage completely changing the balance of power by penetrating important security or economic systems in each and every country in the world and accessing sensitive information, or even by causing the destruction of vital systems. No one disputes non-state actors, like terrorist organizations are using cyberspace as a field enabling small individual players to have influence disproportionate to their size. This asymmetry creates various risks that did not attract attention or provoke action among the major powers in the past. The question is whether the activity of these players in cyberspace constitutes a threat with the potential to cause major and widespread damage, with the ability to operate cyber weapons with strategic significance—weapons that can inflict large scale or lasting damage of the sort causing critical systems to collapse and "brings countries to their knees." And if so, why such damage has not yet occurred?

Can the reality of September 11, 2001—when a terrorist organization planned an attack for two years, including by taking pilot training courses, eventually using simple box-cutters to carry out a massive terrorist attack—repeat itself in cyberspace? Is a scenario in which a terrorist organization sends a group of terrorists as students to the relevant courses in computer science, arms them with technological means accessible to everyone, and uses them and the capabilities they have acquired to carry out a massive terrorist attack in cyberspace realistic or science fiction? In order to answer this question, we must examine the few case studies of cyber-attacks by terror organization and then consider what capabilities a non-state actor can acquire, and whether these capabilities are liable to constitute a real threat to national security.

This chapter assesses whether attacks in cyberspace by terrorist organizations, whose effect until now has usually been tactical, will be able to upgrade (or perhaps have already upgraded) their ability to operate cyber weapons with strategic significance—weapons that can inflict large scale or lasting damage of the sort causing critical systems to collapse and "brings countries to their knees."

This chapter focuses on the activities of non-state organizations with political agendas and goals, even if operated or supported by states. A distinction is drawn between these activities and those conducted directly by countries, which are beyond the scope of this chapter, as are the activities of organizations whose aims are mainly of a criminal nature. For the purpose of this chapter, a terrorist act from a non-state organization in cyberspace will be defined as an act in cyberspace designed to deliberately or indiscriminately harm civilians (see Chapter 2 for other definitions of cyber terrorism).

In order to assess the activities of terrorist organizations in cyberspace, the first stage is the identification of motives for using cyberspace as part of the political struggle being waged by the terrorist organizations. Two principal motives were identified. The first is the use of cyberspace supporting terrorist activity, mainly the acquisition of money and recruits or money laundering in order to finance the activity. The second is the use of tools in cyberspace providing the actual strike against the targets terrorist organizations set for themselves, as well as its use for other violent means. In this context we will analyze the cooperation between non-state organizations and the states operating them supporting their terrorist activity.

The second stage of this study required an examination of terrorist operations in cyberspace, that is, operations whose purpose is to cause deliberate or indiscriminate harm to civilians through action in cyberspace by non-state organizations with political agendas and goals, even if operated or supported by states.

The third stage is an assessment and understanding of the capabilities terrorist organizations can obtain, and by them to generate an effective and significant terrorist attack.

CASE STUDIES—ACTIVITIES IN CYBERSPACE ATTRIBUTED TO TERRORIST ORGANIZATIONS

One of the first documented attacks by a terrorist organization against state computer systems was by the Tamil Tigers guerilla fighters in Sri Lanka in 1998. Sri Lankan embassies throughout the world were flooded for weeks by 800 e-mail messages a day bearing the message, "We are the Black Internet Tigers, and we are going to disrupt your communications systems." Some assert this message affected those who received it by sowing anxiety and fear in the embassies (Denning, 2000). Several years later, on March 3, 2003, a Japanese cult name Aum Shinrikyo ("Supreme Truth") conducted a complex cyber-attack including obtaining sensitive information about nuclear facilities in Russia, Ukraine, Japan, and other countries as part of an attempt to attack the information security systems of these facilities. The information was confiscated, and the attempted attack failed before the organization managed to take action. An attack through an emissary took place in January 2009 in Israel. In this event, hackers attacked Israel's Internet structure in response to Operation Cast Lead in the Gaza Strip. Over five million computers were attacked. It is assumed in Israel the attack came from countries that were formerly part of the Soviet Union and was ordered and financed by Hezbollah and Hamas (Everard, 2008). In January 2012, a group of pro-Palestinian hackers calling itself "Nightmare" caused the Tel Aviv Stock Exchange and the El Al Airlines websites to crash briefly and disrupted the website activity of the First International Bank of Israel. Commenting on this, a Hamas spokesman in the Gaza Strip said, "The penetration of Israeli websites opens a new sphere of opposition and a new electronic warfare against the Israeli occupation" (Cohen and Rotbart, 2013).

The civil war in Syria has led to intensive offensive action by an organization known as the Syrian Electronic Army (SEA)—an Internet group composed of hackers who support the Assad regime (see Chapter 9 for a case study of the SEA). They attack using techniques of denial of services and information, or break into websites and alter their content. The group has succeeded in conducting various malicious operations, primarily against Syrian opposition websites, but also against Western Internet sites. SEA's most recent action was aimed mainly against media, cultural, and news websites on Western networks. The group succeeded in breaking into over 120 sites, including The Financial Times, The Telegraph, The Washington Post, and Al Arabia (Love, 2013). One of the most significant and effective attacks was in April 2013, when the Syrian Electronic Army broke into the Associated Press's Twitter account, and implanted a bogus "tweet" saying the White House had been bombed and the US president had been injured in the attack. The immediate consequence of this announcement was a sharp drop in the US financial markets and the Dow Jones Industrial Average for several minutes (Foster, 2013). The SEA is also suspected of an attempt to penetrate command and control systems of water systems. For example, on May 8, 2013, an Iranian news agency published a photograph of the irrigation system at Kibbutz Sa'ar (Yagna and Yaron, 2013). SEA has also hacked entertainment websites twitter handles outside of their target such as E! Online and The Onion, many surmising it as SEA relishing in the publicity and attempting to broadcast there platforms outside of their spectrum. In January, 2014, SEA hacked and defaced 16 Saudi Arabian government websites, posting messages condemning Saudi Arabia of terrorism, forcing all 16 websites offline (see Chapter 9).

During Operation Pillar of Defense in the Gaza Strip in 2012 and over the ensuing months, the Israeli-Palestinian conflict inspired a group of hackers calling itself OpIsrael to conduct attacks against Israeli websites in cooperation with Anonymous. Among others, the websites of the Prime Minister's Office, the Ministry of Defense, the Ministry of Education, the Ministry of Environmental Protection, Israel Military Industries, the Israel Central Bureau of Statistics, the Israel Cancer Association, the President of Israel's Office (official site), and dozens of small Israeli websites were affected. The group declared Israel's violations of Palestinian human rights and of international law were the reason for the attack (Buhbut, 2013).

In April 2013, a group of Palestinian hackers named the Izz ad-Din al-Qassam Cyber Fighters, identified with the military section of Hamas, claimed responsibility for an attack on the website of American Express. The company's website suffered an intensive DDoS attack continuing for two hours and disrupting the use of the company's services by its customers. In contrast to typical DDoS attacks, such as those by Anonymous, which were based on a network of computers that were penetrated and combined into a botnet controlled by the attacker, the Izz ad-Din al-Qassam attack used scripts operated on penetrated network servers, a capability allowing more bandwidth to be used in carrying out the attack. This event is part of an overall trend toward the strengthening of Hamas's cyber capabilities, including through enhancing its system of intelligence collection against the IDF and the threat of a hostile takeover of the cellular devices of military personnel, with the devices being used to expose secrets (Zook, 2013).

In contrast to the recruitment of terrorist operatives in the physical world, in cyberspace it is possible to substantially enlarge the pool of participants in an activity, even if they are often deceived into acting as partners by terrorist organizations using the guise of an attack on the establishment. This phenomenon is illustrated by the attacks by hackers against Israeli targets on April 7, 2013, when some of the attackers received guidance concerning the methods and targets for the attack from camouflaged Internet sites. The exploitation of young people's anti-establishment sentiments and general feelings against the West or Israel makes it possible to expand the pool of operatives substantially and creates a significant mass facilitating cyber-terror operations. For example, it has been asserted during Operation Pillar of Defense over one hundred million cyber-attacks against Israeli sites were documented (Globes, 2013) and it was speculated the campaign, was guided by Iran and its satellites (Globes, 2013b).

ANALYSIS OF CAPABILITIES

As a rule, a distinction should be drawn among three basic attack categories: an attack on the gateway of an organization, mainly its Internet sites, through direct attacks, denial of service, or the defacement of websites; an attack on an organization's information systems; and finally, the most sophisticated (and complex) category—attacks on an organization's core operational systems for example, industrial control systems. Cyber terror against a country and its citizens can take place at a number of levels of sophistication, with each level requiring capabilities in terms of both technology and the investment made by the attacker. The damage caused is in direct proportion to the level of investment.

An Attack at the Organization's Gateway: The most basic level of attack is an attack on the organization's gateway, that is, its Internet site, which by its nature is exposed to the public. The simplest level of cyber terrorism entails attacks denying service and disrupt daily life but do not cause substantial, irreversible, or lasting damage. These attacks, called "distributed denials of service" (DDoS), essentially saturate a specific computer or Internet service with communication requests, exceeding the limits of its ability to respond and thereby paralyzing the service. Suitable targets for such an attack are, among others, banks, cellular service providers, cable and satellite television companies, and stock exchange services (trading and news). Another method of attacking an organization's gateway is through attacks on Domain Name System (DNS) servers—servers used to route Internet traffic. Such an attack will direct people seeking access to a specific site or service toward a different site, to which the attackers seek to channel the traffic. A similar, but simpler, attack can be conducted at the level of an individual computer instead of the level of the general DNS server, meaning communications from a single computer will be channeled to the attacker's site rather than the real site which the user wishes to surf. Damage caused by such attacks can include theft of information; denial of service to customers, resulting in business damage to the attacked service; and damage to the reputation of the service. The attacker can redirect traffic to a page containing propaganda and messages he wants to present to the public.

One popular and relatively simple method of damaging the victim's reputation at the gateway of the organization is to deface its Internet site. Defacement includes planting malicious messages on the home page, inserting propaganda the attackers wish to distribute to a large audience and causing damage to the organization's image (and business) by making it appear unprotected and vulnerable to potential attackers.

An Attack against the Organization's Information Systems: The intermediate level on the scale of damage in cyberspace includes attacks against the organization's information and computer systems, such as servers, computer systems, databases, communications networks, and data processing machines. The technological sophistication required at this level is greater than that required for an attack against the organization's gateway. This level requires obtaining access to the organization's computers through employees in the organization or by other means. The damage potentially caused in the virtual environment includes damage to important services, such as banks, cellular services, and e-mail.

A clear line separating the attacks described here from the threat of physical cybernetic terrorism: usually these attacks are not expected to result in physical damage, but reliance on virtual services and access to them is liable to generate significant damage nevertheless. One such example is the attack using the Shamoon computer virus, which infected computers of Aramco, the Saudi Arabian oil company, in August 2012. In this incident, malicious code was inserted into Aramco's computer system, and 30,000 computers were put out of action as a result. Even though the attack did not affect the company's core operational systems, it succeeded in putting tens of thousands of computers in its organizational network out of action while causing significant damage by erasing information from the organization's computers and slowing down its activity for a prolonged period.

An Attack on the Organization's Core Operational Systems: The highest level on the scale of attack risk is an attack on the organization's core operational and operating systems. Examples include attacks against critical physical infrastructure, such as water pipes, electricity, gas, fuel, public transportation control systems, or bank payment systems, which deny the provision of essential service for a given time, or in more severe cases, even cause physical damage by attacking the command and control systems of the attacked organization. This is the point a virtual attack is liable to create physical damage and its effects are liable to be destructive. Following the exposure of Stuxnet, awareness increased of the need to protect industrial control systems, but there is still a long way to go before effective defense is actually put into effect. Terrorist groups can exploit this gap, for example, by assembling a group of experts in computers and automation of processes for the purpose of creating a virus capable of harming those systems (Langner, 2012) (see Chapter 9).

TECHNOLOGICAL CAPABILITIES, INTELLIGENCE GUIDANCE, AND OPERATIONAL CAPACITY

Development of attack capabilities, whether by countries or by terrorist organizations, requires an increasingly powerful combination of capabilities for action in cyberspace in three main areas: technological capabilities, intelligence guidance for setting objectives (generating targets), and operational capacity.

TECHNOLOGICAL CAPABILITIES

The decentralized character of the Internet makes trade in cyber weaponry easy. Indeed, many hackers and traders are exploiting these advantages and offering cyber-tools and cyberspace attack services to anyone who seeks them. A variegated and very sophisticated market in cyber products trading for a variety of purposes has thus emerged, with a range of prices varying from a few dollars for a simple one-time denial of service attack to thousands of dollars for the use of unfamiliar vulnerabilities and the capabilities to enable an attacker to maneuver his way into the most protected computer system.

The tools of the cybernetic underworld can be of great assistance in DDoS attacks and in stealing large quantities of sensitive information from inadequately protected companies (for example, information about credit cards from unprotected databases), which will almost certainly arouse public anxiety. Terrorists still have a long way to go, however, before they can cause damage to control systems, which is much more difficult than stealing credit cards, and toward which cybernetic crime tools are of no help. With respect to the intermediate level described above concerning attacks on an organization's information systems, it appears the underworld possesses tools capable of assisting cyber terrorism. Some adjustment of these tools is needed, such as turning the theft of information into the erasure of information, but this is not nearly such a long process, and the virus developers will almost certainly agree to carry it out for terrorist organizations, if they are paid enough.

INTELLIGENCE-GUIDED CAPABILITY

One of the key elements in the process of planning a cyber-attack is the selection of a target or a group of targets, damage to which will create the effect sought by the terrorist organization. Toward this end, a terrorist entity must assemble a list of entities constituting potential targets for attack. Technology providing tools facilitating the achievement of this task is already available free of charge. It is also necessary to map the computer setup of the attacked organization, and to understand which computers are connected to the Internet, which operating systems and protective software programs are installed on them, what authorizations each computer has, and through which computers the organization's command system can be controlled.

Organizations with critical operational systems usually use two computer networks: one external, which is connected to the Internet, and one internal, which is physically isolated from the Internet and is connected to the organization's industrial control systems. The Internet census does not include information about isolated internal networks because these are not accessible through the Internet. Any attack on these networks requires intelligence, resources, and a major effort, and it is doubtful any terrorist organizations are capable of carrying out such attacks.

OPERATIONAL CAPABILITY

After collecting intelligence and creating or acquiring the technological tools for an attack, the next stage for planners of cybernetic terrorism is operational—to carry out an actual attack by means of an attack vector. This concept refers to a chain of actions carried out by the attackers in which each action constitutes one step on the way to the final objective, and which usually includes complete or partial control of a computer system or industrial control system. No stage in an attack vector can be skipped, and in order to advance to a given step, it must be verified all the preceding stages have been successfully completed.

The first stage in an attack vector is usually to create access to the target. A very common and successful method for doing this in cyberspace is called spoofing, that is, forgery. There are various ways of using this method, with their common denominator being the forging of the message sender's identity, so the recipient will trust the content and unhesitatingly open a link within the message. The forging of e-mail is an attack method existing for many years. Defensive measures have accordingly been developed against it, but attackers have also accumulated experience. Incidents can now be cited of completely innocent-looking e-mail messages tailored to their recipients, containing information relating to them personally or documents directly pertaining to their field of business. The addresses of the senders in these cases were forged to appear as the address of a work colleague. As soon as the recipients opened the e-mail, they unknowingly infected their computers with a virus.

The forgery method can be useful when the target is a computer connected to the Internet and messages can be sent to it. In certain instances, however, this is not the case. Networks with a high level of protection are usually physically isolated from the outside world, and consequently there is no physical link (not even wireless) between them and a network with a lower level of security. In this situation the attacker will have to adopt a different or additional measure in the attack vector—infecting the target network with a virus by using devices operating in both an unprotected network and on the protected network. One such example is a USB flash drive ("Disk on Key" or "memory stick"), used for convenient, mobile storage of files. If successful, the attacker obtains access to the victim's technological equipment (computer, PalmPilot, smartphone), and the first stage in the attack vector—creating access to the target—has been completed. Under certain scenarios, this step is the most important and significant for the attacker. For example, if the terrorist's goal is to sabotage a network and erase information from it, then the principal challenge is to gain access to the target, that is, access to the company's operational network. The acts of erasure and sabotage are easier, assuming the virus implanted in the network is operated at a sufficiently high level of authorization. Under more complex scenarios, however, in which the terrorist wishes to cause significant damage and achieve greater intimidation, considerable investment in the stages of the attack vector is necessary, as described below.

Within the offensive cyber products market, terrorists will find accessible capabilities for a non-isolated target. In the same market, they will also find attack products, and presumably they will likewise find products for conducting operations on the target network (similar to the management interface of the SpyEye Trojan Horse; MacDonald, 2011). Despite this availability, Internet-accessible tools have not yet been identified for facilitating an attack on an organization's operational systems. Access to these tools is possible in principle (Rid, 2013), but the task requires large-scale personnel resources (spies, physicists, and engineers), monetary investment (for developing an attack tool and testing it on real equipment under laboratory conditions), and a great deal of time in order to detect vulnerabilities and construct a successful attack vector.

CONCLUSION

The low entry threshold for certain attacks and the access to cybernetic attack tools have not led the terrorist organizations to switch to attacks with large and ongoing damage potential. Until now, the terrorist organizations' cyber-attacks have been mainly against the target organization's gateway. The main attack tools have been denial of service attacks and attacks on a scale ranging from amateur to medium level, primarily because the capabilities and means of terrorist organizations in cyberspace are limited, and to date they have lacked the independent scientific and technological infrastructure necessary to develop cyber tools capable of causing significant damage. Given terrorist organizations lack the ability to collect high quality intelligence for operations, the likelihood they will carry out a significant cyber-attack appears low.

In order for a terrorist organization to operate independently and carry out a significant attack in cyberspace, it will need a range of capabilities, including the ability to collect precise information about the target, its computer networks, and its systems; the purchase or development of a suitable cyber tool; finding a lead for penetrating an organization; camouflaging an attack tool while taking over the system;

and carrying out an attack in an unexpected time and place and achieving significant results. It appears independent action by a terrorist organization without the support of a state is not self-evident. The same conclusion, however, cannot be drawn for organizations supported and even operated by states possessing significant capabilities.

There is also the possibility of attacks by terrorist organizations through outsourcing. A group of hackers named Icefog concentrates on focused attacks against an organization's supply chain (using a hit-and-run method), mainly in military industries worldwide. This is an example for outsourcing cyber-attacks (Kaspersky, 2013). Another development is the distribution of malicious codes using the crime laboratories of the DarkNet network, which has increased access to existing codes for attack purposes. Criminal organizations are already using the existing codes for attacks on financial systems by duplicating them and turning them into mutation codes.

On the one hand, the array of capabilities and means at the disposal of terrorist organizations in cyberspace is limited because of its strong correlation with technological accessibility, which is usually within the purview of countries with advanced technological capabilities and companies with significant technological capabilities. On the other hand, access to the free market facilitates trade in cybernetic weapons and information of value for an attack. One helpful factor in assembling these capabilities is countries that support terrorism and seek to use proxies in order to conceal their identity as the initiator of an attack against a specific target. In addition, the terrorist organization must train experts and accumulate knowledge about ways of collecting information, attack methods, and means of camouflaging offensive weapons in order to evade defensive systems at the target.

This study reveals to date terrorist organizations have lacked the independent scientific and technological infrastructure necessary to develop cyber tools with the ability to cause significant damage. They also lack the ability to collect high quality intelligence for operations. The ability of terrorist organizations to conduct malicious activity in cyberspace will, therefore, be considered in light of these constraints.

The ability to carry out an attack includes penetration into the operational systems and causing damage to them is quite complex. The necessity for a high level of intelligence and penetration capabilities, which exists in only a limited number of countries, means any attack will necessarily be by a state. For this reason, no successful attack by a non-state player on the core operational systems of any organization whatsoever has been seen to date. Although no such attack has been identified, there is a discernable trend toward improvement of the technological capabilities of mercenaries operating in cyberspace for the purposes of crime and fraud. Presumably, therefore, in exchange for suitable recompense, criminal technological parties will agree to create tools carrying out attacks on the core operational systems of critical infrastructure and commercial companies. These parties will also be able to put their wares at the disposal of terrorist organizations.

There is a realistic possibility in the near future, terrorist organizations will buy attack services from mercenary hackers and use mutation codes based on a variation of the existing codes for attacking targets. This possibility cannot be ignored in assembling a threat reference in cyberspace for attacks on the gateway of an organization or even against its information systems. It is, therefore, very likely terrorist organizations will make progress in their cybernetic attack capabilities in the coming years, based on their acquisition of more advanced capabilities and the translation of these capabilities into attacks on organizations' information systems (not only on the organization's gateway).

REFERENCES

Buhbut, A., 2013. Cyber Attack: Prime Minister's Office, Ministries of Defense, Education Websites Put out of Action, Walla News, April 7, http://news.walla.co.il/?w=/90/2630896 (Hebrew).

Cohen, D., Rotbart, A., 2013. The proliferation of weapons in cyberspace. Military Strategic Affairs 5 (1) (May 2013).

Denning, D.E., 2000. Cyberterrorism, Testimony before the Special Oversight Panel on Terrorism. Committee on Armed Services, U.S House of Representatives, May 23, 2000, p. 269, http://www.cs.georgetown.edu/~denning/infosec/cyberterror.html.

Everard, P., 2008. NATO and cyber terrorism. Response to Cyber Terrorism. *Edited by* Center of Excellence Defence Against Terrorism, Ankara, Turkey, pp.118–126..

Foster, P., 2013. 'Bogus' AP tweet about explosion at the White House wipes billions off US markets. The Telegraph, April 23, 2013. http://www.telegraph.co.uk/finance/markets/10013768/Bogus-AP-tweet-about-explosion-at-the-White-House-wipes-billions-off-US-markets.html.

Globes, 2013. Steinitz: Military Threat against Israel Has Also Become a Cyber Terror Threat. Globes. http://www.globes.co.il/news/article.aspx?did=1000860690 (Hebrew).

Globes, 2013b. See the statement by Prime Minister Benjamin Netanyahu on this subject: "Netanyahu: Iran and Its Satellites Escalating Cyber Attacks on Israel". Globes. http://www.globes.co.il/news/article.aspx?did=1000851092 (Hebrew).

Kaspersky Lab Exposes 'Icefog': A new Cyber-espionage Campaign Focusing on Supply Chain Attacks. September 26, 2013. http://www.kaspersky.com/about/news/virus/2013/Kaspersky_Lab_exposes_Icefog_a_new_cyber-espionage_campaign_focusing_on_supply_chain_attacks.

Langner, R., 2012. Lecture on the subject of securing industrial control systems, Annual Cyber Conference, Institute for National, Security Studies, September 4, 2012, http://youtu.be/sBsMA6Epw78.

Love, D., 2013. 10 Reasons to Worry about the Syrian Electronic Army. Business Insider, May 22, 2013, http://www.businessinsider.com/syrian-electronic-army-2013-5?op=1#ixzz2h728aL8P.

Macdonald, D., 2011. A guide to SpyEye C&C messages. Fortinet, February 15, 2011, http://blog.fortinet.com/a-guide-to-spyeye-cc-messages.

Rid, T., 2013. Cyber-Sabotage Is Easy. Foreign Policy, July 23, 2013. http://www.foreignpolicy.com/articles/2013/07/23/cyber_sabotage_is_easy_i_know_i_did_it?pa.

Yagna, Y., Yaron, O., 2013. Israeli Expert Said, 'Syrian Electronic Army Attacked Israel' – and Denied It. Haaretz, May 25, 2013, http://www.haaretz.co.il/news/politics/1.2029071 (Hebrew).

Zook, N., 2013. Cyber Attack: Izz ad-Din al-Qassam Fighters Hit American Express. Calcalist, April 2, 2013, http://www.calcalist.co.il/internet/articles/0,7340,L-3599061,00.html (Hebrew).

Social media and Big Data

14

Alessandro Mantelero, Giuseppe Vaciago

INTRODUCTION

Social media represent an increasing and fundamental part of the online environment generated by the Web 2.0, in which the users are authors of the contents and do not receive passively information, but they create, reshape and share it. In some cases, the interaction among users based on social media created communities, virtual worlds (e.g., Second Life, World of Warcraft) or crowdsourcing projects (Wikipedia). Although there are significant differences in the nature of these outputs, two aspects are always present and are relevant in the light of this contribution: large amount of information, user generated contents.

The social media platforms aggregate huge amounts of data generated by users, which are in many cases identified or identifiable (Ohm, 2010; United States General Accounting Office, 2011; See also Zang and Bolot, 2011; Golle, 2006; Sweeney, 2000b; Sweeney, 2000a; Tene and Polonetsky, 2013).[1] This contributes to create a peculiar technological landscape in which the predictive ability that distinguishes Big Data (The Aspen Institute, 2010; Boyd and Crawford, 2011; see also Marton et al., 2013)[2] has relevant impact not only in terms of competitive advantage in the business world (identifying in advance emerging trends, business intelligence, etc.) but also in terms of implementation of social surveillance systems by states and groups of power.

From this perspective, the following pages consider these phenomena of concentration of digital information and related asymmetries, which put in the hands of few entities a large amount of data, facilitating the attempts of social surveillance

---

[1] See below par. 3.

[2] The creation of datasets of enormous dimension (Big Data) and new powerful analytics make it possible to draw inferences about unknown facts from statistical occurrence and correlation, with results that are relevant in socio-political, strategical and commercial terms; Despite the weakness of this approach, more focused on correlation than on statistical evidence, it is useful to predict and perceive the birth and evolution of macro-trends, that can be later analyzed in a more traditional statistical way in order to identify their causes.

by governments and private companies. The aim of this chapter is to suggest some possible legal and policy solutions both to boost a more democratic access to information and to protect individual and collective freedom.

BIG DATA: THE ASYMMETRIC DISTRIBUTION OF CONTROL OVER INFORMATION AND POSSIBLE REMEDIES

Big Data is not something new, but currently at the final stage of a long evolution of the capability to analyze data using computer resources. Big Data represents the convergence of different existing technologies that permit enormous data-centers to be built, create high-speed electronic highways and have ubiquitous and on-demand network access to computing resources (cloud computing). These technologies offer substantially unlimited storage, allow the transfer of huge amounts of data from one place to another, and allow the same data to be spread in different places and re-aggregated in a matter of seconds.

All these resources permit a large amount of information from different sources to be collected and the petabytes of data generated by social media represent the ideal context in which Big Data analytics can be used. The whole dataset can be continuously monitored by analytics, in order to identify the emerging trends in the flows of data and obtaining real-time or nearly real-time results in a way that is revolutionary and differs from the traditional sampling method (The Aspen Institute, 2010).

The availability of these new technologies and large datasets gives a competitive advantage to those who own them in terms of capability to predict new economic, social and political trends.

In the social media context, these asymmetries are evident with regard to the commercial platforms (e.g., Twitter, Google+, etc.), in which the service providers play a substantial role in term of control over information. Conversely, when the social media are based on open, decentralized and participative architectures, these asymmetries are countered; for this reason in the following paragraphs we will consider the role assumed by open architectures and open data in order to reach a wider access to information and a lower concentration of control over information.

In order to control and limit the information asymmetries related to Big Data and their consequences, in terms of economic advantages and social control, it seems to be necessary the adoption of various remedies, as the complexity of the phenomenon requires different approaches.

First of all, it is important to achieve a better allocation of the control over information. For this purpose, it is necessary to adopt adequate measures to control those who have this power, in order to limit possible abuses and illegitimate advantages. At the same time, we need to increase access to the information and the number of subjects able to create and manage large amounts of data, spreading the informational power currently in the hands of a few bodies.

The need to control these great aggregations of data is also related to their political and strategic relevance and should lead the introduction of a mandatory notification of the creation of a big and important database—as happened at the beginning of the computer age when there was a similar concentration of power in the hands of a few subjects due to the high cost of the first mainframes (Article 29 Data Protection Working Party, 2005; Article 29 Data Protection Working Party, 1997; Bygrave, 2002)[3]—and the creation of specific international independent authorities. These authorities will be able to control the invasive attitude of governmental power with regard to large databases and the power of the owner of Big Data, but can also have an important role in the definition of specific standards for data security.

This will be a long and tortuous journey, as it is based on international cooperation; nevertheless, it is important to start it as soon as possible, using the existing international bodies and multilateral dialogues between countries. At the same time, any solutions should be graduated in an appropriate manner, avoiding the involvement of every kind of data-farm built somewhere in the world, but considering only the data-farms with an absolutely remarkable dimension or a considerable importance because of the data collected (e.g., police or military databases).

Access to data and data sharing are other two central aspects that should be considered in order to limit the power of the owners of Big Data and give society the opportunity to have access to knowledge. From this perspective, a key role is played by open data (Veenswijk et al., 2012; Executive Office of the President, National Science and Technology Council, 2013)[4] and the above-mentioned policies about transparency of the information society (i.e., notification), which permit to know who holds great informational power and ask to these entities to open their archives.

Opening public databases and potentially private archives (Deloitte, 2012; Enel, 2013; Nike Inc., 2013; ASOS API project, 2013; Canadian Goldcorp Inc., 2013) to citizens and giving them raw data not only reduces the power of the owners of information, in terms of the exclusive access to the data, but also limits their advantage in terms of technical and cultural analysis skills (Open Knowledge Foundation, 2004; Cyganiak and Jentzsch, 2011; Kroes, 2011).[5]

---

[3] See Article 8 (a) of the Convention for the Protection of Individuals with regard to Automatic Processing of Personal Data, opened for signature in Strasbourg on 28 January 1981, recital 48 in the preamble to Directive 1995/46 and Articles 18–21 of Directive.

[4] On the differences and interactions between Big Data and open data see A. Marton, M. Avital and T. Blegind Jensen, 2013, above at fn. 2, which point out that "while Big Data is about distributed computation and infrastructures, open data is about standards on how to make data machine-readable, and hence linkable." From a European perspective, see the recent approved Directive 2013/37/EU of the European Parliament and of the Council of 26 June 2013, amending Directive 2003/98/EC on the re-use of public sector information. Available: http://eur-lex.europa.eu/JOHtml.do?uri=OJ:L:2013:17 5:SOM:EN:HTML [Dec. 10, 2013].

[5] The access to data does not mean that everyone will immediately have new knowledge and predictive capacity, because, as mentioned above, technical equipment is necessary. However, the availability of the data permits citizens to put together their economic and cultural resources, even without a business-oriented action, in order to constitute groups dedicated to the analysis and processing of the raw data; see the projects and activities of the Open Knowledge Foundation (OKF), which is a non-profit organisation founded in 2004 and dedicated "to promoting open data and open content in all their forms – including government data, publicly funded research and public domain cultural content"; From this perspective, social media offer clear examples of the virtues of open data and open architecture (e.g., Dbpedia, Wikipedia, etc.).

Finally, it is necessary to address the critical issues concerning the geopolitical distribution of informational power, which represents an emerging problem for Europe. Even though big European companies are able to collect and analyze a large amount of data, the main commercial social media are based in U.S. and this element puts this nation in a better position to control the world's informational flows generated by the users of these kinds of services.

From a geo-political perspective, this situation represents a weakness for the E.U., in terms of the loss of control over the data of its citizens due to the need to entrust the management of strategic information to foreign entities. In order to reduce this risk, the European industry is being urged to assume a more important role in ICT sector (Kroes, 2011) and, at the same time, the E.U. is strengthening the protection of personal data.

BIG DATA AND SOCIAL SURVEILLANCE: PUBLIC AND PRIVATE INTERPLAY IN SOCIAL CONTROL

The risks related to the concentration of the control over information in the social media context and in general are not restricted to the democratic access and distribution of information and knowledge, but also to the potential systems of social surveillance that can be realized using this information.

From this perspective, the recent NSA case (European Parliament, 2013c; Auerbach et al., 2013; European Parliament, 2013a; European Parliament, 2013b)[6] is being the more evident representation of the potential consequences of monitoring online interaction, although it is just the latest in a series of programs adopted by governmental agencies in various nations to pursue massive social surveillance (European Parliament, 2001; European Parliament 2013a; European Parliament 2013b; DARPA. Total Information Awareness Program (TIA), 2002; National Research Council, 2008; Congressional Research Service. CRS Report for Congress, 2008).[7]

In western democratic nations, the modern social surveillance is no longer realized only by intelligence apparatus, which autonomously collects a huge amount of information through pervasive monitoring systems. The social surveillance is the result of the interaction between the private and public sector, based on a collaborative model made possible by mandatory disclosure orders issued by courts or administrative bodies and extended to an undefined pool of voluntary or proactive collaborations from big companies (Council of Europe, 2008).

In this way, governments obtain information with the indirect "co-operation" of the users who probably would not have given the same information to public entities

---

[6] See the various articles publish by The Guardian. Available: http://www.guardian.co.uk; See also the various documents available at https://www.cdt.org [Dec. 10, 2013].

[7] See also more sources on TIA are available at http://epic.org/privacy/profiling/tia/.

if requested. Service providers, for example, collect personal data on the base of private agreements (privacy policies) with the consent of the user and for their specific purposes (Reidenberg, 2013) but governments exploit this practice by using mandatory orders to obtain the disclosure of this information. This dual mechanism hides from citizens the risk and the dimension of the social control that can be realized by monitoring social networks or other services and using Big Data *analytics* technologies.

Another relevant aspect of the control deriving from Big Data is the amount of it. Analyses focused on profiling enable to predict the attitudes and decisions of any single user and even to match similar profiles. In contrast, Big Data is not used to focus on individuals, but to analyze large groups and populations (e.g., the political sentiment of an entire country).

Although, in many cases, intelligence activities have little to do with general data protection regulations—since they are authorized by specific legislative provisions introducing exceptions to general principles (Cate et al., 2012; Swire, 2012; Bailey, 2012; Wang, 2012; Brown, 2012; Tsuchiya, 2012; Pell, 2012; Cate and Cate, 2012; Svantesson, 2012; Tene, 2012; Schwartz, 2012; Abraham and Hickok, 2012; See also Brown, 2013; European Parliament, 2013b), regulations on data protection and privacy can play a relevant role in terms of reduction of the amount of data collected by private entities and, consequently, have an indirect impact on the information available for purposes of public social surveillance.

The interaction between public and private in social control could be divided in two categories, both of which are significant with regard to data protection. The first concerns the collection of private company data by government and judicial authorities (see Section "Array of Approved eSurveillance Legislation"), whilst the second is the use by government and judicial authorities of instruments and technologies provided by private companies for organizational and investigative purposes (see Section "Use of Private Sector Tools and Resources").

ARRAY OF APPROVED ESURVEILLANCE LEGISLATION

With regard to the first category and especially when the request is made by governmental agencies, the issue of the possible violation of fundamental rights becomes more delicate. The Echelon Interception System (European Parliament, 2001) and the Total Information Awareness (TIA) Program (European Parliament, 2001; European Parliament 2013a; European Parliament 2013b; DARPA. Total Information Awareness Program (TIA), 2002; National Research Council, 2008; Congressional Research Service. CRS Report for Congress, 2008) are concrete examples which are not isolated incidents, but undoubtedly the NSA case (European Parliament, 2013c; Auerbach et al., 2013; European Parliament, 2013a; European Parliament, 2013b)[8] has clearly shown how could be invasive the surveillance in the era of global data flows and Big Data. To better understand the case, it's quite

---

[8] See fn. 6.

important to have an overview of the considerable amount of electronic surveillance legislation which, particularly in the wake of 9/11, has been approved in the United States and, to a certain extent, in a number of European countries.

The most important legislation is the Foreign Intelligence Surveillance Act (FISA) of 1978[9] which lays down the procedures for collecting foreign intelligence information through the electronic surveillance of communications for homeland security purposes. The section 702 of FISA Act amended in 2008 (FAA) extended its scope beyond interception of communications to include any data in public cloud computing as well. Furthermore, this section clearly indicates that two different regimes of data processing and protection exist for U.S. citizens and residents (USPERs) on the one hand, and non-U.S. citizens and residents (non-USPERs) on the other. More specifically the Fourth Amendment is applicable only for U.S. citizens as there is an absence of any cognizable privacy rights for "non-U.S. persons" under FISA (Bowden, 2013).

Thanks to FISA Act and the amendment of 2008, U.S. authorities have the possibility to access and process personal data of E.U. citizens on a large scale via, among others, the National Security Agency's (NSA) warrantless wiretapping of cable-bound internet traffic (UPSTREAM) and direct access to the personal data stored in the servers of U.S.-based private companies such as Microsoft, Yahoo, Google, Apple, Facebook or Skype (PRISM), through cross-database search programs such as X-KEYSCORE. U.S. authorities have also the power to compel disclosure of cryptographic keys, including the SSL keys used to secure data-in-transit by major search engines, social networks, webmail portals, and Cloud services in general (BULLRUN Program) (Corradino, 1989; Bowden, 2013). Recently the United States President's Review Group on Intelligence and Communications Technologies released a report entitled "Liberty and Security in a Changing World." The comprehensive report sets forth 46 recommendations designed to protect national security while respecting our longstanding commitment to privacy and civil liberties with a specific reference to on non-U.S. citizen (Clarke et al., 2014).

Even if the FISA Act is the mostly applied and known legislative tool to conduct intelligence activities, there are other relevant pieces of legislation on electronic surveillance. One need only to consider the Communications Assistance For Law Enforcement Act (CALEA) of 1994,[10] which authorizes the law enforcement and intelligence agencies to conduct electronic surveillance by requiring that telecommunications carriers and manufacturers of telecommunications equipment modify and design their equipment, facilities, and services to ensure that they have built-in surveillance. Furthermore, following the Patriot Act of 2001, a plethora of bill has been proposed. The most recent bills (not yet in force) are the Cyber Intelligence Sharing and Protection Act (CISPA) of 2013 (Jaycox and Opsahl, 2013), which would allow Internet traffic information to be shared between the U.S. government and certain

---

[9] Foreign Intelligence Surveillance Act (50 U.S.C. § 1801-1885C).
[10] See Communications Assistance for Law Enforcement Act (18 USC § 2522).

technology and manufacturing companies and the Protecting Children From Internet Pornographers Act of 2011,[11] which extends data retention duties to U.S. Internet Service Providers.

Truthfully, the surveillance programs are not only in the United Sattes. In Europe, the Communications Capabilities Development Program has prompted a huge amount of controversy, given its intention to create a ubiquitous mass surveillance scheme for the United Kingdom (Barret, 2014) in relation to phone calls, text messages and emails and extending to logging communications on social media. More recently, on June 2013 the so-called program TEMPORA showed that UK intelligence agency Government Communications Headquarters (GCHQ) has cooperated with the NSA in surveillance and spying activities (Brown, 2013).[12] These revelations were followed in September 2013 by reports focusing on the activities of Sweden's National Defense Radio Establishment (FRA). Similar projects for the large-scale interception of telecommunications data has been conducted by both France's General Directorate for External Security (DGSE) and Germany's Federal Intelligence Service (BDE) (Bigo et al., 2013).

Even if it seems that E.U. and U.S. surveillance programs are similar, there is one important difference: In the E.U., under Data Protection law, individuals have always control of their own personal data while in U.S., the individual have a more limited control once the user has subscribed to the terms and condition of a service.[13]

FORCED "ON CALL" COLLABORATION BY PRIVATE ENTITIES

Other than government agencies' monitoring activities, there are cases in which Internet Service Providers collaborate spontaneously or over a simple request from the law enforcement agencies. The exponential increase in Big Data since 2001 has provided a truly unique opportunity. In this respect, a key role has been played by Social Media. One need only reflect on the fact that Facebook, Twitter, Google+, and Instagram, all of which are situated in Silicon Valley, boast around 2 billion users throughout the world[14] and many of these users are citizens of the European Union. Facebook's founder may have intended "to empower the individual," but there is no doubt that Social Network Services (SNSs) have also empowered law enforcement (Kirkpatrick, 2013).

---

[11] Protecting Children From Internet Pornographers Act of 2011.

[12] See Letter from John Cunliffe (UK's Permanent Representative to the EU) to Juan Lopez Aguilar (Chairman of the European Parliament Committee on Civil Liberties, Justice and Home Affairs), 1 October 2013. Available: http://snurl.com/282nwfn [Jan. 31, 2014].

[13] See United States v. Miller (425 US 425 [1976]). In this case the United States Supreme Court held that the "bank records of a customer's accounts are the business records of the banks and that the customer can assert neither ownership nor possession of those records". The same principle could be applied to an Internet Service Provider.

[14] Google+ currently has 400 million users, Instragram 90 million, Facebook 963 million e Twitter 637 million. Retrieved October 28th, 2013, from http://bgr.com/2012/09/17/google-plus-stats-2012-400-million-members/; http://www.checkfacebook.com [Jan. 31, 2014]; http://socialfresh.com/1000instagram/ [Jan. 31, 2014]; http://twopcharts.com/twitter500million.php [Jan. 31, 2014].

Data Collection for Crime Prediction and Prevention

To stay on the topic of information acquisition by the law enforcement, there are two interesting cases of the collection of Big Data for crime prevention purposes:

The *first* is the "PredPol" software initially used by the Los Angeles police force and now by other police forces in the United States (Palm Beach, Memphis, Chicago, Minneapolis and Dallas). Predictive policing, in essence, cross check data, places and techniques of recent crimes with disparate sources, analyzing them and then using the results to anticipate, prevent and respond more effectively to future crime. Even if the software house created by PredPol declares that no profiling activities are carried out, it becomes essential to carefully understand the technology used to anonymize the personal data acquired by the law enforcement database. This type of software is bound to have a major impact in the United States on the conception of the protection of rights under the Fourth Amendment, and more specifically on concepts such as "probable cause" and "reasonable suspicion" which in future may come to depend on an algorithm rather than human choice (Ferguson, 2012).

The *second* example is X1 Social Discovery software.[15] This software maps a given location, such as a certain block within a city or even an entire particular metropolitan area, and searches the entire public Twitter feed to identify any geo-located tweets in the past three days (sometimes longer) within that specific area. This application can provide particularly useful data for the purpose of social control. One can imagine the possibility to have useful elements (e.g., IP address) to identify the subjects present in a given area during a serious car accident or a terrorist attack.

Legitimacy

From a strictly legal standpoint, these social control tools may be employed by gathering information from citizens directly due the following principle of public:

> *"Where someone does an act in public, the observance and recording of that act will ordinarily not give rise to an expectation of privacy".*

(Gillespie, 2009)

In the European Union, whilst this type of data collection frequently takes place, it could be in contrast with ECHR case law which, in the *Rotaru vs. Romania* case,[16] ruled that "public information can fall within the scope of private life where it is systematically collected and stored in files held by the authorities." As O'Floinn observes: "Non-private information can become private information depending on its retention and use. The accumulation of information is likely to result in the obtaining of private information about that person" (O'Floinn and Ormerod, 2001).

In the United States, this subject has been addressed in the case *People vs. Harris*,[17] currently pending in front of the Supreme Court. On January 26, 2012,

---

[15] See http://www.x1discovery.com/social_discovery.html [Jan. 31, 2014].
[16] See Rotaru v Romania (App. No. 28341/95) (2000) 8 B.H.R.C. at [43].
[17] See 2012 NY Slip Op 22175 [36 Misc 3d 868].

the New York County District Attorney's Office sent a subpoena to Twitter, Inc. seeking to obtain the Twitter records of user suspected of having participated in the "Occupy Wall Street" movement. Twitter refused to provide the law enforcement officers with the information requested and sought to quash the subpoena. The Criminal Court of New York confirmed the application made by the New York County District Attorney's Office, rejecting the arguments put forward by Twitter, stating that tweets are, by definition, public, and that a warrant is not required in order to compel Twitter to disclose them. The District Attorney's Office argued that the "third party disclosure" doctrine put forward for the first time in *United States vs. Miller* was applicable.[18]

USE OF PRIVATE SECTOR TOOLS AND RESOURCES

The second relationship concerns the use by the state of tools and resources from the private company for the purposes of organization and investigations. Given the vast oceans of Big Data, U.S. governmental authorities decided to turn to the private sector, not only for purposes of software management but also in relation to management of the data itself. One example is the CTO's Hadoop platform (CTO labs, 2012), which is capable of memorizing and storing data in relation to many law enforcement authorities in the United States. Similarly, a private cloud system has emerged which conveys the latest intelligence information in near-real time to U.S. troops stationed in Afghanistan (Conway, 2014). Another example is the facial recognition technology developed by Walt Disney for its park and sold to the U.S. military force (Wolfe, 2012).

Considering costs saving and massive computing power of a centralized cloud system, it is inevitable that law enforcement, military forces and government agencies will progressively rely on this type of services. The afore-mentioned change will entail deducible legal issues in terms of jurisdiction, security and privacy regarding data management. The relevant legal issues might be solved through a private cloud within the State with exclusive customer key control. However, it is worth considering that, in this way, private entities will gain access to a highly important and ever expanding information asset. Therefore, they will be able to develop increasingly sophisticated and data mining tools, thanks to cloud systems' potential. This scenario, which is already a fact in the United States, might become reality also thanks to the impulse of the Digital Agenda for Europe and its promotion of Public Private Partnership initiatives on Cloud (Commission of the European Communities, 2009; see also The European Cloud Partnership (ECP), 2013). This is why it is important that European cloud services should be based on high standards of data protection, security, interoperability and transparency about service levels and government access to information as it has recently been recognized by the European Commission (European Commission, 2013).

---

[18] See United States v. Miller (425 US 425 [1976]).

THE ROLE OF THE E.U. REFORM ON DATA PROTECTION IN LIMITING THE RISKS OF SOCIAL SURVEILLANCE

The framework described above shows that modern social control is the result of the interaction between the private and public sector. This collaborative model is not only based on mandatory disclosure orders issued by courts or administrative bodies, but has also extended to a more indefinite grey area of voluntary and proactive collaboration by big companies. It is difficult to get detailed information on this second model of voluntary collaboration; however, the predominance of U.S. companies in the ICT sector, particularly with regard to the Internet and cloud services, increases the influence of the U.S. administration on national companies and makes specific secret agreements of cooperation in social control easier (European Parliament, 2013a; European Parliament, 2012).

Against this background, the political and strategic value of the European rules on data protection emerges. These rules may assume the role of a protective barrier in order to prevent and limit access to the information about European citizens.[19] In this sense, the E.U. Proposal for a General Data Protection Regulation (European Commission, 2012) extends its territorial scope (Article 3 (2), 2013) through "the processing of personal data of data subjects in the Union by a controller or processor not established in the Union, where the processing activities are related to:

(a) the offering of goods or services, irrespective of whether a payment of the data subject is required, to such data subjects in the Union; or
(b) the monitoring of such data subjects".[20]

It should be noted that various commentators consider that the privacy risks related to Big Data analytics are low, pointing out the large amount of data processed by analytics and the de-identified nature of most of this data. This conclusion is wrong. Anonymity by de-identification is a difficult goal to achieve, as demonstrated in a number of studies (*see* Ohm, 2010; United States General Accounting Office, 2011; See also Zang and Bolot, 2011; Golle, 2006; Sweeney, 2000b; Sweeney, 2000a; Tene and Polonetsky, 2013). The power of Big Data analytics to draw unpredictable inference from information undermines many strategies based on de-identification (Mayer-Schönberger and Cukier, 2013; Schwartz and Solove, 2011). In many cases a reverse process in order to identify individuals is possible; it is also possible to identify them using originally anonymous data (*see* Ohm, 2010; United States General Accounting Office, 2011; See also Zang and Bolot, 2011; Golle, 2006; Sweeney, 2000b; Sweeney, 2000a; Tene and Polonetsky, 2013). Here, it is closer to the truth to affirm that each data is a piece of personal information than to assert that it is possible to manage data in a de-identified way.

---

[19] Although only information regarding natural persons are under the European regulation on data protection, the data concerning clients, suppliers, employees, shareholders and managers have a relevant strategical value in competition.
[20] See also Recital 21, PGDPR and Recital 21, PGDPR-LIBE_1-29.

Although the Proposal for a new regulation does not regard the data processed by public authorities for the purposes of prevention, investigation, detection, prosecution of criminal offences or the execution of criminal penalties,[21] its impact on social control is significant, since in many cases the databases of private companies are targeted by public authority investigations. For this reason, reducing the amount of data collected by private entities and increasing data subjects' self-determination with regard to their personal information limit the possibility of subsequent social control initiatives by government agencies.

However, the complexity of data processes and the power of modern analytics along with the presence of technological and market lock-in effects drastically reduce the awareness of data subjects, their capability to evaluate the various consequences of their choices and the expression of a real free and informed consent (Brandimarte et al., 2010). This lack of awareness facilitates the creation of wider databases, which are accessible by the authorities in cases provided by the law, and is not avoided by giving adequate information to the data subjects or by privacy policies, due to the fact that these notices are read only by a very limited number of users who, in many cases, are not able to understand part of the legal terms usually used in these notices (Turow et al., 2007).

These aspects are even more relevant in a Big Data context rendering the traditional model of data protection to be in crisis (Cate, 2006; See also Cate and Mayer-Schönberger, 2012; Rubinstein, 2013). The traditional model is based on general prohibition plus "notice and consent"[22] and the coherence of the data collection with the purposes defined at the moment in which the information is collected. However, nowadays much of the value of personal information is not apparent when notice and consent are normally given (Cate, 2006; See also Cate and Mayer-Schönberger, 2012; Rubinstein, 2013) and the "transformative" (Tene and Polonetsky, 2012) use of Big Data makes it often impossible to explain the description of all its possible uses at the time of initial collection.

The E.U. Proposal, in order to reinforce the protection of individual information, interacts with these constraints and shifts the focus of data protection from an individual choice toward a privacy-oriented architecture (Mantelero, 2013a).[23] This approach, which limits the amount of data collected through "structural" barriers and introduces a preventive data protection assessment (Article 23, 2013), also produces a direct effect on social control by reducing the amount of information available.

---

[21] This area will fall under the new Proposal for a Directive on the protection of individuals with regard to the processing of personal data by competent authorities for the purposes of prevention, investigation, detection or prosecution of criminal offences or the execution of criminal penalties, and the free movement of such data, COM(2012) 10 final, Brussels, 25 January 2012 (hereinafter abbreviated as PDPI). Available at http://eur-lex.europa.eu/LexUriServ/LexUriServ.do?uri=COM:2012:0010:FIN:EN:PDF [Dec. 10, 2013]; see the Explanatory Memorandum of the Proposal.

[22] With regard to personal information collected by public entities the Directive 95/45/EC permits the data collection without the consent of data subject in various cases; however, the notice to data subjects is necessary also in these cases. See Articles 7, 8 and 10, Directive 95/46/EC.

[23] See Article 23, PGDPR-LIBE_1-29 and also Article 23, PGDPR.

With regard to the information collected, the E.U. Proposal reinforces users' self-determination by requiring *data portability*, which gives the user the right to obtain a copy of the data undergoing processing from the controller "in an electronic and structured format which is commonly used and allows for further use by the data subject".[24] Portability will reduce the risk of technological lock-in due to the technological standards and data formats adopted by service providers, which limit the migration from one service to another. However, in many cases and mainly in social media context, the limited number of companies providing the services reduces the chances for users not to be tracked by moving their account from one platform to another and, thereby, minimizes the positive effects of data portability.

Finally, the Proposal reinforces the right to obtain the *erasure of data* processed without the consent of the data subject, against his objection, without providing adequate information for him or outside of the legal framework (Mantelero, 2013b). An effective implementation of this right can reduce the overall amount of data stored by service providers, and may limit the amount of information existing in the archives without a legitimate reason for the processing of information. In this manner, the possibility of consulting the history of individual profiles by authorities is also reduced.

All the aspects considered above concur to limit the information available to all entities interested in social control, and therefore, also affect the request of disclosure held by government agencies and courts to private companies. Nevertheless, these powers of search and seizure and their exercise represent the fundamental core of social control.

PRESERVING THE E.U. DATA PROTECTION STANDARD IN A GLOBALIZED WORLD

In order to analyze this aspect in the scenario of the future European data protection framework it is necessary to consider both proposals by the European Commission:

- the Proposal for a new General Data Protection Regulation (PGDPR) (see European Commission, 2012) and
- the less debated Proposal for a Directive in the law enforcement sector (PDPI).[25]

Although the second proposal is more specific on governmental and judicial control, the first considers this aspect from the point of view of the data flows.

The new Proposal for a new General Data Protection Regulation, as well as the currently in force Directive 96/46/EC, allows trans-border data flows from the Europe to other countries only when the third country provides an adequate level of data protection (Mantelero, 2012). When evaluating the adequacy of data protection in a given country, the Commission should also consider to the legislation in force in third countries "including concerning public security, defense, national security and

---

[24] See Article 15, PGDPR-LIBE_1-29 and also Article 18, PGDPR.
[25] See above fn. 21.

criminal law".[26] Consequently, the presence of invasive investigative public bodies and the lack of adequate guarantees to the data subject assume relevance for the decision whether to limit the trans-border data flows between subsidiaries and holdings or between companies. Once again this limit does not affect public authorities, but restricts the set of information held by private companies available for their scrutiny.

Without considering the NSA case that is still on-going, an explanatory case on the relationship between trans-border data flows, foreign jurisdiction and the possible effects on citizens and social control is provided by the SWIFT case; the same criticism applies and has been expressed by commentators with regard to the U.S. Patriot Act. These two cases differ because in the NSA case non-E.U. authorities requested to access information held by a company based in the E.U., whereas in the SWIFT case the requests were directed to U.S. companies in order to have access to the information they received from their E.U. subsidiaries.

In the SWIFT case (Article 29 Data Protection Working Party, 2006b) the Article 29 Data Protection Working Party clarified that a foreign law does not represent the legal base for the disclosure of personal information to non-E.U. authorities, since only the international instruments provide an appropriate legal framework enabling international cooperation (Article 29 Data Protection Working Party, 2006b; see also Article 29 Data Protection Working Party, 2006a). Furthermore, the exception provided by Art. 26 (1) (b) Directive 95/46/EC[27] does not apply when the transfer is not necessary or legally required on important public interest grounds of an E.U. Member State (Article 29 Data Protection Working Party, 2006b).[28]

In contrast (as emerged in the PATRIOT Act case and also with reference to the wider, complex and dynamic system of powers enjoyed by the U.S. government in the realm of criminal investigations and national security (van Hoboken et al., 2012)[29]), the U.S. authorities may access data held by the E.U. subsidiaries of U.S. companies.[30] However, it is necessary to point out that there is a potential breach of protection of personal data of European citizens and that this happens not only with regards to U.S. laws, but also in relations with other foreign regulations, as demonstrated by the recent draft of the Indian Privacy (Protection) Bill[31] and Chinese laws on data protection (Greenleaf and Tian, 2013; The Decision of the Standing Committee of the National People's

---

[26] See Article 41 (2) (a), PGDPR-LIBE_30-91 and also Art. 41 (2) (a), PGDPR.

[27] Art. 26 (1) (b) justifies the transfer that is necessary or legally required on important public interest grounds, or for the establishment, exercise or defence of legal claims (Article 26 (1) (d) of the Directive.

[28] "Any other interpretation would make it easy for a foreign authority to circumvent the requirement for adequate protection in the recipient country laid down in the Directive".

[29] See above § 2.

[30] It is necessary to underline that the guarantees provided by the U.S. Constitution in the event of U.S. government requests for information do not apply to European citizens, as well as, legal protection under specific U.S. laws applies primarily to U.S. citizens and residents.

[31] See Privacy (Protection) Bill, 2013, updated third draft. Available: http://cis-india.org/internet-governance/blog/privacy-protection-bill-2013-updated-third-draft [Jan. 31, 2014].

Congress on Strengthening Internet Information Protection 2012; Ministry of Industry and Information Technology Department Order, 2011; Greenleaf, 2013).

In order to reduce such intrusions the draft version of the E.U. Proposal for a General Data Protection Regulation limited the disclosure to foreign authorities and provided that

> *"no judgment of a court or tribunal and no decision of an administrative authority of a third country requiring a controller or processor to disclose personal data shall be recognized or be enforceable in any manner, without prejudice to a mutual assistance treaty or an international agreement in force between the requesting third country and the Union or a Member State".*[32]

The draft also obliged controllers and processors to notify national supervisory authorities of any such requests and to obtain prior authorization for the transfer by the supervisory authority (See also European Parliament, 2013c; European Parliament, 2013a; European Parliament, 2013b).[33] These provisions had been dropped from the final version of the Commission's Proposal on 25 January 2012, but have now been reintroduced by the European Parliament, as a reaction to the NSA case.[34]

In addition to the Proposal for a General Data Protection Regulation, the above-mentioned Proposal for a Directive on the protection of individuals with regard to the processing of personal data by competent authorities (PDPI) establishes some protection against a possible *violation* of *EU citizens' privacy.*

The goal of this Directive is to ensure that "in a global society characterized by rapid technological change where information exchange knows no borders" the fundamental right to data protection is consistently protected.[35] One of the main issues at E.U. level is the lack of harmonization across Member States' data protection law and even more "in the context of all E.U. policies, including law enforcement and crime prevention as well as in our international relations" (European Commission, 2010). Whilst a directive may not have the same impact on harmonizing national regulations currently in force in various Member States (For a critical view on this point see Cannataci, 2013; See also Cannataci and Caruana, 2014), it does in fact represent the first piece of legislation to have direct effect when compared to the previous attempts by way of Council of Europe Recommendation No. R (87)[36] and Framework Decision 2008/977/JHA.[37]

---

[32] See Art. 42 (1), Proposal for a General Data Protection Regulation, draft Version 56, November 29th, 2011.

[33] See Art. 42 (2), Proposal for a General Data Protection Regulation, draft Version 56, November 29th, 2011. ("[The European Parliament] Regrets the fact that the Commission has dropped the former Article 42 of the leaked version of the Data Protection Regulation; calls on the Commission to clarify why it decided to do so; calls on the Council to follow Parliament's approach and reinsert such a provision").

[34] See Article 43a, PGDPR-LIBE_30-91. This provision does not clearly define the assignment of competence between the National Supervisory Authority and the Judicial Authority with regard to the request of judicial cooperation.

[35] See PDPI, explanatory Memorandum, (SEC(2012) 72 final).

[36] Recommendation No. R (87) 15 regulating the use of personal data in the police sector.

[37] Framework Decision 2008/977/JHA on the protection of personal data processed in the framework of police and judicial cooperation in criminal matters, (2008), Official Journal L 350, pp. 60–71.

The founding principles of this Directive, which are shared with the previous directives referred to, are twofold:

(1) First there is the need for *fair, lawful, and adequate data processing* during criminal investigations or to prevent a crime, on the basis of which every data must be collected for specified, explicit and legitimate purposes and must be erased or rectified without delay (Art. 4, PDPI and Art. 4b, 2013).

(2) Then there is the obligation to make a clear distinction between the various *categories of the possible data subjects* in a criminal proceeding (persons with regard to whom there are serious grounds for believing that they have committed or are about to commit a criminal offence, persons convicted, victims of criminal offense, third parties to the criminal offence).

For each of these categories there must be a different adequate level of attention on data protection, especially for persons who do not fall within any of the categories referred above.[38]

These two principles are of considerable importance, although their application on a practical level will be neither easy nor immediate in certain Member States. This is easily demonstrated by the difficulties encountered when either drafting practical rules distinguishing between several categories of potential data subjects within the papers on a court file, or attempting to identify the principle on the basis of which a certain court document is to be erased.

In addition to these two general principles the provisions of the Directive, are interesting and confirm consolidated data protection principles. Suffice to mention here the prohibition on using measures solely based on automated processing of personal data which significantly affect or produce an *adverse legal effect* for the data subject,[39] as well as the implementation of *data protection by design and by default* mechanisms to ensure the protection of the data subject's rights and the processing of only those personal data.[40]

Furthermore, the proposal for a Directive in the law enforcement sector entails the obligation to designate a data protection officer in all law enforcement agencies in order to monitor the implementation and application of the policies on the protection of personal data.[41]

These principles constitute a significant limitation to possible data mining of personal and sensitive data collection by law enforcement agencies. If it is true that most of these provisions were also present in the Recommendation No. R (87) of Council of Europe and in the Framework Decision 2008/977/JHA, it is also true that propelling data protection *by design* and *by default* mechanisms and measures could encourage data anonymization and help to avoid the indiscriminate use of automated processing of personal data.

---

[38] Art. 5, PDPI-LIBE.
[39] Art. 9a, PDPI-LIBE.
[40] Art. 19, PDPI.
[41] Art. 30, PDPI.

REFERENCES

Abraham, S., Hickok, E., 2012. Government access to private-sector data in India. Int. Data Privacy Law 2 (4), 302–315.

Article 3 (2), Proposal for a regulation of the European Parliament and of the Council on the protection of individual with regard to the processing of personal data and on the free movement of such data (General Data Protection Regulation),(COM(2012)0011 – C7 0025/2012 – 2012/0011(COD)), Compromise amendments on Articles 1-29 (hereinafter abbreviated as PGDPR-LIBE_1-29). http://www.europarl.europa.eu/meetdocs/2009_2014/documents/libe/dv/comp_am_art_01-29/comp_am_art_01-29en.pdf [Dec. 10, 2013]. See also Article 3 (2), PGDPR.

ASOS API project at http://developer.asos.com/page [Sept. 29, 2013].

Article 23, Proposal for a regulation of the European Parliament and of the Council on the protection of individual with regard to the processing of personal data and on the free movement of such data (General Data Protection Regulation),(COM(2012)0011 – C7 0025/2012 – 2012/0011(COD)), Compromise amendments on Articles 30-91 (hereinafter abbreviated as PGDPR-LIBE_30-91). http://www.europarl.europa.eu/meetdocs/2009_2014/documents/libe/dv/comp_am_art_30-91/comp_am_art_30-91en.pdf [Dec. 15, 2013].

Art. 4, PDPI and Art. 4b, Proposal for a directive of the European Parliament and of the Council on the protection of individuals with regard to the processing of personal data by competent authorities for the purposes of prevention, investigation, detection or prosecution of criminal offences or the execution of criminal penalties, and the free movement of such data (COM(2012)0010 – C7-0024/2012 – 2012/0010(COD)) (hereinafter abbreviated as PDPI-LIBE). Available: http://www.europarl.europa.eu/meetdocs/2009_2014/organes/libe/libe_20131021_1830.htm [Nov. 15, 2013].

Article 29 Data Protection Working Party, 2006a. Opinion 1/2006 on the application of the EU data protection rules to internal whistleblowing schemes in the fields of accounting, internal accounting controls, auditing matters, fight against, banking and financial crime.

Article 29 Data Protection Working Party, 2006b. Opinion 10/2006 on the processing of personal data by the Society for Worldwide Interbank Financial Telecommunication (SWIFT).

Article 29 Data Protection Working Party, 2005. Article 29 Working Party report on the obligation to notify the national supervisory authorities, the best use of exceptions and simplification and the role of the data protection officers in the European Union, Bruxelles. http://ec.europa.eu/justice/policies/privacy/docs/wpdocs/2005/wp106_en.pdf [10.12.13].

Article 29 Data Protection Working Party, 1997. Working Document: Notification, Bruxelles. http://ec.europa.eu/justice/policies/privacy/docs/wpdocs/1997/wp8_en.pdf [10.12.13].

Auerbach, D., Mayer, J., Eckersley, P., 2013. What We Need to Know About PRISM, June 12. https://www.eff.org [10.12.13].

Bailey, J., 2012. Systematic government access to private-sector data in Canada. Int. Data Privacy Law 2 (4), 207–219.

Barret, D., 2014. Phone and email records to be stored in new spy plan, in The Telegraph. http://www.telegraph.co.uk/technology/internet/9090617/Phone-and-email-records-to-be-stored-in-new-spy-plan.html [31.01.14].

Bigo, D., Carrera, S., Hernanz, N., Jeandesboz, J., Parkin, J., Ragazzi, F., Scherrer, A., 2013. The US surveillance programmes and their impact on EU citizens' fundamental rights, Study for the European Parliament, PE 493.032, Sept. 2013.

Boyd, D., Crawford, K., 2011. "Six Provocations for Big Data," presented at the "A Decade in Internet Time: Symposium on the Dynamics of the Internet and Society". Oxford

Internet Institute, Oxford, United Kingdom, Available: http://papers.ssrn.com/sol3/papers.cfm?abstract_id=1926431 [10.12.13].

Bowden, C., 2013. The US surveillance programmes and their impact on EU citizens' fundamental rights, Study for the European Parliament, PE 474.405, 15 October 2013.

Brandimarte, L., Acquisti, A., Loewenstein, G., 2010. Misplaced Confidences: Privacy and the Control Paradox. Internet, presented at the 9th Annual Workshop on the Economics of Information Security, Cambridge, MA, USA. http://www.heinz.cmu.edu/~acquisti/papers/acquisti-SPPS.pdf [15.02.13].

Brown, I., 2012. Government access to private-sector data in the United Kingdom. Int. Data Privacy Law 2 (4), 230–238.

Brown, I., 2013. Lawful Interception Capability Requirements. *Computers & Law*, Aug./Sep. 2013. http://papers.ssrn.com/sol3/papers.cfm?abstract_id=2309413.

Brown, I., 2013 Expert Witness Statement for Big Brother Watch and Others Re: Large-Scale Internet Surveillance by the UK. Application No: 58170/13 to the European Court of Human Rights. http://papers.ssrn.com/sol3/papers.cfm?abstract_id=2336609, Sept. 27, [31.01.14].

Bygrave, A.L., 2002. Data Protection Law. Approaching Its Rationale, Logic and Limits, Kluwer Law International. London, New York, The Hague.

Cannataci, J.A., Caruana, M. Report: Recommendation R (87) 15—Twenty-five years down the line. http://www.statewatch.org/news/2013/oct/coe-report-data-privacy-in-the-police-sector.pdf [31.01.14].

Cannataci, J.A., 2013. Defying the logic, forgetting the facts: the new European proposal for data protection in the police sector. Eur. J. Law Technol. 3 (2). Available: http://ejlt.org/article/view/284/390.

Canadian Goldcorp Inc. case at http://www.ideaconnection.com/open-innovation-success/Open-Innovation-Goldcorp-Challenge-00031.html [Sept. 10, 2013].

Cate, F.H., Cate, B.E., 2012. The Supreme Court and information privacy. Int. Data Privacy Law 2 (4), 255–267.

Cate, F.H., Mayer-Schönberger, V., 2012. Notice and Consent in a World of Big Data. Microsoft Global Privacy Summit Summary Report and Outcomes. http://www.microsoft.com/en-au/download/details.aspx?id=35596 [15.09.2013].

Cate, F.H., Dempsey, J.X., Rubinstein, I.S., 2012. Systematic government access to private-sector data. Int. Data Privacy Law 2 (4), 195–199.

Cate, F.H. The failure of fair information practice principles. In: Winn, J. (Ed.), Consumer Protection in the Age of the Information Economy. Aldershot-Burlington, Ashgate, 2006, pp. 343–345. http://papers.ssrn.com/sol3/papers.cfm?abstract_id=1156972.

Clarke, R., Morell, M., Stone, G., Sunstein, C., Swire, P., Liberty and Security in a changing World, Report and Recommendations of The President's Review Group on Intelligence and Communications Technologies. http://www.whitehouse.gov/sites/default/files/docs/2013-12-12_rg_final_report.pdf [31.01.14].

Commission of the European Communities, 2009. Communication from the Commission to the European Parliament, the Council, the European Economic and Social Committee and the Committee of the Regions, October 28. http://eur-lex.europa.eu/LexUriServ/LexUriServ.do?uri=COM:2009:0479:FIN:EN:PDF [31.01.14].

Congressional Research Service. CRS Report for Congress, 2008. Data Mining and Homeland Security: An Overview. www.fas.org/sgp/crs/homesec/RL31798.pdf [10.12.13].

Conway, S., 2014. Big Data Cloud Delivers Military Intelligence to U.S. Army in Afghanistan, in Datanami, 6 February 2012. http://snurl.com/284ak5j [31.01.14].

Corradino, E., 1989. The fourth amendment overseas: is extraterritorial protection of foreign nationals going too far? Fordham Law Rev. 57 (4), 617.

Council of Europe, 2008. Guidelines for the cooperation between law enforcement and internet service providers against cybercrime, Strasbourg, 1–2 April 2008. http://www.coe.int/t/informationsociety/documents/Guidelines_cooplaw_ISP_en.pdf.

CTO labs, 2012. White Paper: Big Data Solutions for Law Enforcement. http://ctolabs.com/wp-content/uploads/2012/06/120627HadoopForLawEnforcement.pdf [31.01.14].

Cyganiak and A. Jentzsch, A. "The Linking Open Data cloud diagram". Internet: http://lod-cloud.net/, Sept. 19, 2011 [Sept. 4, 2013].

DARPA. Total Information Awareness Program (TIA), 2002. System Description Document (SDD), Version 1.1. http://epic.org/privacy/profiling/tia/tiasystemdescription.pdf [10.12.13].

Deloitte,2012.Opendata.Drivinggrowth,ingenuityandinnovation.London,pp.16–20.Available: http://www.deloitte.com/assets/dcom-unitedkingdom/local%20assets/documents/market%20insights/deloitte%20analytics/uk-insights-deloitte-analytics-open-data-june-2012.pdf [10.12.13].

http://data.enel.com/ [Sept. 29, 2013] project that shares data sets regarding Enel, an Italian multinational group active in the power and gas sectors.

European Commission, 2010. Study on the economic benefits of privacy enhancing technologies or the Comparative study on different approaches to new privacy challenges, in particular in the light of technological developments. http://ec.europa.eu/justice/policies/privacy/docs/studies/new_privacy_challenges/final_report_en.pdf [31.01.14].

European Commission, Proposal for a regulation of the European Parliament and the Council on the protection of individuals with regard to the processing of personal data and on the free movement of such data (General Data Protection Regulation), COM(2012) 11 final, Brussels, 25 January 2012 (hereinafter abbreviated as PGDPR). Available: http://ec.europa.eu/justice/data-protection/document/review2012/com_2012_11_en.pdf [Dec. 10, 2013].

European Commission, 2013. "What does the Commission mean by secure Cloud computing services in Europe?", MEMO/13/898, 15 October. http://europa.eu/rapid/press-release_MEMO-13-898_en.htm.

European Parliament, Directorate General for Internal Policies, Policy Department C: Citizens' Rights and Constitutional Affairs, Civil Liberties, Justice and Home Affairs, 2013a. The US National Security Agency (NSA) surveillance programmes (PRISM) and Foreign Intelligence Surveillance Act (FISA) activities and their impact on EU citizens. http://info.publicintelligence.net/EU-NSA-Surveillance.pdf [10.12.2013], pp.14–16.

European Parliament, Directorate General for Internal Policies, Policy Department C: Citizens' Rights and Constitutional Affairs, Civil Liberties, Justice and Home Affairs, 2013b. National Programmes for Mass Surveillance of Personal data in EU Member States and Their Compatibility with EU Law. http://www.europarl.europa.eu/committees/it/libe/studiesdownload.html?languageDocument=EN&file=98290 [10.12.13], pp.12–16.

European Parliament, Directorate-General for Internal Policies, Policy Department Citizens' Right and Constitutional Affairs, 2012. Fighting cyber crime and protecting privacy in the cloud. http://www.europarl.europa.eu/committees/en/studiesdownload.html?languageDocument=EN&file=79050 [31.01.14].

European Parliament, 2001. Report on the existence of a global system for the interception of private and commercial communications (ECHELON interception system). http://www.fas.org [10.12.2013].

European Parliament, 2013c. Resolution of 4 July 2013 on the US National Security Agency surveillance programme, surveillance bodies in various Member States and their impact on EU citizens' privacy. http://www.europarl.europa.eu/sides/getDoc.do?pubRef=-//EP//TEXT+TA+P7-TA-2013-0322+0+DOC+XML+V0//EN [10.12.13].

Executive Office of the President, National Science and Technology Council, 2013. Smart Disclosure and Consumer Decision Making: Report of the Task Force on Smart Disclosure. Washington.   http://www.whitehouse.gov/sites/default/files/microsites/ostp/report_of_the_task_force:on_smart_disclosure.pdf [10.12.13].

Ferguson, A., 2012. Predictive policing: the future of reasonable suspicion. *Emory Law J.* 62, 259–325. http://www.law.emory.edu/fileadmin/journals/elj/62/62.2/Ferguson.pdf [31.01.14].

Gillespie, A., 2009. Regulation of Internet Surveillance. Eur. Human Rights Law Rev. 4, 552–565.

Golle, P., 2006. Revisiting the uniqueness of simple demographics in the US population. In: Proc. 5th ACM Workshop on Privacy in Electronic Society. pp. 77–80.

Greenleaf, G., Tian, G., 2013. China Expands Data Protection through 2013 Guidelines: A 'Third Line' for Personal Information Protection (With a Translation of the Guidelines). *Privacy Laws Business Int. Rep.* 122, 1. http://papers.ssrn.com/sol3/papers.cfm?abstract_id=2280037 [25.10.13].

Greenleaf, G., 2013. China: NPC Standing Committee takes a small leap forward. Privacy Laws Business Int. Rep. 121, 1–7.

Jaycox, M.M., Opsahl, K., 2013. CISPA is Back. https://www.eff.org/cybersecurity-bill-faq [31.01.14].

Kirkpatrick, D., 2013. The Facebook Effect: The Inside Story of the Company That Is Connecting the World. Simon and Schuster, New York.

Kroes, N., 2011. The Digital Agenda: Europe's key driver of growth and innovation. SPEECH/11/629. Brussels. http://europa.eu/rapid/press-release_SPEECH-11-629_en.htm [10.12.13].

Mantelero, A., 2012. Cloud computing, trans-border data flows and the European Directive 95/46/EC: applicable law and task distribution. Eur. J. Law Technol 3 (2). http://ejlt.org//article/view/96.

Mantelero, A., 2013a. Competitive value of data protection: the impact of data protection regulation on online behaviour. Int. Data Privacy Law 3 (4), 231–238.

Mantelero, A., 2013b. The EU Proposal for a General Data Protection Regulation and the roots of the 'right to be forgotten'. Computer Law Security Rev. 29, 229–235.

Marton, A., Avital, M., Blegind Jensen, J., 2013. Reframing Open Big Data, presented at ECIS 2013, Utrecht, Netherlands, http://aisel.aisnet.org/ecis2013_cr/146 [10.12.2013].

Mayer-Schönberger, V., Cukier, K., 2013. Big Data: A Revolution That Will Transform How We Live, Work and Think. John Murray Publishers, London, pp. 154–156.

Ministry of Industry and Information Technology Department Order, Several Regulations on Standardizing Market Order for Internet Information Services, published on 29 December 2011. http://www.miit.gov.cn/n11293472/n11293832/n12771663/14417081.html [25.10.13].

National Research Council, 2008. Protecting Individual Privacy in the Struggle Against Terrorists: A Framework for Program Assessment. Washington, D.C., Appendix I and Appendix J.

Nike Inc., http://www.nikeresponsibility.com/report/downloads [Sept. 29, 2013].

O'Floinn, M., Ormerod, D., 2001. Social networking sites RIPA and criminal investigations. Crim. L.R. 24, 766–789.

Ohm, P., 2010. Broken Promises of privacy: responding to the surprising failure of anonymization. UCLA L. Rev. 57, 1701–1777.

Open Knowledge Foundation (OKF), http://okfn.org [Sept. 10, 2013].

Pell, S.K., 2012. Systematic government access to private-sector data in the United States. Int. Data Privacy Law 2 (4), 245–254.

Reidenberg, J., 2013. The Data Surveillance State in the US and Europe. *Wake Forest Law Rev.* http://papers.ssrn.com/sol3/papers.cfm?abstract_id=2349269#!.

Rubinstein, I.S., 2013. Big Data: the end of privacy or a new beginning? *Int. Data Privacy Law* 3 (2), 74–87. http://papers.ssrn.com/sol3/papers.cfm?abstract_id=2157659.

Schwartz, P.M., 2012. Systematic government access to private-sector data in Germany. Int. Data Privacy Law 2 (4), 289–301.

Schwartz, P.M., Solove, D.J., 2011. The PII problem: privacy and a new concept of personally identifiable information. New York University L. Rev. 86, 1841–1845.

Svantesson, D.B.J., 2012. Systematic government access to private-sector data in Australia. Int. Data Privacy Law 2 (4), 268–276.

Sweeney, L., 2000a. Foundations of Privacy Protection from a Computer Science Perspective. In: Proc. Joint Statistical Meeting. AAAS, Indianapolis.

Sweeney, L., 2000b. Simple Demographics Often Identify People Uniquely. Data Privacy Working Paper 3 Carnegie Mellon University, Pittsburgh.

Swire, P., 2012. From real-time intercepts to stored records: why encryption drives the government to seek access to the cloud. Int. Data Privacy Law 2 (4), 200–206.

Tene, O., Polonetsky, J., 2013. Big Data for all: privacy and user control in the age of analytics. Nw. J. Tech. Intell. Prop 11, 239–274. http://papers.ssrn.com/sol3/papers.cfm?abstract_id=2149364 [10.12.13].

Tene, O., Polonetsky, J., 2012. Privacy in the age of big data: a time for big decisions. Stan. L. Rev. Online 64, 63–69.

Tene, O., 2012. Systematic government access to private-sector data in Israel. Int. Data Privacy Law 2 (4), 277–288.

The Aspen Institute, 2010. *The Promise and Peril of Big Data*. David Bollier Rapporteur, Washington. http://www.aspeninstitute.org/sites/default/files/content/docs/pubs/The_Promise_and_Peril_of_Big_Data.pdf [10.12.13].

Zang, H., Bolot, J., 2011. Anonymization of location data does not work: a large-scale measurement study. In: Proc. MobiCom '11 Proceedings of the 17th Annual International Conference on Mobile Computing and Networking. pp. 145–156.

The Decision of the Standing Committee of the National People's Congress on Strengthening Internet Information Protection, adopted at the 30th Session of Standing Committee of the 11th National People's Congress on December 28, 2012. http://ishimarulaw.com/strengthening-network-information-protectionoctober-china-bulletin/ [25.10.13].

The European Cloud Partnership (ECP), https://ec.europa.eu/digital-agenda/node/609 [Dec. 10, 2013].

Tsuchiya, M., 2012. Systematic government access to private-sector data in Japan. Int. Data Privacy Law 2 (4), 239–244.

Turow, J., Hoofnagle, C., Mulligan, D., Good, N., Grossklags, J., 2007. The Federal Trade Commission and Consumer Privacy in the Coming Decade. *ISJLP* 3, 723–749. http://scholarship.law.berkeley.edu/facpubs/935.

United States General Accounting Office, 2011. Record Linkage and Privacy. Issues in creating New Federal Research and Statistical Information. http://www.gao.gov/assets/210/201699.pdf [10.12.13].

van Hoboken, J.V.J., Arnbak, A.M., van Eijk, N.A.N.M., 2012. Cloud Computing in Higher Education and Research Institutions and the USA Patriot Act. Institute for Information

Law University of Amsterdam. http://www.ivir.nl/publications/vanhoboken/Cloud_Computing_Patriot_Act_2012.pdf [25.10.13].

Veenswijk, M., Koerten, H., Poot, J., 2012. Unravelling Organizational Consequences of PSI Reform—An In-depth Study of the Organizational Impact of the Reuse of Public Sector Data. ETLA, Helsinki, http://www.etla.fi/en/julkaisut/dp1275-en/ [10.12.13].

Wang, Z., 2012. Systematic government access to private-sector data in China. Int. Data Privacy Law 2 (4), 220–229.

Wolfe, N., 2012. The new totalitarianism of surveillance technology. Guardian [On-line]. http://www.theguardian.com/commentisfree/2012/aug/15/new-totalitarianism-surveillance-technology [31.01.14].

Social media and its role for LEAs: Review and applications

15

P. Saskia Bayerl, Babak Akhgar, Ben Brewster, Konstantinos Domdouzis,
Helen Gibson

INTRODUCTION

Social media has become a major aspect of online activity, and thus an essential part of cybercrime and cyber terrorism-related operations. As LEA's (law enforcement agencies) focus on cybercrime and cyber terrorism threats increases, so does the requirement to consider the potential application of social media as a vital aspect of any cyber defense strategy. In order to develop an understanding of cyber-related activity, an appreciation of social media's role in society is required to enable the development of strategies that tackle not only cybercrime and cyber terrorism, but also crimes facilitated through the use of social media. These include its potential exploitation in combatting a wide variety of criminal threats, such as those identified in the scenarios in the section "LEA Usage Scenarios for Social Media," and ultimately in the development of competitive advantage over a wide variety of illicit criminal activity.

Although social media is often associated with large network services such as Facebook and Twitter, the term social media refers to a larger family of service platforms. These services can be clustered into six groups (Kaplan and Haenlein, 2010):

1. Collaborative projects (e.g., Wikipedia)
2. Blogs, including microblogs (e.g., Twitter)
3. Content communities (e.g., YouTube)
4. Social networking sites (e.g., Facebook, LinkedIn)
5. Virtual game worlds (e.g., World of Warcraft)
6. Virtual social worlds (e.g., Second Life)

The difference between social media and "traditional" media is the potential for users to create and exchange content that they themselves have created (Kaplan and Haenlein, 2010). This shift has resulted in users moving away from the passive reception of content to actively participating in the creation of online content.

In this process, social media has begun to serve a number of disparate purposes. Ji et al. (2010) differentiate between five main functions:

1. *Communication*: conversations with friends and the conveyance of individual opinions through the network
2. *Connection*: maintenance of relationships created offline
3. *Content sharing*: sharing or distribution of content such as information, music, videos, etc.
4. *Expert search*: search for people, who hold professional knowledge and expertise that users wish to access
5. *Identity*: publishing of own characteristics, emotions, moods, etc., to express users' identity online

These functions are not necessarily linked to specific social media platforms. In fact, often one social media platform can serve multiple functions. LinkedIn, a professional social networking site, accommodates all five: building connections with offline acquaintances such as colleagues, the sharing of content such as documents and links, searching for subject matter experts as well as the representation of the user's own professional identity. It can also be used for communication purposes that range from the sending and receipt of personal emails to the advertisement of business services.

For many citizens social media has become an integral part of everyday life. Currently, estimates state that around 30% of the world's population use social networking sites (Gaudin, 2013a), and while established networks such as Facebook may be seeing a stagnation in their user numbers or at least a shift in the demographics of their users, the general trend of growth in the use of social media remains unbroken. As of 2013, 73% of US adults have memberships to at least one social networking site, with around 42% using multiple sites (Duggan and Smith, 2013).

In Facebook's ten-year existence it has developed from a small network of college students to a global platform that boasts 1.19 billion users. Further, rival platforms such as Google+and Twitter each boast around 500 million users each, with LinkedIn having 238 million users. And despite the fact that the most prevalent social media services are still US-based, the most engaged users in terms of average hours spent using social networks per month hail from Israel, Argentina, Russia, Turkey and Chile (Statistics Brain, 2014).

Given its almost ubiquitous nature, social media has become a vital tool for LEAs in developing competitive advantage against organized criminal threats. To this end, social media serves three main purposes (Denef et al., 2012; Kaptein, 2012):

1. Distribution of information to the public regarding security issues to enhance preventive police tasks,
2. The improvement of operational efficiency by broadening public participation, and
3. The improvement of public trust in the police by raising accessibility and transparency.

In addition to this, social media also enables the acquisition of intelligence (see section on LEA usage scenarios for social media in this chapter).

The diversity of purposes served by social media means that one can differentiate between a performative aspect and a relational aspect of its use by LEAs. The ***performative*** aspect refers to the use of social media as an instrument for the support of operations, either through the distribution or acquisition of information. Individual examples showcasing the application of services such as Twitter and Facebook in crime prevention and criminal conviction can be used to demonstrate their potential use case. For instance, in October 2008, a status note on Facebook aided in the resolution of a first degree murder case in the Canadian city of Edmonton, while Belgian police have had positive experiences in using Facebook to prevent violent attacks between known hostile groups. According to the latest survey by the International Association of Chiefs of Police (IACP), the value of social media for police forces lies in its high potential for information dissemination in emergency and disaster situations, crime investigations, and public relations and community outreach initiatives (IACP, 2013). According to the same survey, 95.9% of US police forces now employ social media in their investigations, with 80.4% of those claiming that social media had aided in the resolution of a crime.

Next to the performative function, processes such as community outreach and public relations illustrate the ***relational aspect*** of social media use. Relational usage refers to the building and maintenance of relationships with members of the public with a focus on increasing the trust in, and legitimacy of LEAs. This is established through positive engagement with the public on social media services.

In this chapter, we focus primarily on the performative aspect of social media for LEAs and more specifically on intelligence gathering with regard to its explicit application in this context. Social media now pervades the everyday lives of many people including those breaking the law and conducting other nefarious activities. It is the ease with which communication is facilitated by social media services that makes them so attractive. Due to its often-open nature, these activities are regularly conducted in plain sight. Yet the sheer amount of information sent through social media makes detection of these activities difficult. News outlets often pick up on information from social media in post-event reports that may have provided early indications of the impending crime. However, identifying these posts prior to the event is akin to finding a needle in a haystack (Brynielsson et al., 2013). These kinds of threat indicators therefore often go ignored, potentially leading to lone-wolf scenarios and school shootings (to give two examples). Only in the aftermath of the event are these indicator signals picked up by LEAs.

LEA's utilization of social media relies on citizen participation, consisting of both public observers and the criminal perpetrators themselves. This participation can take the form of status updates, geographic information or pictures and videos, containing potentially incriminating information. Also, seemingly innocent information may prove a key link in the chain of connecting the dots between disparate social media postings and other sources of intelligence. This so-called open-source intelligence (Best, 2008) may then go on to increase situational awareness and/or create actionable intelligence.

For this process to work it is important to be aware of the "typical" user characteristics and behaviors as well as the type of information social media users post online.

In this chapter we review the current knowledge around social media users, their reasons for engagement in social media, and the factors that influence user behavior including the trustworthiness of user information. Further, we review a number of potential use-cases for social media within the context of law enforcement for investigative purposes. These include events such as lone-wolf scenarios, hostage situations, and human trafficking. Following this, we discuss public engagement as a crucial issue for garnering wide-reaching and on-going support for crowd-sourcing and other applications of social media in combating online crime, and crime facilitated through social media use.

FEATURES OF SOCIAL MEDIA USERS AND USE
DIFFERENCES IN DEMOGRAPHICS ACROSS NETWORKS

In employing social media services as a potential intelligence source, it is important to understand the composition of the various respective user groups. Below are findings from the latest Pew survey (Duggan and Smith, 2013) highlighting the user characteristics in the most prevalent examples of social media services:

- *LinkedIn* is especially popular among college graduates and users from higher income households.
- *Twitter* is frequented mostly by younger adults, urban dwellers, and non-whites.
- *Instagram* is frequented mostly by younger adults, urban dwellers, and non-whites; also users that live in urban as opposed to rural environments.
- *Pinterest* attracts about four times as many women as men and has a slightly higher amount of users with higher degrees of education and higher rates of income amongst its users.
- *Facebook* is used more often by women than men, but shows a nearly equal distribution across ethnicity groups (white-non Hispanic, Hispanic, black-non Hispanic), educational levels, pay scale, and urban versus suburban and rural environments.

These disparities demonstrate that social media services differ in the people they attract, especially with respect to the age, gender and educational level of their users. This has consequences for the style, frequency of postings and type of content that can be expected on disparate services. It also has consequences for the way users approach different networks.

Interestingly, users tend to stay with the services they know (Manso and Manso, 2013). This "stickiness" not only creates comparatively stable user groups, but also creates challenges for the introduction of new apps (e.g., specialized apps for crisis communication).

RATIONALES FOR SOCIAL MEDIA USE

While people once went online to seek anonymity (McKenna and Bargh, 2000), to-day one of the main purposes of online activities is socializing. Still, the main reason to use social media in this sense is not for the creation of new relationships with strangers, but the maintenance of existing relationships (e.g., Campbell and Kwak, 2011; Ellison et al., 2007). Estimates are that 85–98% of participants use social media to maintain and reinforce existing offline networks consisting of friends, family or of people sharing similar interests (Choi, 2006; Lenhart et al., 2013). Users of mobile technologies thus tend to stay within close-knit networks, so-called monadic groups (Gergen, 2008). These groups tend to be closed to external influences and hard to approach online, unless someone is part of their offline communities.

Individuals vary greatly in their approaches to social media use. In general, five distinct user types can be differentiated (Brandtzæg, 2012):

1. *Sporadic users*: This group is closest to nonusers, as they connect only rarely. Their main reason for SNS (Social Network Service) use is to check whether someone has been in touch with them.
2. *Lurkers*: The main reasons of SNS use for this group is the passive consumption of content others have provided online, for instance to look at photos, find information about friends, see if somebody has contacted them or simply to "kill time."
3. *Socializers* are interested in using SNS primarily for social activities with friends, family and like-minded people.
4. *Debaters* actively contribute content by writing and uploading their own contributions, especially through participation in discussions and debates.
5. *Advanced users* are the most active group on SNS and show the broadest and most diverse range of behaviors.

Differentiation of these user groups is important, as they vary in the likelihood with which they may engage in activities put forth by LEAs, such as requests for help in investigations, and the reasons and ways in which they may be engaged online (i.e., attracting socializers may need a different approach than attracting, for instance, debaters or lurkers). This differentiation may be especially relevant as content creators, i.e., the more active user groups, tend to be from relatively privileged backgrounds in terms of education and socio-demographic standing (Brake, 2014). This not only means that social media content may be biased toward these groups, but also that disadvantaged groups may be harder to reach and activate.

INFLUENCES ON SOCIAL MEDIA BEHAVIORS

Online behaviors and the perception of what is acceptable to post or not are influenced by a number of factors most prominently user characteristics such as gender, personality and national culture, attitudes toward the service or people approaching them online as well as the technological setup of social media services themselves.

User characteristics. Early studies of internet usage suggested that introverted people used the internet more heavily than their more outgoing counterparts (Amichai-Hamburger et al., 2002). This is no longer the case, with social media now attracting people with a high level of extraversion and openness for new experiences

(Ross et al., 2009; Zywica and Danowski, 2008). Especially among younger users there is a strong link between extraversion and heavy social media use (Correa et al., 2010). In addition, heavier social media use is also linked with a higher degree of emotional instability, albeit only for men (Correa et al., 2010). Emotional (in)stability also plays a role in the number of times and the length of time spent on social networking sites. Individuals who are less stable emotionally tend to spend longer on the sites, while more emotionally stable and more introverted users frequent sites more often (Moore and McElroy, 2012). Emotional instability further impacts the type of information posted. Users with a lower level of emotional stability are more likely to post problematic content such as substance abuse or sexual content on their profile, as are compulsive internet users (Karl et al., 2010).

Gender impacts social media use in that women tend to use social networking sites for longer periods and post more photos and more comments about themselves than men. On the other hand, men tend to use the sites more frequently than women (Moore and McElroy, 2012).

National culture impacts user expectations as well as usage behaviors. Comparing, for instance, US, Korean and Chinese users, Ji et al. (2010) found that individuals from Korea and China use social networking sites as a tool to search for experts to obtain advice for important decisions and for emotional support. US users are interested rather in the formation of relationships, in which the sharing of content plays an important role. The link between content sharing and relationships was not found for Korean and Chinese users. Comparing US students with German students further suggests that US students are more likely to post problematic behaviors such as substance abuse or sexual content on their Facebook page (Karl et al., 2010).

Minority status impacts behaviors too, as members of minority groups tend to use social media more commonly for occupational than private purposes, while members of a majority group are more interested in the social potential of social media (i.e., chatting and personal relations with family and friends) (Mesch, 2012). Minority groups also seem less willing to use social media services offered by the police (Bayerl et al., 2014).

These are clear indications that online behavior is shaped by demographics as well as national contexts and their cultural norms and standards. These differences are relevant when LEAs try to engage with disparate user groups as well as for better understanding of the disparities of online information provided by users.

Attitudes towards services or people. Generally speaking, trust precedes information sharing. The more people trust another person, the more willing they are to grant even intrusive information requests, at least if they feel that the interaction will remain private (Joinson et al., 2010). If the communication partner is trusted, sensitive information is provided even in a situation where privacy is low (Joinson et al., 2010). Online trust can go so far that even pretending to be a friend can be enough to bring users to divulge personal information (Jagatic et al., 2007). The central role of trust is also relevant for the engagement of LEAs with individuals on social media, as user's willingness to engage is linked to their trust in the organization with which they are engaging (Bayerl et al., 2014).

Technical setup. Site features, such as the ability to set status messages, send private correspondence or provide public feedback to other users' content strongly influences how people behave as well as the type of information they choose to reveal online (Skog, 2005). In addition Hampton et al. (2010) identified that not only physical features of social networks impact user behaviors, but also the social setting in which the users are conducting their interactions, with users commonly using online networks in order to maintain existing networks when using social networks in a social environment. Further, power users (i.e., highly expert technophiles) rate the quality of content higher when it has a customizable interface, while non-power users tend to prefer personalized content (Sundar and Marathe, 2010).

DISCLOSURE AND TRUSTWORTHINESS OF INFORMATION

A great deal of discussion exists around the question of whether information provided online is trustworthy. Do users report who they really are or do they consciously fake and falsify information? Teens, for instance, often provide false information on purpose in their profiles (Lenhart et al., 2013). It is also common that users consciously include or omit personal information such as age or relationship status to achieve an interesting, "well-rounded" personality (Peluchette and Karl, 2010; Zhao et al., 2008).

Generally, women are more risk aware and risk adverse when it comes to divulging information online than men (Fogal and Nehmad, 2009; Hoy and Milne, 2011). Yet, privacy concerns often fail to lead to more privacy-oriented behavior (the so-called privacy paradox; Barnes, 2006). Aspects such as the social relevance of a network in influencing a user's general willingness to disclose personal information seem to be more prevalent when deciding whether personal information is posted publicly or not: the higher the relevance of a network for maintaining social relationships, the stronger a person's generalized willingness to reveal private information is (Taddicken, 2013). Individuals also tend to disclose more information in blog entries, when they are more visually identifiable (i.e., share a picture of themselves) (Hollenbaugh and Everett, 2013); while people with higher levels of privacy concerns tend to use fewer social media applications (Taddicken, 2013).

Users concerned about their privacy may choose three approaches to mitigate possible risks: avoidance (e.g., choosing ways other than the internet to communicate, buy products, etc.), opt-out (e.g., opt-out of third-party collection of information), and proactive self-protection (e.g., using privacy-enhancing technologies, erasing cookies, etc.). The choice of the method seems to be influenced by cultural factors. For example, in Sydney and New York users were unlikely to choose an avoidance strategy, while users in Bangalore or Seoul were more likely to avoid the internet than employ privacy-enhancing technologies (Cho et al., 2009). Attitudes toward privacy seem to differ along a North-South and South-East divide, at least in Europe (cp. Lancelot-Miltgen and Peyrat-Guillard, 2013): Users in Northern European countries considered privacy as a question of personal responsibility, whereas users in the South saw it rather as a question of trust. Users in South-European countries further considered the disclosure of information as a personal choice, while users in Eastern countries saw it rather as a forced choice.

Disclosure and falsification of private information are thus linked to demographics and trust (Joinson et al., 2010), but are also a question of the larger environment in which the user operates.

RELEVANCE TO LEAs

In the acquisition of intelligence, LEAs may want to utilize this information in their models and assumptions. If different demographics vary with respect to the reasons and ways they employ social media, LEAs need to consider these disparities when tracking and garnering intelligence from groups of interest. Further, because offline relationships often precede online relationships, inferences can be made about an individual's social circle. Understanding the normal pattern of engagement with social media for a particular user may also prove to be an indicator of critical changes in attitudes. For example, gradual changes in language may indicate radicalization, while a single threatening post out of the blue may warrant more attention than if an individual posts such comments on a continuous basis, but are clearly not serious. In this respect it is important to know that such behaviors are also impacted by personality and cultural differences, which makes the application of a single standard of "normal" versus "problematic" online behaviors questionable. LEAs need to be able to match online profiles with real people. In this respect, knowing the attitudes toward the falsification of personal information across user groups is vital to appraise likelihood as well as possible motivations to differentiate "normal" from possibly "problematic" behaviors.

LEA USAGE SCENARIOS FOR SOCIAL MEDIA

The continued growth in popularity and diversity in the behaviors exhibited by social media users as discussed in the section "Features of Social Media Users and Use" has led to a wide range of events, and prospective scenarios upon which there is potential for LEAs to leverage available information to improve their investigative capability.

In this section, we put forward a number of relevant and current use-cases for the potential application of social media in specific law enforcement centric scenarios. In the previous section, we have seen how the use of social media varies across different demographics and cultures as well as the reasons for and types of usage. The expectations and behaviors displayed also differ across cultures, gender, personality traits and emotional states while how much trust users put in information found online and what they decide to disclose about themselves all affect how LEAs need to structure their intelligence gathering processes and the assumptions they make about the data they find. Here we apply that knowledge into practical examples of how and why LEAs would engage with social media and what they can expect to get out of it in terms of enhancing investigative capability and effectiveness. Five scenarios are provided where the use and understanding of social media may benefit LEAs. These include that of a lone-wolf attacker, a hostage situation, the detection of organized crime, a crowd-sourcing application and the trafficking of human beings.

In recent years, an increasing number of police arrests have arisen in response to threats made online in relation to shootings, bombings and other criminal activities. In instances such as those at Skyline High school in Sammamish, Washington in 2012 (Seattle Times, 2012), Pitman High School, New Jersey on January 6, 2014 (Polhamous, 2014), and the case of Terri Pitman, in Council Pitt, Iowa in 2013; a mother who threatened to shoot up her sons bullying classmates on Facebook (Gillam, 2013), local police were made aware of social media postings threatening to commit shootings at the respective locations via tip-offs from online observers. In all three of the cases identified police were able to evacuate and search the premises prior to the materialization of any threat. However, in all the cases cited police were reliant on the reports of independent observers such as classmates, parents and other onlookers for awareness of the emergent situation.

A brief search online uncovers a number of incidents, not only isolated to school shooting threats, whereby bombing, shooting, and perpetrators of other criminal activity were charged with intent to commit crimes due to posts made using social media sites such as Twitter, Facebook and Tumblr. In comparing modern scenario's such as those identified previously, with scenarios from just ten to fifteen years ago such as the Columbine school shootings in Jefferson, Colorado it is clear that the emergence and ubiquitous use of technologies including mobile communications and social media has resulted in a cultural shift, forging a new environment that necessitates an evolution in the policing mechanisms required to respond to threats such as these effectively.

To access and detect this information LEAs must monitor social media intelligently. Social network analysis can be used to identify criminal networks, and match profiles across social media platforms and closed police records further assisted by technologies such as facial recognition to build up a complete, integrated picture of the criminal entities, their online profiles, and networks as shown by the model in LEA usage scenarios for social media.

As well as textual content posted on social media; pictures and videos, such as those captured by services like Instagram, Flickr and Twitter also provide a potentially useful resource. These images regularly come attached with textual meta-data, such as "hashtags" and content descriptions, as well as comments and feedback from other users of the platform that describes the media content in question. Searching through these images manually, one by one is impossible due to the sheer amount of content present on the platforms. Since tagging and geo-tagging are common-place, data mining and analytical processing can be used to speed up and automate the extraction of information. Text mining techniques can also extract further metadata such as names, places, or actions related to criminal activities.

Data mining and analysis techniques can be applied in a variety of ways in order to improve the quality of information available to police investigations. Technologies such as the use of artificial neural networks for the extraction of entities from police narrative reports, the use of an algorithmic approach based on the calculation of Euclidean Distances for the identification of identity deceptions by criminals, the tracing of identities of criminals from posted messages on the Web using learning algorithms, such as Support Vector Machines, and the use of Social Network Analysis for uncovering structural patterns from criminal networks can all aid in improving the quality and diversity of information being fed into the intelligence operations of LEAs.

SOCIAL MEDIA IN "LONE-WOLF" SCENARIOS FOR EARLY ASSESSMENT AND IDENTIFICATION OF THREATS

Currently, policing intelligence relies on reports from the public, or the recipients of threats in order to take appropriate action in response to the posts made online indicating possible criminal behavior. Due to this reliance on public reporting, there is potential for these threats to go ignored, or to be drowned out by the noise of the sheer unquantifiable amount of information being posted to social media sites each day. Often in cases such as those identified, the perpetrators are not acting on behalf of a wider criminal organization, or executing a planned course of action. Instead, these threats are regularly instinctive attacks that are unplanned and irrational, and in response to events that draw emotion, executed by individuals out for vengeance, often with histories of social instability and psychological problems. In cases such as this LEAs are unable to draw upon robust intelligence sources to identify a current or emergent threat from the individual as, one off, unplanned events such as the lone-wolf school shooting scenarios identified previously rarely have a bread-crumb trail of evidence that can be picked up by LEA's existing intelligence operations.

Recent reviews of the US intelligence infrastructure have led to the development and formation of "fusion centers" aiming to coordinate intelligence and serve law enforcement agencies (LEAs) across entire states in the acquisition, analysis and dissemination of intelligence (U.S. Department of Justice, 2005). Within these fusion centers, there is potential for the application and integration of social media analytics in the crawling and analysis of social media as an open-source intelligence repository in response to emergent, unplanned "lone-wolf" scenarios such as those discussed in Chapter 10. In these situations, there are two potential streams of information that is of potential value to LEAs. Firstly, there is the identification of posts made by the perpetrator containing explicit signals of intent to cause harm, and secondly, the sentiment being expressed by situational stakeholders in regards to the threats and actions of the individual.

Through the application of technologies such as Natural Language Processing (NLP) and sentiment analysis techniques, it is possible to identify specific postings that (a) contain criminal intent and (b) contain references to specific concepts such as target locations, and methods to be used by the individual(s). Named entity and concept extraction techniques provide the user (in this case envisaged to be an analyst within the fusion centre setting) with explicit reference to the location and nature of the threat being made, in addition to the name and location of the individual making the threat. From this information, the threat can then be analyzed and cross referenced using robust, "closed-source" intelligence sources such as the healthcare and criminal records of the individual making the threat, and the individual's proximity to the location that the threat is being made against. This cross-referencing of intelligence then builds up a robust portfolio of knowledge that then can be used to assess the severity and validity of the threat being made, which in turn can be filtered down to operational officers in instances where further, on scene action is required.

A key concern that has been associated with applying data mined from social media in this way is that it is considered extremely challenging to separate genuine threats from the emotional outbursts and tongue-in-cheek musings of disgruntled individuals. This is where an understanding of different types of user behavior on social media is of significance. The cross-referencing of threat indicators from social media with robust closed-source intelligence sources is extremely valuable in aiding to distinguish likely and probable threats from the "noise" of social media. For further validity, threat indication can also trigger additional analysis of an individual's social media presence, as individuals commonly use the same alias' and user-names across services, looking to identify any other potential indicators that the individual may be capable, and intent upon committing the crime to which they have been threatening across a range of social media platforms. For example, this process could entail the identification that an individual has photographs of themselves posing with weapons, thus providing further validity to the case that the individual is capable of carrying out the threat to which they have eluded.

SOCIAL MEDIA-BASED APPROACH IN A HOSTAGE SCENARIO

Hostage situations are defined as events whereby the actor(s) (i.e., the hostage taker(s)) are holding one of more persons captive against their will. The motives for these attacks can be diverse, and vary from expressive motives such as voicing an opinion or religious view to instrumental motives such as for financial gain through ransom demands (Alexander and Klein, 2009). There are a number of possibilities for communication and the use of social media during hostage situations with the victims, hostage takers, LEAs, media outlets and public bystanders all possessing the potential to comment and monitor the situation before, during, and after the event itself.

In addition, the hostage takers may monitor the outside situation and make identity checks on hostages using social media profiles and web searches such as that exemplified during the Mumbai attacks (Oh et al., 2011); they may also select their hostages via social media by monitoring movements or personal possessions. On rare occasions, hostages themselves may also be able to covertly contact family, friends or LEAs, real-time comments and updates can also be posted by news organizations and bystanders, LEAs are also able to use social media to communicate official information while they can also obtain background information on hostage takers' political, religious, and personal standpoints posted online to facilitate negotiation by understanding their motives. For example, two scenarios where LEAs could use social media are for the prevention of the spread of sensitive operational details and to understand the motives behind a given hostage situation.

While the public can often be helpful, providing key information to LEAs, social media also provides an outlet where people often post without thinking, unaware of the potential consequences of their actions (Gaudin, 2013b). The posting online of current tactics or operational details, such as that which happened during the Mumbai bombing attacks, poses a risk to the success of any operation. Finding ways to mitigate the spread of this information when it is beyond the immediate control of the LEAs is vitally important—the police cannot put a cordon around Twitter—to help in the successful resolution of these situations. While LEAs cannot force people to remove information, by crawling tweets in real-time, identifying those with relevant information, and contacting those who have posted potentially sensitive operational information to request its remove, the threat of information leakage can be mitigated. Natural language processing can be used to identify keywords and hashtags that are associated with the event, and systems put in place to facilitate the provision of an automated, credible response to alleviate the spread of damaging rhetoric and foster a virtual community of moderate, trustworthy advice and positive reinforcement. Keeping this communication from the hostage takers is also a key objective. Otherwise this would act as a red flag toward important information.

A second scenario is based around understanding the motives of the hostage takers and how to bring the situation to a resolution. Without understanding the background to a hostage situation it is difficult to take the necessary steps to resolve it peacefully without further incident, or potentially aggravating the situation further. Assembling all potential evidence rapidly and connecting the dots from the intelligence garnered from social media postings and profiles arms negotiators with the knowledge to do their job more effectively. LEAs need to quickly mine relevant and discard irrelevant information about the hostage taker(s), their social interactions, and their political or religious sympathies to rapidly build up a user profile, complementing pre-existing information already held on file by the police. This information may be taken from social networks, forums, blogs, personal websites and video postings such as those on YouTube. While this may not represent their complete profile it may give vital clues about their personality and motives that negotiators can latch on to and use to their advantage (Mandak, 2012).

Two potential use-cases for the use of social media during a hostage situation have been presented: the control of the spread of information in these scenarios, and the use of social media for conducting background checks against hostage takers. By using the social media profiles LEAs can identify the demographics the hostage takers identify with, their motivations based on content sharing or identify their relationships through their online interactions and use this understanding to inform decision makers on how best to act and proceed with the negotiation.

ORGANIZED CRIME SOCIAL MEDIA DATA ANALYSIS

The arrest of Bernardo Provenzano, a senior member of the Sicilian Mafia, in 2006, after 43 years on the run, brought to light the question of how could a criminal figure such as this evade authorities and at the same time, continue to run a criminal empire.

Provenzano was constantly on the move, communicating using pizzini, tiny typed notes, delivered to him by hand by his trusted assistants (Timelists, 2014). After his arrest, Provenzano was found to be in possession of five copies of the Bible, one of which was littered full of cryptic notes. Arturo Castellanos, a leader of the Mexican Mafia in one of America's toughest prisons, Pelican Bay State in Northern California, sent a letter to Florencia 13, a multi-generational street gang in south Los Angeles. Castellanos, through his letter, underlined a number of rules, or *reglas*, on how he believed the Mafia should be run at a street level. Specifically, these rules outlined how street gangs and their sub-groups should be governed, how drug sales, prostitution and other illegal activities should be realized, and how disputes should be settled (McCarthy, 2009). In both cases, it is shown clearly that communication plays a major role in the way that organized criminal entities perform their illicit activities in order to remain anonymous. It is safe to suppose that organized crime leaders use social media, such as Twitter or Facebook, in order to communicate with their groups in the same way. This communication can again be conducted in a cryptic manner, using social media accounts with fake personal information and pictures, using specific terms in order to pass on their messages. The complexity of organized crime organizations makes it even more difficult to monitor the communication between members.

A social network can be seen as a structure of nodes (often representing people), connected together by some kind of relationship (Snasel et al., 2008). Text-mining algorithms can be used in order to extract suspicious keywords from social media accounts. The operation of these accounts can then be monitored and all their posts can be collected. A formal context from the collected posts can be developed. Formal Concept Analysis (FCA) software can be used in order to extract the most significant concepts of these posts and visualize them as a concept lattice. The study of the concept lattice will identify keywords that appear most frequently in the collected posts. Based on these keywords, the accounts that have used them can be collected for analysis so that more in-depth conclusions can be formulated. Formal Concept Analysis is but one example of a technology that can be applied to aggregate and summarize data.

Formal Concept Analysis (Priss, 2006) can be very useful in the analysis of social media-based communication between Mafia members. The data collected can clarify the way organized criminals communicate with each other and the hierarchy that they follow. Furthermore, it can clarify the roles of each member in the criminal organization, how a criminal activity is organized and how future criminal activities organized by Mafia organizations can be predicted and prevented. In addition, the application of Formal Concept Analysis in a social media setting can result in easier penetration of mafia-type organizations by the police, so that the dismantling of such groups can be realized (see Chapter 4).

CROWD-SOURCING WITH A COLLECTIVE INTELLIGENCE PLATFORM

Crowd-sourcing data are of great significance in crisis situations. Crowd-sourcing enables information to flow quickly and efficiently between emergency management specialists and the public. There are a number of tools, such as Pathfinder

(Luther et al., 2009), Sense.us (Heer et al., 2007) and Many Eyes (Viegas et al., 2007), that are used for the analysis of crowd-sourced information. Platforms such as Ushahidi (http://www.ushahidi.com/) and Google crisis maps (http://www. google.org/crisisresponse/) are already used to crowd-source information in disaster response situations. Crowdsafe (Shah et al., 2011), a mobile application that allows users to input crime data to help identify hotspots also helps users to plot routes home that avoid them. As well as using crowd-sourcing to coordinate the relief effort, LEAs may also wish to crowd-source information during and after a crisis event to provide both situational awareness and to piece together the true nature of the events, as trawling manually through this data is nigh on impossible. Involving LEAs in the crowd-sourcing loop is also necessary but, as the Boston Bombings in 2013 showed; crowd-sourced, public data alone does not necessarily lead to the correct investigative conclusions (Lee, 2013).

Similar to crowd-sourcing, collective intelligence (Bonabeau, 2009) is the result of the collective and collaborative efforts of a number of people with a common aim or goal. A collective intelligence platform combines data from a number of different sources (e.g., open-source intelligence repositories). Data received through crowd-sourcing appeals via social media and closed data that is not exposed to the public is then combined with the domain-specific knowledge of LEA officers, domain experts and analysts in order to produce actions, outcomes, or knowledge building blocks. The results of these analyses may go back out into the public domain to refine and re-organize the actions of scenario stakeholders based on the intelligence provided by LEAs. This type of platform would not only be useful in a crisis management situation but also to track events such as organized crime involving arms trading, drug trafficking, and money laundering gangs (see Chapters 3 and 10).

A number of technologies can be utilized and integrated within a collective intelligence platform. Formal Concept Analysis is one such example of this and may be used for the analysis of data generated by social media that is potentially related to criminal incidents.

In FCA an object can usually only be placed at a certain hierarchy level if it contains all the attributes that are present at that given level. When analyzing textual data in particular, the wide range of expressions someone can use to explain exactly the same situation is problematic. Two potential ways of tackling this problem are to use a lexical database such as Wordnet (Miller, 1995) to map synonyms for each of the attributes and the second is to introduce fault tolerance for FCA. That is to accept objects at a particular level of the hierarchy even if they do not match all the attributes but match a number of them beyond a predefined threshold. This prevents near misses slipping through FCA's metaphorical net. This means the collective intelligence platform can be refined as more information is added and further analytical techniques such as machine learning, clustering and additional classification can also be applied to further enhance and refine the results.

The dynamics of a crisis situation mean that events can change rapidly. Example technologies such as FCA could mean a constant re-evaluation of the number of objects appearing at different positions in the hierarchy and the introduction of new terms. An increase in objects further down the hierarchy indicates a change in situation or visibility that LEAs may need to react too. An addition of a new term may indicate a new event, for example the word "gunman" may keep appearing with a specific place name but five minutes later a second place name starts being picked up by the system and the objects are divided between the two. This might indicate that there is more than one gunman or that they are on the move.

This type of information usually takes the form of unstructured texts, unverified or partial reports, and human knowledge that is not necessarily included in the paper trail. However, bringing all this information from disparate sources and connecting the dots between them is vital for tracking organized crime. A collective intelligence platform is required to import, aggregate, filter, analyze, visualize and also to present this information in a concise manner. News aggregator app Summly (www.summly. com; now Yahoo News Digest; Kelion, 2014) pioneered the idea of mixing news and social media while recognizing that most users do not want long reports but short summary snippets. The same reasoning can be applied to developing crisis situations to provide reports to first responders, the public and those in control centers.

Crowd-sourcing in particular requires the public to get involved and contribute information. Debaters and the advanced users of SNSs are perhaps mostly likely to participate and LEAs should be aware of any demographic biases that may influence the information they receive. LEAs also have to consider how they want to receive their information as users prefer to stick with services they are familiar with. Users may also have privacy concerns about divulging geo-tagged information or attracting unwanted attention.

APPLICATION OF SOCIAL MEDIA IN HUMAN TRAFFICKING SCENARIOS

Human Trafficking is a diverse and complex international problem. Due to its globalized, cross-border and varied nature, any response to Human Trafficking must be similarly scoped (Rankin and Kinsella, 2011). Human Trafficking consists of any efforts to transport humans illegally across borders by force, or through the use of threats such as abduction, fraud, deception and coercion, with criminal organizations constantly identifying and exploiting new routes, modes of transportation and pretences upon which to illegally traffic human beings (UNODC, 2004). As well as being a global issue, Human Trafficking is also a growing one, with the UK's NCA (National Crime Agency) reporting a 9% year-over-year increase on the number of Human Trafficking-related convictions in the UK in 2012 (UKHTC, 2013). In order to improve the architectural underpinnings of Human Trafficking defense strategies, a co-ordinated, multi-disciplinary approach is required to combine the requirements to maximize the identification of criminal activity, and the reprehension of the individuals and illicit organizations responsible for it (UNODC, 2012).

Social Media provides a potential source of competitive advantage for LEAs over criminal organizations perpetrating crimes such as Human Trafficking (Gottschalk, 2010), and is frequently considered to be an under-utilized repository of open-source intelligence that is traditionally under-valued in the minds and practices of police officers as a result of culturally ingrained bias that are deeply embedded within the culture and organizational mechanisms of modern policing (Reiner, 2010). Deep-rooted resistances such as these require any new approaches to be underpinned by knowledge management-enabled organizational mechanisms, facilitating the integration of any new intelligence-led approaches to combatting organized crime threats such as Human Trafficking. In response to this requirement, social media is but one of the resources which can be leveraged in response to the ever diversifying threat of human trafficking through the use of text mining enabled information extraction, categorization and analysis. Although agents of trafficking themselves are unlikely to be detailing the nature of their activities in the text and images they post to social media, observers of the environment (i.e., the general public) are potentially quite likely to make posts in reference to behavior that is suspicious or out of the ordinary.

In a recent case of Human Trafficking in south-east England, a Hungarian trafficking gang were convicted for transporting more than 50 teenage girls into the UK for the purposes of running an illegal prostitution ring. Incidents such as this provide a potential use case to illustrate the application of social media analytics and information extraction in combatting the threat of Human Trafficking. During the case identified, a number of trafficking victims were smuggled into halls of residence at the University of Sussex for prostitution purposes (Campbell, 2014). In events such as this, it is likely that other residents at the halls, and local university students would have made inquisitive posts to social media sites such as Twitter and Facebook in regards to the unusual nature of having a number of eastern European women suddenly appearing at the premises, and rarely being seen or heard from. Although the posts of observers may not have been inferring that the individuals were in fact victims of human trafficking, and operating within a forced prostitution ring, analytical techniques such as natural language processing (NLP) and named entity extraction, enabled through web crawling technologies, can be used in conjunction with a knowledgebase containing the specialist domain knowledge of Human Trafficking experts that could extract textual information from social media indicating multiple reports of unusual behavior being present from the same location that would then be categorized to indicate that it may in fact be related to potential illicit activity, such as Human Trafficking.

By filtering and fusing information sources, law enforcement analysts can begin to accumulate enough information to form a representation of the environment being observed, through the aggregation of information based upon the geo-tagged location data that is embedded within social media content. The repository aspect of any proposed system would be populated with domain knowledge consisting of likely indicators of Human Trafficking activity, both in terms of the victims, the properties being used by those involved and the characteristics of the perpetrators themselves, all tied to linguistic rules designed to pick out slang terms, and posts from social media which would reference activity that coincides with that stored in the knowledgebase. In the past, the police and LEAs would be reliant on the direct reporting of suspicious activity from observers, however in the new environment emergent as a result of the information age, this same information is dispersed within the social media postings of passive, situational observers, enabling the early identification of illicit activities based upon the aggregation of weak indicators expressed via social media platforms such as Twitter and Facebook.

PUBLIC ENGAGEMENT ON SOCIAL MEDIA

Efforts at crowd-sourcing, for instance, for support in crime investigations or during crises depend on the willingness of citizens to support and engage with LEAs on social media. This may not be a logical step for all citizens, as demonstrated by the variances in potential user characteristics outlined in the section "Features of Social Media Users and Use." Services like Amber Alert (a US department of justice program aimed at increasing public awareness of missing persons) require a stable community that is available on a continuous basis. But how can LEAs attract and bind citizens to their social media presence?

A non-governmental organization in Kosovo, InternewsKosova together with the Balkan Investigative Reporting Network (BIRN) created an online platform (www.kallxo.com) for citizens of Kosovo to report cases of corruption through social media, SMS and the web. One year after the launch of the platform, 900 cases have been reported and around 30 municipalities in Kosovo have placed an iFrame of the platform in their websites (United Nations Development Program, 2014). The UK released a public service (http://www.police.uk) showing crime statistics for every address in the country allowing UK citizens to view crime statistics about their local area (Garbett et al., 2010).

A recent study on police social media services with citizens in Czech Republic, Romania, the Former Yugoslav Republic of Macedonia and the UK revealed that trust in police is one of the main deciding factors, of whether people are willing to use such services or not (Bayerl et al., 2014). In this case, LEAs are treated the same as individual users (e.g., Joinson et al., 2010). Furthermore, the lack of knowledge and skills related to the use of Information Technology are restrictive factors in the use of social media for crime reporting by a significant proportion of the populous (Garbett et al., 2010). Also people want to be certain that their anonymity is secured when they report a crime, something that is not always possible or clear when considering social media. LEAs try to attract people to report information about a crime through financial rewards, but even in the case of social media many people are afraid of providing such information.

Yet, while trust is often created offline, LEAs can work on their presentation of social media services and their own behavior toward the citizens who use them. The acceptance of the virtual delivery of public services is linked to the following four aspects: expectations for the performance of the site, social presence (i.e., "the sense of being with each other"; Biocca et al., 2003), social influences by relevant others, who think using the sites is positive, and computer anxiety. Especially affective aspects, and mostly social presence, are important when considering acceptance. This suggests that media that allow for immediate and personal communication that closely resemble face-to-face encounters are more readily adopted by citizens than platforms that allow only intermittent, textual exchanges. For example, when it comes to Virtual Crime Reporting technology, some resistances are identified due to the absence of real human contact. Whether an individual is willing to use a technology or not depends on the individual's cognitive, conative and affective responses. Cognitive responses are related to personal beliefs, conative responses are related to the individual's willingness to engage, and affective responses are related to the individual's emotions (Hoefnagel et al., 2012).

Once a social media platform is established, binding users to the platform becomes an important issue, in order to foster an active, constant community. Reacting and responding to the posts of users is one of the most powerful ways to commit users to a service, as it increases the value of participation in the eyes of the users themselves (Utz, 2009). Hence getting a reply to an initial post increases the likelihood that his person will post again (Joyce and Kraut, 2006).

Further it is crucial that the information on networks is perceived as truthful; otherwise confidence in, and the perceived value of the service will decline (Gentzkow and Shapiro, 2006). Who communicates information also plays a role. Sadly, gender still seems to play a role in how credible information is perceived. For instance, weblogs by male authors are often considered more credible than weblogs from female authors (Armstrong and McAdams, 2009). Furthermore, credibility of information is also higher if the source is official rather than unofficial, but only if the communications are from a male source (Armstrong and Nelson, 2005).

FROM SOCIAL MEDIA TO LEA INTELLIGENCE

Figure 15.1 shows a representative model of the processes LEAs must go through in order to exploit social media effectively as part of their wider intelligence strategies. As social media is now ubiquitous it can be applied to many LEA scenarios, as demonstrated earlier in the section "LEA Usage Scenarios for Social Media."

There is a diverse and extensive range of social media platforms available today; and the number and variety of these platforms continues to increase. There are three main ways in which social media can be utilized by LEAs:

1. Crawling and monitoring social media sources by tracking public comments and scraping criminal profiles and posts
2. LEAs direct communication and interaction with public from their own social media accounts
3. LEA coordinated crowd-sourced information

After the collection of these data LEAs must extract, clean, filter and aggregate the unstructured data into machine readable formats. The types of data retrieved can include:

- Unstructured text from tweets and other postings
- Video and images
- Geographic information

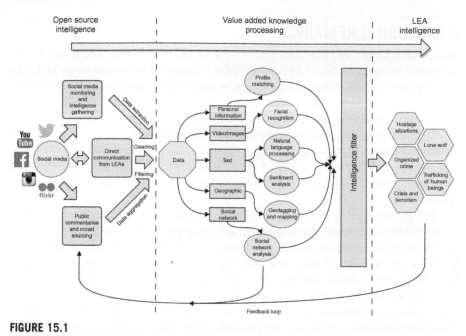

FIGURE 15.1

From social media to LEA intelligence.

- Social network information
- Personal details including age, location, family, likes, dislikes, etc.

Having gathered all these data, it needs to be processed and analyzed so that it can be used as by LEAs in a meaningful way. Examples of such techniques are:

- Facial recognition and matching from picture to images held on file
- Profile matching between social media platforms and police reports
- Natural language processing to make sense of unstructured text
- Sentiment analysis to monitor public opinion
- Geo-tagging and location resolution to track movements and key places
- Social network analysis to map friends, acquaintances and interactions

These disparate analyses can then be filtered, processed and consolidated into actionable, credible information and further assessed by those with domain expertise. The results of these processes may then be applied to a number of scenarios such as organized crime, lone-wolf, human trafficking, hostage situations and crisis and terrorist events as described earlier in this chapter. This, however, is not the end of the loop. Throughout the process as more intelligence is harvested it is fed back into the search to refine and make the tools more accurate and targeted, enabling it to account for new information to strengthen the potential outcomes for LEAs and increase the validity of their intelligence.

CONCLUDING REMARKS

As criminal threats and practices evolve with the environment around them, the intelligence resources offered by social media become an important asset in LEAs investigative armory. Social media offers an unrivalled repository for intelligence-led policing operations; the analysis of which plays a significant role in assessing the validity, credibility and accuracy of the information acquired from open-source intelligence repositories such as social media. Techniques such as text mining, NLP (natural language processing) and sentiment analysis provide a varied toolset that can be applied to better inform LEA decision-makers and lead to the identification of where a crime is likely to happen, who is likely to commit it and the nature of the threat itself.

Yet, in this context not only the technical details of how to mine and analyze social media information are needed, but also in-depth knowledge about the people using the services, their motivations and behaviors. In this chapter, we offered a short overview of the current knowledge around social media usage including user characteristics and the factors that influence user behaviors online. We further offered an overview of usage scenarios to demonstrate how social media can support LEAs in their operations. These scenarios establish use-cases for the application of social media in the prevention, prediction and resolution of a wide variety of criminal threats, thus demonstrating the potential capacity of social media for LEAs.

REFERENCES

Alexander, D.A., Klein, S., 2009. Kidnapping and hostage-taking: a review of effects, coping and resilience. J. R. Soc. Med. 102 (1), 16–21.

Amichai-Hamburger, Y., Wainapel, G., Fox, S., 2002. On the internet no one knows I'm an introvert: extraversion, neuroticism, and internet interaction. Cyberpsychol. Behav. 5 (2), 125–128.

Armstrong, C.L., McAdams, M.J., 2009. Blogs of information: how gender cues and individual motivations influence perceptions of credibility. J. Comput.-Mediated Commun. 14 (3), 435–456.

Armstrong, C.L., Nelson, M.R., 2005. How newspaper sources trigger gender stereotypes. J. Mass Commun. Q. 82 (4), 820–837.

Barnes, S., 2006. A privacy paradox: social networking in the United States. First Monday 11 (9). http://firstmonday.org/issues/issue11_9/barnes/index.html (accessed 06.06.11).

Bayerl, P.S., Horton, K., Jacobs, G., Akhgar, B., 2014. Who want's police on social media. Paper Presented at the 1st European Conference for Social Media, July 10-11, 2014, Brighton, U.K.

Best, C., 2008. Open source intelligence. In: Mining Massive Data Sets for Security: Advances in Data Mining, Search, Social Networks and Text Mining, and Their Applications to Security, IOS Press, Amsterdam, Netherlands, 19. p. 331.

Biocca, F., Harms, C., Burgoon, J.K., 2003. Toward a more robust theory and measure of social presence: review and suggested criteria. Presence: Teleoper. Virtual Environ. 12, 456–480.

Bonabeau, E., 2009. Decisions 2.0: the power of collective intelligence. MIT Sloan Manage Rev 50 (2), 45–52.

Brake, D.R., 2014. Are we all online content creators now? Web 2.0 and digital divides. J. Comput. Mediat. Comm. 19 (3), 591–609.

Brandtzæg, P.B., 2012. Social networking sites: their users and social implications—a longitudinal study. J. Comput. Mediat. Comm. 17 (4), 467–488.

Brynielsson, J., Horndahl, A., Johansson, F., Kaati, L., Mårtenson, C., Svenson, P., 2013. Harvesting and analysis of weak signals for detecting lone wolf terrorists. Secur. Inf. 2 (1), 11.

Campbell, C., 2014. BBC NEWS: Hungarian woman used as prostitute 'locked in room and raped'. http://www.bbc.co.uk/news/uk-england-25641460.

Campbell, S.W., Kwak, N., 2011. Political involvement in "mobilized" society: the interactive relationships among mobile communication, network characteristics, and political participation. J. Commun. 61 (6), 1005–1024.

Cho, H., Rivera-Sánchez, M., Lim, S.S., 2009. A multinational study on online privacy: global concerns and local responses. New Media Soc. 11 (3), 395–416.

Choi, J.H., 2006. Living in Cyworld: contextualising Cy-Ties in South Korea. In: Bruns, A., Jacobs, J. (Eds.), Use of Blogs (Digital Formations). Peter Lang, New York, pp. 173–186.

Correa, T., Hinsley, A.W., De Zuniga, H.G., 2010. Who interacts on the Web? The intersection of users' personality and social media use. Comput. Hum. Behav. 26 (2), 247–253.

Denef, S., Kaptein, N., Bayerl, P.S., Ramirez, L., 2012. Best Practice in Police Social Media Adaptation. Public Report COMPOSITE Project. [online]. http://www.composite-project.eu/index.php/publications-669.html.

Duggan, M., Smith, A., 2013. Social Media Update. Pew Internet and the American Life Project. Available at: http://www.pewinternet.org/Reports/2013/Social-Media-Update.aspx (accessed 14.02.14).

Ellison, N., Steinfield, C., Lampe, C., 2007. The benefits of Facebook "friends": exploring the relationship between college students' use of online social networks and social capital. J. Comput. Mediat. Comm. 12 (4), 1143–1168.

Fogal, J., Nehmad, E., 2009. Internet social network communities: risk taking, trust, and privacy concerns. Comput. Hum. Behav. 25 (1), 153–160.

Gaudin, S., 2013a. One out of seven people use social networks, study shows. Available at: http://www.computerworld.com/s/article/9244251/One_out_of_seven_people_use_social_networks_study_shows (accessed 14.02.14).

Gaudin, S., 2013b. Twitter etiquette: the do's and don'ts of tweeting. Computerworld. Available at: http://www.computerworld.com/s/article/9240533/_Twitter_etiquette_The_do_s_and_don_ts_of_tweeting?taxonomyId=10 (accessed 07.02.14).

Gergen, K.J., 2008. Mobile communication and the transformation of the democratic process. In: Katz, J.E. (Ed.), Handbook of Mobile Communication Studies. MIT Press, Cambridge, MA, pp. 353–366.

Gillam, C., 2013. IOWA mom arrested for post threatening shooting at son's school. Available at: http://www.reuters.com/article/2013/12/17/us-usa-iowa-mom-dUSBRE9BG14320131217 (accessed 06.02.14).

Gottschalk, P., 2010. Knowledge management technology for organized crime risk assessment. Inf. Syst. Front. 12 (3), 267–275.

Hampton, K.N., Livio, O., Sessions Goulet, L., 2010. The social life of wireless urban spaces: Internet use, social networks, and the public realm. J. Commun. 60 (4), 701–722.

Heer, J., Viégas, F.B., Wattenberg, W., 2007. Voyagers and voyeurs: supporting asynchronous collaborative information visualization. In: Proceedings of the SIGCHI Conference on Human Factors in Computing Systems. ACM.

Hoefnagel, R., Oerlemans, L., Godee, J., 2012. Acceptance by the public of the virtual delivery of public services: the effect of affect. Soc. Sci. Comput. Rev. 30 (3), 274–296.

Hollenbaugh, E.E., Everett, M.K., 2013. The effects of anonymity on self-disclosure in blogs: an application of the online disinhibition effect. J. Comput.-Mediated Commun, 18 (3), 283–302.

Garbett, A., Linehan, C., Kirman, B., Wardman, J., Lawson, S., 2010. Using social media to drive public engagement with open data, Digit. Engagement 11, Newcastle, UK.

Gentzkow, M., Shapiro, J., 2006. Media bias and reputation. J. Polit. Econ. 114, 280–316.

Hoy, M., Milne, G., 2011. Gender differences in privacy-related measures for young adult Facebook users. J. Interact. Adv. 10 (2), 28–45.

IACP Center for Social Media, 2013. 2013 IACP Social Media Survey. Available at: http://www.iacpsocialmedia.org/Resources/Publications/2013SurveyResults.aspx.

Jagatic, T.N., Johnson, N.A., Jakobsso, M., 2007. Social phishing. Commun. ACM 50 (10), 94–100.

Ji, Y.G., Hwangbo, H., Yi, S.J., Rau, P.L.P., Fang, X., Ling, C., 2010. The influence of cultural differences on the use of social network services and the formation of social capital. Int. J. Hum. Comput. Interact. 26 (11–12), 1100–1121.

Joinson, A.N., Reips, U.-D., Buchanan, T., Schofield, C.B.P., 2010. Privacy, trust, and self-disclosure online. Hum.-Comput. Interact. 25 (1), 1–24.

Joyce, E., Kraut, R.E., 2006. Predicting continued participation in newsgroups. J. Comput. Mediat. Comm. 11 (3), 723–747.

Kaplan, A.M., Haenlein, M., 2010. Users of the world, unite! The challenges and opportunities of Social Media. Bus. Horiz. 53 (1), 59–68.

Kaptein, N., 2012. Digital transformation in public security and policing. Eur. J. ePract. 17, 44–50.

Karl, K., Peluchette, J., Schlaegel, C., 2010. Who's posting Facebook faux pas? A cross-cultural examination of personality differences. Int. J. Sel. Assess. 18 (2), 174–186.

Kelion, L., 2014. CES 2014: Yahoo unveils news summary app. BBC News. Available at: http://www.bbc.co.uk/news/technology-25647209 (accessed 07.02.14).

Lancelot Miltgen, C., Peyrat-Guillard, D., 2013. Cultural and generational influences on privacy concerns: a qualitative study in seven European countries. Eur. J. Inform. Syst. 23 (2), 103–125.

Lee, D., 2013. Boston bombing: How internet detectives got it very wrong. BBC News . http://www.bbc.co.uk/news/technology-22214511 (accessed 07.02.14).

Lenhart, A., Madden, M., Cortesi, S., Duggan, M., Smith, A., Beaton, M., 2013. Teens, Social Media and Privacy. Pew Internet and American Life Project Report. Available at: http://www.pewinternet.org/2013/05/21/teens-social-media-and-privacy/ (accessed 10.02.14).

Luther, K., Counts, S., Stecher, K., Hoff, A., Johns, P., 2009. Pathfinder: an online collaboration environment for citizen scientists. In: Proceedings of the 2009 ACM Conference on Human Factors in Computing Systems (CHI 2009), pp. 239–248.

Mandak, J., 2012. Police Get Social Media Training In Pittsburgh As Hostage-Takers Post To Facebook. Huffington Post. Available at: http://www.huffingtonpost.com/2012/09/26/police-social-media-training_n_1915059.html (07.02.14).

Manso, M., Manso, B., 2013. The role of social media in crisis: a European holistic approach to the adoption of online and mobile communications in crisis response and search and rescue efforts. In: Akhgar, B., Yates, S. (Eds.), Strategic Intelligence Management. National

Security Imperatives and Information and Communications Technologies. Elsevier, Oxford, pp. 93–107.

McCarthy, C., 2009. How the Mafia conquered social networks. Available at: http://news.cnet.com/8301-13577_3-10274060-36.html (accessed 07.02.14).

McKenna, K.Y.A., Bargh, J.A., 2000. Plan 9 from cyberspace: the implications of the Internet for personality and social psychology. Person. Soc. Psychol. Rev. 4 (1), 57–75.

Mesch, G.S., 2012. Minority status and the use of computer-mediated communication: a test of the social diversification hypothesis. Commun. Res. 39 (3), 317–337.

Miller, G.A., 1995. WordNet: a lexical database for English. Commun. ACM 38 (11), 39–41.

Moore, K., McElroy, J.C., 2012. The influence of personality on Facebook usage, wall postings, and regret. Comput. Hum. Behav. 28 (1), 267–274.

Oh, O., Agrawal, M., Rao, H.R., 2011. Information control and terrorism: tracking the Mumbai terrorist attack through twitter. Inform. Syst. Front. 13 (1), 33–43. http://dx.doi.org/10.1007/s10796-010-9275-8.

Peluchette, J., Karl, K., 2010. Examining students' intended image on Facebook: "what were they thinking?" J. Educ. Bus. 85 (1), 30–37.

Polhamous, A., 2014. Pitman police evacuate high school for 'potential threat'. Available at: http://www.nj.com/gloucester-county/index.ssf/2014/01/pitman_police:evacuate_high_school_for_potential_threat.html (accessed 02.06.14).

Priss, U., 2006. Formal concept analysis in information science. Annu. Rev. Inform. Sci. Technol. 40 (1), 521–543.

Rankin, G., Kinsella, N., 2011. Human trafficking—the importance of knowledge information exchange. In: Akhgar, B., Yates (Eds.), Simeon Intelligence Management. Springer London, pp. 159–180.

Reiner, R., 2010. The Politics of the Police. Oxford University Press, Oxford.

Ross, C., Orr, E.S., Sisic, M., Arseneault, J.M., Simmering, M.G., Orr, R.R., 2009. Personality and motivations associated with Facebook use. Comput. Hum. Behav. 25 (2), 578–586.

The Seattle Times, 2012. Threat closes skyline high school in sammamish. Available at: http://seattletimes.com/html/localnews/2019206262_apwasammamishschoolthreat.html (accessed 16.02.14).

Shah, S., Bao, F., Lu, C.-T., Chen, I.-R., 2011. CROWDSAFE: crowd sourcing of crime incidents and safe routing on mobile devices. In: Proceedings of the 19th ACM SIGSPATIAL International Conference on Advances in Geographic Information Systems. ACM, New York, NY, USA, pp. 521–524. http://dx.doi.org/10.1145/2093973.2094064.

Skog, D., 2005. Social interaction in virtual communities: the significance of technology. Int. J. Web Based Commun. 1 (4), 464–474.

Snasel, V., Horak, Z., Abraham, A., 2008. Understanding social networks using Formal Concept Analysis. In: 2008 IEEE/WIC/ACM International Conference on Web Intelligence and Intelligent Agent Technology, pp. 390–393.

Statistics Brain, 2014. Social Networking Statistics. Available at: http://www.statisticbrain.com/social-networking-statistics/ (accessed 14.02.14).

Sundar, S.S., Marathe, S.S., 2010. Personalization versus customization: the importance of agency, privacy, and power usage. Hum. Commun. Res. 36 (3), 298–322.

Taddicken, M., 2013. The 'privacy paradox' in the social web: the impact of privacy concerns, individual characteristics, and the perceived social relevance on different forms of self-disclosure. J. Comput.-Mediated Commun. 19 (2), 248–273.

Timelists, 2014. The Boss of All Bosses. Available at: http://content.time.com/time/specials/2007/article/0,28804,1683530_1683532_1683538,00.html (07.02.14).

United Kingdom Human Trafficking Centre (UKHTC), 2013. Available at: http://www.ecpat. org.uk/sites/default/files/ext-6538_ukhtc_strategic_assesssment_on_human_trafficking_2012_v1.01.pdf.

United Nations Office on Drugs and Crime (UNODC), 2004. United Nations convention against transnational organised crime and the protocols thereto.

United Nations Office on Drugs and Crime (UNODC), 2012. Global Report on Trafficking in Persons. http://www.unodc.org/documents/data-and-analysis/glotip/Trafficking_in_Persons_2012_web.pdf.

U.S. Department of Justice, 2005. Intelligence-led policing: the new intelligence architecture. The bureau of justice assistance - new realities: Law enforcement in the post-9/11 era.

Utz, S., Matzat, U., Snijders, C., 2009. Online reputation systems: the effects of feedback comments and reactions on building and rebuilding trust in online auctions. Int. J. Electron. Commer. 13 (3), 95–118. http://dx.doi.org/10.2753/JEC1086-4415130304.

Viegas, F.B., Wattenberg, M., Van Ham, F., Kriss, J., McKeon, M., 2007. Manyeyes: a site for visualization at internet scale. IEEE Trans. Visual. Comput. Graphics 13 (6), 1121–1128.

Zhao, S., Grasmuck, S., Martin, J., 2008. Identity construction on Facebook: digital empowerment in anchored relationships. Comput. Hum. Behav. 24 (5), 1816–1836.

Zywica, J., Danowski, J., 2008. The faces of Facebookers: investigating social enhancement and social compensation hypotheses. J. Comput.-Mediated Commun. 14 (1), 1–34.

The rise of cyber liability insurance

16

Gary Hibberd, Alan Cook

A BRIEF HISTORY OF INSURANCE

Whilst "cyber threats" may be new, the need to protect businesses against threats and losses incurred in the event of a major calamity is almost as old as civilization itself. People throughout history have employed risk management techniques to reduce the likelihood of loss or reduce the impact should a threat crystallize and occur. As early as the second century Chinese merchants travelling across dangerous rivers would distribute their goods across many ships to minimize their losses should they lose one or more in the troubled waters and it was the Romans and Greeks who introduced the concept of life and health insurance, where relatives of those lost in battle or at sea would benefit by receiving payments to cover funeral and future living expenses.

Insuring against losses has been with us for centuries, from the early Babylonians through to the Romans and the Greeks. More recently, in the seventeenth century Edward Lloyd's coffee house in London embarked on a new journey as they swiftly became known as the place to obtain marine insurance. In a world ever more reliant upon shipping and produce from around the world, the need to protect businesses trading on these dangerous waterways made perfect sense to everyone involved. Lloyds of London was firmly established as a world player in maritime insurance when a young man by the name of Cuthbert Heath joined Lloyds in 1877. Cuthbert Heath, an underwriter in Lloyds was soon developing policies for non-marine-related insurance and reinsurance including fire insurance, burglary insurance including policies for the American market. This moved Lloyds out of the shipping lanes and opened up new and emerging markets and set the template which Lloyds still follows today, priding itself on covering new and complex risk areas.

BUSINESS INTERRUPTION INSURANCE

The world today is very different than it was in 1877 but what Lloyds did was to set the mold for modern-day Business Interruption Insurance (BI Insurance) which many businesses today still rely upon. Dependent upon the cover, BI Insurance provides cover for a company's loss of earnings or profits in the unlikely event that they should be closed for a period of time for any number of reasons, including (but not limited to); fire, flood, earthquake, or acts of terrorism.

Typically there are three types of BI Insurance cover available:

- **"Business interruption"** insurance compensates the insured for income lost during the period of restoration or the time necessary to repair or restore the physical damage to the covered property;
- **"Extended business interruption"** (EBI) offers cover which is typically limited by a period of time, for the **income** lost after the property is repaired but before the income returns to its pre-loss level; and
- **"Contingent business interruption"** (CBI) offers cover for the insured's loss of income resulting from physical damage, not to its own property but to the property of third-parties (i.e., the damage did not affect the insured's property— but affected someone they rely upon and therefore affects their profit).

BI Insurance in whichever form is recognized as a very valuable and necessary type of insurance and one which many businesses see as the basic level of insurance they need in order to trade. But whilst BI Insurance and its variants cover for loss of profit, reimbursement of costs and compensate for damages to physical assets such as property, they rarely if ever cover the cost of non-physical assets. This means that BI Insurance may reimburse a claimant for the loss of the computer but it is unlikely to compensate them for the data which sits upon it, even though the data which this device holds may be worth many times the value of the device itself.

This gap some may feel is bridged by an additional form of insurance known as Professional Indemnity Insurance (PI Insurance) which can help protect a business if claims are brought against it by a client who believes some form of negligence or error has occurred (intentional or unintentional). In professional services organizations, such as financial services or legal entities this form of insurance is crucially important as the risk of litigation is often extremely high. This form of insurance may also cover the cost of penalties or fines arising from a data breach and brings us closer to a new form of insurance which has begun to grow in prominence and is quickly becoming the next "must have" for businesses operating in the modern era; Cyber Insurance Liability.

WHAT IS CYBER LIABILITY?

As we have seen, historically it was considered prudent to protect the physical assets of a business through insurance (BI Insurance) and later, claims for damage due to error or negligence (PI Insurance). But as the world becomes ever more interconnected and our dependency upon technology increases, the threat of unauthorized access or loss of personal information has resulted in the need to protect against previously uninsurable risks. So the Insurance market responded by creating the "Cyber Liability Insurance" (CL Insurance) product. CL Insurance is intended to cover risks associated with data breaches, which according to the Privacy and

Electronic Communications Regulations (2011), include the *"accidental or unlawful destruction, loss, alteration, unauthorized disclosure of, or access to, personal data transmitted, stored or otherwise processed."*

Although CL Insurance is relatively new the products are developing quickly as businesses and Insurance companies alike recognize the growing risks associated with operating in cyberspace. This growth is being driven by a number of factors including the speed and growth of the use of the Internet and our dependency upon technology. In 2013 the network company CISCO wrote a paper entitled "The Internet of Everything for Cities" which discussed *"Connecting People, Process, Data, and Things to improve the 'Livability' of Cities and Communities."* In this paper it states how the "Internet of Things" (IoT), interconnected systems will become the *"Internet of Everything (IoE) a network of networks where billions or even trillions of connections create unprecedented opportunities as well as new risks."* As we enter this era of the "Internet of Everything" several things become apparent:

- The world becomes more interconnected;
- the underlying infrastructure becomes more complex;
- the average user craves simplicity and "ease of use"

This means that

- We do not need to understand how the technology works to use it
- Information becomes easier to share between people and organizations
- Information is more likely to be retained for longer (disk storage is cheaper than ever)
- Information is more likely to exist on multiple devices (it no longer sits in secure computer rooms)
- Information can be sent to thousands of people with the click of a button
- We can communicate (using Social media) with thousands of people
- We can remain anonymous or create new identities behind which to hide
- We can connect to like-minded people around the world

As our reliance upon technology and information increases organizations are beginning to recognize their exposure is increasing, driven largely by high-profile cyber-related breaches and increased regulatory scrutiny and legislative requirements. As awareness increases, organizations are realizing that cyber risks are not solely concerned with the loss or unauthorized disclosure of personal data or information. Although there are a wide range of cyber risks, including those associated with business interruption and denial of service there are in fact just two forms of CL Insurance available (although these are not mutually exclusive as one can impact the other):

FIRST-PARTY CYBER LIABILITY

First-party insurance refers to a policy which provides protection for the asset owned by the insured organization and in reference to cyber risks typically includes a data breach of a company's own information and services (e.g., website hacked and defaced or Denial of Service (DoS) attack). Additional first-party liability can include business interruption caused by a network or system failure, loss or damage to digital assets, theft of digital assets (including money), cyber extortion and reputational damage.

THIRD-PARTY CYBER LIABILITY

Third-party cyber liability refers to a policy which provides protection against cyber risks which puts at risk customer or partner information the organization is contracted to keep safe. For example, a website hacked which results in the exposure of customer credit card details or an IT Cloud provider who experiences an outage resulting in the loss of client information. This form of cover also provides indemnification against the losses incurred through investigations, defense costs and fines resulting from a breach and can include the costs associated with notifying and compensating customers affected by the breach.

Both forms of liability can be equally damaging with first-party liabilities impacting upon the capability of the primary business to operate, whilst third-party liabilities may impact their clients and customers which may affect the entire reputation and brand of all those involved. Organizations therefore need to take account of an array of cyber risks, understand their exposure to them and then evaluate the potential for using insurance as a control mechanism. As we become more connected and rely increasing on cyberspace to provide services the need to protect against losses increases with it.

CYBER RISKS—A GROWING CONCERN

According to Government website, www.gov.uk, internet-related market in the UK is now estimated to be worth £82 billion a year while British businesses earn £1 in every £5 from the internet. This demonstrates the importance of the internet for businesses and individuals alike but research sponsored by Department for Business Innovation & Skills in 2013 revealed that in 2012 in the UK, 93% of large organizations had a security breach, with 87% of small businesses suffering a breach. The report estimated that costs incurred as a result of a security breach ranged between £450k-£850k and £35k-£65k respectively. It is likely because of these significant costs related to breaches, that security budgets have increased by 16% in 2013 (over 2012). This echoes further data from the Department for Business Innovation & Skills that 81% of senior management teams in large organizations are becoming increasingly concerned about security and see it as high or very high priority.

It is easy to understand the growing concern of those in large (and small) businesses when security breaches appear to be on the increase and the headlines are filled with almost daily stories of businesses being compromised. Cases include high-profile names such as "Yahoo!" (400 thousand passwords exposed), "LinkedIn" (6.5 million passwords exposed), and "Adobe" (38 million records breached [unofficially this number is reported to be far higher and estimated to exceed 150 million]). Many more stories are reported and countless more go unreported, all illustrating the growing need to understand the growing risks associated with "cyber." The following examples offer further evidence of the diverse nature of cyber risks:

- On 29th of August 2013 two individuals were charged in connection with an attempt to blackmail a Manchester internet company via a cyber-attack. The investigation into this incident is currently ongoing, led by Greater Manchester Police in association with the Serious and Organised Crime Agency. This incident highlights the expanding threat Cyber Extortion poses to UK business.
- A multinational insurance company had to pay a multi-million pound sum to UK regulators when it was proved they had misplaced the server back-up tapes of their IT system containing the private details of over 40,000 of their policy holders.
- In 2011 the UK high street cosmetics company "Lush" was hacked via a third-party email provider. The hackers were able to access the payment details of 5000 customers who had previously shopped on its website. Lush did not fully meet industry standards relating to card payment security and faced a potential fine of £500,000 from The Information Commissioner's Office.

These incidents and many more like them demonstrate the multitude and variety of risks faced by organizations today not only from direct losses from the event itself, but from the risks associated to impact upon reputation (requiring a structured and often costly PR response) and from increased fines and claims for damages.

THE CYBER THREAT

The cyber threat for organizations comes in a variety of shapes and sizes and dependent upon who they are, they may be seen as a primary target, as collateral damage or merely as a "playground" in which the cyber-infant hones their "Hacking" skills. These threats can include: Hacktivism, theft of IP (intellectual property), Cyber-stalking, Extortion, virus dissemination, identity theft, vandalism, and fraud. Many businesses could also find themselves unwittingly playing a part in attacks on other computer networks as they become "infected" by tools which enable an attacker to take command and control over their computers and use them at their will in a "Distributed Denial of Service" (DDOS) attack on another organization or critical infrastructure.

Stanley Konter, CEO of Savannah's Sabre Technologies once stated "The problem has gotten more prevalent with always-on, high-speed internet access. Attackers are always out there looking for that type of computer." He was referring to the fact that computers are often left switched on and connected to the internet, even when not in use and this connection can be used both ways by people wishing to do us harm. These threats range between state-sponsored terrorists looking to disrupt national infrastructures through to individuals and groups of individuals who are doing it for "lulz" (slang for the term "for laughs").

Whilst it must be recognized that the cyber threat can come from an external source businesses are in need to be reminded that they are far more likely to be the victims of a cyber-related incident from within their own organization than that of an external source. Many organizations are already taking steps to protect themselves and their businesses from the cyber threat with Firewall technology, Antivirus protection and Intrusion Detection Systems. However internally, their processes have not evolved to protect themselves and the information they hold at the same pace. The incidents relayed earlier demonstrate that having good security controls in place will not prevent someone "misplacing" backup files containing masses of information. Nor will it prevent staff from throwing away physical documentation which contains personal information in the trash. The cyber threat therefore is far from being purely related to online information, a matter which the regulatory framework, worldwide is trying to address.

A CHANGING REGULATORY LANDSCAPE

Increased scrutiny by regulatory bodies (worldwide) and threats of increased fines have clearly raised the need for appropriate protection. In Europe, January 2012 the European Commission proposed a reform of the EU's 1995 data protection rules in a bid to strengthen online privacy rights. This was seen as a key requirement due in part because the 27 EU Member States had implemented the 1995 rules differently, resulting in divergences in enforcement. The intention is to create a single law which will reduce the cost of administration (of the legal frameworks) and is seen as a way to raise confidence in online services (see Chapters 1 and 14).

This chapter is not intended to be an in-depth review of the new regulation but there are key elements of the standard which are worthy of exploration as they directly impact the growing need for CL Insurance.

ICO NOTIFICATION

The regulation which is due to come into force in 2014 (possibly 2015) empowers each supervisory authority to impose administrative sanctions in accordance with the regulation and stipulates that within 24 h and provide a full report within 3 days of the event. The wording of Article 31 of the regulation states:

> *In the case of a personal data breach, the controller shall without undue delay and, where feasible, not later than 24 hours after having become aware of it, notify the personal data breach to the supervisory authority. The notification to the supervisory authority shall be accompanied by a reasoned justification in cases where it is not made within 24 hours.*

The regulation stipulates the information which is required and also the manner in which it should be reported. Furthermore, Article 79 ("Administrative Sanctions") outlines the administrative sanctions the supervisory authority can levy against organizations who breach the regulations and states that the sanction *"shall be in each individual case effective, proportionate and dissuasive"* (Article79.2). Article 79 of the regulation goes on to state that the amount of the administrative fine shall

> *be fixed with due regard to the nature, gravity and duration of the breach, the intentional or negligent character of the infringement, the degree of responsibility of the natural or legal person and of previous breaches by this person, the technical and organisational measures and procedures implemented [pursuant to Article 23] and the degree of cooperation with the supervisory authority in order to remedy the breach.*

The above passage clearly indicates that organizations must be in a position to understand their risks and have clear understanding of how they are protecting themselves against these risks becoming incidents. The regulation goes on to stipulate the kinds of sanctions which the supervisory authority can impose and it is these sanctions which organizations are becoming increasingly aware and concerned about, leading them to consider the uptake of some form of insurance which mitigates the increased risk of fines. These sanctions include fines of between €250,000 and €1,000,000 or between 0.5% and 2% of the annual worldwide turnover dependent upon the circumstances of the breach and the level of protection and mitigation that can be demonstrated.

As regulations therefore become more comprehensive businesses need not only to consider the most appropriate ways to improve their security controls (e.g., by adopting the international standard for information security, ISO27001:2013) but they must also look for ways to mitigate the potential losses from fines imposed by their local supervisory authority through the use of appropriate insurance.

WHAT DOES CYBER LIABILITY INSURANCE COVER?

It is important to state at this stage that CL Insurance should not be seen as a method for organizations to simply transfer their risks to an insurer and make no other effort to protect themselves against potential incidents. Like many insurance products, CL Insurance products carry a series of exemptions and exclusions to protect the insurer from underwriting bad risks. Cyber Liability insurance is intended to mitigate losses from a variety of cyber-related incidents including those stated previously. With the new regulation on the horizon and the increasingly complex and interconnected environment businesses operate in; it is easy to see why cyber insurance is so desirable to businesses.

A good CL Insurance product should protect against the financial impact of a data leak, a data loss or a breach of a company's IT system and may include ancillary cover for such elements as Cyber Extortion or costs associated with PR management. Current products vary in what they will and will not cover, but essentially range from the loss of information from an individual laptop to the hacking of an entire network or cloud storage facility. The impact of any of the above can have a serious effect on a company's IT system, their market reputation and most importantly their financial stability.

The impact of a data breach can be far reaching but Cyber liability coverage essentially falls into three distinct areas of cover:

- **Loss or Damage of Data**—Data which is lost, stolen, corrupted or damaged by any means including intentional or unintentional actions. Costs incurred may include compensation claims, fines, investigations, remediation or recovery costs.
- **Cyber Extortion**—An increasing risk where hackers or "hacktivists" threaten to disrupt your business by introducing a virus or shutting down your website via a "Denial of Service" (DoS) attack, unless a sum of money is provided. Additional risks include the threat of having defamatory (or inappropriate) material injected into their websites or online catalogues to discredit the company. Cyber Extortion also includes the release of confidential information unless a fee is paid.
- **Command & Control**—Specialist knowledge may be required to manage the incident and ensure all necessary actions are taken to minimize the disruption to the business and ensure all interested parties are informed of actions being taken (including customers, clients, suppliers, and regulators). This can also include costs associated with external PR agencies to manage communication to the wider community and finally will include costs associated with the provision of Credit Protection Services to those affected.

As highlighted above in "Command & Control" the wider cover provided by some cyber polices extends to the public relations cost that can result from a business that is exposed as having a cyber breach. A company's reputation can be quickly soured as customers lose confidence in their security. Having a speedy and professional PR Team to help manage the crisis and restore customers confidence is paramount in the digital age.

WHO OFFERS CYBER LIABILITY INSURANCE AND WHAT SHOULD CUSTOMERS LOOK OUT FOR?

Cyber Liability Insurance has existed in the insurance market for a number of years but it is only the proposed changes in legislation, increased usage of mobile electronic devices and a series of high profile cyber attacks that have brought Cyber Liability Insurance to the forefront of businesses and broker's attention. Choosing the right broker who understands the covers and the exposure is paramount in ensuring a business has adequate protection.

As the need for meaningful Cyber Liability protection grows there is no shortage of market capacity for this product. The established markets for this cover include AIG, Hiscox, ACE, Chubb, and Zurich; however, choosing the right policy is key to ensuring adequate cover is provided. A comprehensive Cyber Liability product should give cover for the following key areas:

- Defense Cost & Damages covered for First and Third Party losses
- Business interruption for Server Downtime
- A Forensic Investigation and Support Service to manage a breach and help restore a company's system
- A Public Relations response service to help mitigate negative publicity following a cyber breach
- Cover offered in respect of Cyber Extortion

It is important also to consider if the provider offering the Cyber liability product understands the Cyber "space" they are operating within. Responding effectively to the threat is of paramount importance and understanding the process for notification and management will offer confidence to the purchaser that should the need arises, everyone will understand what will happen.

CONCLUSION

From the details provided on cyber threats and cyber-attacks it is clear that every businesses or organization operating a web site or conducting business in cyber-space needs protection from an ever increasing array of risks and need to take pro-active steps to protect themselves from incidents occurring. These measures should include a basic understanding and implementation of appropriate security controls. What "appropriate" means is different from industry to industry and business to business, but every organization should at the very least have adopted the principals of Data Protection and considered the appropriateness of the international standard for information security, ISO27001.

Good information security processes have always mandated that there should be good incident management in place and this is where CL Insurance steps into the frame. CL Insurance provides a level of comfort that, if (or "when") a breach occurs there is something that the claimant can ultimately rely upon to help reduce the impact on their organization should there be legal or regulatory scrutiny (or sanctions) or there is a need for specialist or expert knowledge.

As more and more business is transacted in cyber-space, the use of mobile electronic devices increases and "Big Data" gets bigger the likelihood of something going wrong is undoubtedly going to increase too (see Chapter 14). The potential direct or indirect losses which could occur due to theft, loss, destruction of critical data, libel, defamation, copyright or trademark infringement, vandalism, threats or denial of service attacks are increasing and show no sign of slowing down.

Regulatory and legislative changes regarding data protection and breach notification could see fines and penalties becoming much more prevalent so businesses need to acknowledge the risk that Cyber Liability presents and carefully consider the security controls required to ensure data protection is in place. Whilst there are a variety of approaches to this which should be carefully assessed and understood, the benefits of a comprehensive and effective Cyber Liability policy will not be fully understood until they are needed.

The insurance market is historically slow to develop products which have little or no statistical information available but as this details surrounding breaches becomes more readily available the provision of CL Insurance will increase along with the demand in the market place. The future of CL Insurance is secured and will undoubtedly evolve over the coming years. The only question is how quickly CL Insurance will evolve into full Data Protection Insurance. This is a step which has yet to be taken but undoubtedly needs to happen.

Responding to cyber crime and cyber terrorism— botnets an insidious threat

17

Giovanni Bottazzi, Gianluigi Me

INTRODUCTION

One of the most insidious cyber threats for the IT community is currently represented by a diffusion of networks containing infected computers (called bots or zombies), which are managed by attackers and are called botnets.

The use of botnets is very common in various IT contexts, from cybercrime to cyber warfare. They are able to provide a very efficient distributed IT platform that could be used for several illegal activities such as launching Distributed Denial of Service (DDoS), attacks against critical targets or starting with a "sample" attack followed up with an email or other communication threatening a larger DDoS attack (if a certain amount of money is not paid—cyber extortion), malware dissemination, phishing and frauds (e.g., banking information gathering) or to conduct cyber-espionage campaigns to steal sensitive information.

In these scenarios, the controller of a botnet, also known as botmaster, controls the activities of the entire structure giving orders to every single zombie through various communication channels.

The diffusion of the botnets measures their level of dangerousness and depends on the capabilities of managers to involve the largest number of machines trying to hide the activities of the malicious architecture too—a particular kind of "hide and seek" game.

A critical phase in the botnets arrangement is represented by its constitution. Attackers can recruit bots diffusing a malware, typically via phishing or sending the malicious agent via email.

Infected machines receive commands from Command & Control (C&C) servers that instruct the overall architecture how to operate to achieve the purpose for which it has been composed.

The diffusion of botnets has recently increased due to various factors such as:

- increased availability of powerful internet connectivity and hosts (to be understood not only as personal computers, but as objects of everyday life more and more interconnected and smart). Fifty to one hundred billion things are expected to be connected to the Internet by 2020. This paradigm is usually referred as "*Internet of Things*";

- possibility of malware customization (introduced by Zeus botnet and its Software Development Kit);
- presence in the underground/black market of cyber criminals that rent services and structures that compose the malicious systems.

There are various classifications of botnets based on the overall topology and the command and control channels used, through which they can be updated and directed, the developing technology used and the scope of the services implemented.

Emerging trends show that newer architectures are migrating toward completely distributed topologies (P2P networks) instead of centralized structures, mobile implementations of malwares and the use of TOR networks and social platforms as C&C server hiding techniques. The high sophistication and spread of botnets has led to the emergence of a new criminal business model that can be synthesized with "Cybercrime-as-a-Service" (CaaS). This chapter is a botnet essay (with two use cases included) and related countermeasures.

A BOTNET ROADMAP

The malwares that both have introduced the concept of victim machine connected to a communication channel to listen for malicious commands, beginning with the so-called botnet-era, were "Sub7" and "Pretty Park"—a Trojan and worm, respectively. These two pieces of malware first emerged in 1999 and botnet innovation has been steady since then (Ferguson, 2010).

During 2002, there were a couple of major developments in botnet technology with the release of both SDBot and Agobot. SDBot was a single small binary, written in C++, marketed by its creator who has also made the source code widely available. As a result, many bots later include code or ideas taken from SDbot. Agobot, instead, introduced the concept of a modular attack. The initial attack installed a "back door", the second tried to disable the antivirus software and the third has blocked access to the websites of security vendors. These two malwares started the huge increase in variants and the expansion of functionalities.

Malware authors gradually introduced encryption for Ransomware (hostage taking of encrypted files), HTTP and SOCKS proxies allowing them to use their victims for onward connection or FTP servers for storing illegal content.

Steadily botnets migrated away from the original IRC Command & Control channel—the protocol is easily identified in network traffic and TCP ports seldom opened through firewalls—and began to communicate over HTTP, ICMP and SSL ports, often using custom protocols. They have also continued the adoption and refinement of peer-to-peer communications, as would be demonstrated 5 years later by another famous botnet known with the name of Conficker.

It was around 2003 that the criminal interest in botnet capabilities began to become apparent. At the start of the decade, spamming was still a "home-work" occupation with large volumes of Spam sent from dedicated Server Farms, Open Relays or compromised servers.

Bagle and Bobax were the first spamming botnets and the malware Mytob was essentially a blend of earlier mass mailing worms MyDoom and SDbot. This enabled criminals to build large botnets and distribute their spamming activities across their entire victim PCs, giving them agility and flexibility and helping them to avoid the legal enforcement activity that was starting to be aggressively pursued.

In 2005, a Russian group of five developers known as UpLevel started developing Zeus, a "Point-and-Click" program for creating and controlling a network of compromised computer systems (Lemos, 2010). The following year they released the first version of the program, a basic Trojan designed to hide on an infected system and steal information. In 2007, the group came out with a more modular version, which allowed other underground developers to create plug-ins to add to its functionality. Five years of development later, the latest version of this software (which can be downloaded for free and required low technical skill to operate), is one of the most popular botnet platforms for spammers, fraudsters, and people who deal in stolen personal information (note that there was an increase of actions you can perform with a malware). The latest Zeus platform allows users to build custom malicious software to infect target systems, manage a wide network of compromised machines, and use the resulting botnet for illegal gain. The construction kit contained a program for building the bot software and Web scripts for creating and hosting a central Command and Control server (Figure 17.1).

A survey conducted by a security firm—Atlanta-based Damballa—found Zeus-controlled programs to be the second most common inside corporate networks in 2009. Damballa tracked more than 200 Zeus-based botnets in enterprise networks. The largest single botnet controlled using the Zeus platform consisted of 600,000 compromised computers.

Consequently, independent developers have created compatible "exploit packs" capable of infecting victims' systems using vulnerabilities in the operating system or browser. Other developers focus on creating plug-in software to help "wannabe" cybercriminals in making money from a Zeus botnet. For example some add-ons focus on phishing attacks, delivering images and Web pages needed to create fraudulent banking sites. With the mentioned features it is very hard for antivirus software to identify a Zeus payload (Binsalleeh et al., 2010; Falliere and Chien, 2009; Wyke, 2011).

Zeus obviously is not the only tool available for building a botnet, but its birth is a milestone for the entire cybercriminal sector since it was designed with the "nonexpert" user in mind, including simple point-and-click interfaces for managing infected machines (for these reasons called ZeuS Crimeware family). For example ZeroAccess botnet—specialized in click fraud attacks and apparently disrupted in 2013—was probably wider than Zeus (it is estimated millions of infections globally in 2012, with up to 140,000 unique IPs in the US and Europe).

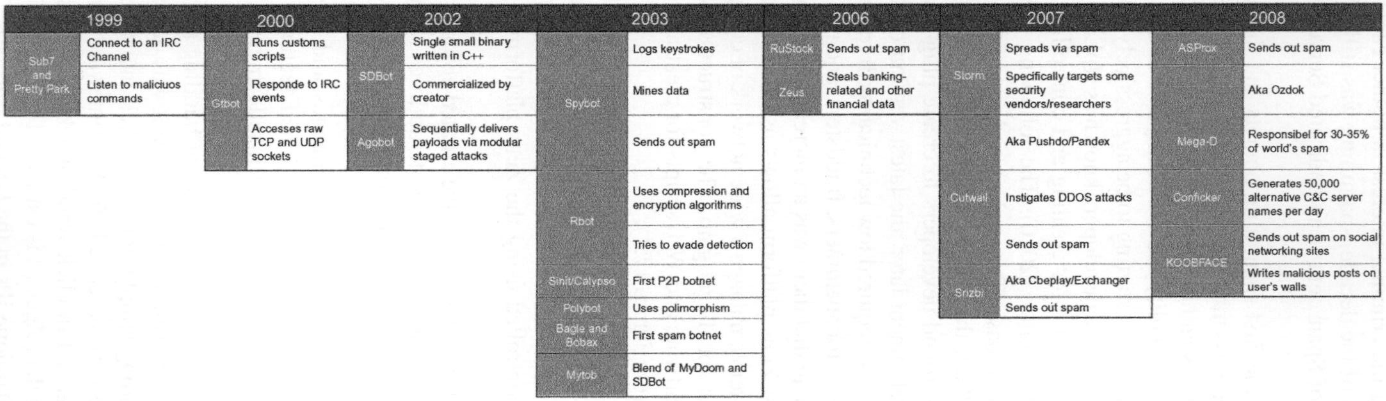

	1999	2000	2002	2003	2006	2007	2008
Sub7 and Pretty Park	Connect to an IRC Channel	Runs customs scripts	Single small binary written in C++	Logs keystrokes	Sends out spam	Spreads via spam	Sends out spam
	Listen to malicious commands						
		SDBot Responde to IRC events	Commercialized by creator	Mines data	Steals banking-related and other financial data	Specifically targets some security vendors/researchers	Aka Ozbok
		Gtbot Accesses raw TCP and UDP sockets	**Agobot** Sequentially delivers payloads via modular staged attacks	Sends out spam		Aka Pushdo/Pandex	Responsibel for 30-35% of world's spam
				Rbot Uses compression and encryption algorithms		Instigates DDOS attacks	Generates 50,000 alternative C&C server names per day
				Tries to evade detection		Sends out spam	Sends out spam on social networking sites
				Sinit/Calypso First P2P botnet		**Srizbi** Aka Cbeplay/Exchanger	Writes malicious posts on user's walls
				Polybot Uses polimorphism		Sends out spam	
				Bagle and Bobax First spam botnet			
				Mytob Blend of MyDoom and SDBot			

Row headers spanning years: **Storm** (2007), **RuStock** (2006), **Zeus** (2006), **Cutwail** (2007), **ASProx** (2008), **Mega-D** (2008), **Conficker** (2008), **KOOBFACE** (2008), **Spybot** (2003).

FIGURE 17.1

Botnets roadmap.

Just as Zeus was the cornerstone of the next-generation botnets, Blackhole is definitely the cornerstone of the next-generation exploit kits. Since it emerged in late 2010, the Blackhole exploit kit has grown to become one of the most notorious exploit kits ever encountered (Howard, 2012).

Over the last few years the volume of malware seen in the field has grown dramatically, thanks mostly to the use of automation and kits to facilitate its creation and distribution. The term "crimeware," already used for Zeus, was coined specifically to describe the process of "automating cybercrime." Individuals no longer profit just from writing and distributing their malware. Today's malware scene is highly organized, structured and professional in its approach, where individuals can choose the criminal role which best fit.

Kits, as an intrinsic part of crimeware, provide the tools for criminals to create and distribute malware, but also the systems used to manage networks of infected machines. Some of these kits focus on creation and management of the malware payload—Zeus is perhaps the best example of this. Other kits are those that focus on infecting users through web attacks, specifically attacks known as drive-by downloads. It is this latter group of kits that are commonly referred to as exploit kits or exploit packs (the terms are used interchangeably).

There are several versions of Blackhole exploit kit, the first being v1.0.0 (released in late 2010). The kit consists of a series of PHP scripts designed to run on a web server (all protected with the commercial ionCube encoder). This is presumably to help prevent other miscreants stealing their code (there are many exploit kits which are little more than copies of others), and to hinder analysis.

The general characteristics of the Blackhole exploit kit are listed below:

- The kit is Russian in origin.
- Configuration options for all the usual parameters (querystring parameters, file paths for payloads or exploit components, redirect URLs, usernames, passwords, etc.).
- MySQL backend.
- Blacklisting/blocking (only hit any IP once, maintain IP blacklist, blacklist by referrer URL, import blacklisted ranges).
- Auto update (of course).
- Management console provides statistical summary, breaking down successful infections by exploit, OS, country, affiliate/partner (responsible for directing user traffic to the exploit kit) and by browser.
- Targets a variety of client vulnerabilities.
- Antivirus scanning add-ons.

However, there are some features that are (or were at first release) unique to Blackhole:

- "Rental" business model. Historically, exploit kits are goods (pay-per-use) that are sold to individuals and then used as they desire. Blackhole includes a rental strategy, where individuals pay for the use of the hosted exploit kit for some period of time. Figure 17.2 illustrates the pricing model (translated from Russian) for the first release of Blackhole.
- Management console optimized for use with PDAs.

Annual licence: $ 1500
Hal-year license: $1000
3-month license: $700

Update cryptor $ 50
Changing domain $ 20 multidomain $ 200 to license.
During the terme of the license all the updates are free.

Rent on our server:

1 week (7 full days): $ 200
2 weeks (14 full days): $ 300
3 weeks (21 full days): $ 400
4 weeks (31 full days): $ 500
24-hour test: $ 50

There is restriction on the volume of incoming traffic to a leasehold system, depending of the time of the contract.

Providing our proper domain included.The subsequent change of the domain: $ 35
No longer any hidden fees, rental includes full support for the duration of the contract

FIGURE 17.2

Blackhole pricing model.

The whole purpose of Blackhole is to infect victims with some payload. The payloads are typically polymorphic, packed with custom encryption tools and designed to evade antivirus detection (a process which is helped with the built-in AV checking functionality of Blackhole). The most prevalent payloads installed in the past few years include fake AV, Zeus, ZeroAccess rootkit and Ransomware.

One of the most important new features of Blackhole is the automation through which you can exploit servers and clients by a large amount of vulnerabilities (remember that both Zeus and Blackhole are networks constantly managed and updated remotely). Web Servers with some vulnerability (compromised servers) may be used to host Blackhole directly or to redirect clients toward "ad-hoc-builded" Blackhole Web Sites.

An attacker can use a compromised server in order to steal information of all users of the same server also known as a Watering Hole attack. The attackers study the behavior of people who work for a target organization, to learn about their browsing habits. Then they compromise a web site that is frequently used by employees—preferably one hosted by a trusted organization which represents a valuable source of information. Ideally, they will use a zero-day exploit. So when an employee visits a web page on the site, they are infected, typically a backdoor Trojan is installed allowing the attackers to access the company's internal network. In effect, instead of chasing the victim, the cybercriminal sits in a location that the victim is highly likely to visit—hence the watering-hole analogy (Kaspersky, 2013; Symantec, 2013).

The other important aspect, from the criminal point of view, is the change of the criminal business model. Older versions of malware were offered for sale at very high prices. Actually early versions are distributed free of charge and often these former versions have been "backdoored" by criminals, meaning that the novice thief (so called lamer) also becomes the victim.

In the recent past, instead, the glut of freely available criminal tools has lowered the cost barrier of entry into cybercrime and encouraged more wannabe cybergangsters (lamer) into online crime. As mentioned today's malware scene is highly organized, structured, and professional in its approach.

The spread of the Internet, especially for government and commercial purposes, has led to an evolution of the business model of the criminal market behind the modern threats. It is possible to imagine a layered reverse-pyramid structure (in terms of organizations involved, the size of these organizations, skills and goals) (Figure 17.3).

Organizations with more technical skills (probably the less numerous and comparable to a kind of Cyber-Mercenaries) are those who design and distribute various types of crimeware (payloads and exploit kits) according to different modes of diffusion (spam, phishing, social engineering, drive-by or watering-hole), but do not take any particular action. In many cases, the cyber mercenaries instead of monetizing botnet activities by directly implementing fraud schemas rent a series of services to other criminals—a trend confirmed by the constant monitoring of the underground market offers. The prepared infrastructure is ready to be "sold" or better "rent" to the highest bidder. The rental model showed better revenue than the sale one. In fact many criminals made their money simply by renting access to their botnets rather than engaging in Spam, DDoS or information theft campaigns of their own devising (remember that the so-called Blackhole "landing page" could be the compromised sever by itself or an hosting server).

Those who pay to take criminal action do not need a high technical skill, but their attacks are usually more motivated and more numerous. The two most common reasons are socio-political (Hacktivist) and economic (Cyber Criminal). Criminals

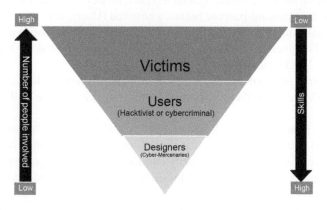

FIGURE 17.3

Criminal business model.

Pay-per-Use (PPU) to thousands of already compromised machines or provide additional malwares to these computers already infected.

Spam bots can provide secondary information, for example, via stealing malware, fake antivirus software and Ransomware, to increase the flexibility of the infected machines and to maximize the potential revenue of each infected computer.

To give an idea of the economic impact of the botnets, the "F-Secure 2012 Threat Report" revealed that the ZeroAccess threat reportedly clicks 140 million ads a day. It has been estimated that the botnet is costing up to USD 900,000 of daily revenue loss to legitimate online advertisers. Moreover, as we will see later, in one of the two use cases, Eugrograbber earned 36+ million euros.

The third level is obviously composed by Victims (owner of the infected machines) that, depending on the type of attack, may be a generic Internet user (if the number of the victims is the most important variable, e.g., in DDoS campaign) or belonging to a particular category of people (if the quality of the information to be subtracted is the most important variable).

Moreover, the users layer, is not necessarily monolithic, but can be further divided into intermediate levels (e.g., organizations most experienced in malware development could be not equally in its distribution) and consists of various criminal figures in a kind of partnership program where the higher level guarantees a minimum number of "customers" to the lower one (see ZeroAccess Pay-per-Install—PPI—business model).

The previous pyramid, as well as criminal business model, is considered as a measure of the real threat (the more the victim layer is wide the most of the threat is disruptive).

The mentioned botnet monetization models (PPI and PPU) affect both the direction and the magnitude of the "criminal value flows." Moreover, in the specific case of the PPU model, the entity of a flow is proportional to the dangerousness of the threat.

In fact, while for a click-fraud-oriented botnet, money flows and their size are almost certain, for a general-purpose botnet, a criminal (User), who wants to attack for example a bank, might be willing to invest a larger amount of money to buy or rent a botnet (by Designers) sufficiently wide and sufficiently skilled for bank account exfiltration or DDOS campaigns.

So the botnet economic flows, in the two monetization models, can be represented as in Figure 17.4 (the thickness of the arrows is indicative of the amount of money).

A possible value chain for "Designers," believed to be to most "e-structured," can be represented by using models such as Porter's model chart which is very similar to what can be generated for a generic software-house with a prevalence of the trustee element (for customers and suppliers) linked to the fact that the added-value will be directly or indirectly related to criminal activities.

Based on Porters model we can identify two sets of activities:

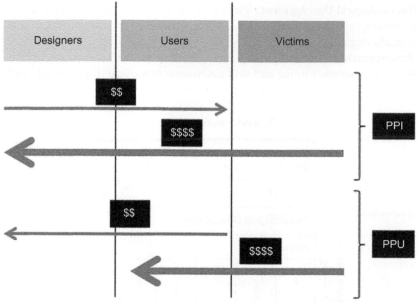

FIGURE 17.4

Money flows.

PRIMARY ACTIVITIES:

- **Inbound Logistics:** all the needed logistical activities for the implementation of services for sale or rent. Hw & Sw logistics, bulletproof hosting services rental and anonymous connectivity.
- **Operations:** the core business. Develop payloads, customizable crimewares, exploit kits and back-end infrastructures for building, hiding and accessing C&C servers (maybe hosted on bulletproof domains), malware distribution methods/services, etc.
- **Outbound Logistics:** Hw & Sw for managing secure e-marketing, e-sales and e-money transfer infrastructures.
- **Marketing and Sales: MARKETING:** post on forums, black markets, rate and target of success. **SALES:** sell/rent all is made by Operations.
- **Services:** Botnet amplitude, steadily updated malware features (Spam, DDOS, Exfiltration, etc.).

SUPPORT ACTIVITIES:

- **Firm Infrastructure:** Labs, C&C server owned, technologies for anonymous connectivity and/or VPNs with Countries with poor legislation on cybercrime.
- **Human Resource Management:** Employees skilled and trusted.

- **Technological Development:** Variants to Crimeware SDK or brand new payloads, exploit kits, bulletproof C&C host, secure e-payments, secure e-marketing.
- **Procurement:** Forecasting and planning of criminal market requests, secure payment systems, trusting and skill assessment procedures for providers and partners (PPI business model) (Figure 17.5).

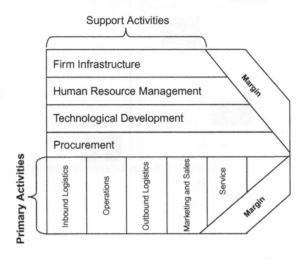

FIGURE 17.5

The Porter's value chain.

BOTNETS HOW DO THEY WORK. NETWORK TOPOLOGIES AND PROTOCOLS

As mentioned in the introduction a botnet is a network of infected computers (bots or zombies) managed by attackers, through one or more Command & Control Server and due to the inoculation of malware. The controller of a botnet, also known as Botmaster, controls the activities of the entire structure (from specific orders to software updates) through different communication channels.

The level of diffusion of the botnets depends on the capabilities of botmasters to involve the largest number of machines trying to hide both the activities of the malicious architecture and the location of the C&C servers.

We will not make reference to infection or dissemination practices of the payload because already mentioned in the introduction (e.g., Blackhole) and because it is intimately linked to the exploitation of the vulnerabilities of compromised systems (out of scope).

Trying to categorize the concept of botnet is not an easy task. There are many purposes for which these architectures are designed and created. They inevitably influence factors such as the malware used to compromise victims, rather than the technology involved (Balapure, 2013; Paganini, P., 2013a, 2013b, 2013c).

Botnets could be discriminated, for example, by their architecture. Some networks are based on one or more C&C, every bot is directly connected with Command & Control servers. The C&C manages a list of infected machines, monitors their status and gives them operative instructions.

This type of architecture is quite simple to organize and manage, but has the drawback of being very vulnerable, since turning-off the C&C server(s) would cause the malfunction of the entire botnet. The server(s) in fact represent a single point of failure since the operation of the whole botnet is functional to the capacity of its bots to reach the control systems.

Initially C&C IP addresses were hardcoded into each bot, which made their identification easier and resulted in their eventual disruption by researchers, but the "attackers" learn from their failures every time. For example a natural evolution could be the use of a reverse proxy (in some environments called rendez-vous point) to address a C&C server. In this way is easier to hide C&C IP addresses and the botmaster identities (but we have just moved the single point of failure from the C&C to the Reverse Proxy). This is the case of centralized architectures (Figure 17.6).

A more radical and increasingly popular way to increase botnet resilience is to organize the botnet in decentralized architectures as a Peer-to-Peer (P2P) network. In a P2P botnet, bots connect to other bots to exchange C&C traffic, eliminating the need for centralized servers. As a result, P2P botnets cannot be disrupted using the traditional approach of attacking centralized infrastructures.

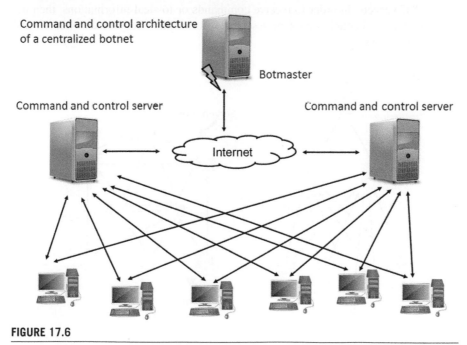

FIGURE 17.6

Botnet centralized architecture.

So the bots are not necessarily connected to the C&C servers, but they compose a mesh structure where commands are also transmitted "zombie-to-zombie." Each node of the network has a list of addresses of "neighbor" bots with which they exchange commands. In a similar structure, each bot could send orders to others and attackers to control the entire botnet, but they need access to at least one computer.

Tracking of P2P botnets requires the complete node enumeration, while in ordinary botnets it is necessary to find only the C&C servers. The security community has been trying to identify the infected machines in this way, collecting the IP addresses of the participating nodes. The collected items can be used by security defense systems to identify sources of infection, but it is very hard because in many cases, bots are behind firewalls or NAT devices (Figure 17.7).

Symantec security researchers detected a variant of the popular Zeus malware that relies on P2P communication as a backup system in case the C&C servers were not reachable. The variant isolated by Symantec does not use C&C servers implementing an autonomous botnet.

This type of botnet is really concerning and is hard to fight due to the absence of a single point of failure as represented in classic botnet architecture. Despite the fact that destroying a decentralized botnet is more difficult (or maybe impossible?), this type of architecture presents a higher management complexity (Wang, 2013).

It should now be clear that C&C play an essential role for botnets functionality, which are generally hosted on hacked, bought or rented servers. Moreover, regardless of the architecture used, a botnet has the need to connect every single bot with one or more C&C servers, in order to receive commands or to steal informations, then the communication channel is another essential discriminator for botnets (Lanelli and Hackworth, 2005).

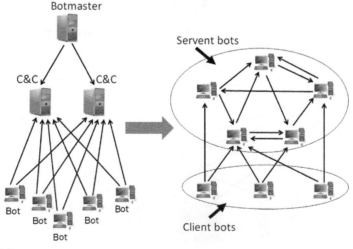

FIGURE 17.7

From centralized botnet to hybrid peer-to-peer botnet.

So botnets can also be classified on the basis of network protocol used. An old botnet scheme was the classic IRC-oriented, that is, on the basis of the Internet Relay. Every bot receives a command via an IRC channel from an IRC-Bot. An IRC bot is composed of a set of scripts connecting to Internet Relay Chat as a client.

Since then, there have been numerous developments, however, all geared to obfuscate and/or encrypt the communication channel. Most advanced botnets use their own protocols based on protocols such as TCP, ICMP or UDP. For example before Zeus P2P variant, the expert noted that authors implemented communication through UDP protocol.

Historically, the UDP protocol has already been used in the past as a real data transmission channel (fake DNS A-queries carrying a payload), but it is the UDP protocol, or rather the DNS protocol, that has been heavily used by the bots to identify the domain name of their own C&C servers. Botmasters have coded algorithms into their malware, automatically and dynamically generating a high number of Internet Fully Qualified Domain Names, also known as Domain Generation Algorithm (DGA). In this way authors, executing the same algorithms, can hide their C&C servers behind different and highly dynamic domain names. Obviously, all domains that are generated by a DGA have a short life span, since they are used only for a limited duration, and generate a lot of NXDomain traffic. They also need some collaboration from particular type of hosting providers that guarantee the operators that they would not respond to abuse complaints nor cooperate with takedown requests. These providers are commonly known as "bulletproof hosting" and are widely used in the cybercrime ecosystem (however, their services are typically more expensive and they might not be 100% reliable).

Of course we must not forget web-based botnets which are a collection of infected machines controlled through World Wide Web. HTTP bots connect to a specific web server, receiving commands and sending back data. This type of architecture is very easy to deploy and manage and very hard to track if encryption (HTTPs) is added.

The Nugache botnet (Rossow, 2013), which appeared in early 2006, was one of the first to use strong encryption. Commands were signed with a 4096-bit RSA key, in order to prevent unauthorized control, and the communications between peers was encrypted using session keys which were individually negotiated and derived from a particular RSA scheme.

The highlight value of botnets is the ability to provide anonymity through the use of both a multi-tier C&C architecture and different communication channels. The use of standard application protocols such as HTTPS can also facilitate the spread to corporate networks. Instead the use of custom protocols (typical of P2P botnet), while providing greater flexibility, may be neutralized by firewall systems.

Finally, the individual bots may not be physically owned by the botmaster (criminal reverse-pyramid in previous paragraph), and may be located in several locations all around the globe. Differences in time zones, languages, and laws make it difficult to track malicious botnet activities across international boundaries.

CASE STUDY—EUROGRABBER (2012)

This is a case study about a sophisticated, multi-dimensional and targeted attack which stole an estimated 36+ million Euros from more than 30,000 bank customers from multiple banks across Europe. The attacks began in Italy, and soon after, tens of thousands of infected online bank customers were detected in Germany, Spain and Holland. Entirely transparent, the online banking customers had no idea they were infected with Trojans, or that their online banking sessions were being compromised, or that funds were being stolen directly out of their accounts.

This attack campaign was discovered and named "Eurograbber" by Versafe and Check Point Software Technologies (Kalige and Burkley, 2012). The Eurograbber attack employs a new and very successful variation of the ZITMO, or Zeus-In-The-Mobile Trojan. To date, this exploit has only been detected in Euro Zone countries, but a variation of this attack could potentially affect banks in countries outside of the European Union as well.

The multi-staged attack infected the computers and mobile devices of online banking customers and once the Eurograbber Trojans were installed on both devices, the bank customer's online banking sessions were completely monitored and manipulated by the attackers. Even the two-factor authentication mechanism used by the banks to ensure the security of online banking transactions was circumvented in the attack and used by the attackers to authenticate their illicit financial transfer. Further, the Trojan used to attack mobile devices was developed for both the Blackberry and Android platforms in order to facilitate a wide "target market" and as such was able to infect both corporate and private banking users and illicitly transfer funds out of customers' accounts in amounts ranging from 500 to 250,000 euros each. This case study provides a step-by-step walkthrough of how the full attack transpired from the initial infection through to the illicit financial transfer.

To improve security for online transactions, the banks added a second authentication mechanism, different from account number and password that validates the identity of the customer and the integrity of the online transaction. Specifically, when the bank customer submits an online banking transaction, the bank sends a Transaction Authentication Number (TAN) via SMS to the customer's mobile device. The customer then confirms and completes their banking transaction by entering the received TAN in the screen of their online banking session. Eurograbber is customized to specifically circumvent even this two-factor authentication.

Bank customer's issues begin when they click on a "bad link" that downloads a customized Trojan onto their computer. This happens either during internet browsing or more likely from responding to a phishing email that entices a customer to click on the bogus link. This is the first step of the attack and the next time the customer logs into his or her bank account, the now installed Trojan (customized variants of the Zeus, SpyEye, and CarBerp Trojans) recognizes the login which triggers the next phase of the attack.

It is this next phase where Eurograbber overcomes the bank's two-factor authentication and is an excellent example of a sophisticated, targeted attack. During the customer's first online banking session after their computer is infected, Eurograbber injects instructions into the session that prompts the customer to enter their mobile phone number. Then they are informed to complete the "banking software security upgrade," by following the instructions sent to their mobile device via SMS. The attacker's SMS instructs a customer to click on a link to complete a "security upgrade" on their mobile phone; however, clicking on the link actually downloads a variant of "Zeus in the mobile" (ZITMO) Trojan. The ZITMO variant is specifically designed to intercept the bank's SMS containing the all-important "transaction authorization number" (TAN). The bank's SMS containing the TAN is the key element of the bank's two-factor authorization. The Eurograbber Trojan on the customer's mobile device intercepts the SMS and uses the TAN to complete its own transaction to silently transfer money out of the bank customer's account. The Eurograbber attack occurs entirely in the background. Once the "security upgrade" is completed, the bank customer is monitored and controlled by Eurograbber attackers and the customer's online banking sessions give no evidence of the illicit activity.

In order to facilitate such a sophisticated, multi-stage attack, a Command & Control (C&C) server infrastructure had to be created. This infrastructure received, stored and managed the information sent by the Trojans and also orchestrated the attacks. The gathered information was stored in an SQL database for later use during an attack. In order to avoid detection, the attackers used several different domain names and servers, some of which were proxy servers to further complicate detection. If detected, the attackers could easily and quickly replace their infrastructure thus ensuring the integrity of their attack infrastructure, and ensuring the continuity of their operation and illicit money flow.

THE INFECTION

Step 1: The customer's desktop or laptop is infection.

Step 2: The Eurograbber Trojan intercepts the banking session and injects a javascript into the customer's banking page. This malicious Javascript informs the customer of the "security upgrade" and instructs them on how to proceed.

Step 3: The Eurograbber Trojan then delivers the bank customer's mobile information to the dropzone for storage and use on subsequent attacks.

Step 4: Receipt of the customer's mobile information triggers the Eurograbber process to send an SMS to the customer's mobile device. The SMS directs the customer to complete the security upgrade by clicking on the attached link. Doing so downloads a file onto the customer's mobile device with the appropriate mobile version of the Eurograbber Trojan.

Step 5: Simultaneous with the SMS being sent to the bank customer's mobile device, the following message appears on the customer's desktop instructing them to follow the instructions in the SMS sent to their mobile device in order to upgrade the system software to improve security. Upon completion they are

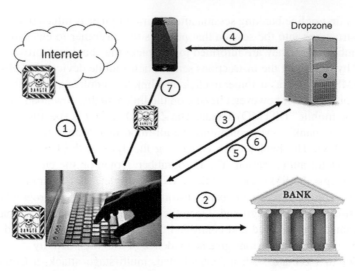

FIGURE 17.8

Anatomy of the attack.

to enter the installation verification code in the box below to confirm that the mobile upgrade process is complete.

Step 6: Upon completing the installation this text box appears in the customer's native language acknowledging the successful installation and displays the verification code the user is to enter in the prompt on their computer.

Step 7: Eurograbber completes the process by displaying messages on a customer's desktop informing the user of successful completion of the "security" upgrade and that they can proceed with their online banking activities (Figure 17.8).

THE MONEY THEFT

Step 1: A banking customer logs into their online bank account.

Step 2: Right after the bank customer's login, the cybercriminal initiates Eurograbber's computer Trojan to start its own transaction to transfer a predefined percentage of money out of the customer's bank account to a "mule" account owned by the attackers.

Step 3: Upon submission of the illicit banking transaction, the bank sends a Transaction Authorization Number (TAN) via SMS to a user's mobile device.

Step 4: However, the Eurograbber mobile Trojan intercepts the SMS containing the TAN, hides it from the customer and forwards it to one of many relay phone numbers setup by the attackers. The SMS is then forwarded from the relay phone number to the drop zone where it is stored in the command and control

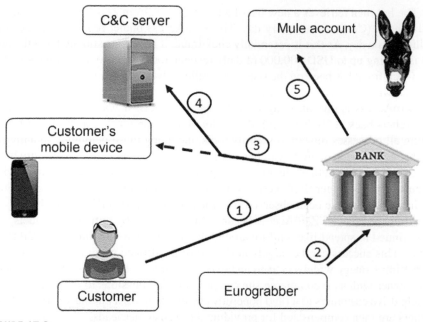

FIGURE 17.9

The money theft.

database along with other user information. If the SMS was forwarded straight to the drop zone it would be more easily detected.

Step 5: The TAN is then pulled from storage by the computer Trojan which in turn sends it to the bank to complete the illicit transfer of money out of a bank customer's account and into the attacker's "mule" account. The customer's screen does not show any of this activity and they are completely unaware of the fraudulent action that just took place (Figure 17.9).

At this point, the victims' bank account will have lost money without their knowledge. Cybercriminals are being paid off via mule accounts. This entire process occurs every time the bank customer logs into his or her bank account.

CASE STUDY—ZEROACCESS (2013)

The fastest growing botnet was surely ZeroAccess, which racked up millions of infections globally in 2012, with up to 140,000 unique IPs in the US and Europe (F-Secure 2012). The actual malware that turns users' computers into bots is typically served by malicious sites which the user is tricked into visiting. The malicious site contains an exploit kit, usually Blackhole, which targets vulnerabilities on the user's machine while they are visiting the site. Once the machine is compromised, the kit drops the malware, which then turns the computer into a ZeroAccess bot.

The bot then retrieves a new list of advertisements from ZeroAccess's command and control (C&C) server every day. The ZeroAccess botnet reportedly clicks 140 million ads a day. As this is essentially click fraud, it has been estimated that the botnet is costing up to USD 900,000 of daily revenue loss to legitimate online advertisers. Click fraud has been on the rise as the online advertisement vendors realistically have no way to differentiate between a legitimate click and a fraudulent one.

ZeroAccess is one of today's most notable botnets. It was first discovered by researchers back in 2010, when it drew a lot of attention for its capability for terminating all processes related to security tools, including those belonging to antivirus products. When too many researchers focused on this self-protection capability however, ZeroAccess's authors decided to drop the feature and focus more on improving its custom peer-to-peer (P2P) network protocol, which is unique to ZeroAccess. Four distinct variants have been observed (Neville and Gibb, 2013) (Figure 17.10):

After the change, ZeroAccess became easier to spot by antivirus products, yet it continued to spread like wildfire around the world due to the improved P2P technique. This success can be largely attributed to its affiliate program, a well-known marketing strategy widely used by many e-commerce websites. Essentially, a business owner with an e-commerce site can promote commissions to other site owners to help drive customers to it (and hopefully eventually make a purchase). The website owners are then compensated for providing these customer leads.

Adopting this concept, ZeroAccess' author or operator(s) has managed to distribute the program to a large number of machines with the help of its enlisted partners. The ZeroAccess team advertises the malware installer in Russian underground forums, actively looking for distributor partners. Their objective was to seek other cybercriminals who are more capable in distributing the malware and do so more efficiently. The malware distributors generally consist of experienced affiliates, each of

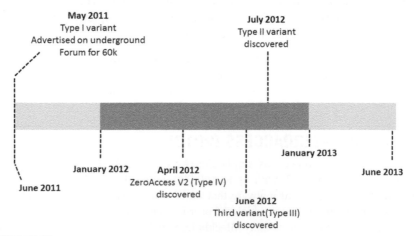

FIGURE 17.10

ZeroAccess variants roadmap.

them employing their own methods of distributing the Zeroaccess installers, in order to fulfill the recruiter's requirements.

The most popular distribution methods seen involve exploit kits, spam e-mails, trojans-downloaders, and fake media files available on P2P file-sharing services and video sites, although the specific details depend on the distributor handling the operations. The variety of distribution schemes, and methods used by the numerous affiliates have contributed to the volume of "Trojan dropper" variants detected by antivirus products every day.

They are all driven by the same motive which is to collect attractive revenue share from the gang. The partners are compensated based on a Pay-Per-Install (PPI) service scheme and the rate differs depending on the geographical location of the machine on which the malware was successfully installed. A successful installation in the United States will net the highest payout, with the gang willing to pay USD 500 per 1000 installations in that location.

Given the rate of pay, it is no surprise that ZeroAccess is widespread in the US alone. After the US, the commission rate sorted from highest to lowest are Australia, Canada, Great Britain, and others. Some distributors even post screenshots of the payment they have received in underground forums to show the reliability of their recruiter. The ZeroAccess team can afford to pay such high incentives to its recruits because the army of bots created by the affiliate's efforts is able to generate even more revenue in return. Once the malware is successfully installed on the victim machines, ZeroAccess will begin downloading and installing additional malware onto the machines, which will generate profit for the botnet operators through click fraud operations.

The affiliate program, as an interesting criminal business model, encourages the spread of malware and attracts more cybercriminals due to the botnet operators' established reputation for reliably paying its affiliates and adjusting commission rates to maintain their attractiveness. The criminal organizations behind the botnet have shown that they are willing to experiment and modify their "product" in order to increase their ability to make money.

The Europol's European Cybercrime Centre (EC3), supported by Microsoft Corporation's Digital Crimes Unit and other industry partners, announced that has successfully disrupted ZeroAccess network in 2013, but, as we know, P2P networks are very resilient to disruption and some backfire are expected (EC3, 2013).

COUNTERMEASURES FOR FIGHTING BOTNETS OR MITIGATING BOTNETS EFFECTS

Due to the high level customization of malwares, it is quite difficult to adopt an effective and efficient countermeasure through code analysis and fingerprint definition which, of course, is what well known Antivirus systems practice. So we need methods that analyze malware behaviors (regardless of architectures and protocols used, bots need to contact with their C&C—you can hide everything except the network traffic!).

Even behavioral analysis, however, is not easy to manage. Typically a lot of work has already been done in the analysis of standard protocols (typically level 4 and 5 of the TCP/IP stack) in order to distinguish legitimate traffic from the botnet.

Unfortunately the increasing use of high encryption mechanisms and of techniques of traffic customization/obfuscation (as we shall see in the next section), will make this work ineffective in the medium to long term, even because much of the work mentioned in this paragraph have revealed great response only for specific botnet architectures.

First of all, from an operational standpoint, the necessary condition (probably not enough!) where you have to be ready to deal with an in-progress botnet attack, considering for example the two cases for excellence, as a spam campaign and a DDOS, is to verify that:

- firewall facing the Internet has capacity of "Intrusion Detection/Prevention System" and throughput greatly overestimated compared to the normal conditions of work and the Internet bandwidth available;
- Antispam system is configured as rigidly as possible (e.g., only accept messages from the MTA that have the common DNS MX, PTR and A records correctly configured);
- your Internet Service Provider is equipped with monitoring tools that highlight timely surge of traffic to your Internet services and in the worst cases, can quickly disable entire portions of the Internet (e.g., all international routes) to reduce temporarily the firepower of the botnet;

Regarding the goals to be achieved, we formerly need to distinguish two different of approaches. In fact, network and security administrators usually have an interest in detecting the presence of bots and C&C servers on their networks or to withstand a botnet attack (mitigation), while researchers focus their attention on the direct identification of the botnet itself (payload, architectures, protocols, capacity criminals, etc.) to its vulnerability and, consequently, disruption.

In regards to the methodology used, botnet hunting methods can be divided in two key categories:

- **Passive**: such capabilities are usually organized with network monitoring solutions within corporate LANs. These techniques are essentially based on statistical analysis of both TCP and UDP traffic, on specific application protocols analysis such as HTTP or DNS as well as on the pattern recognition of specific keywords or IP addresses to be put in the blacklist.
- **Active**: these techniques are usually based on scanning, crawling or sinkholing of IP address ranges, probing the presence of bots and/or C&C peers as a result of the analysis of specific query answers (usually via honeynet). These practices also attempt to exploit any protocols or C&C servers vulnerabilities.

As previously mentioned, we can assume that botnets are different from other forms of malware in that they use C&C channels which are the essential mechanism that allows a botmaster to direct the actions of bots in a botnet. As such, the C&C channel can be considered the weakest link of a centralized botnet. That is, if we can take down an active C&C or simply interrupt the communication to the C&C, the botmaster will not be able to control the botnet. Moreover, the detection of the C&C channel will reveal both the C&C servers and the bots in a monitored network. Therefore, understanding and detecting the C&Cs has great value in the battle against centralized botnets.

Botnet C&C traffic is difficult to detect because: it follows normal protocol usage and is similar to normal traffic; the traffic volume is low; there may be very few bots in the monitored network and may contain encrypted communication. However, the bots of a centralized botnet demonstrate spatial-temporal correlation and similarities due to the nature of their pre-programmed response activities to control commands. For instance, at a similar time, all the bots within the same botnet will execute the same command and report to the C&C server with the progress/result of the task (and these reports are likely to be similar in structure and content).

Regular network activities are unlikely to show such a synchronized and correlated behavior and, although the traffic is encrypted, might be useful to investigate on traffic generated by groups of clients that have the same (IP, TCP port) destination pair (Gu et al., 2008).

When botnets switch to a peer-to-peer (P2P) structure and utilize multiple protocols for C&C, the above assumptions no longer hold. Consequently, the detection of P2P botnets is more difficult.

One possible approach is to design a particular kind of a "Network Traffic Data Warehouse." Capturing enough network traffic data (training data), the proposed approach can profile (cluster) the behavior of normal application/users activities from other ones. In fact the action sequence differs greatly between the normal user and the botnet. Since the botnet is dynamic: peers in the botnet can be dynamically shut down or removed from the botnet at any time, a bot may first generate traffic to find the online peers on certain ports from its peer list, and then send a command to all the available peers. On the other hand, it is very unlikely that a normal user (or a majority of normal users) generates the normal behavior in this way. Although normal users are capable of choosing arbitrary destinations, they usually associate themselves on a small range of destinations of different popularity. On the other hand, the peers chosen in P2P botnets are random regardless of the destination popularity.

In this way we could be able to compute some statistical measures (e.g., Behavior Proportion based Test or Behavior Mean Distance based Test) in order to identify new samples of network traffic data (Chang and Daniels, 2009).

If the C&C server cannot be taken down, another option is to redirect malicious traffic to sinkholes, a strategy that found its way into recent mitigation techniques, either locally or globally. The sinkholes record malicious traffic, analyze it and drop it afterwards such that it cannot reach the original target it is meant for. One example of sinkholing is DDoS null-routing. In the case where traffic belongs to an ongoing DDoS attempt it is dropped and sometimes counted for later analysis. DDoS null-routing at border-routers is a promising approach to mitigate DDoS attacks but comes with the challenges of reliable identification of attack-related traffic and clean dissection of high-bandwidth data streams at an early stage. This is generally only possible at ISP level (Leder et al., 2009).

Two completely different approaches in botnet hunting are based on protocol failure information analysis (Zhu et al., 2009) and passive DNS protocol analysis (Bilge et al., 2011) to detect zombies. The first one uses a new behavior-based approach to detect infected hosts within an enterprise network. The goal is to develop a system that is independent of malware family and requiring no "a priori" knowledge of malware semantics or command and control (C&C) mechanisms. The approach is motivated by the simple observation that many malware communication patterns result in abnormally high failure rates that is extended to broadly consider a large class of failures in both transport and application TCP/IP levels. In fact a survey conducted on 32 different malwares instances highlighted some commonly failure messages listed in Figure 17.11.

From a quantitative point of view the mentioned survey found that most malware instances (18/24 instances) have triggered DNS failures.

Because of the important role that DNS plays in the operation of the Internet, the second approach is based on exclusive analysis of this protocol. It is not surprising that a wide variety of malicious activities involve the domain name service in one way or another. Bots resolve DNS names to locate their C&C servers, and spam mails contain URLs that link to domains that resolve to scam servers. Thus, it seems effective to monitor the use of the DNS system in order to investigate if a certain name is used as part of a malicious operation.

If the IP address of the C&C is hard-coded into the bot binary, there exists a single point of failure for the botnet. Whenever this address is identified and is taken down, the botnet would be lost. So attackers, by using DNS, give the flexibility and the fault tolerance they need in the malicious architectures that they manage. Furthermore,

Protocol	Layer	Failure Types
DNS	Application	NX DOMAIN (No such domain)
HTTP	Application	400 Bad Request, 404 Not Found, 403 Forbidden, 411 Length Required, 500 Internal Server Error, 501 Not Implemented
FTP	Application	Transient Negative completion reply Permanent Negative completion reply
SMTP	Application	Domain service not available, mailbox unavailable sintax error, command not implemented Machine does not accept mail, mailbox unavailable User not local, requested mail action aborted
IRC	Application	No such nick, no such server, no such channel, Cannot send to channel

FIGURE 17.11

Protocols failure messages.

Feature Set	#	Feature Name
Time-based features	1	Short life
	2	Daily similarity
	3	Repeating patterns
	4	Access ratio
DNS answer-based features	5	Number of distinct IP addresses
	6	Number of distinct countries
	7	Number of domains share the IP with
	8	Reverse DNS query results
TTL value-based features	9	Average TTL
	10	Standard deviation of TTL
	11	Number of distinct TTL values
	12	Number of TTL change
	13	Percentage usage of specific TTL ranges
Domain name-based features	14	% of numerical characters
	15	% of the length of LMS (longest meaningful substring)

FIGURE 17.12

DNS features.

they can hide their critical servers behind proxy services so that they are more difficult to identify and take down.

Hence, by studying the DNS behavior of known malicious and benign domains, as largely as possible in terms of observation time and traffic volume observed, could possibly identify the distinguishable generic features that are able to define the maliciousness of a given domain. For example the 15 different features listed in Figure 17.12 may be indicative to detect malicious behaviors.

There are many other approaches aimed at the identification, enumeration, and poisoning usually referred to the P2P botnet (peer crawling). These approaches commonly deal with very vertical studies of small botnet families, if not the single botnet. The basic idea is to try to join with a particular botnet and contextually understand its architecture, protocols, size and then subsequently outline its disruption or simply mitigation modes.

CONCLUSION AND FUTURE TRENDS (TOR, MOBILE AND SOCIAL NETWORKS)

The temple of botnets relies on three main pillars (Figure 17.13). The pervasive diffusion of the Internet fortifies these three pillars. All devices equipped with internet connectivity can potentially become future zombies. In fact, the main candidates are currently smartphones and tablets and we have already witnessed criminal actions due to the spread of malware for mobile devices (e.g., ZITMO).

Still few people are aware of the risks that can arise from a modern device. The technological convergence is more and more invasive—almost all everyday life objects are "Internet connected" and smart. There will hardly ever be a countertrend.

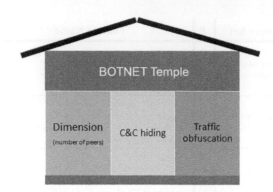

FIGURE 17.13

Botnet pillars

In addition to the widespread use of encryption of communication channels, recently we have seen the spread of using social networks as part of a botnet. One of the primary intents of botmasters is to reach a wide audience of users, so it is natural that they are exploring the possibility to exploit social media platforms, for recruiting new zombies and controlling infected machines (typically creating fake accounts that send encrypted messages to malware on victims), since social networks have monopolized the majority of user's internet experience. Botmasters have begun to exploit social network websites (e.g., Twitter.com) as C&C head-quarters, which turns out to be quite stealthy because it is hard to distinguish the C&C activities from the normal social networking traffic (Kartaltepe et al., 2010). "UPD4T3" is an example of a fake Twitter account owned, of course, by a botmaster.

Moreover, we know that TOR is an anonymity network operated by volunteers which provides encryption and identity protection capabilities. Tor is a great tool that helps people all over the world to protect themselves from Internet censorship. It is widely used by anyone concerned about the privacy and safety of their communications. At the same time though, it does get abused a lot, as in the case we are going to describe.

The potential use of TOR in botnet infrastructure has been discussed several times in the past (e.g., at "Defcon 18 Conference" by Dennis Brown). In September 2012 the German Antivirus vendor G-Data briefly described a similar case.

As we already know, hosting C&C infrastructure on "Internet servers" could expose the botnet. A much stronger infrastructure can be built just by utilizing Tor as the internal communication protocol and by using the Tor Hidden Services functionality.

Hidden services, introduced in 2004, permit the creation of completely anonymous and concealed services accessible through Tor only. An "onion" pseudo-domain is generated, which will then be used to resolve and contact the hidden server. It is very difficult to identify the origin of the hidden service and to revoke or take over the associated onion domain (Figure 17.14).

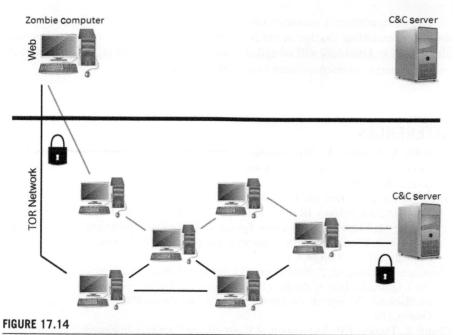

FIGURE 17.14

C&C server as a hidden service.

The advantages of this approach are:

- The traffic is encrypted.
- The hidden services do not rely on public-facing IP addresses.

The threat posed by the spread of botnets is still, unfortunately, a prerogative of worlds that, for various reasons (technical or historical), are closely linked to the words "Internet" and "Computer." Moreover, only recently we have seen concrete examples of its translation into effective criminal activities (monetization of the operational capabilities of a botnet).

Google uses the Internet, e-mail uses the Internet, Home Banking makes use of the Internet. Are we still using the Internet to play with a friend (who lives on the other side of the world) through our home Wi-Fi? Is "Waze App" still using the Internet? Yes, of course.

If you can see YouTube through your Smart TV maybe you need an antivirus or (why not) a firewall installed on it (usually installed on a PC or Laptop).

The countermeasures described in the previous paragraph should be extended to those vendors whose core business to date has been completely different. In a not too distant future, a DOS attack to a "TV broadcasting cable system" or to the VOIP system of a telephony operator—two real examples of critical infrastructure—could foreshadow Cyber Terrorism scenarios.

The aforementioned scenarios pose severe concerns for botnet development in the future, extending the threatened perimeter of the target infrastructures. Hence, a plurality of stakeholders will be called to cope with this problem, via different balance of synergic countermeasures to mitigate the risk.

REFERENCES

Balapure, A., Paganini, P., 2013. InfoSec Institute, Botnets Unearthed – The ZEUS BOT, Available from, http://resources.infosecinstitute.com/botnets-unearthed-the-zeus-bot/ (accessed 08.07.13).

Bilge, L., Kirda, E., Kruegel, C., and Balduzzi, M.; Institute Eurecom Sophia Antipolis, Northeastern University Boston, University of California Santa Barbara. EXPOSURE: Finding Malicious Domains Using Passive DNS Analysis, published in 18th Annual Network & Distributed System Security Symposium Proceedings, NDSS 2011, 6–9 February 2011, San Diego, CA.

Binsalleeh, H., Ormerod, T., Boukhtouta, A., Sinha, P., Youssef, A., Debbabi, M., Wang, L., 2010. On the Analysis of the Zeus Botnet Crimeware Toolkit. published in Eighth Annual International Conference on Privacy Security and Trust (PST), 17–19 August 2010, Ottawa, ON.

Chang, S., Daniels, T.E.; Department of Electrical and Computer Engineering of Iowa State University, Ames, Iowa. P2P Botnet Detection using Behavior Clustering & Statistical Tests, published in Proceedings of the 2nd ACM workshop on Security and artificial intelligence (AISec 2009), 16th ACM Conference on Computer and Communications Security (CCS 2009), 9–13 November 2009, Hyatt Regency Chicago, Chicago, IL.

EC3, 2013. Europol's European Cybercrime Centre (EC3) press release. Notorious botnet infecting 2 million computers Disrupted. https://www.europol.europa.eu/content/notorious-botnet-infecting-2-million-computers-disrupted.

Falliere, N., Chien, E., 2009. Symantec White Paper. Zeus: King of the Bots, November 2009.

Ferguson, R., 2010. Trend Micro White Paper, The Botnet Chronicles, A journey to Infamy, November 2010.

F-Secure Threat Report – Second half (H2) of 2012.

Gu, G., Zhang, J., Lee, W.; School of Computer Science, College of Computing Georgia Institute of Technology Atlanta, GA. BotSniffer: Detecting Botnet Command and Control Channels in Network Traffic, published in 16th Annual Network & Distributed System Security Symposium Proceedings, NDSS 2008, 7–10 February 2008, San Diego, CA.

Howard, F., 2012. Sophos White Paper, Exploring the Blackhole Exploit Kit, March 2012.

Kalige, E., Burkley, D., 2012. Versafe and Check Point software Technologies White Paper. A Case Study of Eurograbber: How 36 Million Euros was Stolen via Malware, Eran Kalige (Versafe), Darrell Burkey (Check Point Software Technologies), December 2012.

Kartaltepe, E.J., Morales, J.A., Xu, S., Sandhu, R., June 2010. Institute for Cyber Security and Department of Computer Science, University of Texas at San Antonio. In: Social Network-Based Botnet Command-and-Control: Emerging Threats and Countermeasures, published in 8th International Conference on Applied Cryptography and Network Security, ACNS 2010, 22-25 June 2010, Beijing, China.

Kaspersky Security Bulletin, 2013. Kaspersky Lab Global Research and Analysis Team.

Lanelli, N., Hackworth, A., 2005. CERT Coordination Center, Carnegie Mellon University. . Botnets as a Vehicle for Online Crime, http://www.cert.org/archive/pdf/Botnets.pdf (accessed 01.12.05).

Leder, F., Werner, T., Martini, P., 2009. Institute of Computer Science IV, University of Bonn, Germany, 2009. In: Proactive Botnet Countermeasures—An Offensive Approach. NATO Cooperative Cyber Defence Centre of Excellence—Cyber Warfare Conference, 17–19 June 2009.

Lemos, R., 2010. MIT Technology Review—Computing, "Rise of the Point-and-Click Botnet", February 23, 2010.

Neville, A., Gibb, R. Symantec White Paper. ZeroAccess Indepth, 4 October 2013.

Paganini, P., 2013a. InfoSec Institute, Botnets and cybercrime – Introduction. http://resources.infosecinstitute.com/botnets-and-cybercrime-introduction/ (published 08.04.13).

Paganini, P., 2013b. InfoSec Institute, Botnets, how do they work? Architectures and case studies – Part 2. http://resources.infosecinstitute.com/botnets-how-do-they-work-architectures-and-case-studies-part-2/ (published 22.04.13).

Paganini, P., 2013c. InfoSec Institute, Botnets and Cybercrime – Botnets hunting – Part 3. http://resources.infosecinstitute.com/botnets-and-cybercrime-botnets-hunting-part-3/ (published 25.04.13).

Rossow C., 2013. Inst. for Internet Security, Gelsenkirchen, Germany; Andriesse, D., Werner, T., Stone-Gross, B., Plohmann, D., Dietrich, C.J., Bos, H. SoK: P2PWNED – Modeling and Evaluating the Resilience of Peer-to-Peer Botnets, published in IEEE Symposium on Security and Privacy (SP), 19–22 May 2013, Berkeley, CA.

Symantec Internet Security Threat Report 2013: Volume 18, April 2013.

Wang, P.; Sch. of Electr. Eng. & Comput. Sci., Univ. of Central Florida, Orlando, FL, USA; Wu, L., Aslam, B., Zou, C.C., 2013. A Systematic Study on Peer-to-Peer Botnets, published in Proceedings of 18th International Conference on Computer Communications and Networks, 2009. ICCCN 2009, 3–6 August 2009, San Francisco, CA.

Wyke, J., 2011. Sophos White Paper, What is Zeus?, May 2011.

Zhu, Z.S., Yegneswaran, V., Chen, Y.; Department of Electrical and Computer Engineering, Northwestern University, Computer Science Laboratory, SRI International, 2009. Using Failure Information Analysis to Detect Enterprise Zombies, published in 5th International ICST Conference on Security and Privacy in Communication Networks. SecureComm, 14–17 September 2009, Athens, Greece.

Evolution of TETRA through the integration with a number of communication platforms to support public protection and disaster relief (PPDR)

18

Hamid Jahankhani, Sufian Yousef

INTRODUCTION

Public Protection and Disaster Relief (PPDR) organizations such as law enforcement, ambulance services, civil emergency management/disaster recovery, fire services, coast guards services, search and rescue services, government administration, etc., are tasked with providing public safety and security service. Public safety services bring value to society by creating a stable and secure environment; and PPDR organizations address situations where human life, rescue operations and law enforcement are at stake. And due to the nature of these situations, mobile communication is a main requirement. PPDR organizations rely extensively on Professional Mobile Radio (PMR) communication systems to conduct their daily operations. Many of these communication networks are based on TETRA, TETRAPOL, GSM, Project 25 specification, etc., however, TETRA has become the widely accepted choice in Europe with TETRAPOL being used in some countries.

PPDR is a priority subject for the citizens, the National Governments and the European Union. Especially since events such as the September 11th world trade centre attacks, the Atocha (Madrid) bombings, the London underground attacks, and the recent major earthquake in Van, Turkey; security, counter-terrorism, and disaster relief have been on top of the agenda of the European decision-makers, at national as well as at EU level. Evidence from these recent disasters shows that public cellular systems are not designed to cope with major incidents and have failed at the time when good communications are needed most, hence, the importance of dedicated PPDR communication network. However, due to the nature of some of these events and the increasing globalization of terrorism (and other security and safety threats), it is very important for future PPDR organizations to work across national borders, which is a limitation of current PPDR communication networks. In Europe, especially during the early 1990s when there was a transition to a borderless society following the Schengen Agreement, the freedom to cross borders has also meant that those with criminal intent would also be able to freely cross borders. As a result it became apparent that there was a need to ensure good communications between the PPDR organizations of each of the countries and enable PPDR officers to travel across borders without losing communications. Neighboring countries' networks must interoperate with one another for both routine day-to-day and disaster relief operations.

PPDR organizations cannot afford the risk of having communication failures in their voice, data and video transmissions; and this can only be ensured by building robust, secure and reliable, modern PPDR mobile communications networks. Also, for these organizations to be adequately prepared to tackle any future events like those we have recently witnessed, they need to be properly equipped. There are needs for new advanced services and applications envisioned in the next generation of PPDR communication systems such as remote personnel monitoring, remote sensor networks (forest fire tracking or water/flood level monitoring), two-way real-time video, 3D positioning and GIS, mobile robots, multi-functional mobile terminals (ID verification, Transfer of images; Biometric data; Remote database access; Remotely controlled devices), etc. Also, the need for a very reliable, secure and resilient communication network for public protection that can cope with threats of terror and disaster at all levels, toward citizens all the way to its communication infrastructure, is necessary. However, this growing demand for a reliable and secure high-speed data communication means that the current capacity for PPDR communication network (i.e., TETRA) will be exceeded, requiring an upgrade or replacement at some stage in the future.

TETRA TECHNOLOGY

TETRA is a modern standard for digital PMR and has enjoyed wide acceptance (especially in Europe) to now be considered one of the most mature and prominent technologies for the PPDR markets. TETRA specifications are constantly being evolved by ETSI (European Telecommunications Standards Institute) and new features are being introduced to fulfill the growing and ever demanding PPDR requirements. The original TETRA standard first envisaged in ETSI was known as the TETRA Voice plus Data (V+D) standard with less emphasis on the data side with just two data services compared with the nine voice services. Because of the need to further evolve and enhance TETRA, the original V+D standard is now known as TETRA 1. Packet Data Optimized (PDO) is a completed part of the TETRA suite of standards produced for only "Data Only" wireless communications applications (i.e., pagers). However, very few manufacturers have developed PDO systems and products because: all traditional PMR users use voice communication as well as data communications; and also the obvious application area for such standard (high data size transfer) would take significant amount of time and power to operate.

Nevertheless, TETRA already provides a comprehensive portfolio of services and facilities. TETRA protocol specifies several standard interfaces to ensure an open multivendor market: (1) Air Interface (AIR IF), (2) Terminal Equipment Interface (TEI), (3) Inter-System Interface (ISI), (4) Direct Mode Operation (DMO).

However, as time progresses, there is a need to evolve and enhance all technologies to better satisfy user requirements, future proof investments and ensure longevity. Like GSM moving to GPRS, EDGE and UMTS/3G, TETRA will also evolve to satisfy increasing user demand for new services and facilities. For this reason, a TETRA 2 standard has been developed and is sufficiently complete for product development purposes. However, product availability will depend on the different manufacturers' R&D plans, but manufacturers have not deployed product yet and take up is slow. At TETRA conferences the opinion was expressed that the earliest deployment of broadband TETRA (or equivalent) was likely to be 2020. This is because the existing network cannot be upgraded to support TETRA 2 due to spectrum availability issues; and some that could be will not because of the cost involved. Hence, there is a need for an upgraded PPDR communication system that would be highly efficient, secure, resilient and flexible with modern and sophisticated applications; and that even when the introduction of TETRA 2 and future releases (Broadband TETRA) become well established, there is a guarantee that the economic and commercial uptake of the network is justified. However, there are issues with the uptake of the network, which would have implications on future networks; and they stem from the disadvantages of the current TETRA network.

CURRENT TRENDS OF PPDR (I.E., TETRA) TECHNOLOGY

The majority of PPDR organizations in Europe currently use dedicated PMR networks, designed specifically to meet their needs, for their communications. Typically TETRA (or TETRAPOL), and operating in the 380-400 MHz spectrum band. These networks offer a range of low rate data services, but the speed and capacity available limits more widespread use of higher-speed data applications. In line with societal trends for access to information on the move, PPDR operations are becoming increasingly information driven, requiring access to a wider range of wideband and broadband applications. Given the limitations in capacity of existing dedicated networks to deliver mobile broadband services, it is considered likely that a new generation of solutions will be required across Europe in the next 5-10 years, too meet future PPDR demands. These solutions, if delivered using new dedicated mobile broadband networks that are designed to meet PPDR requirements, will still require additional spectrum to deliver the required services effectively.

The trend for current and future PPDR mobile data and multimedia applications that is being foreseen to cover a range of needs was highlighted above. Alongside these are a number of specific operational requirements that are essential for PPDR communications, in order to ensure the availability, reliability and integrity of networks, which include: High levels of network availability; High degree of network control (implementing prioritized access for specific user groups or individuals, and reserving capacity where required); Near nationwide geographic coverage (communicating in remote areas); Security; Low latency (end-to-end voice delay of no more than 200 ms);

Interoperability between different PPDR authorities and across borders; Highly resilient networks (various layers of redundancy); and Ability to support mixed traffic.

Within the PPDR sector, the above demand for access to a wider range of applications and services is driven by changes in working practices, which creates requirements for access to a far wider range of data sources (textual, images, and video) that are typical in commercial mobile networks. Sharing of these data is being used in order to establish and maintain a common operational picture between PPDR agencies and between field and central command staff. This is used to improve responsiveness, aid the deployment of resources, and improve timeliness and decision making in daily PPDR operations; when responding to major planned and unplanned events.

As there is a limit to the range and volume of data and multimedia applications that existing (and possibly future) dedicated narrowband and wideband networks (and existing commercial networks) can provide, if a new-generation PPDR network is not made available, some of the envisaged applications would not be delivered. Ultimately, this will affect how already emerging changes to the ways of working within the PPDR sector might evolve, and in the longer term, constrain the further development of the sector.

TECHNOLOGICAL AND ECONOMIC BARRIERS AND ISSUES

The capabilities of existing (and possibly future) narrowband and wideband dedicated mobile networks currently used in the PPDR sector will not be sufficient to meet the envisaged future requirements. This is inevitable, unless a steady growth approach is introduced where PPDR operation methods change gradually, voice remains the dominant method of mission critical communication, and existing data applications continue to be used alongside voice (with a gradual increase in use). However, this is not suitable in the longer term since there is already growing evidence of changes in working methods and trends within the PPDR sector that suggest that this path will not match future demands. A new generation of mobile broadband service is required to accommodate the range of future data, image and multimedia applications that PPDR users demand. The options for delivering this new generation of services are to make use of upgraded commercial networks, or to develop a new generation of dedicated mobile broadband networks for exclusive public safety use. While the new generation of data service could theoretically be delivered through upgrading and re-engineering commercial networks, there are certain barriers, which range from technical to cost and commercial considerations, that might make it difficult to achieve in practice. These include the following:

- The PPDR sector requires very extensive geographic coverage as well as in-depth coverage penetration inside buildings, irrespective of location, which does not match the typical roll-out requirements of commercial network. Commercial operators typically invest in coverage where populations exist, and capacity is designed to maximize revenue generation in those areas, with little incentive to invest in areas of low density population.

- It is likely to be very expensive to re-engineer commercial networks to achieve all the public safety sector's operational requirements, and there are questions about whether sufficient incentives exist for commercial operators to do this. For example, typical requirements include the need for battery back-up to be available at thousands of base station sites across the network, and for networks to be designed to ensure that they are highly resilient (including overlapping coverage, standby power supplies and fall-back sites) and that no single "point of failure" exists either in access or core networks.
- There is the view that commercial networks might be more vulnerable to sabotage by criminals than dedicated networks are.
- There are questions about whether the required Grade of Service for PPDR use can be guaranteed within a network shared with commercial users, particularly in times of very high traffic loading; and whether some PPDR requirements are actually achievable in this network.
- There are conflicting views on whether signaling could be encrypted over air interface in 3G/LTE.
- Ensuring the specific requirements of carriage of "restricted" or "confidential" documents requires careful network planning and approvals, which is complex and costly to achieve.
- It is not clear that networks can be dimensioned to achieve the required immediacy and guaranteed access that PPDR requires.
- There is reluctance for public bodies to be reliant on fully commercial operators, in view of the potential lack of control upon future network investment, business plans and financing.

However, as explained before, the current (and possibly, future) dedicated PMR network (TETRA) would not be able to cope with the trend for current and future PPDR mobile high speed data and multimedia applications that is being foreseen to cover a range of needs.

PROGRESS BEYOND THE STATE-OF-THE-ART
CURRENT PPDR COMMUNICATION NETWORK ARCHITECTURE LANDSCAPE

PPDR organizations currently use a range of different communications networks to meet their operational needs. In Europe, the majority of their personnel now use dedicated networks to provide narrowband mobile communications using TETRA or TETRAPOL technologies operating in the 380-400 MHz band. This spectrum allocation is based on the harmonization of spectrum for public safety that was put in place by the ECC in 1996 and provides recommendations on the harmonization of additional frequency bands for digital PPDR within the 380-470 MHz range. There are significant barriers to the implementation of this decision as the same spectrum is also identified for narrowband and wideband digital land mobile (PMR/PAMR).

In nearly 20 countries, the presence of CDMA 450 networks will impact on the availability of this spectrum for PPDR organizations. Interest is also emerging in the commercial deployment of LTE technology in this band.

Recent years have seen increasingly rapid progress in the capability of technologies deployed in the commercial electronic communications sector, particularly with regard to over the air data rates and the spectrum efficiency that can be achieved. For example, when the first 3G technology standards were agreed in 1999 the maximum bit rate realizable over a 3G mobile network was 2 Mbps, though in practice most users experienced speeds in the range 64-384 kbps. By comparison the digital technology mainly deployed by the PPDR sector (TETRA) could deliver up to 28 kbps. Many of today's 3G networks have been upgraded to the latest High Speed Packet Access (HSPA, HSPA+) technology and can theoretical peak bit rates of up to 21 Mbps (one user per cell only, best case channel, no error protection), with actual user bit rates of 1 Mbps or more in case of several users relatively commonplace in some networks in high density traffic areas, using a 5 MHz bandwidth channel. Newer systems employing such standards as the TETRA Release 2 TEDS component are capable of supporting more advanced data communications, with a theoretical maximum IP throughput of up to 500 kbps in a 150 kHz channel; however there is an increasing gulf between the capabilities of commercial networks and dedicated PPDR networks, as the increasing demands to support broadband data require more spectrally efficient technologies to be developed and implemented faster for the commercial sector.

Despite improvements in spectral efficiency through the deployment of new technologies which will yield some relief to the spectrum shortage, demand growth for frequencies is likely to outstrip growth of supply into the foreseeable future. The spectrum available to existing PPDR operations will not satisfy future needs for these essential services. One example of this is the current situation with TETRA TEDS in that not all EU Members States are able to identify radio channels. Therefore, communications policy must evolve to empower new systems by reallocating spectrum from the Digital Dividend to PPDR mission critical communications. This decision is not to be taken lightly since it sits on the critical path for numerous other decisions necessary before deploying next-generation PPDR networks. Historically, it has been the usual practice to identify suitable spectrum well in advance because of the timescales for releasing the spectrum, development of standards and equipment. It may require as long as 10 years to plan and deploy such networks. Adding to the urgency of the matter is the growing need for new services to emerge due to the increase in terrorist threats, frequency of natural environmental disasters, and normal population growth. The 450-470 MHz band is also widely used in Europe by analog private mobile radio services which in some cases (notably UK and Ireland) are not aligned with relevant CEPT recommendations and it seems unlikely that sufficient harmonized spectrum to support broadband mobile operation could be made available in a reasonable time frame.

In practice, many PPDR users already make use of commercial 3G networks alongside their own dedicated networks; however, the coverage of the commercial networks is inferior, mainly because of commercial considerations in part because of the higher frequencies deployed and the corresponding smaller cell sizes. Moreover, networks are likely to suffer capacity constraints at times of high demand, which would tend to be the case in the aftermath of major public safety incidents. There could be significant benefit in extending the capabilities provided by commercial mobile broadband technologies such as HSPA, LTE, CDMA 2000 EV-DO, and WiMAX to the PPDR sector. Adopting such standards within dedicated PPDR spectrum would overcome the capacity limitations of commercial networks and also provide scope for interoperability with public networks which could facilitate inter-agency communication. Such an approach could also provide economies of scale with only the RF modules differing from standard commercial networks. Such technologies would be well suited to future application trends discussed earlier.

STATE-OF-THE-ART ON MOBILE COMMUNICATION STANDARD

General PMR standards

Professional Mobile Radio (also known as Private Mobile Radio [PMR] in the UK and Land Mobile Radio [LMR] in North America) are field radio communications systems which use portable, mobile, base station, and dispatch console radios and are based on standards such as MPT-1327, TETRA, TETRAPOL and APCO 25 which are designed for dedicated use organizations. Typical examples are the radio systems used by police forces and fire brigades. Key features of professional mobile radio systems can include: Point to multi-point communications (as opposed to cell phones which are point to point communications); Push-to-talk, release to listen (a single button press opens communication on a radio frequency channel); fast call set up; large coverage areas; closed user groups; Use of VHF or UHF frequency bands. The most important factor for the effective and successful deployment of PPDR operatives is secure and reliable communication. In an emergency, the reliability of the communication system can make the difference between human life and death. However, the usefulness of professional mobile radio networks should not be limited to voice communication, but to be able to send sensitive data and information securely and timely. Being able to integrate more sensors (to enable access to more high speed critical data) into the PMR terminals would be very beneficial to emergency response and preventive responses.

TETRAPOL

TETRAPOL is a digital Professional Mobile Radio standard, as defined by the Tetrapol Publicly Available Specification (PAS), in use by professional user groups, such as public safety, military, industry and transportation organizations throughout the world. TETRAPOL is a fully digital, FDMA, Professional Mobile Radio system for closed user groups, standardizing the whole radio network from data and voice terminal via base stations to switching equipment, including interfaces to the Public switched telephone network and data networks. End-to-end encryption is an integral part of the standard just as in TETRA. Matra/EADS developed TETRAPOL and delivered an operational digital trunked radio system at an early date. Among the first users was the French Gendarmerie Nationale in 1988 for its RUBIS system. EADS (Connexity) and Siemens (S-PRO) are among the major manufacturers of professional radio systems based on the TETRAPOL specification. TETRA, however, is a more recent standard than TETRAPOL and trend in Europe is seeing a very significant move to the TETRA standards due to the longevity and evolutionary capability of the TETRA standard as it has moved from TETRA 1 to TETRA 2 and has the potential to evolve to more enhanced functionality and features (similar to the route taken by GSM).

GSM

Global system for mobile communication (GSM) is a globally accepted standard for digital cellular communication. GSM is the name of a standardization group established in 1982 to create a common European mobile telephone standard that would formulate specifications for a pan-European mobile cellular radio system operating at 900 MHz. GSM is a cellular network, which means that mobile phones connect to it by searching for cells in the immediate vicinity. However, GSM was designed with a moderate level of security. Communications between the subscriber and the base station can be encrypted. GSM uses several cryptographic algorithms for security. The A5/1 and A5/2 stream ciphers are used for ensuring over-the-air voice privacy. A5/1 was developed first and is a stronger algorithm used within Europe and the United States; A5/2 is weaker and used in other countries. Serious weaknesses have been found in both algorithms: it is possible to break A5/2 in real-time with a cipher text-only attack, and in February 2008, Pico Computing, Inc. revealed its ability and plans to commercialize FPGAs that allow A5/1 to be broken with a rainbow table attack. The system supports multiple algorithms so operators may replace that cipher with a stronger one.

TETRA

The TETRA standard (originally aimed to the European market) has now become a global standard with a potential worldwide market. TETRA is often used next to established frequency bands with different standards. Usually TETRA's frequency bands are adjacent to important communication bands so they must not interfere in any way with the established adjacent channels. Thus, transmission of TETRA signals must have very low out-of-band signals and spurious frequency output power. Reception of TETRA signals can be virtually in any spectral environment and so TETRA radio receivers require high blocking and linearity specifications. TETRA uses a non-constant envelope modulation which requires a highly linear transmitter to prevent high levels of adjacent channel interference (ACI) due to spectral re-growth. Linear power amplifiers (PA) typically have low efficiency which is undesirable in mobile communications as the efficiency of the PA is one of the most important parameters in a system determining talk time, battery size, etc. The conventional approach for achieving low distortion is to use power amplifiers operating at an output level far below their real capabilities (back-off approach). However, such an approach drastically reduces the power efficiency, increasing the power consumption of the system to unacceptable levels. This has hindered the growth on the user uptake. An important advantage, however, of the TETRA standard is that it has a number of open interface specifications that can be used by application developers to further enhance the capabilities of TETRA. Although TETRA uses many of the principles of GSM, TETRA has been specifically designed to enable communication by the emergency services (Police, Fire, Ambulance, etc.) as it has distinct features from and over GSM including:

- Group communication—the ability of one individual to talk to a large number of other operatives in a walkie-talkie type mode of operation.
- Very quick call setup times to ensure critical communication can occur rapidly.
- Priority/Congestion management techniques to ensure that during overload periods important (potentially life threatening) communication can occur.
- Security of communication. A number of techniques are included in the standard and restrictions are placed on the way the products are designed to ensure that communication cannot be "eaves dropped" and the units tampered with.
- Dependability—through the different levels of grade of services and the way the infrastructure is installed TETRA networks are more resilient during times of emergencies than commercial communication bearers.

TETRA is a clear winner in the commercial battle for a communications technology within the PPDR sector. However, in order for TETRA to deliver its potential and for the advanced services envisioned in the next generation of PPDR communication network to be achieved, significant development is required.

Despite the advantages of TETRA there are a number of issues which prevent TETRA's more widespread adoption. These include: Product Cost; Product Size; Data capability of the products. These are driven by the demanding protocol, performance, and security requirements that differ from a commercial mobile network. These aspects in turn prevent both the full integration of the emergency staff using a secure communication system and critical/useful data not being transferred over secure and guaranteed communication bearers. By improving the technology used by the emergency services within European and specifically TETRA the quality and value for money of the services will be improved.

PROPOSED PPDR COMMUNICATION NETWORK ARCHITECTURAL SOLUTIONS
TETRA OVER MOBILE IP NETWORK
Multi-technology communication mobile IP gateway (MIPGATE)

There has been strong research effort in the last decade on the development and integration of new wireless access technologies for mobile Internet access. Among the main research concepts for taking advantage of the availability of various heterogeneous networking technologies in place, Always Best Connected (ABC), Quality of

Experience (QoE), Bandwidth Aggregation concepts have been at the centre of attention. *Always Best Connected* implies that end-users expect to be able to connect anytime, anywhere—also when on the move—by their terminal of choice. End-users also expect to be able to specify in each situation whether "best" is defined by price or capability. However, the current state-of-the-art solutions, such as IETF Mobile IPv6 (MIP) or the emerging Host Identity Protocol (HIP), mainly focus on mobility management, instead of considering additional user-related issues, such as user preferences, associated cost, access-network operator reputation, and trust and mainly application-related issues like (Quality of Service) QoS and failure recovery in conjunction with mobility. *Quality of Experience (QoE)* reflects the collective effect of service performances that determines the degree of satisfaction of the end-user, e.g., what user really perceives in terms of usability, accessibility, retain-ability and integrity of the service. Seamless communications is mostly based on technical Network QoS parameters so far, but a true end-user view of QoS is needed to link between QoS and QoE. While existing 3GPP or IETF specifications describe procedures for QoS negotiation, signaling and resource reservation for multimedia applications (such as audio/video communication and multimedia messaging, support for more advanced services, involving interactive applications with diverse and interdependent media components) is not specifically addressed. Additionally, although the QoS parameters required by multimedia applications are well known, there is no standard QoS specification enabling to deploy the underlying mechanisms in accordance with the application QoS needs.

One of the early attempts to provide all-IP architecture and integrate different access technologies for public safety communications was by the project MESA (Mobility for Emergency and Safety Applications), an international partnership project by ETSI and TIA dating back to 2000 (Project MESA, 2001). Salkintzis (2002) proposed a solution for integrating WLAN and TETRA networks that fits to the all-IP architecture of MESA and allows TETRA terminals to interface the TETRA infrastructure over a broadband WLAN radio access network instead of the conventional narrowband TETRA radio network, while remaining fully interoperable with conventional TETRA terminals and services. Chiti et al. (2008) propose a wireless network that aims to interconnect several heterogeneous systems and provide multimedia access to groups of people for disaster management. The authors address the issues of heterogeneous network interconnection, full and fault tolerant coverage of the disaster area, localization to enable an efficient coordination of the rescue operations, and security. The focus of this work is on the use of WiMAX-based wireless network as a backbone to provide reliable and secure multimedia communications to operators during the disaster management. Durantini et al. (2008) present a solution for interoperability and integration among Professional Mobile Radio systems (TETRA and Simulcast), public systems (GSM/GPRS/UMTS), and broadband wireless technologies, such as WiMAX, with the aim of enabling distributed service provisioning while guaranteeing always best connection to bandwidth demanding applications provided by an IP-based core network. Furthermore, the authors address the issue of optimizing the quality of service management in a multi-network environment, and propose a QoS mapping between WiMAX QoS classes and TETRA service typologies. There is a multitude of other similar work focusing on the integration of various network technologies in and out of the scope of public safety communications. However, solutions available to date are fragmented and each considers only a subset of the ideal QoE-aware and autonomous connectivity solution that can also simultaneously exploit all available network interfaces. During large scale emergencies and disasters, it is crucial to aggregate the *scarce communication resources of multiple technologies* and be able to use simultaneously, since the left-over capacity of a single technology may suffer due to infrastructural damages.

Multipath TCP

The transmission control protocol (TCP), which serves as the data transport basis of many telecommunication services of today, was designed to work on single links and does not cope well with the simultaneous use of multiple links at the same time. A survey of TCP performance in heterogeneous networks (Barakat, 2000) shows the existing solutions to date and their problems. Magalhaes et al. (2001) present a solution for channel aggregation at the transport layer, called R-MTP (Reliable Multiplexing Transport Protocol), which multiplexes data from a single application data stream across multiple network interfaces (Magalhaes, 2001). The recently finished EU-funded Trilogy project introduced the MultiPath TCP (MPTCP) solution, toward enabling the simultaneous use of several paths by a modification of TCP that presents a normal TCP interface to applications, while in fact spreading data across several subflows (Barré, 2011). An IETF working group has been formed to develop the MPTCP protocol, which is an ongoing effort. However, through extensive evaluation studies over MPTCP, some authors (Nguyen, 2011) report that heterogeneous network environment (Ethernet, Wifi, and 3G) has a great impact on MPTCP throughput and reveals the need of an intelligent algorithm for interface selection in MPTCP.

Security

Terrestrial Trunked Radio (TETRA) supports two types of security: air-interface security and end-to-end security. Air-interface security (TETRA, 2010) protects user's identity, signaling, voice and data between mobile station (MS) and base station (BS). It specifies air-interface encryption, (mutual) authentication, key management (OTAR: over-the-air-rekeying) and enable/disable functionality. End-to-end security (TETRA, 2010) encrypts the voice from MS to MS. Current candidates as encryption algorithms are IDEA (owned by MediaCrypt AG) and AES as the encryption schemes. One of the main challenge for multi-technology communication is the compatibility problem between the security mechanisms (encryption, authentication, integrity, and key management) supported by these technologies. Wireless LAN supports various security mechanisms, uses of which are mostly optional. MAC address filtering and hidden service set identifier (SSID) are the simplest techniques. Today very few access points use Wired Equivalent Privacy (WEP) because many cracking tools are publicly available on Internet. Wi-Fi Protected Access (WPA and WPA2 based on 802.11i) are introduced to overcome this problem but weak passwords are still problem. 802.1x defines the encapsulation of the Extensible Authentication Protocol (EAP), and enables authentication through third-party authentication servers such as Radius and Diameter. End-to-end security can be provided by use of Internet Protocol Security (IPSEC), Transport Layer Security (TLS), Secure Sockets Layer (SSL), Secure Shell (SSH), pretty Good Privacy (PGP), etc. Security of GSM and 3G suffers from similar compatibility problems with TETRA. GSM security defines Subscriber Identity Module (SIM), the MS, and the GSM network. SIM hosts subscribe authentication key (K), Personal Identification Number (PIN), key generation algorithm (A8), and authentication algorithm (A3). MS contains the encryption algorithm (A5) for air interface. Encryption is only provided for the air interface. 3G security builds upon the security of GSM. It addresses the weaknesses in 2G systems with integrity and enhanced authentication as well as with enhanced encryption using longer keys and stronger algorithms. Seamless communication for crisis management (SECRICOM—FP7) project partially addresses this challenge for secure push to talk systems over existing infrastructures (GSM, UMTS networks).

Another challenge in multi-technology communication is that the most of the security mechanisms are optional, and they are maintained based on the policies of different administrative domains. An end-to-end connection between two MS may go through an unsecure public network which may permit in variety of attacks including denial-of-service and man-in-the-middle. Cost of mitigating these attacks on MS side may be higher than the benefit of the connection in terms of Quality of Service (QoS) and Quality of Experience (QoE) metrics. Therefore, QoS and QoE mechanisms must involve related metrics to provide predictable security service levels to the end users (Spyropoulou, 2002).

TETRA OVER MOBILE AD-HOC NETWORK

Mobile Ad-Hoc Networks are multi hop networks where nodes can be stationary or mobile; and they are formed on a dynamic basis. They allow people to perform tasks efficiently by offering unprecedented levels of access to information. In mobile ad-hoc networks, topology is highly dynamic and random; and in addition, the distribution of nodes and their capability of self-organizing play an important role. Their main characteristics can be summarized as follows: The topology is highly dynamic and frequent changes in the topology may be hard to predict; Mobile ad-hoc networks are based on wireless links, which will continue to have a significantly lower capacity than their wired counterparts; Physical security is limited due to the wireless transmission; Mobile ad-hoc networks are affected by higher loss rates, and can present higher delays and jitter than fixed networks due to the wireless transmission; and Mobile ad-hoc network nodes rely on batteries or other exhaustible means for their energy. As a result, energy savings are an important system design criterion. Furthermore, nodes have to be power-aware: the set of functions offered by a node depends on its available power (CPU, memory, etc.).

A well-designed architecture for mobile ad-hoc networks involves all networking layers, ranging from the physical to the application layer. Power management is of paramount importance; and general strategies for saving power need to be addressed, as well as adaptation to the specifics of nodes of general channel and source coding methods, of radio resource management and multiple accesses. In mobile ad-hoc networks, with the unique characteristic of being totally independent from any authority and infrastructure, there is a great potential for the users. In fact, roughly speaking, two or more users can become a mobile ad-hoc network simply by being close enough to meet the radio constraints, without any external intervention.

Routing problems have been addressed through research; where routing protocols between any pair of nodes within an ad-hoc network can be difficult because the nodes can move randomly and can also join or leave the network. This means that an optimal route at a certain time may not work seconds later.

Two of the best multicast protocols to be adopted are MAODV (Multicast Ad-hoc on-demand Distance Vector Routing Protocol) and ODMRP (On Demand Multicast Routing Protocol). The performance measures that were evaluated are the PDR (Packet Delivery Ratio) and the Latency. Previous studies have evaluated these algorithms with respect to the network traffic, the node speed, the area and the antenna range for different simulation scenarios. In general, MAODV performs better for high traffic. ODMRP performs better for large areas and high node speeds but poorer for small antenna ranges. Therefore, MAODV and its derivative AODV ALMA will be adopted in this project. A number of technical challenges are faced today due to the heterogeneous, dynamic nature of this hybrid MANET. The hybrid routing scheme AODV ALMA can act simultaneously combining mobile agents to find path to the gateway and on-demand distance vector approach to find path in local MANET is one of the unique solution. An adaptive gateway discovery mechanism based on mobile agents making use of pheromone value, pheromone decay time and balance index is used to estimate the path and next hop to the gateway. The mobile nodes automatically configure the address using mobile agents first selecting the gateway and then using the gateway prefix address. The mobile agents are also used to track changes in topology enabling high network connectivity with reduced delay in packet transmission to Internet.

Clustering is an effective technique for node management in a MANET. Cluster formation involves election of a mobile node as Cluster head to control the other nodes in the newly formed cluster. The connections between nodes and the cluster head changes rapidly in a mobile ad-hoc network. Thus cluster maintenance is also essential. Prediction of mobility-based cluster maintenance involves the process of finding out the next position that a mobile node might take based on the previous locations it visited. The overhead can be reduced in communication by predicting mobility of node using linear autoregression and cluster formation.

TETRA OVER DVB-T/DTTV NETWORK

Digital Video Broadcasting—Terrestrial (DVB-T) is the DVB European-based consortium standard for the broadcast transmission of digital terrestrial television that was first published in 1997 and the first DVB-T broadcast was in the UK in 1998.

The DVB-T system transmits compressed digital audio, digital video and other data in an MPEG transport stream, using coded orthogonal frequency-division multiplexing (COFDM or OFDM) modulation (ETSI, 2004-2006). Recently, there are many efforts toward the use of the DVB-T infrastructure for emergency warning and alert of the public in the view of disastrous events, as part of integrated Emergency Warning Broadcast Systems (EWBS) (Azmi, 2011). EWBS usually use TV and radio broadcasting networks to alert people about impending disasters and enable them to prepare for emergencies. The EWBS uses special warning or alert signals embedded in TV and radio broadcasting signals to automatically switch on the receiver equipment (if so equipped) in the home, and issue an emergency bulletin, alerting people to an impending disaster such as a tsunami or an earthquake. Besides, at least one special disaster emergency warning system standard for DVB-T which involves a specific message flow architecture and transmitter and receiver standard have been proposed (Shogen, 2009).

However, there are no available implementations of DVB-T-based systems that are especially suited for Public Protection and Disaster Relief (PPDR) environments, essentially being part of an integrated Emergency Response Broadcast System (ERBS). Since TV broadcasting systems, including Digital TV (DTV) systems, are widely available across rural and urban areas, and their operation and RF coverage are not affected by the land type, the terrain morphology or the weather conditions, the use of DVB-T based systems in terms of emerging ERBS systems would be highly beneficial, especially considering: The higher video and audio transmission rate of the DVB-T-based systems compared to their analog counterparts or previous digital TV implementations; The higher spectral efficiency compared to their analogue counterparts; The advanced Forward Error Detection (FEC) capabilities, which also provide a major capacity enhancement; and The improved signal robustness against external influences such as the impact(s) caused by geography, weather conditions and buildings/technical obstacles.

CONCLUSION

In general, it is important to provide a framework which will exploit additional networks (Mobile IP, Ad-Hoc Mobile Networks, and DVB-T) to support emergency relief communications (which at this point and the foreseeable future is going to be TETRA) and resource management during disasters in two aspects:

(i) *guaranteed communication* capabilities and services *among the response teams and units* regardless of the location and level of crisis,

(ii) *communication* opportunities *between responders and general public, affected people and their families*

Involvement of families, citizens and social groups in rescue operations (millions of eyes/agents over the Internet providing unstructured time critical information such as possible locations of trapped people) has already illustrated its benefits during the rescue operations after the recent major earthquake in Van, Turkey.

Earthquake 7.2, Van, Turkey (October 2011): Major GSM operators in Turkey could manage to fix their infrastructures within the first 1-3 h of the earthquake. They also increased capacity of their infrastructures through mobile stations to be able to handle the extra load. They provided free services in earthquake region. These efforts paid off shortly after by the lives saved using GSM and 3G connectivity.

- Yalcin Akay (19 years old) was trapped under a collapsed six-story building with a leg injury. GSM network was up, and he could call Police emergency line (155). Mr. Akay described his position to first response team. He saved himself and three others including two children who were trapped under the same building.
- Saydun Gökşin, secretary-general of Turkish Search and Rescue Society (AKUT), told the reporters that AKUT teams managed to rescue three people who were trapped under collapsed building using information from Twitter. They tweeted. Tweet Location Feature was used to pinpoint their exact co-ordinates. Within 2 h, search teams could reach them.
- Families and friends are organized under "hashtags" to inform first response teams about the locations of the collapsed buildings and locations about the people they know who might have been trapped under these building. This was very critical service for the families all over the Turkey whose members are state employees who were serving in the disaster region (e.g., primary and secondary school teachers, doctors, nurses, soldiers, ...).

In the context, we consider three regions in a disaster area in terms of communication locality: emergency site, first response site, and a local site for additional resources. Each of these regions may have different requirements. For example, *local site for additional resource* may already have an infrastructure to support the operations. *First response site* may be better organized compared to *emergency site* which may be the most challenging environment for providing resilient, secure and high quality communication service. The objective is to create a framework that can adapt itself based on the requirements and available resources in the environment it is operating.

REFERENCES

Chiti, F., Fantacci, R., Maccari, L., Marabissi, D., Tarchi, D., 2008. A broadband wireless communications system for emergency management. Wireless Commun. IEEE 15 (3), 8–14.

Durantini, A., Petracca, M., Vatalaro, F., Civardi, A., Ananasso, F., 2008. Integration of Broadband Wireless Technologies and PMR Systems for Professional Communications, Networking and Services, 2008. ICNS 2008. In: Fourth International Conference, 16–21 March 2008, pp. 84–89.

Project MESA, 2001. http://www.projectmesa.org (accessed January 14).

Salkintzis, A.K., 2002. Wide-Area Wireless IP Connectivity with the General Packet Radio Service. Chapter 3, In: Wireless IP and Building the Mobile Internet. Artech House, ISBN: 1-58053-354-X, pp. 21–39, 2002.

Shogen, K., NHK, 2009. Handbook on EWBS, Technical Department, Asia-Pacific Broadcasting Union, June 2009.

Index

Note: Page numbers followed by *f* indicate figures and *t* indicate tables.

Printed and bound by CPI Group (UK) Ltd, Croydon, CR0 4YY

03/10/2024

01040327-0002